Advance Praise for *Skin in the Game*

"Anwar Elgonemy's *Skin in the Game* is an excellent analysis of the unresolved problems in the post-crisis US financial system—and particularly the real estate sector—that points out looming risks and possible solutions to avert further catastrophe. *Skin in the Game* is an easily accessible, well-written, and essential read from a seasoned practioner."

—Colin Dyer, Chief Executive Officer, Jones Lang LaSalle

"Anwar Elgonemy brings his invaluable perspective as a commercial real estate strategist to the tangled story of the financial crisis and breaks down its many mysteries into clear, thorough, and lively explanations that never lose sight of the most important factor of all: human psychology. For anyone looking for a primer on what went very, very wrong in US real estate, *Skin in the Game* is an excellent resource."

—Alyssa Katz, author of *Our Lot: How Real Estate Came to Own Us* and Adjunct Faculty member at New York University's Arthur L. Carter Journalism Institute

"Anwar Elgonemy's unique background and passion for real estate investments shine through brilliantly in *Skin in the Game*, which provides a critical look at the many factors leading to the failure of the US financial system and its impact on the property market. Whether you are seeking to get in or out of the real estate market, advising investors, or restructuring deals, *Skin in the Game* is an indispensable book. Ending with a note of optimism and concrete suggestions for digging out of our current economic problems,

Elgonemy provides illuminating alternatives to doomsday predictions for both the US financial and real estate markets."
—**Lynn Cadwalader, Partner, Holland & Knight**

"This is a great deep-dive into the world of real estate finance and some of the major factors behind the current malaise in the market. Well-written and impressively researched, the book lays out how a glut of capital, lust for transaction speed, and lack of responsibility—among all participants in the market—led to the real estate market boom and subsequent crash. Entertaining and educational, I recommend this book to both newcomers and seasoned market players alike."
—**Matthew Anderson, Managing Director, Trepp LLC**

"*Skin in the Game* offers Americans faced with the slow economic recovery, lost wealth, and deteriorating lifestyles valuable insight into the causes of the Great Recession: the abundance of capital, deregulation, over-leveraged transactions, non-alignment of interests, and the Wall Street 'fee spree.' Noting the need for a combination of sound macroeconomic market policies, Anwar Elgonemy intelligently explores policy options for a post-crisis future, calling for a renewed commitment to sound underwriting and a lower leverage environment. *Skin in the Game* is a compelling, well-written, and highly informative read from an active market participant."
—**Michael Burrichter, Principal, CBRE Investors**

"Have we learned our lessons from the past? Anwar Elgonemy's compelling and informative book makes a very strong case for how we can minimize the boom and bust cycles that have popped more than a few real estate bubbles. *Skin in the Game* is deep and wise. You will be, too, if you read it."

—Chip Conley, Executive Chairman of Joie de Vivre Hospitality and author of *Peak: How Great Companies Get Their Mojo from Maslow*

"Anwar Elgonemy's new book *Skin in the Game* is a must-read for both seasoned real estate professionals as well as those who want to learn more about the property sector. It is not only an in-depth and informative discussion on the 'hows and whys' of the recent real estate crisis, it is also a very enjoyable read."

—Tom Callahan, Chief Executive Officer, PKF Consulting USA

"Can the American Dream be saved? Anwar Elgonemy's superb treatise guides us through the mortgage crisis and illuminates its long-term ramifications on the economy. Elgonemy's forward-looking insights hold out hope for the reformation of the US real estate system, and the renewal of our dreams as homeowners. *Skin in the Game* is a timely and very rewarding read."

—Stewart Fahmy, President of Calandev LLC and member of the Real Estate Academic Initiative at Harvard University

"Whether you are a beginner in finance or an expert, Anwar Elgonemy's *Skin in the Game* is a fascinating look at not only what got the US real estate market into trouble, but what it will take from a non-partisan, highly lucid, and practical perspective to get us through our changing economy. *Skin in the Game* shows deep understanding of the socio-economic forces at work that have—and will—reform how we think about debt, consumerism, and property value."

—Bob Puccini, Chief Executive Officer, The Puccini Group

"Anwar Elgonemy has objectively uncovered the ramifications to the US economy from a hyper real estate debt-growth period from 2003 through 2007. This hyper debt-growth period was fueled by aggressive lenders and borrowers contributing no skin or cash equity in the real estate debt originated during this period. As Elgonemy has lucidly conveyed, with no risk of cash down-payment equity loss, lenders and borrowers are both exposed to a higher risk of loan default. I highly recommend *Skin in the Game* as a must-read for every leveraged homeowner and real estate investor in the US."

—Marc Thompson, senior banker

"Anwar Elgonemy's *Skin in the Game* offers a fresh perspective on the credit-banking crisis and its impact on real estate markets everywhere. In this extraordinarily well-crafted book, he offers the reader many ways to appreciate and understand the state of our economy, in addition to courageous assertions for its resolution. Elgonemy's background and experience is global and his unique take on the US economy confirms that 'skin in the game' is a critical element missing in the equation."

—Tony Wood, author of *The Commercial Real Estate Tsunami, A Survival Guide for Lenders, Owners, Buyers, and Brokers*

"Anwar Elgonemy's new book, *Skin in the Game*, is the kind of diagnosis and prescription for real estate finance that you might get from an articulate, expert, caring doctor—if doctors could treat the financial sector. The book explains in plain English the nuanced contributing factors that led to the present breakdown in mortgage finance—commercial and residential—and provides a recovery plan with practical suggestions on how to heal the patient. Required reading for financiers, investors, and members of Congress."

—Maura O'Connor, Managing Partner, O'Connor Cochran LLP and former chairman of the Los Angeles Economic Development Corporation

"If you want to understand what is still wrong with real estate investments in America and how its unresolved problems can be fixed, you can't do better than the brilliantly written and researched *Skin in the Game.*"

—Abdul Suleman, Chief Executive Officer, Equinox Hospitality Group

"Elgonemy's highly readable book makes complex financial transactions easily comprehensible to a wide audience. Worth the price of the book for the outstanding diagrams and graphics alone."

—Karen Johnson, President, Pinnacle Advisory Group West

$KIN IN THE GAME

The Past, Present, and Future of Real Estate
Investments in America

ANWAR ELGONEMY

Skin in the Game:

The Past, Present, and Future of Real Estate Investments in America

Includes bibliographical references and index.

Printed in the United States of America by CreateSpace

7290-B Investment Drive

North Charleston, South Carolina 29418

For additional information visit www.skininthegame.info

ISBN: 1463507658

ISBN-13: 9781463507657

LCCN: 2011908701

CreateSpace, North Charleston, South Carolina

To the women of my life: Gigi, Dahlia, and Ameera

Many shall be restored that now are fallen
and many shall fall that now are in honor.

—Horace, *Ars Poetica*

Contents

Appendices:

Introduction

This book is about the bloody crossroads where real estate and high-finance meet. It is intended for a wide audience, from intelligent laymen to financial professionals. It is not a traditional textbook about real estate finance, nor is it one of the numerous post-mortem publications that have covered the intricacies of the subprime mortgage crisis.[1]

As opposed to such treatises, I have concentrated on the underlying fault lines in America's financial system and its hard-hit real estate sector. By discussing these fault lines, my objective is to communicate the different ways in which we can lessen the probability of another *purely* real estate-driven crisis, or mitigate its severity should it occur. In essence, I recommend the changes necessary for the United States property sector to succeed in the long-term.

———

In finance, corporate insiders have "skin in the game" when they use their own money to buy stock in the company they are running. The idea behind creating such a situation is to ensure that corporations are managed by individuals who, like the outside investors, actually share a stake in the company. Executives can talk all they want, but the best vote of confidence is putting one's own money on the line.

When it comes to real estate, mortgage providers have skin in the game—otherwise known as the alignment of interests and the sharing in any losses—when they retain a stake in what they have lent. This forces the providers to vet their borrowers more carefully, reducing the chances of failed loans.

On the other hand, *no* skin in the game means having nothing to lose; being unaffected by the failure or mistakes of a corporation you manage or a loan you provide. Someone with no skin in the game basically doesn't give a damn about what happens to others. This has been, and continues to be, a serious problem in the US financial system.

————

Since the US financial markets change on an hourly basis, the impacts of numerous new regulations have yet to be fully unraveled, and the real estate sector continues its uneven progress, I have abstained from making long-term quantitative predictions about the future. Let's face it, the future is not only unknown—it's *unknowable.* And to paraphrase economist John Kenneth Galbraith, economic forecasts exist to make astrology look respectable!

There are no heroes or manufactured villains in this book, nor are the vast swaths of characters, dates, plots, and events of the financial crisis minutely chronicled. Rather, I have attempted to make the book an easy read, peppered with tidbits and graphic illustrations. As much as possible, I've also avoided tortured financial formulas and needlessly obscure descriptions, focusing instead on the unresolved problems of US real estate.

———

Chapter 1, "Red, White, and Blue," presents the lay of the land, delving into the warped consumerist social fabric of America that indirectly produced the financial crisis of 2008. The purpose of chapter 2, "Mumbo Jumbo," is to demonstrate the unnecessary complexity of derivatives and the need to go back to the basics of banking. In chapter 3, "Drinking the Purple Kool-Aid," I provide a brief recap of the faulty assumptions that caused the financial meltdown. Chapter 4, "Strawberry Pickers and Predators," transitions into the out-of-control US mortgage machine that fleeced immigrants, minorities, and lower middle-class Americans. Chapter 5, "Wicked Incentives," conveys that greed is both innate and rampant in corporate America, culminating in exorbitant CEO compensation packages that have caused great mistrust in the leadership of US corporations. Chapter 6, "Cheese, Sleaze, and Filling in the Boxes," discusses the inner workings of the real estate profession—the incompetence of some appraisers, loan officers, mortgage brokers, and real estate agents—and how it needs urgent fixing at the grassroots level.

Further, chapter 7, "Mixed Signals," gives a snapshot of the plumbing of the US commercial real estate sector and its current challenges. Chapter 8, "Violating the Law of the Lever," analyzes the dangers of excessive leverage, the unsustainable real estate debt growth experienced before the meltdown, and the calamitous missed assessment of real estate debt risk, all fundamental causes of the financial maelstrom. Chapter 9, "Fiddling with the System," discusses how government reform and intervention needs to be more in balance with the US free-market system in the longer-term.

In addition, chapter 10, "The Seeds of Risk," delves into how the leveraged buyouts (LBOs) of the 1980s planted the seeds of misaligned interests and incentives in the capital markets. Chapter 11, "Facing the Music," walks the reader through the unresolved problems in the US economy, focusing on its hard-hit property sector. Specifically, the following five unresolved problems in American real estate are discussed in detail:

1. Misconceptions about housing;
2. Negative home equity;
3. Delinquencies, defaults, and foreclosures;
4. Commercial debt maturities; and
5. Private-label mortgage-backed securities.

Lastly, chapter 12, "An American Renewal," provides possible answers and solutions to the five unresolved problems highlighted above, ending with a glint of optimism that the US will make a comeback only if its unresolved problems are dealt with properly.

Chief among the necessary changes is the idea that debt risk in US real estate must be controlled, coupled with a uniform risk assessment methodology that will help lenders, borrowers, regulators, and the US government make better decisions going forward. Moreover, the notion of having *more* skin in the game threads its way throughout the needed changes, with the underlying thesis being that the interests of stakeholders in US real estate must be more closely aligned.

Since this book pertains to finance, it inevitably includes a smorgasbord of acronyms, especially in chapter 2. A list of abbreviations at the end of the book serves as an easy reference for the reader.

———

Although it had been brewing in my mind for some time, I made the decision to write this book after receiving a mail solicitation from a predatory mortgage broker in March 2010. The letter, which arrived *after* the Great Recession of 2007–09 had officially ended, was offering a home loan with zero down-payment and zero interest for twelve months, a very risky over-extension of credit that was one of the many causes of the real estate meltdown. After receiving the solicitation, I felt that something was still very much wrong with the property sector in America and that it continues to be characterized by conflicting and contradictory interests. It was clear as daylight that no skin in the game and moral hazard were still rampant in the system.[2] The financial crisis was not just a banking phenomenon—America's unresolved problems go much deeper than that.

———

I'm an American, and I love being an American, even though I wasn't born and raised in the United States. As such, I believe it's important for the reader to learn a bit about my perspective and my background. My mother was born in England. My father was born in a small village near the Nile River in Egypt. After earning his PhD in economics in the United States thanks to a scholarship from the Egyptian government, he became a career diplomat at the United Nations. Following retirement, he became a senior fellow at Oxford University in England, where he has published several books.

I was born in Italy in the 1960s. My boyhood and adolescence were spent between Egypt and Italy in the 1970s and 1980s. I

attended an American high school in Rome, and after gradu-
ation I went to Switzerland to get an education in hotel man-
agement, then a master's degree in business administration in
Arizona. I have also lived and worked in England, Portugal, and
Dubai, and can speak four languages. I've been in the United
States since the late 1980s and reside today in the San Francisco
Bay area.

———

My professional career began in the nose-to-the-grindstone
trenches of hotel operations, which made little economic sense
as a long-term career (to me at least) because of the outrageously
long hours and low pay. But since I liked real estate, I decided to
become an advisor to clients looking to invest their hard-earned
cash prudently in property worldwide.

Most of my career has been in the US, where I've worked for
small private firms and large public corporations, reaching the
position of senior vice-president. During my twenty-five-year career
in commercial real estate, I've advised big investment banks, sovereign wealth funds, and billionaire investors, as well as start-up
developers, local lenders, and small property owners.

I've experienced firsthand the free-market zealotry and reckless finance that resulted in the savings and loan crisis of the late
1980s, the spectacular dot-com crash of 2000–02, the free-fall of
real estate in Dubai in 2008–09, and the very worst of the financial
meltdown in the US. My experience has taught me that regardless of the size of an investment, real estate can swiftly become a
creator *or* a destroyer of wealth—an ego-feeding aphrodisiac that
has to be tamed.

Clearly, my background is hardly typical. But its varied nature allows me to be objective when it comes to different points of view and business cultures. I write this book as a Western-educated, neutral observer with a passion for real estate investments.

———

Financial crises have happened before, and—if history is any guide—they will happen again. At some point, the real estate markets and the US economy will fully recover and be moving into another boom, which will most likely contain the seeds of its own downfall. This is not the view of a pessimist or a cynic; I am neither, and I hope that my fellow Americans will not be taken aback by some of the comments I make in this book. I consider myself to be an objective interpreter of real estate cycles and trends; a proponent of constructive criticism who is optimistic that America will gradually rebound as a much-improved bastion of high-finance.

In addition to no skin in the game, the US financial system continues to suffer from excessive aggregate debt. It also suffers from weak growth in gross domestic product and employment, both results of calamitously off-the-mark assessments of real estate debt risk. Despite the attempted financial reforms by the US government, the American property sector still has significant unresolved problems and is unable to withstand a further deterioration in home values.

Therefore, this multi-dimensional book highlights the impending risks in the US financial system and property sector in particular. If these problems are dealt with effectively, real estate in America will get its gallant groove back and be better prepared for inevitable crises in the future.

Chapter 1: Red, White, and Blue

America, from its inception, was a speculation.
—Aaron Sakolski, historian

The makeup of a country in terms of its employment, education, and values is known as its social fabric. Social fabric is the "raw material" of society, and is created from the myriad everyday interactions between people and institutions. Because the financial crisis of 2008 originated in the US, this chapter provides some insight into the social fabric of the society that produced the real estate meltdown.

This chapter is much less technical than the chapters that will follow; it's the bird's-eye view. Moreover, it's an analysis of *indirect* causes, whereas the bulk of the book is an analysis of the direct problems and possible solutions pertaining to US real estate. If readers want to dive right into the nitty-gritty content, they might want to skip to chapter 2 and beyond.

America the Big

The United States is one of the greatest countries to ever exist. The US is also the third-largest country in the world by land area and population.[1] At 3.79 million square miles (including the

Great Lakes), it is larger than China, Brazil, and Australia—and with some 312 million people, its population is surpassed only by China and India.

Compared to other countries, it is uncrowded—according to the US Census Bureau, urban land accounts for only 2.6 percent of total land area in the United States. The US economy is the world's largest, with an estimated 2011 gross domestic product (GDP) of $14.5 trillion, a quarter of global economic activity.

I love this country because of the genuine goodwill of so many of its citizens, its awe-inspiring natural beauty, its never-ending creativity, its relentless ability to reinvent itself, and its extraordinary vastness. But America, like everything else, isn't perfect. It is for that reason that I shall bring to light certain flawed characteristics and aspects of the US social tapestry which, in my view, indirectly caused the financial collapse of 2008.

———

I believe that nearly every aspect of US society is dictated by its sheer physical size, from its semiautonomous fifty states, which I call the "United Economies of America," to its use—and waste—of vast financial and natural resources. America's size is a gigantic pot of gold for corporations that have thousands of discrete markets in which to sell their products. This provides the distribution channels that flood the US market with products that Americans often don't really need but that are bought anyway by consumers who are psychologically hardwired to spend their money on almost anything that is well marketed. In other words, Americans (including myself) are caught up in a never-ending cycle of supply-driven consumption.

The US still offers quasi-endless opportunities for relocation and upward social mobility. Add the Puritan ideal of self-improvement—uplift through work—into the equation and America is probably the most competitive society on the planet in terms of the need to succeed—to attain goals, to obtain money.

These underlying traits render it a stronghold of individualism and, in many ways, a loner society. Moreover, since the United States is so vast, wealthy, competitive, and individualistic, it is also a defender of ego-feeding consumerism. The American philosopher Ayn Rand heroized individual, independent action when she wrote, "I am not *primarily* an advocate of capitalism, but of egoism."[2]

———

Consumerism reigns in the US, and the social values of many Americans tend to orbit around that claim. In the old Aesop's Fables, the grasshopper sings merrily all summer long. He dances during the warm months and laughs at the ant that has no time to celebrate the good times because he is so busy preparing for the bad. In the end, the grasshopper, starving and freezing in the cold of winter, begs the ant for help.

Despite the impact of the recent financial crisis and the real estate meltdown in which we are still mired, the American urge for conspicuous consumption still looms within, and frugality has surfaced only temporarily in this nation of grasshoppers. A survey indicated that 51 percent of American consumers were behind on their savings goals. Of those 51 percent, some 20 percent reported they were buying on impulse, while 17 percent were spending beyond their means.[3] I'm not necessarily saying that these are negative aspects of America. On the contrary, these traits comprise the essence of the nation and its day-to-day reality. It is what it is.

————

The world we live in is often uncontrollable and unpredictable, so the only thing that we can do is to be aware and be prepared for economic changes—the same way that we prepare ourselves for such anxiety-inducing possibilities as illness, natural disasters, death, and, of course, taxes.

Pessimism is not inherent to the American DNA, so to be pessimistic about the future because of the financial crisis would be strikingly un-American. Indeed, I believe that good always comes out of bad. However, we need to be aware of certain aspects of the American social fabric and economy that indirectly toppled the house of cards—and could cause another crisis.

Bubbles, Panics, and Crashes

Speculative bubbles date back to the Dutch tulip mania of 1637, if not earlier, and are not unique to the United States. However, given the country's sheer size and its poorly regulated capitalism, the impacts of its speculative bubbles have been much more vicious and intense.

Throughout its history, America has weathered numerous banking panics, stock market crashes, and other asset-price collapses. A period of economic growth and rising prices usually precedes a period of extreme speculation enabled by an abnormal expansion (or bubble) in the supply of money or credit, or both.[4] Then an exogenous shock, or perhaps just a pause in the increase of asset prices, causes a loss of confidence and a rush to liquidity. Growing numbers of banks, firms, and individuals cannot meet their obligations, so a crisis ensues.[5]

———

Real estate bubbles are periods when property trades in high volumes at prices that are considerably at variance with intrinsic values. The Southern California real estate bubble, which was built up in the 1880s, peaked in 1887 only to burst in 1888. It was a frenzy fueled by fast-spreading and overly optimistic stories about the riches of high rollers—a contagion of speculation, price surges, and a resulting oversupply of homes.

The Florida land bubble that peaked in 1925 was the biggest real estate expansion during the first half of the twentieth century, spreading far beyond the sunshine state and ending with the onslaught of the stock market crash in 1929 and the resulting Great Depression. From 1925 to 1929, home prices declined a total of 31 percent, and the unemployment rate rose to 25 percent at the peak of the Depression. In later years, there were six cyclical production-peaks of new homes (1963, 1972, 1978, 1986, 1998, and 2005) that were soon followed by busts.[6] The United States also suffered severe periodic banking and trading crises, starting as far back as 1775.[7]

Over a period of 233 years (1775–2008), thirty-one financial sector crises (or boom-bust cycles) have hit the United States, an average of one every eight years.[8] In some sense, they seem the inevitable result of the country's vast land area, which encouraged speculators to take excessive risks. Coupled with extreme and unregulated capitalism, the system often bred illogical enthusiasm for quick profits.

As such, future financial shocks are assured. It's part of the American existence. Although very few people know when or how the next crisis will hit, it could be related to the Internet (think cyber-attacks), war, environmental disasters, European sovereign debt defaults, a massive sell off of Treasuries by the Chinese, a commodity-price crash, or the US government's daunting fiscal challenges. It's impossible to accurately predict how these ultra-complex and interrelated factors will play out in the future.

An American Love Affair

Technology played a vital part in delivering the economic and cultural good times that most of America enjoyed since the 1920s. Henry Ford blazed the way with his Model T, selling more than fifteen million of them by 1927. The automobile's popularity and the construction of roads and highways—pouring fresh public funds into the economy—brought tremendous economic prosperity and a new love affair with spending. Canned foods, ready-made clothing, and household appliances, for example, liberated women from much household drudgery. The influence of Ford's methods of mass production and efficiency also enabled other industries to produce a huge variety of consumer appliances.

After World War II, there was a boom in general aviation, both private and commercial, as thousands of pilots were released from military service and many inexpensive war-surplus transport and training aircraft became available. Manufacturers such as Beechcraft, Cessna, and Piper expanded production to provide light aircraft for the new middle-class market, which had the itch for relocation and upward social mobility. The growth in aviation facilitated relocation for new jobs and, as a result, the suburbanization of America and the related proliferation of mega-malls.

———

Before the 1960s, homes were places of quiet refuge. That completely changed with the barrage of mass-marketed mail-order catalogs that enabled consumers to call toll-free to place their orders, and later with TV's twenty-four-hour home-shopping networks.[9] Today the Internet allows people to easily spend away their paychecks at home, on the road, or even while they're at work. While advertisements used to appear exclusively in magazines and newspapers or on billboards and the radio, today they are everywhere: taped up in bathrooms, displayed on airplane tray tables, and even laser-etched on egg shells in supermarkets.

There's little space that our eyes can fall on that doesn't hold some kind of branded image. But perhaps advertising's most worrisome effect is that it *works*, and all this purchasing via such lures is driving us into debt and unhappiness. Many Americans have been powerless to resist the advertiser's siren song and focus on making wise financial decisions. Although people may have more physical objects and possessions now than they had in previous generations, many of them are deeply unhappy. One can only speculate that this condition increased during 2007–11 due to the ill effects of the Great Recession.

———

America is a republic of money that worships commerce, and its love affair with consumption contributed to the real estate meltdown, albeit indirectly. People were willing to forget history and believe that housing prices were headed in only one direction. You could surf the boom and borrow against home equity to pay for all sorts of extravagant expenses—a vacation, a leased Lexus, a flat-screen TV, or the latest electronic gadget. It may have seemed like a lot of debt on paper, but considering that housing prices nearly doubled from 1995 to 2006, there was always a temporary exit: sell the house and make enough money to pay it all back.

The love affair with consumption was crystallized by President George W. Bush's advice when, after the 9/11 attacks, he was asked what Americans should be doing. He urged Americans to keep shopping! In an "only in America" way, consumption is equated with patriotism. Excessive consumption has also created a kind of vicious cycle in which hard times reduce spendable income, which diminishes purchasing power, which weakens production, which piles up inventories, which leads to company closings and layoffs, which further reduces purchasing power. It's very hard to underestimate the impact of consumer spending on the US economy, which was close to a monstrous 71 percent of America's GDP in 2011 (see figure 1-1), after exhibiting a slight dip in 2010. In a spend-happy world, the US consumer *must* consume or the whole system is significantly impacted. Consumption is the glue that keeps America together.

Figure 1-1: US Consumer Spending Share as Percent of GDP

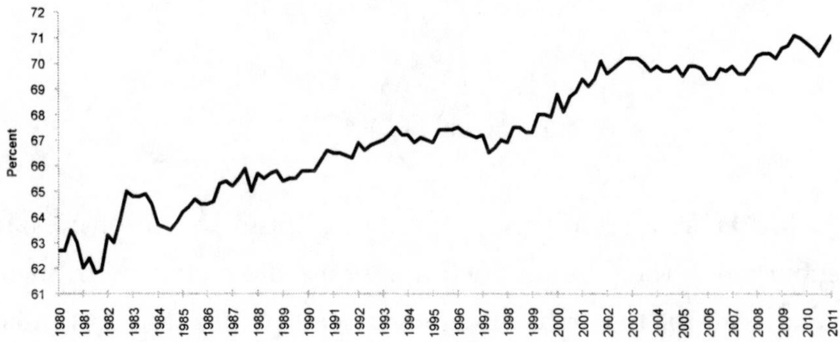

Source: Bureau of Economic Analysis

In post-crisis America, it is the rich shoppers who are driving an increase in spending, helping a recovery that masks unwillingness among less affluent Americans to join in. For example, retail leasing activity on upscale urban streets are up at elite luxury stores, sustained by demand for diamond pendants and plush leather handbags thanks to the wallets of the affluent. At the other end of the economic spectrum, Wal-Mart, the world's largest discount retailer, reported that "everyday Americans" are living paycheck to paycheck as they await an improvement in job prospects. In other words, the heavy lifting is being done by the upper-income households.

Rich shoppers will retain an edge in driving spending, as the top 20 percent of income earners in the United States own approximately 80 percent of equity wealth and half of total housing wealth. In addition, in 2010 President Obama signed into law an $858 billion bill extending George W. Bush-era tax cuts for two years for all income groups, instead of letting them expire for family earnings that exceed $250,000 a year (the cutoff the administration uses for the middle-class). This means that most of the rest of the country is still suffering financially while the wealthy seem to be largely insulated.

Living in Excess

A "McMansion" is a large, pretentious house typical of upscale, suburban developments. Such houses are characterized by steep, complex roof lines, theatrical entrances, plaster-cast Corinthian columns, and backsides that are notably less fussy than their fronts. They are often crowded close together to maximize the developer's short-term yields (benefits) and appeal to people who value perceived social status over anything else. McMansions have been a celebration of a saccharine suburban dream.

According to the US Census Bureau, homes with seven or more rooms had the most vacancies between 2004 and 2008, as well as the greatest increase in vacancy rates. Newer homes had the highest vacancy rate of all housing at close to 20 percent—a rate that has been steadily increasing as the years pass.

Today's homes are huge. The average American home morphed from 983 square feet in 1950 to 2,152 square feet in 2010, a 119 percent increase in size. Even as families have gotten smaller (see figure 1-2), everything about houses has gotten bigger, from the three- and four-car garages to the professional-grade stoves and refrigerators.

Figure 1-2: Number of Average Persons per Household in the US

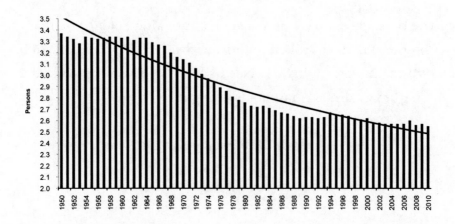

Source: US Census Bureau

With the average number of persons per household in the country at 2.5 in 2010, a decline of nearly 26 percent from 3.4 in 1950, why were Americans buying mega-homes? It's because most of us define financial success by the size and quality of our home. It's also because home developers, with their increasing construction costs, had to build much bigger homes to make higher profit margins—not because people had larger families that required larger square footage. In other words, it was supply-driven by greedy home developers who wanted to crank their yields as high as possible, as quickly as possible, on their cookie-cutter subdivisions.

The result is elevated vacancy rates on gaudy, foreclosed McMansions throughout America, which were mostly owned by people who didn't really need to live in them and couldn't afford them in the first place. It seems that the demand for McMansions was an American fetish instigated by an urge to openly display affluence, which, more often than not, was built on phantom equity.

Unending Impulses, Unending Debt

The personal savings rate (the percent of after-tax income that is not spent) of debt-swollen Americans dropped from 12 percent in 1981 to 1.2 percent in 2005 (see figure 1-3). The decline was due in part to wealthier households saving less.

Figure 1-3: US Personal Savings Rate

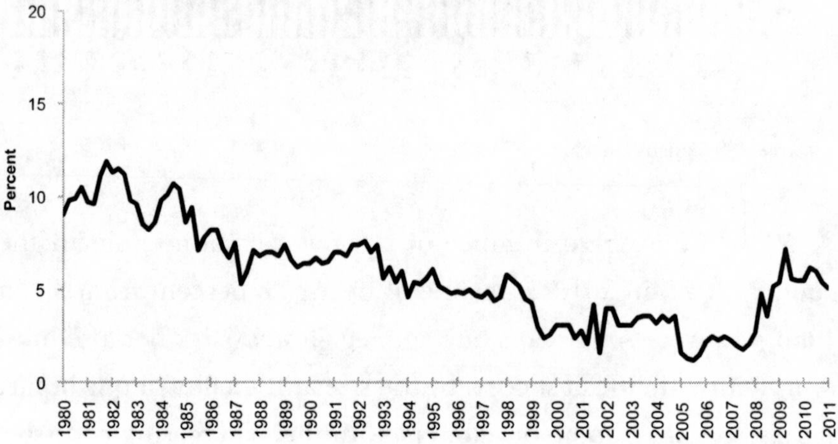

Source: Bureau of Economic Analysis

Affluent Americans had built up their nest eggs during years of strong stock market and real estate gains. The 1987 stock market crash and the 2000–02 tech-stock bust had been only temporary setbacks. An increase in personal savings during 2008–10 could have been a temporary, knee-jerk reaction to the economic recession, because the savings rate again fell. In 2011, Americans were saving only 5.4 percent of their income, down from the more recent peak of 7.2 percent in mid-2009. However, I'm hoping that the decline isn't a long-term trend and that most Americans have woken up from the wealth illusion that for decades was driven by a reckless, buy-now, pay-whatever-whenever approach to money.

————

Personal bankruptcy filings reached 1.5 million in 2010, up 9 percent from 2009.[10] Researchers indicate that new ways of advertising, combined with financial problems and health-related expenses continue to fuel this trend.

Any time an urge strikes, we now have the capability to act on it impulsively, and that creates a much greater challenge for us than ever before. It's only natural that we Americans are having trouble with home mortgage and consumer debt (see figure 1-4). I don't count myself immune to this problem; after college, I racked up more than $40,000 in credit card debt—not in student loans, but because I bought stuff that I didn't really need.

Figure 1-4: US Home Mortgage and Consumer Debt

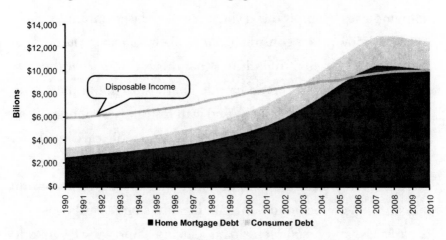

Source: Bureau of Economic Analysis, Federal Reserve Board

Americans are constantly bombarded with challenges to their financial self-control. When we're stressed—meeting deadlines at work, dealing with difficult relationships—we're at risk for spending money simply to feel good, be it on mortgages, gizmos, travel, or frivolities. Life in fast-paced, ultracompetitive America is indeed stressful, so we face daily temptations to spend to release that stress. Although easier said than done, a way to break away from this spending treadmill is to suck it up and live within our means.

Before the deregulation of credit card interest rates in 1978, only wealthier consumers qualified for a credit card, or "plastic." (The first plastic charge card was issued in California in 1958 by American Express and Bank of America). More recently, the credit card industry began soliciting consumers in high school, often offering credit at very high interest rates, without requiring financial qualifications or providing guidance on how the plastic should be prudently used.

Moreover, credit cards condition people into accumulating debt at a very young and vulnerable age. To make matters worse, psychological research shows that credit cards condition us to give in to impulses.[11] Simply displaying a Visa or MasterCard insignia in a store window makes consumers more likely to make a purchase at that store. Research also indicates that this is true even if the consumer does not own a credit card.[12] There is no doubt that credit cards are useful but only when used with restraint and moderation.

Before the financial crisis, the average credit card debt per US household was approximately $15,800, and consumers had on average a total of thirteen credit obligations on record at a credit bureau.[13] These included department store charge cards, gas, and bank cards, and installment loans (such as auto, mortgage, and student loans). In addition, according to a study conducted by the Federal Reserve Bank of Boston, some 56 percent of consumers carry an unpaid balance. It is hoped that these unsustainable numbers will go down with the tightening of lending standards and lower credit limits set by banks and credit card issuers, even though a drop in credit card defaults is emboldening issuers to solicit new customers. US credit card companies mailed 1.4 billion offers for new credit cards in the first quarter of 2011, a 69 percent jump from a year earlier, based on research by Mintel Comperemedia. Credit card mailings haven't rebounded to their gung-ho pre-recession level of 1.8 billion in 2007's fourth quarter. But the surge in 2011 shows that banks are trying aggressively to rev up one of their most profitable types of lending. This means that Americans should be cautious with the renewed onslaught by credit card issuers.

Home Sweet Home

Dubious advertising and illegal pyramid schemes by some mortgage brokers and real estate agents had a strong impact on the pre-crisis housing market by selling homes to people who couldn't afford them. The falling housing market (i.e., the single-family residential sector) has forced a reevaluation, not just of the financial value of a home, but of its intrinsic meaning.

Traditionally, the home is supposed to be a shelter, a space to have a family and raise children that is close to a job and schools, and a place to eat and sleep in privacy. Sadly, in recent years the American home has been transformed into a mere investment opportunity or a cold financial product, an emotionless place where you stay for a short period, create some quick equity or "upside potential," and then move on to the next home-investment.

Historically, America's banks did not lend with "prime" thirty-year amortizing mortgages, but with five-year loans and a balloon payment at the term's end.[14] A family needed to amass a 50 percent down payment, something only a few Americans could do. The word "home" had no investment nuances. The thirty-year mortgage we know today is a legacy of President Franklin D. Roosevelt's New Deal. A US government agency, the Federal Housing Administration (FHA), was inaugurated in 1934 as part of the National Housing Act during President Roosevelt's first term. The goal of the act was to enable homeownership for a broad sector of the American public, and was in response to the deep deprivations of the Great Depression, which included a collapse of the banking system and the consequent mass foreclosures of homes.

When the government introduced long-term mortgages in the 1930s, people could finally afford to buy their dwellings. At the time, a home was an anchor, a stake in the community.[15] Veterans from World War II seized upon FHA and Veterans Affairs (VA) mortgages to establish roots in the suburban middle-class, and one hallmark of middle-class success was the pride of long-term homeownership. The home was more a place to live than a mere investment strategy.

Homeowners hoped to be upwardly mobile, to get promotions, and to find higher-paying jobs. But the house itself was not a financial product designed to increase wealth. People at the time did, of course, move. After a new child, or a promotion, fortunate families moved to larger homes, often in better neighborhoods.

But most home-owning families stayed put, expecting to age in their houses.[16]

In most of the world, homeownership still carries that expectation of rootedness. Home also represents an asset, but an asset that's *illiquid*, that is not expected to provide quick financial returns. Between the late 1990s and 2007, a large single-family home or a condominium became a sexy investment, more a place to buy and sell than to actually live in. For example, between 1997 and 2007, the total number of single-family homes sold (existing and new) increased by 23.9 percent, demonstrating the underlying demand shift in the US residential market.[17]

Americans who lacked the timely insight (or luck) to buy shares in soaring high-tech companies during the dot-com boom could buy a house instead, thus achieving double-digit returns on their investments. People who bought homes expected to sell them at a big profit. Some owners converted their homes into "slush funds," borrowing against the allure of supposedly ever-rising equity.

Mortgage products evolved to let everybody—even people with dodgy credit, low incomes, and no savings—sign purchase agreements. Some other people, who became known as "flippers," a term akin to day-traders of stocks, made their living by frantically buying and selling homes.

Home was where the money was, but eventually contagious optimism—unreceptive to facts and often taking hold when prices are rising—contributed to rising debt, excess supply, and the collapse of residential values. Homes, especially in the "bad boy states" of Florida, Nevada, Arizona, and California—which benefit from ample land and good weather that enables builders to construct homes during most months of the year—were being purchased while still under construction, then being flipped for a profit without the sellers ever having lived in them. The dot-com frenzy of the late 1990s had infiltrated the mindset of US homebuyers.

Particular attention needs to be focused on the bad boy states, which in 2007 had the highest percentages of "sub-prime" mortgages (loans to borrowers with less-than-perfect credit history), measured against the total number of existing housing units in these states.[18] The four states had relatively high proportions of African-American and Hispanic residents who were concentrated in low-income neighborhoods of inner-cities. Tellingly, the four states were among the highest in terms of percentage of housing units in foreclosure in the nation in 2010, due to the abusive practices of gangs of preda-tory lenders.[19] According to RealtyTrac, Nevada had the highest percentage of housing units in foreclosure in 2010 at 9 per-cent. Florida and Nevada saw more Americans move out than move in during 2008. California too had a net loss of domestic migrants because of numerous foreclosures. Hence, residents of these states experienced the impacts of frequent relocation, which can weaken the social fabric and the sense of place and community.

———

The years 2007 and 2008 were a major game-changer in America, awakening many homebuyers from their halcyon dream of ever-rising house values, easy credit, and wild expectations of profit, reminding them that a home can carry significant risk—that the pricing of *all* assets rise and fall. The party may have made many people wealthy (if they left before the music stopped), yet the hangover left many others in a wasteland of financial quicksand.

Born to be Wild

Many of the A-type personalities working in the cut-throat arena of high-finance have wild "animal spirits," so it's no surprise that they despise financial regulations and oversight. That is also probably why for many years America had a benign, even encouraging, lending regulatory environment. But nothing lasts forever, and American-style extreme deregulation eventually took its toll after the onslaught of the financial meltdown in 2008.

Although US mortgage lenders faced state and federal regulations before the crisis, few of these regulations impeded the origination of subprime loans. Furthermore, the system of commercial bank capital requirements provided banks with strong incentives to securitize (or collateralize) many of the subprime mortgage loans they originated, which created a huge house of cards.

Flummoxed US regulators weren't paying attention during the run-up to the financial crisis. There was a chronic lack of effective oversight of the banking system and, above all, inadequate consumer protections. The US capital markets and real estate lending sector were so strongly driven by greed that the best interests of borrowers disappeared from the equation. Wall Street firms, which disdained the need for government regulation in good times, insisted on being rescued by government in bad times. Success was individual achievement; failure was a social problem.[20]

Conclusion

Despite its flaws, the American Dream has not died and the United States will eventually get its big mojo back. The future still belongs to us.

In the grand scheme of world history, America is still a young nation of some 235 years, which pales in comparison to many nations with histories of thousands of years. Therefore, the country is still at the beginning of a long and arduous journey of destiny and is bound to make numerous blunders at the initial stages of its unfolding history, such as the Great Depression of the 1930s and the financial crisis of 2008, among others.

After the 1930s, the United States was able to learn from its mistakes and create institutions like the FHA, the Federal Deposit Insurance Corporation, and the Securities and Exchange Commission to stabilize the turbulence in the financial markets. Its ability to constantly reinvent itself is one of America's greatest attributes, and there is no reason that the country can't become a better society and a more balanced, restrained financial culture after the disarray of the recent crisis.

———

To describe America's positive attributes, one could write an entire book to give the vast topic justice. From the sweet smell of the desert after rain in Arizona, the majesty of its national parks, and the distinctive cultures of Boston, New York, and San Francisco—to the untouchable sacredness of its rule of law, the smooth transition of power after presidential elections, and the endless optimism of its people, America is truly in a league of its own. However, it is still a flawed gem that constantly needs refining.

To be sure, I am not laying the blame of the financial crisis on the American consumer. While certainly consumers were a factor, there is ample evidence that the poorly regulated US financial markets contributed to what really should be considered criminal acts by some financial institutions that created the conditions leading to the crisis. If there were sufficient checks and balances in place, and given that the financial world is prone to excess, such measures might have prevented the numerous excesses from happening.

Moreover, characteristics such as the constant need for instant gratification, out-of-control consumerism, exorbitant debt, and extreme materialism, are maladies that weigh heavily on the American social fabric, and, indirectly, its complex web of financial markets. The prosperity of the 1990s and 2000s was in part stolen from the future. Borrowing allowed for instant gratification, and now the bills are coming due. But with its ever-evolving financial system and its urge for reform and market transparency, the mistakes that we Americans made leading up to the financial crisis can be fixed, although the process of a deep-rooted transformation toward what is better will take some time. During that period, however, we will most likely experience several roller-coaster financial cycles that will enrich certain groups of privileged Americans, and destroy the wealth of many others.

Chapter 2: Mumbo Jumbo

*Derivatives are financial weapons of mass
destruction...designed by madmen.*
—Warren Buffet, billionaire investor

This chapter illustrates how something as basic as a home mortgage or a commercial real estate loan was packaged into unnecessarily complex financial instruments and used for pure speculation. Many of these opaque financial products and their abbreviations appear later in the book, so you may want to use this chapter as a reference. You might also wish to read sections that interest you and refer to others in the context of the following chapters. (To assist the reader, the most pertinent terms are highlighted in bold).

———

As has been well documented by investors, analysts, and academics, the US financial meltdown was caused by an interconnected system of loans improvidently made, inappropriately packaged, imprudently bought, and inadequately capitalized. The global financial system was exposed to the excesses in US mortgages after trillions of dollars of complex securities linked to them were sold to investors around the globe. Mad derivatives were the basic elements of those securities.

The financial collapse that spawned a global crisis revealed the ugly side of American investment banking,[1] which has always tried to cover up its blemishes with Hickey Freeman suits and obscure jargon. Investors faced a cornucopia of financial words and acronyms that added unnecessary opacity to the already complex US financial system. The alphabet soup of financial exotica frequently used by investment bankers ranged from ABSs and MBSs to CDOs and CDSs, to name just a few. The legal fine print of opaque financial contracts mattered enormously and had unpredictable consequences for investors who suddenly stumbled on overlooked interconnection risks. In addition, the rules governing derivative deals occupied hundreds of pages of impenetrable legal prose written by lawyers for whom writing in lucid English is perhaps not one of their selling points.

However, and to give it justice, American investment banking has also displayed its positive side through the vast distribution of capital, market-making, counseling on mergers and acquisitions, and financial research.

And In the Beginning There Was Securitization

In broad terms, **securitization** is the "manufacturing of securities," or the building of bonds from mortgage loans. In technical terms, it is the use of contractual cash flows as collateral for bonds. More specifically, **loan securitization** refers to the pooling of illiquid loans such as mortgages and repackaging them into new investments to be used as collateral for the issuance of **bonds**, financial instruments with which entities raise money. In other words, loan securitization is a process through which large numbers of relatively illiquid mortgages are turned into a smaller number of securities that are more easily sold and traded in the global capital markets.[2]

For example, investors might assemble pools of home loans, then pledge the principal and interest payments as funds for a set of mortgage-backed securities (see figure 2-1). While bank loans are collateralized with balance sheet assets (i.e., buildings and land), securitized bonds are collateralized with contractual cash flows from the underlying mortgages for bondholders. When individual mortgages and other loans are tied together and transformed from a debt agreement into a tradable bond, they are **securitized**, which simply means **collateralized**.

Figure 2-1: Simplified Home Loan Securitization Process

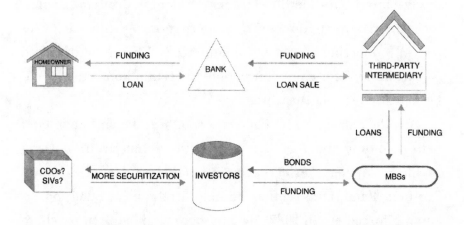

Source: Citibank. Before 2008, third-party intermediaries mainly included the two government-sponsored enterprises Fannie Mae and Freddie Mac. A discussion of CDOs, SIVs, and MBSs is provided later in the chapter.

A **security** can have two meanings, depending on the financial context used. It can be a piece of "paper" that represents the rights to contractual cash flows offered by a borrower to a lender to secure any type of loan. For instance, the security behind a residential mortgage is the *home* being acquired with the proceeds of the loan. On the other hand, a security can be a negotiable *investment instrument* that signifies an ownership position in a corporation (a stock), or a creditor relationship with a corporation, mortgage originator, or government entity (a bond), with both instruments representing financial value. (In this chapter, the words "loan securitization" and "security" are used in the context of the latter meaning).

———

Mortgage-backed securities (MBSs) were invented in 1970 by Lewis Ranieri, a former bond trader at Salomon Brothers. Ranieri is considered the "godfather" of modern mortgage finance for his role in pioneering securitization and MBSs. He coined the word "securitization" for converting home loans into bonds that could be sold anywhere in the world.

A college dropout, he had once sought to be an Italian chef before finding that his asthma prevented him from working in smoky kitchens. After becoming vice-chairman of Salomon Brothers, Ranieri was seen as "too big" in the trade by his bosses and was forced out in 1987. He later became non-executive chairman of Computer Associates and started his own investment firm. In 2008, Franklin Bank in Houston, founded by Ranieri, failed after taking large real estate loan losses.

In 2011, he was running Hyperion Partners, a private equity firm that invests primarily in software startups and mortgage companies. Ranieri is also championing a possible solution for fixing the mess he's accused of enabling in the first place. Ranieri has raised $825 million from thirty-one foundations and corporate and public pension funds, including the South Carolina Retirement Systems, to form the Selene Residential Mortgage Opportunity Fund.

Selene's mission is to buy delinquent mortgages at a deep discount, work with homeowners to get them paying again, and resell stabilized loans for profit. To get homeowners to do their part, Ranieri is taking the radical step of substantially lowering their mortgage balances, known as principal write-downs (which are discussed in chapter 11).

Without securitization, banks generally either held onto the mortgage loans they made or sold them on the secondary market to Fannie Mae or Freddie Mac—government-sponsored enterprises that provide liquidity to the housing market. By buying mortgages, guaranteeing their principal payments, and turning them into MBSs, Fannie and Freddie provide funding for banks to make more mortgages and absorb some of the risks of the market. Because whole mortgages are difficult to trade (since every mortgage is unique), the number of transactions generated by each mortgage originator is small.[3]

Securitization created many new ways for banks to profit. For the banks making the initial mortgages, securitization created a new market for their loans, making it easier for them to recover their cash and lend it out again to another borrower, boosting volume. Investment banks had three ways to make money. They could take fees out of each securitization that they created; they could earn fees selling the new MBSs to investors; or they could earn fees by trading these securities. In each case, the revenues available depended on the *volume* of mortgage-backed securities.[4]

Institutional investors bought MBSs created by investment banks, and the cash flowed to mortgage lenders who no longer needed to be affiliated with traditional banks because they didn't rely on deposits for funding. This flow of money—from investors to special purpose entities created by investment banks to non-bank mortgage lenders to homebuyers—bypassed the traditional banking system, escaping regulation. Large commercial banks also got in on the action, using securitization to tap the capital markets for funds to complement the money deposited by their customers.[5]

Banks, as well as other financial intermediaries that detected a lucrative market opportunity, sought ways of increasing the sources of residential mortgage funding. To attract investors, Wall Street investment bankers eventually developed a financial instrument that isolated defined **mortgage pools** (or *tranches*, which is French for "slices") that treated the mortgages as independent of each other, segmented the credit risk, and structured the cash flows from the underlying residential loans into bonds. Although it took several years to develop efficient mortgage securitization structures, loan originators quickly realized the process was transferable to commercial real estate loans as well. (Appendix A provides an overview of the evolution of US mortgage finance, securitization, and real estate derivatives).

———

Under the umbrella of securitized bonds and their esoteric derivatives (more on this later), there are seemingly endless acronyms.

I'll provide the background of the more commonly used abbreviations and briefly describe them.

Different Twins

MBSs and **asset-backed securities (ABSs)** are both known as "asset-structured products." The typical legal entity for the securitization of MBSs is a **real estate mortgage investment conduit (REMIC)**, a creation of the 1986 Tax Reform Act that allows mortgage-backed securities with multiple bondholder classes to be issued without any adverse tax consequences. MBSs are essentially mortgage-backed trusts that issue bonds, while a **mortgage bond** is a claim on a portion of the cash flows from a pool of thousands of individual home mortgages.

While MBSs are obviously backed by mortgages, ABSs are typically backed by other forms of collateral, such as credit card receivables, auto loans, or home-equity lines of credit. An ABS is subject to prepayment risk, although not as much as an MBS. When originally created, the assumption was that people are more likely to pay off their mortgages by refinancing than they are to pay off credit card debt, student loans, or auto loans.

Another key difference between the two types of securities is the way guarantees are offered by both. Fannie Mae and Freddie Mac MBSs are backed by the government and, therefore, have limited credit risk (similar to US Treasury bonds). An ABS, on the other hand, will entail a credit risk—albeit a small one—due to the differences in the underlying assets within the security.

Just like the mortgage industry, where banks sell securitized home loans to Fannie and Freddie (the two government-sponsored enterprises, or GSEs, that finance nearly all US mortgage-backed securities) to get them off their balance sheets, ABS issuers do the same to issue more and more debt.

Since mid-2010, asset-backed securities have been rebounding in the financial markets, while mortgage-backed securities have been having relatively small issuance volume (to be discussed in chapter 11). MBSs may be further divided into two general categories: (1) Those issued by one of the GSEs, known as agency MBSs; and (2) those that are issued by private financial institutions, known as private-label MBSs. The government-sponsored enterprises are basically charged with enhancing the flow and reducing the cost of credit for housing in the United States.

———

In 2011, the global capital markets still bore deep scars from securitization. Before the financial crisis, markets relied heavily on ABSs and MBSs to fund their lending, suffering greatly when that funding dried up instantly in 2007. The importance of ABSs and MBSs was that they were used to supply a significant amount of mortgage, consumer—and to a lesser extent—corporate financing in the US and foreign markets.

Inevitably, the crisis cost ABSs and MBSs their good name, but not always for the right reasons. It is true that MBSs helped fuel the US housing bubble, and when the bubble burst, the repercussions were magnified by a witch's brew of securitizations spiked with complex derivatives. But securitization's guilt mustn't condemn it to the garbage dumps of finance. Loan securitization isn't necessarily evil, but some derivatives are diabolic because they can create major instability in the financial system due to their profligate leverage and the fact that the counterparties are hidden.

———

The role of securitization is essentially to free credit from direct, relationship-based lending. Asset-backed securities can be taken off banks' balance sheets by end-investors, a way—in principle—of rendering the banking sector more robust and transparent. In the credit boom, of course, the opposite happened. The problem wasn't because the loans were repackaged into tradable bonds, rather it was because the repackaging was done in such a way that rendered end-investors, including the banks themselves, often times unaware of the real risks involved.

Before the meltdown in 2008, about a third of investors in securitization were banks. That concentration of risk, especially in B-piece tranches (discussed later), brought many down and, as a result, few are willing to delve back into securitization today. Other than the likes of JPMorgan Chase, Deutsche Bank, and Goldman Sachs,[6] not many financial institutions seem eager to assume the **liquidity risk** involved (the risk that arises from the difficulty of selling an asset or a financial product).

Apart from the higher capital requirements for banks under the Basel III announcement in September 2010[7], the new rules that force originators of loan securitization to keep 5 percent of each deal (or *more* skin in the game) have made bankers cautious. This has made them think twice about the products they sell, and thus should render the financial markets a relatively safer place. More significantly, companies hoping for a quick balance sheet fix can no longer offload much of their hidden risk as was happening during the Wild West days of the mid-2000s.

Your Home Is Just a Bond

Loan securitization breaks down into several subsectors that are generally characterized as **structured products**. For example, MBSs include both residential and commercial mortgage-backed securities. **Residential mortgage-backed securities (RMBSs)** are essentially bonds—instruments issued that promise to pay investors a fixed amount of interest for a defined period of time.

As we know, subprime RMBSs were at the center of the financial meltdown as the value of trillions of dollars of securities assumed to be safe plunged when the housing market collapsed and mortgage defaults soared. More specifically, the collapse of the US housing market in 2008 resulted in massive losses on **private-label** residential mortgage-backed securities (issued by large non-government agency financial firms), which financed millions of home loans before the crisis and were bought by investors around the world since the 1990s. Many of the senior tranches of such debt proved much riskier than expected and lost their allegedly stellar AAA (triple A) ratings.

Instead of being privately financed, new residential mortgages are almost entirely funded by the US government, through its backing of Fannie Mae and Freddie Mac. Since September 2008, these agencies have bought the vast majority of mortgages from banks and repackaged them into government-guaranteed RMBSs.

Residential mortgage-backed securities are created when a corporation such as Bank of America Merrill Lynch buys a cluster of mortgages from a primary lender—that is, from the company that you actually got your mortgage from—and then uses your monthly payments (and those of thousands of others) as the revenue stream to pay bond investors who bought clusters of the RMBS offering.

A mortgage is like a bond in that it represents a stream of payments, so an RMBS is similar to a bond fund that changes in price with fluctuations in interest rates, the likelihood of default, or the early repayment of the underlying debt. Furthermore, RMBSs allow lenders to sell the mortgages they make, thus adding to their capital and allowing them to lend again and again in a swirling whirlpool of fast-moving debt. For their part, buyers of residential mortgage-backed securities are supposed to feel "safe" with the knowledge that the value of the bond doesn't only rest on the creditworthiness of one borrower but on the collective creditworthiness of a large group of investors.

———

Between July 2007 and April 2008, the three main rating agencies (Standard & Poor's, Moody's, and Fitch) lowered the credit ratings on $1.9 trillion of RMBSs by applying the controversial "mark-to-market" valuation ruling by the Financial Accounting Standards Board, known as FAS 157. Mark-to-market (or "fair value" accounting) refers to quantifying the value of an asset or liability based on the current market price of the asset or liability, or for comparable assets and liabilities.

Mark-to-market accounting made values on the balance sheet change very frequently, as supply and demand conditions change daily. Mark-to-market accounting also had become inaccurate when prices deviated from the fundamental or intrinsic values of assets and liabilities. This is because buyers and sellers were unable to collectively and accurately value the future value of income from securities due to incorrect information from the credit rating agencies, or overly optimistic or excessively pessimistic expectations. Therefore, financial institutions had to lower the value of their residential mortgage-backed securities and acquire additional capital so as to maintain their capital-reserve ratios. The decline in the value of RMBSs held by these highly leveraged companies resulted in their insolvency—the equivalent of bank runs—as investors hastily pulled funds from them.

However, in 2009, the Financial Accounting Standards Board (FASB)—in response to growing concern and following a public comment period in which leading accounting firms offered their feedback—formally made public FAS 157-4. With the changes to rule 157, banks can now value the assets on their books as if they were unloaded in an "orderly" sale rather than dumped in a forced or "distressed" sale. So in order to avoid writing-down a bad loan, all a bank has to do is state that it more than likely will be holding onto an asset for an indefinite period of time without any capital pressure to dispose of it. This method has also caused much confusion in the financial markets because the intrinsic value of assets is obscured.

———

Increasing risk levels (which can be viewed as an "expense") reduce the value of securities that pay a fixed rate of interest; therefore, yields move inversely to bond prices, as explained in Appendix C. When borrowers default on mortgages, the stream of payments available to holders of RMBSs, therefore, declines. In addition, when a firm borrows heavily to finance the purchase and trading of such securities, it doesn't take much of a fall in value to trigger serious repercussions throughout the financial system.

When the housing market was thriving on congenital optimism and interest rates were low, investing in an RMBS appeared to be a no-brainer. So long as homeowners stayed current on their payments, holders of residential mortgage-backed securities received a nice stream of cash flow. Even those investors who bought low quality RMBSs in the hopes of receiving higher interest payments (to compensate them for the higher risk taken) fared well in the frenzied boom. But when the housing markets cratered, even the safest of these investments found themselves in financial quicksand.

———

In the following paragraphs I explain (with the aid of several illustrations) how plain-vanilla residential mortgage-backed securities are created.[8] I illustrate the creation of RMBSs using figures 2-2 through 2-4. Figure 2-2 shows five mortgage loans (each loan is shown as a house), and lists the cash flows from those loans to investors.

Figure 2-2: Cash Flow of Home Mortgage Loans

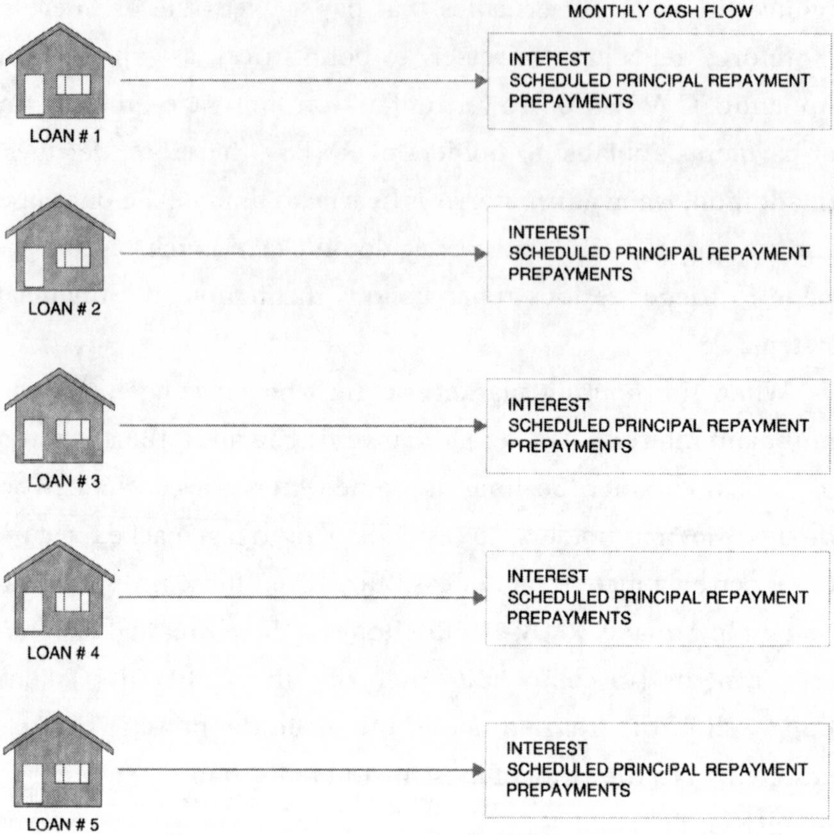

MONTHLY CASH FLOW

INTEREST
SCHEDULED PRINCIPAL REPAYMENT
PREPAYMENTS

LOAN # 1

INTEREST
SCHEDULED PRINCIPAL REPAYMENT
PREPAYMENTS

LOAN # 2

INTEREST
SCHEDULED PRINCIPAL REPAYMENT
PREPAYMENTS

LOAN # 3

INTEREST
SCHEDULED PRINCIPAL REPAYMENT
PREPAYMENTS

LOAN # 4

INTEREST
SCHEDULED PRINCIPAL REPAYMENT
PREPAYMENTS

LOAN # 5

EACH LOAN IS FOR $200,000

TOTAL LOANS: $1 MILLION

For simplicity, I've assumed that the amount of each loan is $200,000, so the aggregate value of all five loans is $1 million. The cash flows are monthly and consist of three components:

1. Interest;
2. Scheduled principal repayment; and
3. Payments in excess of the regularly scheduled principal repayment.

The third component above is referred to as a **prepayment**. It's the amount and timing of this component of the cash flow from a mortgage that make the analysis of RMBSs complex. When the way in which residential mortgage-backed securities are created is examined, it can be seen that the total amount of prepayment risk doesn't change. It is the *distribution* of the risk among numerous investors, rather, that can be altered.

———

Mortgage borrowers typically repay their loans only when interest rates fall, so they can refinance more cheaply, leaving the owner of a mortgage bond holding a pile of cash to invest at lower interest rates. The investor in home loans doesn't know how long his investment will last, only that he will probably get his money back when he *least* wants or expects it. For example, an investor who owns one of the mortgage loans (shown in figure 2-2) faces prepayment risk. For an individual loan, it's difficult to predict prepayments, but if an individual investor purchased all five loans, then he might be able to better predict prepayments on a broader scale. In fact, if there were 500 mortgage loans in figure 2-2 instead of five, the investor might be able to use historical data to improve his predictions about prepayments. (But an investor would have to invest $1 million to buy five loans and $100 million to buy 500 loans, assuming that each loan is for $200,000).

Just Passing Through

What happens if entities, such as Fannie Mae, Freddie Mac, or the Government National Mortgage Association (Ginnie Mae), purchased all five loans in figure 2-2 from a primary lender and pooled them together? The five loans can be used as collateral for the issuance of a bond, with the cash flow from that security reflecting an equal claim of the underlying cash flows from the five loans, as shown in figure 2-3.

Figure 2-3: Creation of a Pass-Through Security

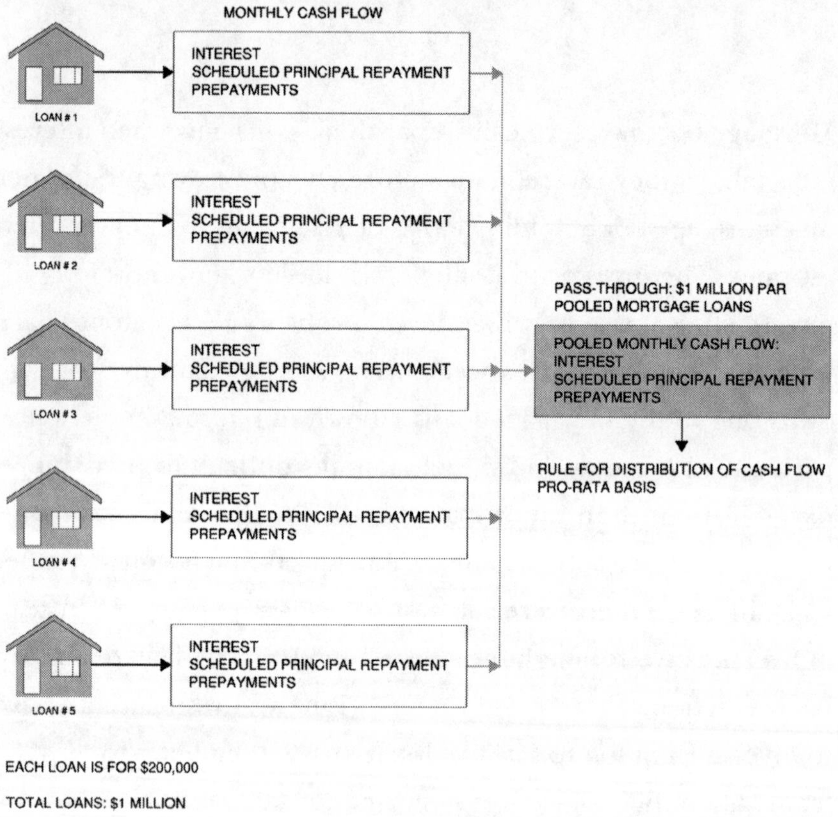

MONTHLY CASH FLOW

INTEREST
SCHEDULED PRINCIPAL REPAYMENT
PREPAYMENTS

LOAN # 1

INTEREST
SCHEDULED PRINCIPAL REPAYMENT
PREPAYMENTS

LOAN # 2

PASS-THROUGH: $1 MILLION PAR
POOLED MORTGAGE LOANS

INTEREST
SCHEDULED PRINCIPAL REPAYMENT
PREPAYMENTS

LOAN # 3

POOLED MONTHLY CASH FLOW:
INTEREST
SCHEDULED PRINCIPAL REPAYMENT
PREPAYMENTS

RULE FOR DISTRIBUTION OF CASH FLOW
PRO-RATA BASIS

INTEREST
SCHEDULED PRINCIPAL REPAYMENT
PREPAYMENTS

LOAN # 4

INTEREST
SCHEDULED PRINCIPAL REPAYMENT
PREPAYMENTS

LOAN # 5

EACH LOAN IS FOR $200,000

TOTAL LOANS: $1 MILLION

Suppose that fifty units of this security are issued. Therefore, each unit is initially worth $20,000 ($1 million divided by fifty), and each unit will be entitled to 2 percent (a 1/50 pro-rata share) of the mortgage bond's cash flow. The security created is called a **pass-through**. A pass-through is basically a tax-efficient security representing pooled debt obligations (or bonds) repackaged as shares that pass income from debtors to investors (via an intermediary) with each bond having an equal claim on the mortgage payments of the pool, thus spreading the risk evenly. A **trustee** is designated as the owner of the mortgages in the pool and ensures that all payments are made to individual security owners. Cash flows from the pool, which consist of principal and interest, are distributed to security holders. That is why the securities are called passthroughs, because cash flows are "passed-through" to the investors by the intermediary (mortgage originator or servicer). By creating such a pass-through, the total amount of prepayment risk has not changed. However, with an amount of less than $1 million, the investor is still exposed to the *total* prepayment risk of all the five loans, rather than face the risk of an individual mortgage loan.

So far this financial structure hasn't resulted in the creation of a novel instrument, since an individual investor could have accomplished the same outcome by purchasing all five loans. But by buying a pass-through, an investor with less than $1 million can acquire a proportionate share of all five loans. Furthermore, by selling a pass-through the investor can dispose of all five loans simultaneously, rather than having to inefficiently dispose of each loan one by one. (The marketability of a pass-through is also greater than that of individual loans).

A pass-through can, therefore, be viewed as a more transactionally efficient vehicle for investing in mortgages than the purchasing of individual ones. Mortgage loans that are included in a pool to create a pass-through are said to be "securitized." As such, the creation of a pass-through is one of the ways comprising the process referred to earlier as "loan securitization."

Divvying It Up

Following the financial crisis of 2008, **collateralized mortgage obligations (CMOs)** have been slow to recover. CMOs are basically a pool of mortgage bonds tranched to reflect the degree of sensitivity to prepayment.

A collateralized mortgage obligation starts its life as a portfolio of MBSs, which turns pools of thirty-year mortgages into collections of two-, five-, and ten-year bonds to appeal to a wide range of investors. As indicated earlier, an investor in a pass-through is still exposed to the total prepayment risk associated with the underlying pool of the five mortgages. However, financial instruments can be created in which investors don't share prepayment risk equally. For example, instead of distributing the monthly cash flow on a pro-rata basis, as in the case of a pass-through, the distribution of the mortgage *principal* is carried out on a prioritized basis. How this is achieved is depicted in figure 2-4, which shows the cash flows of the original five mortgage loans and the pass-through. The figure also shows three classes of CMOs, the par value (that is, the value of a security that is set by the entity issuing it) of each class, and a set of rules indicating how the principal amount from the pass-through is to be distributed to each class (tranche).

Figure 2-4: Creation of a Collateralized Mortgage Obligation

MONTHLY CASH FLOW

INTEREST
SCHEDULED PRINCIPAL REPAYMENT
PREPAYMENTS

LOAN # 1

INTEREST
SCHEDULED PRINCIPAL REPAYMENT
PREPAYMENTS

LOAN # 2

PASS-THROUGH: $1 MILLION PAR
POOLED MORTGAGE LOANS

POOLED MONTHLY CASH FLOW:
INTEREST
SCHEDULED PRINCIPAL REPAYMENT
PREPAYMENTS

INTEREST
SCHEDULED PRINCIPAL REPAYMENT
PREPAYMENTS

LOAN # 3

RULE FOR DISTRIBUTION OF CASH FLOW
PRO-RATA BASIS

INTEREST
SCHEDULED PRINCIPAL REPAYMENT
PREPAYMENTS

LOAN # 4

INTEREST
SCHEDULED PRINCIPAL REPAYMENT
PREPAYMENTS

LOAN # 5

EACH LOAN IS FOR $200,000

TOTAL LOANS: $1 MILLION

COLLATERALIZED MORTGAGE OBLIGATION (THREE CLASSES)

RULE FOR DISTRIBUTION OF CASH FLOW TO THE THREE CLASSES

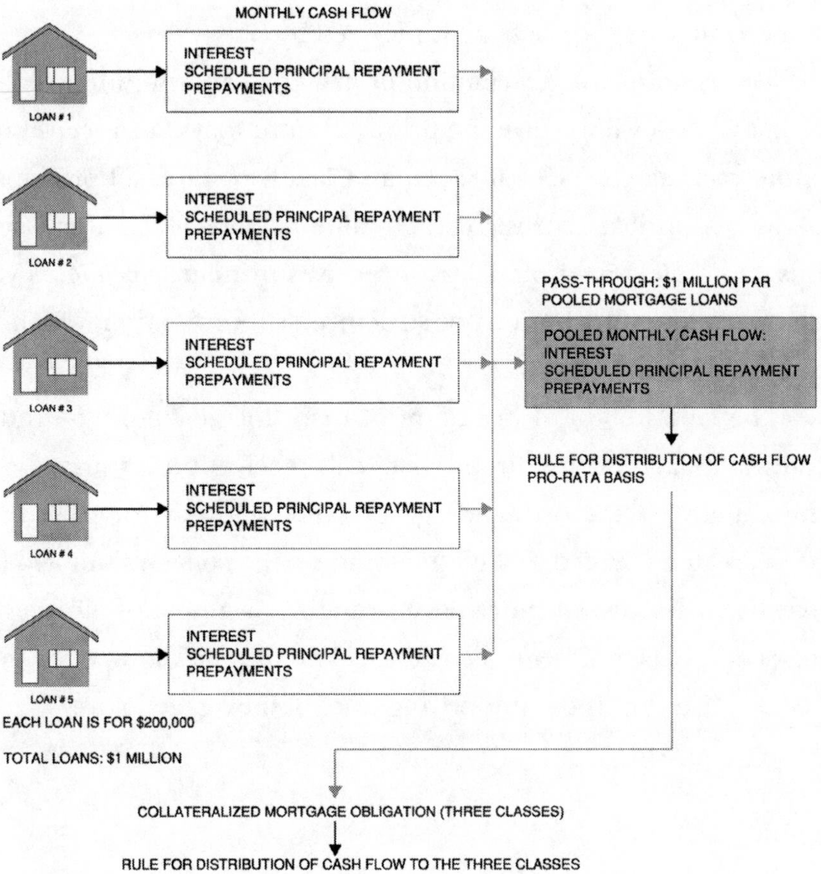

CLASS (PAR VALUE)	INTEREST	PRINCIPAL
A. ($500,000)	PAY EACH MONTH BASED ON PAR AMOUNT OUTSTANDING	RECEIVES ALL MONTHLY PRINCIPAL UNTIL COMPLETELY PAID OFF
B. ($300,000)	PAY EACH MONTH BASED ON PAR AMOUNT OUTSTANDING	AFTER CLASS A PAID OFF, RECEIVES ALL MONTHLY PRINCIPAL UNTIL COMPLETELY PAID OFF
C. ($200,000)	PAY EACH MONTH BASED ON PAR AMOUNT OUTSTANDING	AFTER CLASS B PAID OFF, RECEIVES ALL MONTHLY PRINCIPAL

The sum of the par values of the three classes (A, B, and C) is equal to $1 million. Though not shown in figure 2-4, for each of the three classes there would be units representing a proportionate interest in a class of CMOs. For example, suppose that for

Class A, which has a par value of $500,000, there are fifty units issued. Each unit would, therefore, receive a proportionate share (2 percent, or 1/50) of what is received by Class A.

The rule for the distribution of principal shown in figure 2-4 is that Class A will receive the principal until that class receives its entire par value of $500,000. Then, Class B receives all principal payments until it receives its par value of $300,000. After Class B is completely paid off, Class C receives principal payments via this cascading distribution (or structured subordination, which is discussed later).

The rule for the distribution of cash flow in figure 2-4 indicates that each of the three classes will receive interest based on the amount of the outstanding par value. The security that has been created is called a CMO. In addition, the collateral for a loan may be either one or more pass-throughs, or a pool of mortgage loans that have not been securitized. The ultimate source for the CMO's cash flow is the underlying pool of mortgage loans.

———

What has been accomplished so far? Once again, the total prepayment risk for the CMO is the same as the total prepayment risk for the five mortgage loans. However, the prepayment risk has been distributed among the three classes of the CMO. The result of this is that Class A will effectively have a shorter-term security than classes B and C, while Class C will have the longest maturity (the date at which the debt instrument is due and payable).

Certain investors—mainly institutional—would be attracted to the different classes, given the nature of their liability structure (what they owe) and the effective maturity of each CMO class. In addition, the uncertainty about the maturity of each class of the collateralized mortgage obligation is far less than the uncertainty pertaining to the maturity of the pass-through security. Therefore, by redirecting the cash flow from the underlying mortgage pool, different tranches have been created that satisfy the liability objectives and risk parameters of investors better than a pass-through. A CMO is not an innovative market instrument, since it simply represents the *redirecting* of the cash flows. However, it is a transactionally efficient instrument for distributing prepayment risk by divvying up the principal amounts.

To recap, the collateralized mortgage obligation illustrated in figure 2-4 has a simple set of rules for prioritizing the distribution of the principal. The purpose is to provide specific CMO classes with less uncertainty about prepayment risk. But this elevated comfort level for one class can occur only if the reduction in prepayment risk is absorbed by the *other* classes in the CMO structure.

As demonstrated, the simplest financial product—the home mortgage—is an instrument for which the underlying cash flow is uncertain because the borrower/homeowner has an option to prepay part, or the entire loan, at any time. The value of mortgage bonds is particularly sensitive to *when* homeowners repay the mortgages. If the mortgages are refinanced, the bonds backed by the mortgages are repaid at par, meaning that investors would lose any amount of foregone cash flow above that. The uncertainty about when a borrower/homeowner will prepay a mortgage is called **prepayment risk**, and if it were not for this risk, the analysis of RMBSs would be much less complex. In addition, when interest rates decline—causing an increase in the prepayment of mortgages—interest payments to investors decline and these investors lose a portion of their investment, thus complicating the analysis.

The Pecking Order

The most common internal credit enhancement mechanism in the MBS market is known as the senior-subordinate structure.[9] It was very common for subprime loan pools to be carved up into tranches such that cash flows from bonds would suit particular investor requirements. The idea is that the senior pieces are designed to get paid preferentially, while the subordinated tranches get paid only to the extent that the underlying collateral permits. Of course, and as compensation, the higher-risk pieces offer a higher expected yield. This aspect of the senior-subordinate credit enhancement, or pecking order, is called **structured subordination** or a "waterfall."

For example, when a pre-crisis residential mortgage-backed security (RMBS) deal was structured, bonds of various levels of credit risk were created to generate cash flow streams from borrowers to investors. Following the process of credit tranching, the securitized loans were divided into different classes according to their level of risk. The top tranches were the low-risk AAA-rated bonds, and below these were the higher-risk, higher-return classes. At the highest risk level was the equity tranche or "first-loss" piece—which was not rated by the rating agencies—in a structure that was intended to have the equity tranche protect and absorb the defaults of the other tranches (see figure 2-5).

Figure 2-5: RMBS Tranche Structure

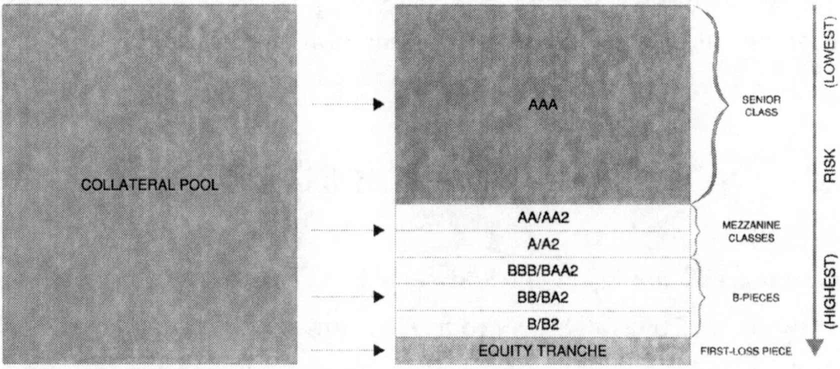

Source: Citibank, Society of Actuaries

Put another way, the buyer of the first tranche (equity) was like the owner of the ground floor in a flood: he got hit with the first wave of mortgage prepayments. In exchange, he received a higher interest rate. The buyer of the second tranche—the second story of the building—took the next wave of prepayments and in exchange received the second highest interest rate, and so on. The investor in the top floor of the building (the AAA tranche) received the lowest rate of interest but had the greatest assurance that his investment wouldn't end before he wanted it to.[10]

Through this credit tranching process, it was possible for the senior pieces to obtain senior class/investment-grade status, even though the underlying collateral was subprime mortgage debt. This was because the AAA tranche wasn't backed by specific loans, only by a set of rules governing the cash flows from the loans. Therefore, depending on the level of subordination (the percentage of principal of the deal that's designated as subordinate), the senior tranches were protected from losses up to a predetermined level. Such a set of rules is an example of a pool of securities that was tranched into various credit classes, where the pool was rated by credit rating agencies and sold to bond investors under the moniker of a collateralized mortgage obligation (CMO).

Rising From the Ashes of Collapse

Commercial mortgage-backed security (CMBS) loans were originally created by Wall Street to free up additional sources of capital in the non-residential real estate market, which primarily includes office, retail, industrial, apartment, and hotel properties. They've been around since the mid-1980s, but they gained popularity during the euphoric run-up in commercial property values from 2005 to 2007. Similar to RMBSs, CMBS loans differ from conventional bank loans in that they are pooled together and offered as bonds to investors based on credit ratings given by the likes of Standard & Poor's, Moody's, and Fitch.

The prepayment risk level is lower in the case of CMBSs compared to RMBSs, as most commercial mortgages have fixed terms and prepayment penalties. That is, commercial mortgages often contain "lock-out" provisions after which they can be subject to defeasance and yield maintenance clauses to protect the bondholders.[11] In addition, CMBSs are not supported by the two government-sponsored enterprises (GSEs), Fannie Mae and Freddie Mac.

———

As a lending vehicle, commercial mortgage-backed securities usually offer borrowers lower interest rates and higher leverage. All are typically non-recourse loans (in the event of a default, the lender is allowed to pursue only the collateral and cannot seek payment directly from individuals, although there are some exceptions to this clause). In addition, unlike portfolio loans—which continue to be held by the originating lender through maturity—many commercial real estate senior loans originated since the mid-1990s were securitized CMBS lending products.

In a CMBS transaction, many single mortgage loans of varying size, property type, and location are pooled and transferred to a trustee/custodian, typically a major bank, which holds title to the loans pursuant to an "indenture trust agreement" for the benefit of the bondholders—the investors to whom interests in the CMBS pool of loans are sold.[12] A series of bonds are issued that may vary in yield, duration, and payment priority. The nationally recognized rating agencies assign credit ratings to the various bond classes ranging from investment-grade to below investment-grade, and an unrated class (equity) that is subordinate to the lowest rated bond class.[13]

———

Investors are able to choose which CMBS bonds to purchase based on the level of credit risk they want to assume, the yield they desire (yields go up as risk goes up), and the duration (maturity) they seek.[14] Each month the interest received from all of the pooled CMBS loans is paid to the bondholders, starting with those holding the highest rated bonds, until all accrued interest is paid on those bonds. Then interest is paid to the holders of the next highest rated bonds, and so on. The same process occurs with the principal amount, as payments are received by the CMBS trustee.[15]

This sequential payment hierarchy, including the priority of paying operating expenses, real estate taxes, and mezzanine loan debt service, is generally referred to as the **cash waterfall** and is typically set forth in one or more cash management agreements.[16] If there is a shortfall in contractual loan payments from the borrowers, or if the loan collateral is liquidated and doesn't generate sufficient proceeds to meet payments on all the bond classes in the capital stack, investors in the most subordinate (higher risk) bond class will incur a loss, with any further losses impacting the more senior classes.[17]

Pools of CMBS loans are typically placed into a real estate mortgage investment conduit (REMIC), also known as a trust or a special purpose entity. The REMIC allows the investment structure to qualify as a pass-through-issuing entity not subject to tax at the trust level. Since bondholders base their investment decisions on the assumption that the REMIC will not be subject to taxation at the trust level, strict compliance with REMIC tax regulations is essential.[18]

———

CMBSs became an attractive capital source for commercial real estate lending because the bonds backed by a pool of loans were generally worth more than the sum of the value of all the loans. The enhanced liquidity and structure of CMBSs attracted a broader range of investors to the commercial mortgage market. This apparent value creation allowed loans intended for securitization to be aggressively priced, benefiting borrowers (and thus driving up commercial real estate values).[19]

A typical CMBS is stuffed with mortgages on a diverse group of properties—often fewer than one hundred—with loans ranging from a couple of million dollars to more than $100 million. Table 2-1 provides a summary of the pros and cons of CMBSs.

Table 2-1: The Pros and Cons of Commercial Mortgage-Backed Securities

Pros	Cons
• Contribute to financing-liquidity in the commercial real estate sector. • Offer lower interest rates. • Higher loan-to-value (LTV) as a result of tranching. • Non-recourse to the borrower. • Can be applied to nearly any property type or location. • Closing period is quicker than portfolio loans.	• Typically unable to prepay interest with a CMBS loan. • In a workout situation, the special servicer must follow the pooling and servicing agreement, which often gives little flexibility to modify the loan. • CMBS loans divide responsibilities among many parties who often don't know each other. • Special servicers focus only on maximizing recovery for the bondholders.

Source: Harvard Business School

———

Commercial mortgage-backed securities got white-hot in the market rocket-ride of 2005–07, and the underlying loans were extremely aggressive. Some were interest-only, and they were high leverage (the excessive use of other people's money). They basically did things local banks wouldn't have done.

As odd as this may sound, banking should basically be staid, and thorough credit analysis should dominate over so-called financial engineering. "Boring banking" did not constrain the financing of innovation and development in America. Instead, it facilitated a phase of tremendous growth in economic output and prosperity between the 1940s and the 1980s, before deregulation paved the way for an out-of-control financial system.[20] Bankers should be successful again if they apply the basics of banking, compared to, say, the intricate web of derivatives dealings. After all, real estate is not supposed to be a casino that thrives on fantasy stuff and murky dealings.

Figure 2-6: Back to Boring Banking?

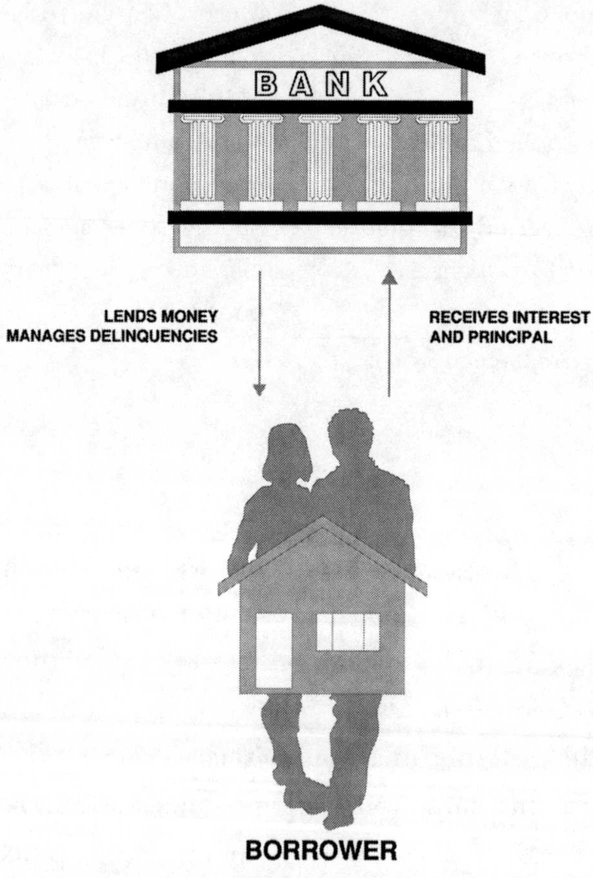

LENDS MONEY
MANAGES DELINQUENCIES

RECEIVES INTEREST
AND PRINCIPAL

BORROWER

Loan securitization was a leading source of real estate financing until the meltdown of 2008. The securitized share of subprime mortgages (those passed to third-party investors via RMBSs) increased from 54 percent in 2001 to 75 percent in 2006. In 2007, Wall Street sold $230 billion of commercial mortgage-backed securities, a record. In contrast, there were only $2.6 billion in new CMBS issues in 2009, $11.6 billion in 2010, with some $32 billion in issuances projected for 2011.

Default rates on US CMBSs were hitting record levels in 2011 after a big jump in defaults on such bonds in 2010, according to Fitch Ratings. Bonds backed by loans on trophy (core) office buildings and hotels increased in value as investors rushed into markets based on optimism that an economic recovery would help reduce defaults on property investments. Despite the relatively improved sentiment in the commercial real estate sector, the losses on CMBSs, especially those sold in the run-up to the financial crisis in 2007, have continued to rise. Total defaults rose to 10.6 percent in 2010, up from 6.6 percent in 2009. Fitch expected the overall default rate on CMBSs to exceed 11 percent by the end of 2011. However, Fitch indicated some slowing in the pace of new defaults, but noted that it was too early to predict a meaningful decline in default rates in the near future due to commercial real estate fundamentals lagging the overall economic environment. There remained a huge difference in defaults depending on the year the loan was originated. For example, of the $22 billion of CMBS defaults in 2010, Fitch found nearly 50 percent were from 2007 vintage deals.

———

The securitization markets shut-down completely in August 2007, and while they were virtually stagnant after the financial crisis, by

2011 CMBSs were slowly rising from the ashes (see figure 2-7). However, some investors were still spooked by the potential loss rates on CMBS deals.

Figure 2-7: US Commercial Mortgage-Backed Securities Issuance

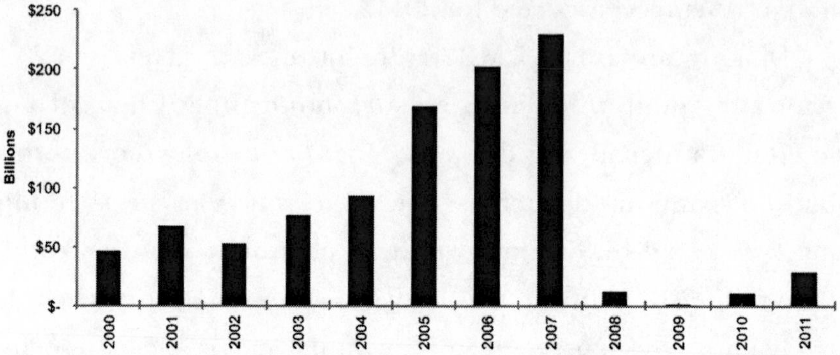

Source: *Commercial Mortgage Alert,* Commercial Real Estate Finance Council, Standard & Poor's

The narrow focus on high quality, stabilized assets in prime markets is one of the main obstacles to renewed commercial mortgage-backed security volume. New CMBS deals are backed almost exclusively by the upper crust of commercial properties— trophy assets that command excellent locations in major markets. By definition, that excludes investors with properties outside the best urban areas, or with properties operating with some level of vacancy. As such, a steady flow of new origination or refinancing activity trickling down to tertiary markets and locations had yet to be seen in 2011.

Investors want to buy more securitizations but many are concerned that they still cannot properly analyze CMBS deals, underlining the complexities of rebuilding an overall securitization market that was at the epicenter of the financial crisis. In addition, the securitization sector's efforts to restart CMBSs have been made difficult by the complex nature of deals and the various structures in place in the global markets. Because so many are tailored transactions, it's still hard to compare cash flows across two seemingly similar deals, since each has a slightly different set of rules governing which group of bondholders gets their cash flow first.

———

The typical pre-crisis CMBS deal flowed like this: After the commercial banks, mortgage bankers, and insurance companies—known collectively as loan originators—closed their loans, many of the mortgages were sold off to investment banks, at which point the originators essentially exited the deals. The CMBS loans were then placed into tax-efficient real estate mortgage investment conduits (REMICs), or trusts. Then pass-through certificates (mortgage bonds) were pooled, packaged, and securitized with other loans by the fixed-income departments of big Wall Street investment banks and sold to a variety of investors worldwide after being euphorically blessed by the credit rating agencies. (As fixed-income securities, the bonds were technically a "fractional ownership" in the CMBS trust). The mortgage pools were sliced to create multiple classes (tranches) of bonds, each of which had a different seniority, risk profile, and credit rating relative to the others. A trustee then administered the sale of the various classes of bonds to investors based on their appetite for risk and return. A CMBS servicer (usually a large financial institution) hired by the trustee collected monthly payments from the borrowers and passed the money on to the institutional investors that bought the bonds.

———

As presented in figure 2-8, which shows how convoluted the CMBS process was, the notes backed by the mortgage pool's income reflect different levels of risk given by the credit rating agencies. Senior notes were usually considered the least risky and were sold with AAA credit ratings. The BBB tranches were riskier as they absorbed any losses on the mortgage pool first and could easily get wiped out.

The trustee shown in figure 2-8 is the nominal owner of all the assets in a commercial mortgage-backed security trust. His primary responsibility is to hold the assets for CMBS investors. Borrowers won't generally hear from the trustee. Through power of attorney, the trustee delegates the day-to-day administration of the loans to the master servicer, although in the event of a fore-closure such action is taken in the name of the trustee (after title passes, it's held in the name of the trustee).[21]

Upon uncured monetary defaults (such as a sixty-day or more delinquency on debt service) or other circumstances—includ-ing failure in certain non-monetary default covenants that could affect the CMBS—the master servicer can refer the loan file to a special servicer. Special servicers have significantly more influ-ence in the restructuring of the debt.

Prior to 2009, special servicers generally didn't permit loan modifications unless there was an actual default on the loan. (This is a key point since a loan modification prevents a default and postpones the day of reckoning). However, certain changes made to the rules governing REMICs in 2009 allow for some loan modification when default is either imminent or anticipated. Specifically, the 2009 changes referred to two items: the "principally secured test" and the "imminent default test."[22]

Figure 2-8: The Seven Convoluted Steps of the CMBS Securitization Process

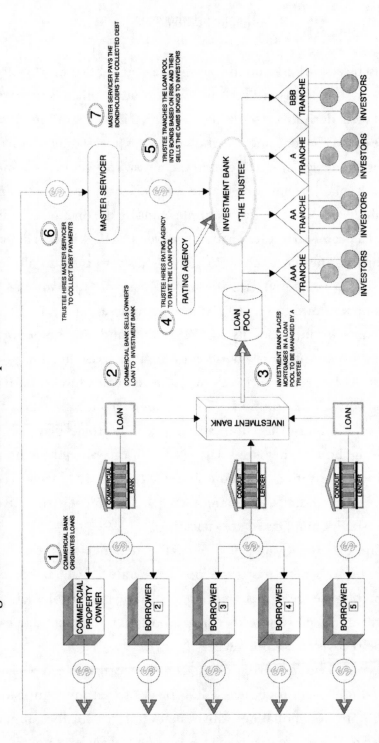

Source: Harvard Business School

Diabolic Derivatives

As discussed earlier, a bond is a relatively straightforward security. A not-so-straightforward security is a derivative, which is bond-*like*. The word **derivative** (short for derivative instrument) itself can cause confusion for someone who's not completely familiar with the English language, not to mention the messy world of high-finance.

In layman's terms, a derivative is a piece of "paper" that *derives* its value from an asset. For example, a mortgage on a house (also called a **promissory note** or the borrower's "IOU") is such a piece of paper. (The term "paper" is loosely used to refer to all debt issued by a company). To simplify, let's assume that you are an investor who owns a securitized mortgage on a house, the house maintains or increases its market value, and the homeowner makes the mortgage payments on a regular basis, meaning that you should be a content person. However, you can also be happier if you sell that derivative (the value of which is based on the note on the house) to another investor, thus avoiding any direct risk if the homeowner stops paying and/or the value of the house declines. Derivatives can combine real, or "hard," assets (i.e., gold, land, buildings, equipment, etc.) with other instruments in increasingly complicated cocktails.[23]

The economic value of a derivative depends on three risky characteristics of a mortgage pool: the rate at which borrowers prepay (redeem their mortgages early); their probability of default; and the loss severity (the proportion of the debt that cannot be recovered if a borrower defaults).

As noted earlier, investors who acquire mortgages can package and bundle them together, selling pieces to yet more investors, and so on, in a global derivatives marketplace. But the ultimate holder of the mortgage, or pieces of a mortgage, may not always know the market value of the mortgaged property or how that value may be changing. Therefore, to offload that additional risk the mortgages are sold and resold repeatedly through ultra-complex securitization (i.e., CDOs-squared and CDOs-cubed). In the meantime, the actual values of the homes could be plummeting, causing the value of the derivatives to decline in tandem. This results in yet more transfer of risk onto another investor to get rid of the unwanted securitized mortgages (read: phantom financial products) that are being tossed around. Ultimately, this game of "hot potato" can stop and the pile of mortgage paper collapses into a worthless heap of financial garbage.

————

Derivatives based on subprime mortgages were diabolic because they were side bets on the debts of ordinary and less creditworthy Americans. The subprime mortgage loans they were based on were, in essence, a cheat—a rip-off that nibbled away at a wholesome slice of pure Americana. What made such derivatives even more diabolic was that many people on Wall Street, who didn't give a damn about what they were selling, didn't understand them.

This, however, doesn't mean that *all* derivatives are diabolic. Derivatives can be highly useful, but only if they price in all the risk they embody. For example, futures, swaps, and options for commodities such as cotton, crude oil, and pork bellies—or those related to interest rates and foreign currency exchange rates—appropriately fulfill their purpose of hedging risk, because the party with the risk, like the Midwest farmer, is protecting his future. That means that such derivatives can also help companies smooth out their earnings over multiple periods, or reduce their tax bills by deferring earnings into the future.

If You Play with Fire...

The degree to which derivatives had created havoc via dangerously interlinked capital markets became clear after the infamous
breakdown of AIG (American International Group), Bear Stearns,
and Lehman Brothers in 2008. The default by one bank at the
center of a tangled web of derivatives contracts with dizzying complexity paralyzed the whole financial system. That's because the
derivatives became worthless as the underlying mortgage-backed
securities declined significantly in value.

Looking back at the crisis of 2008 we see that excessive aggregate
real estate debt is basically what brought down the financial system
(discussed in chapter 8). Sloppy lending, driven by poor underwriting standards, also contributed to the meltdown. Screwed-up derivatives led to the most *purely* real estate-driven disaster in history.

For example, a large portion of AIG's position was taken via
high-risk derivatives infested with underlying real estate mortgage uncertainty. Fannie Mae and Freddie Mac, with combined
losses topping $160 billion, had colossal real estate exposure
through derivatives. Washington Mutual and Wachovia were victims of severe residential mortgage problems. Both banks were
very active creating collateralized debt obligations (which are
explained later) out of subprime mortgages and other opaque
debt structures. Bear Stearns was "rescued" by being gobbled up
by JPMorgan Chase, but nearly $30 billion of its deadly real estate
exposure was left at the Federal Reserve Board (the Fed)—the
nation's key financial regulator and probably the world's most
powerful institution.

Lehman, of course, failed spectacularly, its demise being the
result of soured real estate investments. Countrywide Financial,
America's largest mortgage lender at the time, was acquired by

Bank of America (several months before it bought Merrill Lynch in September 2008). Others, such as Independent National Mortgage Corporation (IndyMac), American Home Mortgage, and New Century Mortgage, failed as well. Dozens of other banks with more than $1 billion of assets failed because of real estate problems that spread like a lethal virus throughout the globally wired derivatives markets. Moreover, property severely impaired the entire credit insurance industry (also known as the monoline sector comprised of groups like Ambac and PMI Group), which tried to diversify from insuring the rather dull world of public finance (municipal and local governments) but drove its business into the ground.

———

Better risk management of the mortgage market would be much more effective if it was more focused on excessive real estate debt risk. The casualties of the financial crisis were not only the victims of property-linked derivatives—rather, they were the victims of aggressive lending and a missed assessment of real estate debt risk, which are bound to resurface again if effective measures aren't implemented.

Repackaged Crappy Loans

Mortgage-backed securities are a subset of a financial instrument known as a **collateralized debt obligation (CDO)**. A CDO is a bond-like security with cash flows that are derived from other bonds backed by mortgages, thus making it a derivative. Note that a CDO is fundamentally similar to a collateralized mortgage obligation (CMO), which was discussed earlier, in that the risk of a portfolio of bonds has been bundled and redistributed so that some buyers have far less risk and some have far more, depending on their risk tolerance. The only difference is that a CMO is designed to redistribute *prepayment* risk, whereas a CDO is designed to redistribute *default* risk. That is, a CMO takes a portfolio of mortgage-backed securities and divvies up the principal payments, while a CDO takes a portfolio of credit-risky bonds and divvies up the **credit losses**. (Commercial banks take charge-offs on loans that have defaulted and increase their reserves in tandem for loans they expect to go bad, which they label as "credit losses").

––––––

The collateralized debt obligation has a suspect pedigree. The first basic CDO was issued in 1987 by bankers at Drexel Burnham Lambert for Imperial Savings Association. Drexel Burnham had collapsed in the wake of insider trading scandals that sent financier Michael Milken to prison. Imperial later became insolvent and was taken over in 1990 by the Resolution Trust Corporation (RTC) during the savings and loan crisis of the late 1980s. A decade later, collateralized debt obligations emerged as the fastest-growing sector of the derivatives market. This reflected the increasing appeal of CDOs for a growing number of asset managers and investors, which included insurance companies, hedge funds, commercial and investment banks, and pension funds, among others.

––––––

A collateralized debt obligation is also quite similar to a regular mutual fund that buys bonds. In simpler terms, a CDO is an arrangement that raises money primarily by issuing its own mort-gage-backed securities and then invests the proceeds in a port-folio of bonds.[24] (Typically, a pre-crisis CDO had an underlying portfolio of roughly one hundred bonds).

Payments on the portfolio were the main source of funds for repaying a CDO's own securities. Most collateralized debt obliga-tions had actively managed portfolios, and before the financial crisis a typical deal had a management company that collected fees for managing the portfolio (similar to a mutual fund).

As part of the smoke and mirrors culture of Wall Street, a CDO composed of nothing but the riskiest, mezzanine layer of subprime mortgages was not called a "subprime-backed CDO," but a more bespoke-sounding "structured finance CDO." There was so much confusion about the different terms, and in the course of trying to figure them out, many investors realized that there's a reason why they didn't make sense to them. It's because they *didn't* make sense. The subprime mortgage bond market had a special talent for obscuring what needed to be clarified. Bond market terminology was designed less to convey meaning than to confuse outsiders—to add intrigue and mystique with sexy-sound-ing words and acronyms.

———

Table 2-2 shows a basic CDO capital structure with four issued classes of securities of $300 million derived from a collateral pool of debt designated as:

- Senior class or high-grade debt (takes priority over other unsecured debt owed by the issuer);

- Mezzanine class debt (so-named because it exists in the middle of the capital structure);
- B-pieces (holders have a claim on assets only *after* the senior and mezzanine debt holders' claims have been satisfied); and
- Equity or first-loss piece (the residual claim of the most junior class of investors in assets, after all debts are paid). The equity class is the riskiest in the capital stack.

Table 2-2: Capital Structure of a Basic Collateralized Debt Obligation

Class	Amount (millions)	Percent of the Deal*	Subordination Percentage**	Ratings by Credit Agencies
Senior	$243	81.0%	25.5%	AAA/AA-
Mezzanine	$24	8.0%	19.0%	A+/A-
B-pieces	$18	6.0%	13.0%	BBB+/B- or lower
Equity	$15	5.0%	0.0%	Not rated

Source: Nomura Securities International. *Although this example shows that the mezzanine tranche comprises 8 percent of the overall capital structure, many CDOs based on mortgage bonds were comprised of a much higher portion of risky mezzanine tranches. **The subordination percentage of a security is the percentage of the total capital which is subordinate to the security in question. Thus, the security will not suffer any losses until *after* that percentage of capital has been lost.

Logically, investors demand higher yields on classes exposed to greater credit risk. In table 2-2 above, the senior securities would command the lowest yield because they carry the highest ratings (and lowest risk). Conversely, the equity class would command the highest risk because of its station at the very bottom of the deal's capital structure.

In 2009–11, the global issuance of collateralized debt obligations had virtually stopped (see figure 2-9). CDOs had been the fastest-growing debt market—outpacing corporate and municipal bond sales by total dollar amount—with about $510 billion sold in 2006, up from $95 billion in 2003. But the benefit of owning even "highly-rated" CDOs containing subprime loans experienced a sharp decline in mid-2007, when two high-profile Bear Stearns hedge funds that were holding subprime collateralized debt obligations collapsed.

The Bear Stearns hedge fund implosion demonstrated how misleading credit ratings of CDOs were, and how risky they actually were as structured products—a sentiment that is still shared today by investors. Exposure to such instruments proved toxic for the banks and investors who bought them, causing hundreds of billions of dollars of losses, but substantial profits for the hedge funds that sold them at the right time.

Figure 2-9: Global Collateralized Debt Obligations Issuance

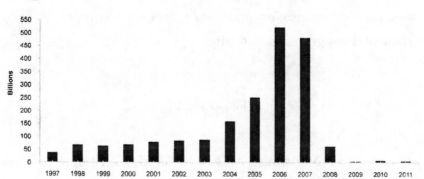

Source: Hammond Associates, Securities Industry and Financial Markets Association (SIFMA)

———

According to research conducted by economist Yuliya Demyanyk of the Federal Reserve Bank of Cleveland, although the subprime mortgage market comprised about 16 percent of all US mortgage debt in 2008, the financial crisis radiated out from failures connected to that relatively small market. The reason is the complexity of the securities that were derived from subprime mortgages. Not only were the securities traded directly, they were also repackaged to create more complicated derivatives, such as CDOs. The derivatives were again split into various tranches, repackaged, re-split and repackaged again many times over. According to Demyanyk, this was one of the mechanisms that significantly amplified problems in the subprime securitized market, and the subsequent subprime-related losses.

Each stage of the securitization process increased the leverage financial institutions were taking on—as they were purchasing the securities and derivatives with borrowed money—and made it more difficult to value their holdings of those financial instruments. With the growing leverage and inability to accurately value the securities, uncertainty about the solvency of a number of large financial firms grew dramatically.

A License to Kill

The plot thickens. Another type of sick and twisted derivative is a **credit-default swap (CDS)**. At its most basic, the pricing of a CDS measures how much a buyer has to pay to purchase (and how much a seller demands to sell) protection from default on an issuer's debt.

For example, a company raises cash by selling bonds. The buyer of a credit-default swap—a pessimist in this scenario—does so to insure against a default on his acquired bonds, or simply to bet that the default risk will rise. In exchange for regular payments over a fixed period of time, the seller of the CDS agrees to make a large payout to the buyer if the acquired bonds default.

———

Before the financial crisis, a credit-default swap was essentially an unregulated insurance-like policy on corporate debt (such as a bond or a loan) where the CDS buyer paid a quarterly premium and the CDS seller promised to cover the losses on the debt should it go into default.[25] When a bondholder purchased a CDS contract as protection against the risk of default of the bond, he would be reimbursed in full for the face value of the bond when a default occurred.

Like an automobile owner whose car is "totaled," once he's paid off he no longer cares about the true value of the bond. If that value changes because the position of the bond in the liability structure changes after default, the bondholder (the buyer) cares little about the effects on the recovery value of the bond. However, the CDS *seller* (the insurer) cares a lot about getting the best value for the defaulted bond because the lower the bond price, the more the CDS seller must pay out. In other words, it was a deadly zero-sum game in which one party's loss was the other's profit.

———

When you buy a bond, you are taking on two types of risk: interest rate risk and default risk. **Interest rate risk** is the peril that interest rates (the cost of borrowed money) in general will go up. If they do, the value of your bond goes down (see Appendix C for an explanation of this inverse relationship). **Default risk** is the hazard that the bond issuer goes bankrupt and doesn't pay you back. In addition, a CDS is called a "swap" because you are swapping the default risk—but not the interest rate risk—to another party (the insurer).[26]

This sounds pretty simple so far. So why did CDS become such a scary acronym? There are two reasons. First, in order to buy CDSs you don't actually have to own the bonds in question. These are **over-the-counter (OTC)** derivative contracts, meaning they are individually negotiated between buyers and sellers. As a result, CDSs became the tool of choice for betting on the likelihood of a company going bankrupt. For example, if you thought the chances of company X going bankrupt were higher than everyone else thought they were, you would buy a CDS on company X. Three months later, when everyone else realized company X was in trouble, the market prices for CDSs would have gone up, and you could either sell your CDS to someone else at the higher price, or you could sell a new one at a higher price. (In the latter case, you still have your original contract, and you would write a new contract with a new buyer).

As a result, there were lots of CDSs out there that were supposed to protect investors against bond defaults. The volume of CDSs outstanding increased one hundred-fold from 1998 to 2007, with estimates of the debt covered by CDS contracts at the height of the market in 2007 at approximately $60 trillion (which means the total face value of the bonds *insured* was $60 trillion).[27]

Second, CDSs were not regulated. In 2008, there were actually no central clearing houses to honor credit-default swaps in the event a party to a CDS proved unable to perform the obligations under a contract. At the height of the frenzy, speculators were buying CDSs en masse to bet against the failure of CDOs backed by subprime mortgages of lower middle-class Americans. It was a big financial bordello of the first order.

As 2008 rolled around, bonds started going bad. There were CDSs not just for traditional corporate debt, but also for mortgage-backed securities and CDOs. During the boom, when everyone was drinking the purple Kool-Aid, CDSs for these exotic products were cheap; when they started failing, the price of CDSs shot up and anyone who had sold these swaps was looking at major losses on them.[28] So CDSs were one way that losses on subprime mortgages triggered massive write-downs at financial institutions.

This only got worse as banks, such as Bear Stearns and Lehman, started failing, and people who had sold CDSs on their debt faced even larger losses. So the most basic problem with CDSs is that the insurers selling them (and many of the companies selling them were not insurance companies) had sold CDSs at excessively low prices, therefore they faced major losses.[29]

———

In addition, you have the risk that the insurance companies won't be able to pay. If a financial institution—say, AIG—sold a lot of CDSs based on the debt of a particular company—say, Lehman—there was a risk that it wouldn't be able to honor all of those swap contracts. In that case, their counterparties (other banks) were looking at losses they *thought* they were insured against.[30] Therefore, CDSs were one of the credit-derivatives that created major uncertainty in the banking sector. A bank may look healthy, but it may be counting on CDS payouts from other banks that you can't see, so if you can't be sure it's healthy you won't lend to it.[31]

The cumulative effect of CDSs is to supposedly spread risk, but to spread risk in unpredictable and invisible ways is dangerous because CDSs are a big gambling scheme. One of the reasons why the government refused to let AIG fail—one day after letting Lehman tank—was that AIG was a large net seller of CDSs, and if it had defaulted on those swaps, no one could predict what the implications would have been for the rest of the global financial sector. It would be a mistake to blame the whole crisis on CDSs, but they had the effect of amplifying and spreading uncertainty in ways that significantly reduced confidence in the US financial markets.[32]

———

Different forms of CDSs have been in existence since the early 1990s, with UK-born Blythe Masters of JPMorgan credited for inventing the world's first credit-default swap.[33] In that instance, JPMorgan (part of today's JPMorgan Chase) had extended a $4.8 billion credit line to Exxon, which faced the threat of $5 billion in punitive damages for the *Exxon Valdez* oil spill in Alaska in 1989. A team of high-flying JPMorgan investment bankers transferred the credit risk using credit-derivatives to the European Bank for Reconstruction and Development (EBRD) to cut the reserves that JPMorgan was required to hold against Exxon's default, thus improving the bank's own balance sheet. Then in 1997, JPMorgan developed a funky-sounding product called BISTRO (Broad Index

Securitized Trust Offering). BISTRO used the underlying concept of a credit-default swap to "clean up" a bank's balance sheet, which later evolved into the **synthetic CDO**.[34] The advantage of BISTRO was that it used securitization to split up the credit risk into little pieces, which smaller investors found more digestible since most investors lacked EBRD's capability to accept $4.8 billion in credit risk all at once.

————

As the net worth of banks and other financial institutions rapidly deteriorated in 2008 because of massive losses related to subprime mortgages, the likelihood increased that those providing the credit-default swaps would have to pay the entity with whom they obtained the CDSs from (that is, to make them "whole"). This created extreme uncertainty throughout the financial system, as investors wondered which companies would be required to pay to cover mortgage defaults because of a lack of transparency in the CDS market. With oversight in shambles and risk management practically nonexistent, investors focused their frustration on CDSs that wreaked havoc on their portfolios.

As their 401(k)s melted away, the investing public also began howling for the blood of CDS traders. Nobel Prize-winning economist Joseph Stiglitz captured the crux of the contribution of credit-default swaps to the financial meltdown: "With this complicated intertwining of bets of great magnitude, no one could be sure of the financial position of anyone else—or even of one's own position."[35] Describing the credit-default swaps, retired currency trader and hedge fund manager George Soros said at a meeting in

Beijing in 2009, "It's like buying life insurance on someone else's life and owning a license to kill."[36]

––––––

There are many types of derivative instruments that, due to the lack of oversight, contributed to the financial meltdown (such as mezzanine CDOs, CDOs-squared, and CDOs-cubed, to name just a few), but as they are extremely technical they are beyond the scope of this book. Figure 2-10 shows just how complex multilay-ered real estate-related derivatives can be. Is it any surprise that very few people *really* understood what was going on in the dark bowels of these diabolic instruments?

Figure 2-10: The Absurd Complexity of Multilayered Real Estate Derivatives

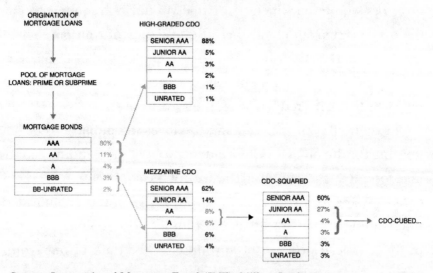

Source: International Monetary Fund (IMF), Milken Institute

Dancing in the Shadows

In 2007, derivative contracts between buyers and sellers of at least $600 trillion in face value swirled around the world's financial system, the equivalent of more than ten years of global economic output.[37] Only about 3 percent of such contracts have historically been traded on exchanges such as the NASDAQ index and the New York Stock Exchange (NYSE), with the balance traded in private markets under secretive terms directly struck between buyers and sellers.[38] Hence, a behemoth market that grew dramatically in recent decades and without direct oversight crashed, wiping out trillions of dollars in savings and investments. All too obviously, the US financial innovation machine was running amok.

Under the regulations of the Dodd-Frank Wall Street Reform and Consumer Protection Act, which was signed into law in 2010, an entirely new rulebook was drawn up for this privately traded part of the financial markets called over-the-counter (i.e., customized) derivatives, which involve bilateral trades between financial firms.

OTC derivatives, such as credit-default swaps, have been partially blamed for increasing systemic risk (affecting an entire system). These derivatives were originally created to serve a specific role in financial markets, but deficiencies in the markets' design and infrastructure—coupled with blind greed, conflicts of interest, opacity, and a lack of understanding—allowed for the misuse of these instruments, aggravating the financial meltdown. Moreover, the risk of some derivatives, due to their total opacity, was not discovered until disaster ensued.

———

The biggest intra-day drop—998.5 points—in Dow Jones Industrial Average history is known as the "flash crash." The flash crash on May 6, 2010, was a terrifying reminder of how the US financial system can exert its venomous volatility and erase massive amounts of wealth instantaneously. Although the Securities and Exchange Commission claimed that a single algorithm connected to a $4.1 billion sale of complex stock index futures by the money manager Waddell & Reed was the primary cause, the crash was a reminder of the never-ending tangle of interconnections of the securities and derivatives markets. Such chilling and panic-fanning events will most likely happen again. But when and how is impossible to know.

———

Following the recession of 1990–91, which many economists attribute to the savings and loan crisis of the late 1980s, the US commercial real estate sector started to undergo rapid change, as Wall Street securitized the sector's capital markets. Commercial real estate mortgages were pooled and placed into trusts. Bonds, with varying maturities, returns, and risk profiles—all secured by such diversified mortgage pools—were issued to a vast array of investors worldwide, including banks.

The so-called **shadow banking system** emerged as the role of the real estate portfolio lender diminished. Large banks and a host of other institutions became aggressive loan originators, ready to make big fees with no risk as the loans they underwrote were sold and taken off their books quickly by the securitization process. This total lack of skin in the game was one of the main factors that caused the financial crisis.

———

The securitization food chain is part of the reason the US financial system could pump hundreds of billions of dollars into subprime home loans. Being able to repackage obligations and distribute them allowed ordinary borrowers to tap into the global capital markets. However, along with the growth came some serious problems and unintended consequences. Because of the financial crisis some investors now consider loan securitization to be a Bernie Madoff-style scheme. But that's probably true when the process is unregulated and opaque—layered with out-of-control, ultra-complex derivatives with no skin in the game.

Securitization, or its functional equivalent, is essential, and prudent loan securitization is important for the economy as it allows financial institutions and companies to take some risk off their balance sheets and sell it to investors who are seeking higher yields. With the loans offloaded, lenders can expand their business while avoiding excessive exposure to one financial product. The correct response to these instruments would be to make market-based credit products do their jobs better. That means fixing the root problems, namely: (1) Ignorance about what these financial products contain; (2) conflicts of interest leading too many to present the securities as being safer than they actually are; and (3) setting standards that ensure that sellers of mortgage-backed securities have skin in the game. Bringing the loan securitization market back to health is a job the financial industry must do itself—most importantly by making MBSs much more transparent so they can be priced and monitored correctly.

———

Financial institutions had a strong incentive to avoid making and keeping mortgages and other types of loans on their balance sheets, temporarily holding MBSs instead. Commercial banks were more than happy to originate mortgages—processing borrowers and accepting origination fees—but less interested in actually funding the loans which required them to hold more capital in reserve, meaning that they would be forced to lend less. As such, funding for loans came increasingly from non-traditional bank institutions. These institutions were a mixed bag; they included investment banks, hedge funds, and money-market funds, as well as newly invented entities called asset-backed conduits and structured investment vehicles (SIVs). Together they formed the shadow banking system, which was subject to little regulatory oversight and also not required to publicly disclose much about itself.[39] Sounds absurd, right?

The US financial labyrinth (see figure 2-11), driven by unsustainable real estate debt growth, created a spectacular house of cards of derivative instruments linked to numerous types of subprime mortgages. A large number of lenders and financial institutions joined Fannie Mae and Freddie Mac in packaging shaky mortgages into residential mortgage-backed securities that they then sold to investors, flooding the US housing markets with ever-more liquidity. Countrywide Financial and other mortgage lenders like them would use the cash they received at sale to make even more loans—to satisfy the insatiable desire for higher yields that pumped the securitization pipeline.

Investors assumed that a residential mortgage-backed security was a good investment opportunity because of the "stellar" (read: rigged) reviews they received from the credit rating agencies. From 2000 to 2007, Moody's rated nearly 45,000 mortgage-backed securities as AAA. This compares with just six private-sector companies in the US that carried this coveted rating in 2010. In addition, in

Figure 2-11: An Incomprehensible Galaxy

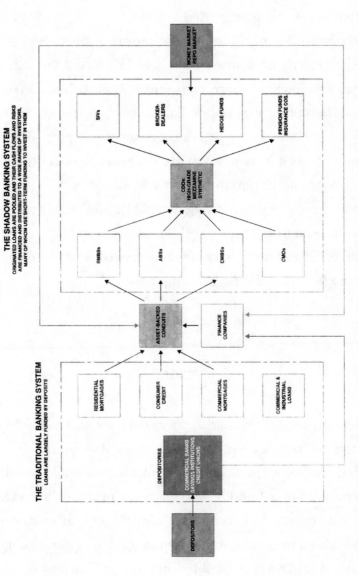

Source: Mark Zandi, Moody's Economy.com. It has been assumed above that the CDS contracts between sellers and buyers of debt securities were being made within the shadow banking system. *"Repo" —short for repurchase agreement—is a contract for the sale and future repurchase of a financial asset, most often Treasury securities.

2006 alone Moody's put its bogus AAA stamp of approval on thirty mortgage-backed securities *every* working day.[40] The results were, of course, disastrous: 83 percent of the mortgage securities rated AAA that year were downgraded.

No one in this pipeline of toxic mortgages had enough skin in the game. The firms involved believed they could offload their risks on a moment's notice to the next fool in line. They were wrong. When borrowers stopped making mortgage payments, the losses—amplified by toxic real estate derivatives—gushed through the pipeline. As it turned out, these losses were concentrated in a set of systemically important financial institutions.[41]

In the end, the system that created millions of mortgages has proven to be difficult to unwind. Its complexity has erected barriers to modifying mortgages and has created further uncertainty about the health of the US housing market.[42]

Conclusion

This lengthy chapter should be beneficial to understanding the unnecessary complexity of the derivatives that caused so much financial mayhem. Financial innovation is by no means evil, and I'm certainly not a Luddite who's against prudent financial creativity. I'll refrain from using the term "financial engineering" because it's an over-glamorized, hyped-up description. Real engineers build bridges and satellites, not financial products that bet on the default of millions of home mortgages.

Housing is a basic need and it must be treated as such, based on tried and true, common-sense underwriting practices. When you start getting into the realm of reckless departure from the basic standards and principles of real estate lending, you are building a one-way road paved with avarice leading to financial hell. You have to be very careful when you mix basic bricks and mortar with esoteric, massively leveraged financial instruments like subprime mortgage bonds inside CDOs. It's perhaps too much to expect the people who run big Wall Street firms to speak plain English, since so much of their livelihood depends on folks believing that what they do cannot be translated into plain English.[43]

———

Securitization is currently a fraction of what it was at the height of the real estate bubble, but it should gradually rebound following intense scrutiny by regulators and the implementation of more-skin-in-the-game rules. Before the financial crisis, a huge proportion of new mortgages were packaged and sold to investors through the securitization markets, in effect enabling all intermediaries to clear their balance sheets so they could quickly make new loans. This process ground to a halt in August 2007 as securitization became synonymous with the toxic US subprime loans that triggered the credit meltdown.

Before the housing boom, certain regulations imposed rules on banks regarding the amount of capital they had to hold in reserve to cover loan or investment losses. These capital requirements varied based on the expected risk of the investment. If a bank held relatively safe government bonds, for example, they were required to hold *less* capital to guard against losses. This was known as risk-weighting, and it made sense as long as the rules reflected the inherent risks of a particular asset or investment.[44] For years, AAA-rated residential mortgage-backed securities, collateralized debt obligations, and similar financial instruments had been assigned relatively low-risk weights, and regulators thought they were safe. As it turned out, the assessment of risk in the financial system was completely off target, and the big Wall Street firms, seemingly so shrewd and self-interested, had somehow become the dumb money.[45]

————

The missed assessment of real estate debt risk (discussed in chapter 8) is one of the main reasons for this difficult situation we are in today. The aggregate debt growth rate above 8 percent of GDP between 2004 and 2007 was the reason for the collapse of the underlying collateral values supporting mortgage-backed securities.[46] All the financial products sold as derivatives linked to subprime mortgages (i.e., CDOs and CDSs) collapsed at record speeds because of excessive default covenants requiring immediate redemptions or pay offs. This caused the liquidity crisis and systemic risks never before observed in modern times. In some cases, subordinate tranches were wiped out in a collateralized debt obligation structure because more senior tranches required immediate redemption due to a downgrade of the entire CDO.

Ever-higher home prices, which were out of step with fundamentals (i.e., a bubble waiting to burst) and lax mortgage underwriting criteria, specifically in the subprime market, helped drive home prices higher while expanding home construction and ownership. An explosion in the use of complex securitization products and derivatives facilitated both of the above (see figure 2-12).

Figure 2-12: How the Cookie Crumbled

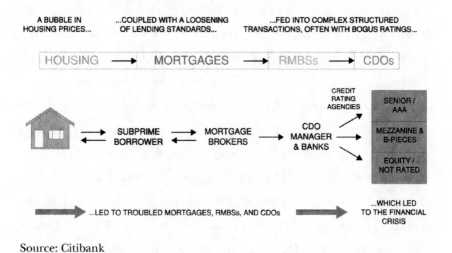

Source: Citibank

Because of surging "animal spirits," the financial industry did not stop with the plain-vanilla residential mortgage-backed securities. More and more strategies were hatched, limited only by high-living bankers' unbounded imaginations and, doubtless, egos and greed. Many firms began packaging up large numbers of complex MBSs (and pieces of these financial instruments) into CDOs that could be sold and resold to investors worldwide: European pension funds, German banks, Japanese farmers' unions, and Taiwanese insurance companies, among many others. The initial goal was to offer opportunities for investment, provide a broader portfolio, and of course, for lenders to make a lot of money—the barn door was wide open.

CDOs were dummy corporations—legal fictions organized for the purpose of buying and selling bonds.[47] Created by Wall Street banks and similar operators, the CDO introduced a second level of securitization. Instead of buying mortgages directly, the CDO was a security that invested in other, first-order securities that themselves had acquired mortgages. The CDO thus introduced an additional layer of complexity into the process, with the result that the ultimate investor was further removed and less equipped to scrutinize the quality of the underlying mortgages.[48]

In an attempt to reduce risk, financial institutions created the underpinnings of disaster, adding yet another layer to this house of junk in the form of credit-default swaps that insured CDOs, which were like a license to kill. Holders of collateralized debt obligations created contracts with firms such as AIG. The CDO owner made payments to AIG (easy money, so they thought), which in return promised to purchase the CDO at an agreed-upon price if the CDO declined in value. Given the extent of the house of junk built on mortgages and bonds, one can easily assume that it was hard for anyone to clearly know what was behind these securities and their derivatives. For that reason, some forms of securitization are likely to vanish forever, having been an artifact of excessively loose credit conditions and mad finance. That assumes that the hard lessons have actually been learned—and are remembered—once the economy turns around and money is plentiful once again.

———

Another of the culprits in the whole mess were the credit rating agencies that were out of touch with reality, and too often incestuously hired by investment banks and obscure hedge funds to evaluate the quality of bonds in their securitization structures. The mortgage owners, investment banks, and hedge funds, were all using the analysis of a large number of very smart people to evaluate the securities themselves. Meanwhile, other big firms were evaluating these bonds as well, as they considered purchasing them, or wrote credit-default swap contracts on CDOs owned by other firms. But as we know, all this sophisticated analysis of mumbo jumbo led to a numbing financial calamity triggered by unwarranted optimism and a US mortgage implosion that brought the global financial system to its knees. Everyone was drinking the purple Kool-Aid.

Chapter 3: Drinking the Purple Kool-Aid

I would tell audiences that we were facing not a bubble but a froth—lots of small bubbles that never grew to a scale that could threaten the health of the overall economy.
—Alan Greenspan, previous Fed Chairman, in his book, *The Age of Turbulence*

The combined effect of the financial crisis has severely impacted America's credibility around the world, has caused a corrosive loss of trust in the US financial system, and has left many wondering whether anybody really understood how the mechanics of the capital markets work.

But how could this happen in a country that worshiped its malls and outlet stores, perfected its obsession with debt-driven consumption, and invented the master of business administration degree? What kind of financial system allows the forking out of mortgages with 110 percent loan-to-value ratios? What kinds of borrowers are willing to take on such absurd risk? And how could the United States, the pinnacle of laissez-faire capitalism and a key source of intellectual leadership in investment theory, have been so wrong?

———

We are painfully aware that the spark that ignited a string of events that caused the Great Recession of 2007–09 was set off by hundreds of billions of dollars of "safe" securities linked to US mortgages plunging in value, with major adverse consequences for banks and financial markets around the globe. In this chapter, I briefly remind the reader of the most pertinent factors leading to the financial crisis, as well as the faulty assumptions that caused the meltdown. The greatest tragedy would be to surrender to the notion that no one could have seen the crisis coming and, there-fore, nothing could have been done to prevent it. If we accept this complacent conception, it is bound to happen again.

Shaky Foundations

Homeownership is the cornerstone of the American Dream, closely related to how people identify themselves socially. During the nirvana years before 2007, homeownership was at center stage in an unfolding mega-drama that proved the world can be a pro-foundly unpredictable and uncontrollable place.

The US homeownership rate increased from 64 percent in 1994 (where it had been since 1980) to an all-time high of 69 percent in 2004, and subprime lending was a contributor to the increase in homeownership rates, which drove prices higher.[1] People had bet that home prices would continue to rise and buy-ers would continue to make their mortgage payments.

Home prices in the United States rose for more than thirty consecutive years before the financial panic, as the federal gov-ernment aggressively advocated increased homeownership as a national policy. The government provided incentives to homeowners and touted the capital gains and interest-payment tax benefits generated by owning a house.

It's worth noting that over the long-term, the overall appreciation in US home prices averaged approximately 1 percent per year above the national rate of inflation, more or less tracking the growth in real (adjusted for inflation) incomes. But from 2000 through 2005, when inflation was averaging about 2.7 percent (see figure 3-1), median home prices grew by 7.6 percent, one of the fastest extended price increases ever. So the appreciation in home prices net of inflation was 4.9 percent but without any obvious demographic reason.[2] It was a gargantuan sector of the US economy (with an estimated value of $20.1 trillion in 2006) that was morphing on over-optimism and speculation.

Figure 3-1: US Consumer Price Index and
Median Home Sale Prices

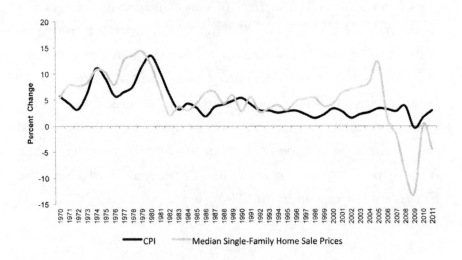

Source: Bureau of Labor Statistics, National Association of Realtors (NAR)

Even though housing prices were escalating, people weren't making any more money. From 2000 to 2006, the median household income stayed flat. Therefore, the more prices rose, the more fragile the residential sector's house of cards became. Slack lending standards allowed an arsenal of exotic loan products created by a Vegas-style mortgage machine to push already debt-swollen people into homes they couldn't possibly afford.

The fact that the median household income has been flat for many years should not be overlooked, as it most likely contributed to the high consumer debt levels that are haunting the US economy. In a materialistic country where people are constantly bombarded by ads, the urge to spend is huge. But with stagnant incomes, the only way to buy more and more stuff is by using debt.

While housing prices were increasing, consumers were saving less and borrowing and spending more. Household debt grew from $705 billion in 1974 (60 percent of after-tax personal income), to $5.9 trillion in 2000, and finally to $12.8 trillion in 2008, (a whopping 134 percent of personal income). In 2009 and 2010 US mortgage debt declined (see figure 3-2), attributed to lower interest payments due to loan modifications, homes being foreclosed upon, and less Americans buying homes. While total household debt as a percentage of after-tax income has fallen from its peak, it remains at about 120 percent—well above the 89 percent it averaged in the 1990s.

Figure 3-2: Total Household Debt

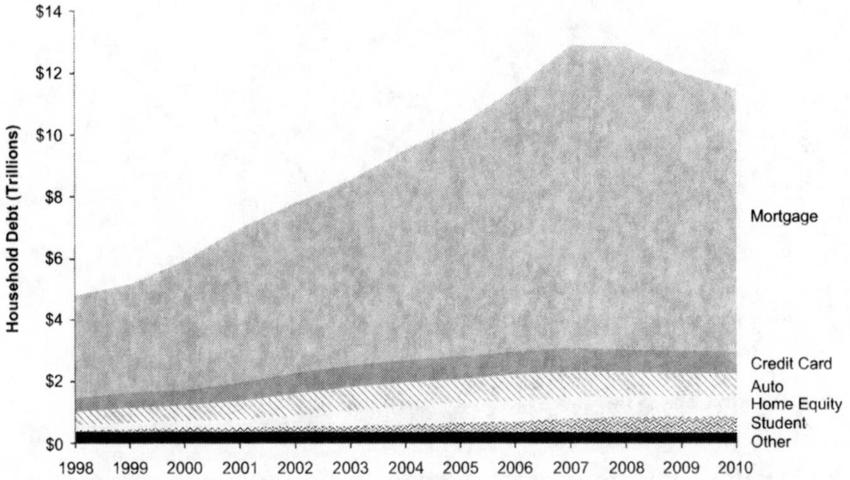

Source: Federal Reserve Board

Total US home mortgage debt relative to GDP increased from an average of 47 percent during the 1990s to 79 percent in 2009. This credit and house-price explosion led to a building boom and eventually to a surplus of unsold homes, especially in the second-home market, which caused US housing prices to peak and begin declining in August 2006.

The excess US housing supply had a big impact on prices. In order to capture the high immediate profits made possible by rising home prices, developers that served booming housing markets raised their annual production of new units to levels that were unsustainable over time. Homebuilders increased production levels by selling homes into what normally would have been future demand, especially in 2004–06, when close to two million new homes were built each year (see figure 3-3).

Figure 3-3: US Total Housing Starts

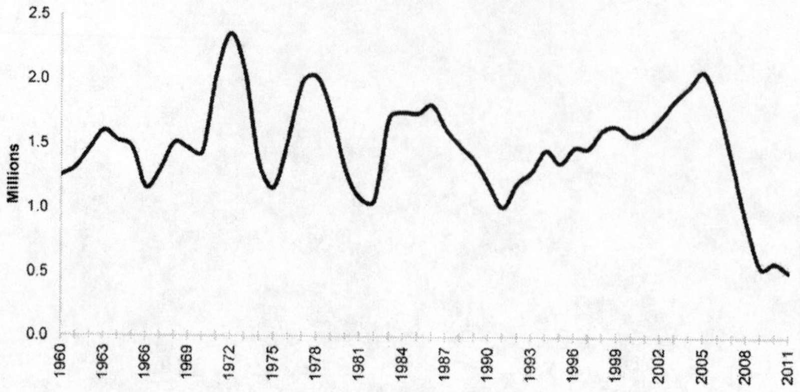

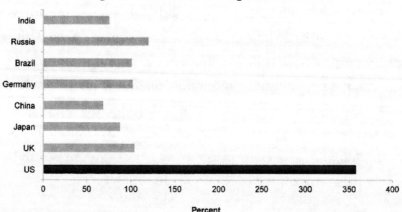

Source: US Census Bureau. Data includes manufactured homes.

At the same time, the average loans-to-deposits ratio of US banks in 2008 was an outrageous 358 percent, meaning that American banks lent 3.58 times their clients' deposits (see figure 3-4). This alarming ratio continues to be the highest in the world. (The loans-to-deposits ratio is the amount of a bank's loans divided by the amount of its deposits at any given time. The higher the ratio, the more the bank is relying on borrowed funds).

Figure 3-4: Loans-to-Deposits Ratio

Source: Merrill Lynch (2008 data)

Because it involves a panoply of banks, savings institutions, insurance firms, appraisers, developers, accountants, lawyers, mortgage brokers, and real estate agents, housing finance is *the* Achilles heel of the US financial system. Housing is a huge part of the US economy, not to mention that it's very slow to unravel given the highly illiquid nature of property. That is why the financial crisis, which began in the nation's residential markets, has been having such a profound impact on the US capitalist system and how it is viewed around the world today. Gone are the days of cozy complacency in America.

Up, Up, and Away With the Fairies

Most US banks were selling Americans champagne hopes and caviar dreams. Homeowners were brainwashed into believing they could quickly refinance at more favorable terms and withdraw capital from the escalating equity accumulated in their homes. But once interest rates began to rise in mid-2007 and housing prices started their rapid decline, refinancing became basically impossible in many parts of the country.

Starting in 1995, house prices practically doubled within a decade. The run-up in values was not just unprecedented, it was dangerous. That begs an equally obvious question: if no one intervened to pop that bubble, is anyone likely to do so next time round?

The housing market peaked in mid-2006, with the US single-family median home price reaching close to $222,000, compared to $147,000 in 2000, indicating a nearly 7 percent compound annual growth rate (see figure 3-5).[3] High default rates on deadly loans such as subprime, Alt-A, and adjustable rate mortgages (ARMs) began to increase significantly. (See pages 395–403 for a detailed description of these types of mortgages). The end of house price appreciation meant the end to an effortless accumulation of homeowner equity, a phenomenon that had previously made life very easy for weak borrowers. It also meant the end to a story that was too good to be true.

Figure 3-5: Median Single-Family Home Prices by Region

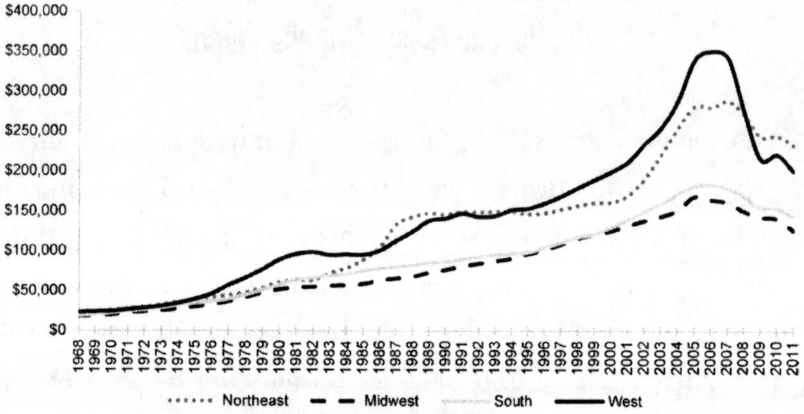

Source: National Association of Realtors (NAR)

An increase in loan incentives such as initial "teaser" terms, and an extended trend of rising housing prices encouraged borrowers to assume beyond-their-means mortgages, accompanied by the delusion of ever-increasing home prices in the future—all factors that added helium to the housing balloon.

It's Just an Illusion

By 2006, the average home cost nearly four times what the average American family made (historically it was between two and three times).[4] Then mortgage originators noticed something they had not seen before. People would sign all the mortgage papers, buy a home, and then default on their very first payment. No loss of a job, no medical emergency—they were instantly "underwater" (the value of their home was less than their mortgage). Even worse, a record level of 40 percent of homes purchased were not intended as primary residences.[5] Speculators started to leave the market in October 2006, causing home investment sales to fall much faster than the primary ownership market. Although no one could hear it, that was probably the moment when the largest bubble in modern economic history imploded and financial bedlam was about to be unleashed.

———

The year 2006 represented a price bubble on top of a credit bubble—a double bubble. Figure 3-6 shows what went terribly wrong with home values in the United States. Buyers expected that the value of their homes would appreciate in a straight-line and that their increase in equity (the difference between a home's value and the underlying mortgage) would widen forever. Reality, of course, was harshly different, with home values taking a nose dive and wiping out the created equity.

What is needed for every homeowner who is underwater is that as the housing market reaches a bottom, values start to increase, and the vanished equity is recreated once again. This should happen, but it will take a long time as many housing markets still face a long, flat spell with prices bouncing along a bottom.

Figure 3-6: Diminished Equity

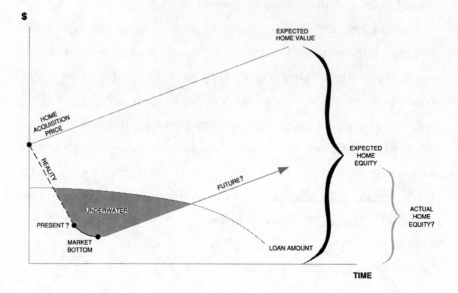

Defaults and foreclosures increased dramatically as the easy initial terms of predatory lenders expired, home prices failed to continue to increase as was naïvely anticipated, and ARM rates reset to higher levels. (According to the Fed, nearly 60 percent of US mortgages issued to borrowers in 2007–08 were ARMs).

As indicated earlier, falling prices also resulted in homes becoming worth less than the remaining amounts owed on their mortgages (negative equity), providing a double-edged incentive for borrowers to enter into foreclosure. That destructive trend was accentuated by the fact that 80 percent of houses with second-mortgages at origination had an LTV of 100 percent or more.

There were some cases in which banks wanted to foreclose because borrowers were close to paying off their mortgages, and it was more profitable for the lenders that way. The foreclosure virus that commenced in 2007 continues to be a major unresolved problem in the aftermath of the financial crisis, sucking wealth from consumers and businesses, and placing risk on the stability of bank balance sheets. Foreclosure filings in the US have declined (see figure 3-7), but that has been due to banks reworking their documentation procedures following claims that they improperly repossessed homes. Weak demand from hesitant buyers is also making it difficult for lenders to sell the distressed properties that they already have on their books.

Figure 3-7: US Delinquent Loans and Foreclosures

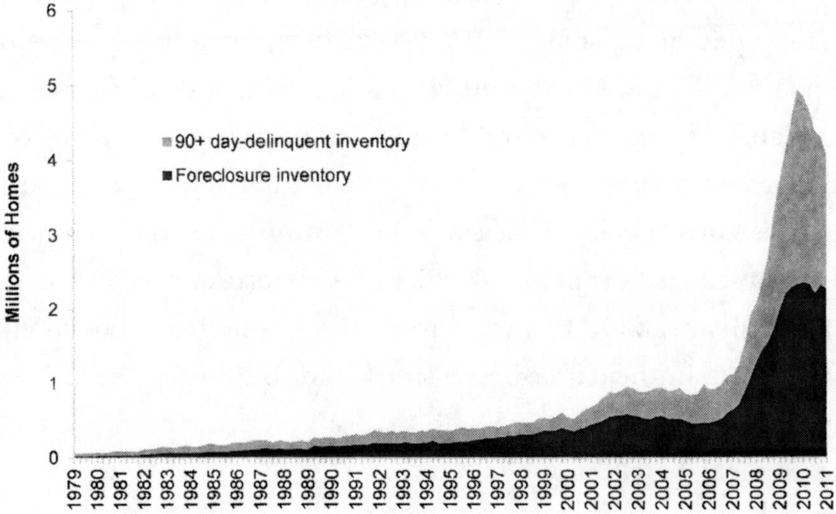

Source: Mortgage Bankers Association

Doom Loops

As more borrowers stopped paying their mortgage payments, foreclosures and the supply of homes for sale increased dramatically. This placed downward pressure on housing prices, which further lowered homeowners' phantom equity. The decline in mortgage payments also reduced the net worth and financial health of numerous banks. In addition, as housing prices peaked and then began to decline in 2006–07, many borrowers began to default on their mortgages. Since many of these mortgages were the underlying collateral for many securitizations, the markets for private-label securitized products saw a decrease in liquidity and, in some cases, significant declines in value. Furthermore, as assets became less valuable, stock prices fell as anticipated consumption and future corporate earnings declined, resulting in negative investor sentiment.

Government agency mortgage-backed security markets also experienced some shorter-lived disruptions, but generally remained liquid. On the other hand, the amount of financing available to consumers and businesses that were dependent on the private-label (non-agency) markets became severely restricted and its costs increased—a condition known as a credit crunch. Lenders started dropping like flies as foreclosures rose and lending guidelines were tightened to the point that many borrowers were stuck in their time-bomb loans, and thus began the vicious cycle. As shown in figure 3-8, this vicious cycle was at the core of the financial meltdown.

Figure 3-8: Vicious Cycle of the Mortgage Crisis

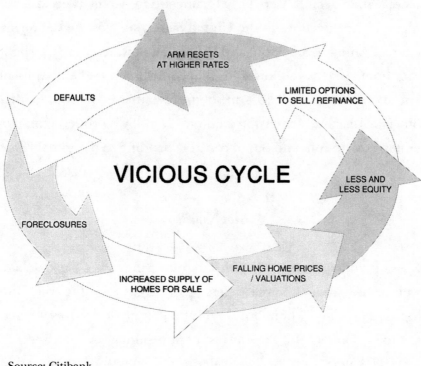

Source: Citibank

The US housing markets, of course, continue to struggle, causing major challenges for sustaining a fragile recovery. Without effective government initiatives to reduce interest payments and principal balances, the housing market could remain locked in the vicious circle in which supply outstrips demand for years to come. If the cost of a thirty-year fixed rate mortgage goes back up to 5 percent, half the borrowers will be outside the "refinancing threshold," and the rest will most likely be locked out due to damaged credit or falling home prices.

"Strategic defaults," when homebuyers abruptly and intentionally abandon their mortgages—a glorified name for dumping houses on banks—became a new buzz word in the drama-seeking media. Such defaults were heavily concentrated in markets with the highest price declines in the United States, such as the California cities of Antioch, Stockton, and Vallejo, all of which were overbuilt with homogeneous subdivisions that contributed to the occasional ennui of suburbia. Vallejo is one of the few cities in the country that officially declared bankruptcy due to dwindling property tax revenues, corruption, and out-of-control spending in the mid-2000s.

Hot Money

Investment banks created, sold, and traded mortgage-backed securities (MBSs), which were carelessly rated by monolithic credit rating agencies, and when morphed into opaque derivatives, turned out to be some of the worst investment products ever devised.

The American public was caught up in a grand delusion that housing prices would *never* fall. In 2005, the median down payment for first-time homebuyers was only 2 percent, with 43 percent of those buyers making no down payment whatsoever.[6] In 1995, the government-sponsored enterprises (GSEs) Fannie Mae and Freddie Mac began receiving government tax incentives for purchasing MBSs, which included risky ARMs to low-income borrowers. By 2008, Fannie and Freddie owned (either directly or through mortgage pools they sponsored) $5.1 trillion in residential mortgages, about 57 percent of the total US mortgage market. Along with the Federal Housing Administration (FHA), they now own approximately 90 percent of the residential lending sector.[7]

As part of this illusory-credit prosperity period, the number of MBSs—which derive their values from mortgage payments and home prices—increased significantly. Such so-called financial innovations enabled institutions around the world to invest in the US housing market because of the higher returns offered commensurate to the underlying risk related to purchasing subprime-linked MBSs. As home prices declined, major global financial institutions that borrowed and invested heavily in MBSs reported key losses.

As the securities backed by high-risk mortgages lost most of their value, the result was a decline in the capital of many banks, causing an unprecedented drought of global credit—a massive liquidity shortfall. Defaults and losses on other loan types also increased dramatically as the crisis expanded from the housing market to other segments of the economy, including commercial real estate and manufacturing.

In the 2003–06 period preceding the crisis, huge amounts of foreign capital sloshed into the United States from the growing economies of Asia and the Middle East (see figure 3-9).

**Figure 3-9: Foreign Capital Flows into US
Commercial Real Estate Markets**

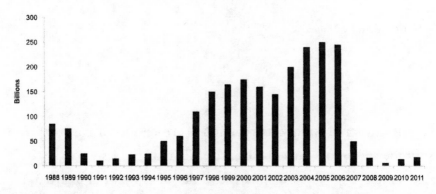

Source: Peter Linneman Associates, Real Capital Analytics, Jones Lang LaSalle, ULI. Includes both public and private equity and debt.

This inflow of funds, coupled with low interest rates in 2003 (thirty-year, fixed-rate mortgages were at a then-low of 5.9 percent), fueled unprecedented credit conditions (see figure 3-10). Aggressively peddled by some lenders and mortgage brokers who were acting like drug pushers, loans of various types were ridiculously easy to obtain and consumers assumed a record debt load. The spend-and-pretend cycle was in full swing.

Figure 3-10: US Average Home Mortgage Interest Rates

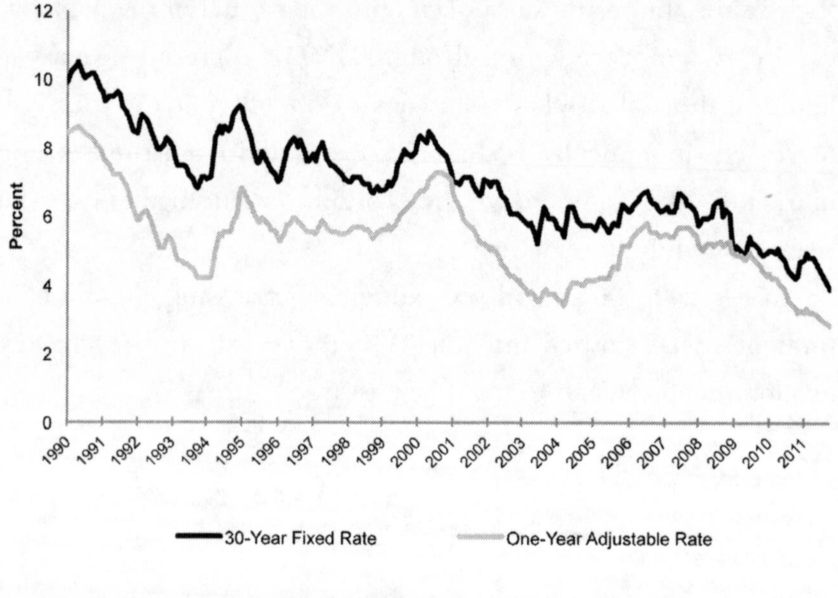

Source: Freddie Mac

While the credit markets reached a crescendo in early 2007, a number of factors caused the entire US financial system to become extremely exposed to the headwinds of fragility. Policymakers did not recognize the increasingly important role played by certain financial entities such as elitist investment banks, opaque off-balance-sheet conduits, and elusive hedge funds, known collectively as the shadow banking system described in chapter 2.

These institutions had become as important as traditional commercial banks in providing credit to the US economy, but they weren't subject to the same regulations, if any at all. These institutions, as well as numerous Fed-regulated banks, had assumed massive debt burdens. They provided mortgage, credit card, and auto loans galore, yet without a sufficient financial cushion to absorb monstrous MBS losses, which were extremely difficult to quantify or value. These losses halted the ability of financial institutions to lend, bringing economic activity in the United States to a virtual standstill by October 2008. The global capital markets were in panic mode.

———

Another indirect contributor to the mess was deregulation of the banking system in the 1990s, which allowed US commercial banks to get involved in more "sophisticated" types of mortgages and to lend more money relative to their capital reserves than ever before. As a result, housing was a gargantuan house of cards in the US economy, contributing approximately 20 percent to GDP in 2005.[8]

Deep concerns regarding the stability of financial institutions made central banks take action to inject funds and cut interest rates to encourage lending and to try to restore faith in the short-term (commercial paper) debt markets that are essential for the funding of basic business operations. Governments also bailed out key financial institutions, assuming colossal capital commitments in the process.

The REIT Red Flag

Real estate investment trust (REIT) stocks are a barometer of property performance in general, and a reflection of investor sentiment toward real estate as an asset class at any point in time. The Financial Times Stock Exchange (FTSE) National Association of Real Estate Investment Trusts (NAREIT) Equity REIT Index is one of the better measures of property investments in the United States and the most visible cornerstone of American real estate finance.

Wednesday, February 7, 2007, was a major red flag for the American property sector. On that day, the FTSE NAREIT Equity Index[9] reached its apex of 10,981, an increase of 298 percent above its July 2000 level, reflecting the shift that had been favoring real estate investments up until then (see figure 3-11).

Figure 3-11: NAREIT Equity Index

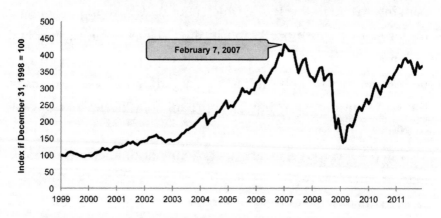

Source: National Association of Real Estate Investment Trusts (NAREIT)

In the past, most investment firms had avoided buying property because they viewed real estate as being too illiquid, cumbersome, and demanding too much specialized knowledge of local markets to be attractive investments. However, the free-fall of stock prices globally in 2000–02 caused by the dot-com crash, coupled with the superior returns being offered by real property and mortgage-backed securities, made many yield-hunting institutional investors view property as the darling asset class in which they should place a much bigger share of their total capital. A me-too herd mentality and a speculative mania clouded the real estate capital markets.

This shift in investor sentiment was bolstered by the wider use of securitized lending and REIT shares for investing in real estate, as both instruments had the allure of high liquidity, compared to the time- and capital-intensive ownership of property directly, especially when involving trophy assets.[10]

For the most part, owning real estate in some form was considered desirous because it enhanced the diversity of portfolios. In addition, while nearly all stocks were plummeting in value and bonds were vulnerable to potential increases in inflation, residential and commercial property prices kept on rising. But between February 2007 and February 2009, the NAREIT Index declined by nearly 70 percent, sending shivers down the spines of already-anxious investors. Real estate became a byword for "bad investment," forcing many terrified investors to run for the hills.

In a spooky coincidence, on that very same day—February 7, 2007—the capital markets sent conflicting signals to investors. HSBC, the world's largest bank at the time, wrote down its holdings of subprime mortgage-backed securities by $10.5 billion, the first major subprime-related loss to be reported. From then on, it was all downhill.

Skating on Thin Ice

The irrational public enthusiasm for owning and/or investing in residential real estate can be attributed to a number of specific factors enveloping the housing and credit markets that emerged between 2003 and 2007. Known causes include the inability of homeowners to make their mortgage payments, as well as the reasons reiterated below.

- Unnecessary complexity of the market for mortgage-backed securities and derivatives that was built on phantom equity and borrowed money.
- Reckless government policies that pushed homeownership on millions of Americans with poor credit.
- Runaway credit markets and an oversupply of capital (easy money).
- High personal debt levels driven by excessive consumption (silly money).
- Too much money managed by fast-moving investors chasing the same yields.
- Unwise investment in risky assets and an excessive degree of trust in the judgments of others.
- Speculation and overbuilding by developers (excess supply).
- Excessive dilution of home equity via refinancing cash-outs.
- Disregard for the fundamental relationship between household income and housing affordability.
- Ignorance about the interaction of complex financial regulations by bankers and regulators that fomented a global loss of trust in the banking system.

A distorted incentive system implicit in the mortgage securitization process, arrogance among financial market operators, mediocre monetary policies, and poor underwriting standards by lenders also played a destructive role within the US housing finance system. For the most part, no skin in the game lay at the heart of many of these mechanisms.

Faulty Assumptions

It's important to remind the reader that there were several assumptions underlying the US financial system as a whole that contributed to the crisis. These faulty assumptions included the following:

- The future is both known *and* knowable; that is, the activity of capital markets can be predicted with scientific precision.
- Free markets, supported by "sophisticated financial engineering," will always produce fundamentally correct asset prices; therefore, the financial sector can be left to its own devices (known as the Efficient Market Hypothesis, developed by Eugene Fama and Merton Miller at the University of Chicago in the 1960s and 1970s).
- Esoteric concepts embedded in applied mathematics, physics, and engineering (developed by "quant jocks" and the "high priests" of the Efficient Market Hypothesis) could be directly applied to the capital markets in the form of idolized financial models used to evaluate credit risk and uncertainty.
- Risks can be evenly distributed throughout the financial system.

- There's a philosophical tendency in the West, following Plato, to conclude that if a theory isn't working, there must be something wrong with reality. What goes up will continue to go up, known as the Great Fool Theory, was proven to be ever so wrong.
- Most investors are rational, far-thinking people.
- Borrowers will always pay their mortgages.
- Market economies are not always vulnerable to chancers and spivs who sell over-priced products to ill-informed customers.
- The sensation-mongering media, which glorified the stories of home flippers, was being objective in its reporting.
- Economic imbalances such as low savings rates indicative of over-consumption were sustainable.
- Regulation and oversight of the over-leveraged shadow banking system and the opaque derivatives markets was not needed.

The deadly mixture of aforementioned reasons and faulty assumptions resulted in financial pandemonium and a system that was extremely susceptible to a self-reinforcing asset-price feedback loop. It was a surreal capital feeding frenzy that had spun rapidly out of control and turned the American Dream into a fitful reverie.

Conclusion

In chapter 1, I discussed several underlying characteristics of American society and its flawed financial system that have culminated over generations into an aggregate mindset that, in my view, indirectly led to the real estate meltdown and the resulting financial crisis.

The American consumer's desire to spend and live well beyond his or her means circuitously contributed to the crisis. But the "spend-it-before-we-earn-it" consumerism habits were in place long before the housing boom took shape, slowly forming a huge bubble that burst into a financial screw-up of epic proportions. Through seemingly endless appreciation and recycled home equity, most people were able to refinance out of their debt loads, creating ever-larger debts, while some lucky others took their equity and quickly cashed-out from their homes.

The financial meltdown is well known to have been an accumulation of different factors, ranging from rampant consumerism and greed, keeping up with the Joneses, and buying everything on credit to the predatory lenders who offered loans with easy to qualify "don't-ask-don't-tell" guidelines and the lack of regulatory oversight.

There is plenty of blame to go around. Tempting, low-rate loans, often with artificial payments, were pushed by greedy, unscrupulous loan officers. They found easy marks in gullible buyers who wanted the dwelling of their dreams at any cost and as quickly as possible.

Let's not forget the shady mortgage brokers and money-grubbing real estate agents who only wanted to close the sale, demanding that the transaction close or they would pull the deal from homebuyers because they had already referred the "opportunity" to an incentivized loan officer, who in turn placed the loan with the lender to satisfy the lifestyle of the voracious American consumer.

Just as some dodgy mortgage brokers and real estate agents are guilty of playing a role in the financial crisis, so, in different ways, are average American homeowners who were the "sacrificial lambs" of ruthless investment bankers. All these players are the offspring of a culture of extreme consumerism, excessive use (or abuse) of debt, and lax regulations that created the biggest boot of financial looting in US history. It was a team effort. We all screwed up. Government. Rating agencies. Wall Street. Commercial banks. Regulators. Investors.[11]

———

During the boom years of 2004–06, the possibility of buying a home was a seductive one. Whether through a contract-for-deed, rent-to-own, ARM, or a zero-down and zero interest for twelve months scam—the promise was the same.[12] Responding to cunning advertising tactics, including highly visible road signs, low-income families and recent immigrants in Florida, Nevada, Arizona, and California who didn't understand the complex process of credit and borrowing were the most frequent victims. It can be assumed that these families seldom had access to an honest real estate agent, loan officer, or attorney to guide them through the stressful home buying process—they were often dealing with the low-end of the real estate profession who would make a salesman of replica watches in a bazaar in Dubai look like an angel.

———

These underlying characteristics are social distractions that keep people from paying close attention to what's happening in the complex financial system, not to mention the fine-grain details of their mortgage agreements. They are distractions that most likely lured many people into financial deep water, as well as behavioral shortcomings that are due to inattention to developing good judgment and insightful decisions. In the words of Yale economist Robert Shiller, "One might say that the fundamental cause of the subprime crisis was that many people simply did not pay attention. They fell into traps of one sort or another because they did not know or understand what was happening in the marketplace. When their attention lapses, consumers are more likely to accept whatever financial contract is offered."[13]

Moreover, homeowners with nothing down basically had no risk retention mandate—no skin in the game. When home values fell, they were quickly underwater, with little incentive to keep paying their mortgages, even if they could. Mortgage brokers who acted as pass-through agents also had no skin in the game. Businesses failed, but someone else was always left holding the bag. Lenders and mortgage companies that peddled loans had no skin in the game either, unless, as often happened, they couldn't resist keeping high-yield loans in their own portfolios and then selling them off to the next sucker in the chain of capital.

———

When investment markets digest expectations only, it is a bubble in the making. Investors and bankers can easily get caught up in a feedback-loop that reinforces a sense of tunnel vision or expectations "group-think." This makes them repeat the same mistakes again and again. It seems as if a strong belief in the efficient US market lulled many investors and bankers into a lethal state of complacency. When the prices of assets spiraled upwards during the credit boom, many assumed that this reflected a genuine increase in their underlying value. That is, there was an assumption that American markets were "always right." Because so many investors had had similar training in the United States and were looking at the system in a homogeneous way, that faulty assumption made it hard to identify the scale of the credit bubble, and the looming financial crisis. As a result, they tended to act in a similar, mechanical way until it was too late.[14] It seems that they didn't "get" the big picture.

Additionally, the Fed wasn't totally aware of what was happening in the market. While Fed officials were aware that the nation's rapid increase in housing prices was coming to an end, they significantly underestimated how much damage the popping of the real estate bubble would cause in the rest of the economy. In his first meeting as Fed chairman, in March 2006, Ben Bernanke noted the slowdown in the housing market. But he said he shared the view that "strong fundamentals support a relatively soft landing in housing," adding: "I think we are unlikely to see growth being derailed by the housing market."[15]

Lastly, the data-overload experienced by Americans due to the constant bombardment from some deceitful mortgage brokers and "*me* first" real estate agents convinced the inexperienced to buy homes they couldn't afford. Their downfall was further quickened by the absence of reader-friendly mortgage lending forms and the jungle of financial jargon that baffled the average American homebuyer trying to decide whether to take a leap into the marketplace. Little wonder that consumers found themselves free-falling into a world ruled by greed, uncertainty, and money predators.

Chapter 4: Strawberry Pickers and Predators

It is not the want, but rather abundance
that creates avarice.
—Michel Eyquem De Montaigne, essayist

The real estate boom covered a multitude of sins in American business, banking, and financial regulation. When the housing market was white-hot in 2004–05, people who signed up for unaffordable loans could easily sell their homes and make a quick profit. But once the US housing market started to decline, the rug was pulled back to show the rot underneath, revealing thousands of cases of the darkest side of the property sector: predatory lending.

One of the causes of the real estate bust can be traced to the super-sophisticated manipulations of highly educated MBA and PhD types, all playing with newly developed algorithms designed to game the system. But on a much lower level, you had garden-variety con-men selling snake oil to the unsophisticated. High-level manipulators concentrated on big targets like pension funds. Low-life bamboozlers, on the other hand, went after the Aunt Minnies of the country. The goal of each was the same: to manipulate the unwary.

Greasing the Machine

Predatory lending has struck at the very core of American society, and because of the vulnerability of the victims it was one of the ugliest. A predatory loan is basically an unsuitable mortgage designed to exploit susceptible borrowers, where the lender doesn't care if the borrower can't make his payments because then the lender can pick up the home cheaply. Predatory loans are a subset of subprime mortgages made to people with less-than-perfect credit. A predatory loan, which is riddled with fraud, typically has one or more of the following features:[1]

- Charges more in interest and fees than is required to cover the added risk of lending to borrowers with credit imperfections;
- Contains abusive terms and conditions that trap borrowers and lead to increased indebtedness;
- Does not take into account the borrower's ability to repay the loan; or
- Violates fair-lending laws by deliberately targeting women, minorities, retirees, and communities of color.

More specifically, characteristics of predatory lending that were rampant before the financial crisis included the following (summarized by category of fraud).[2]

Table 4-1: Characteristics of Predatory Lending

Sales and Marketing Fraud	Mortgage Loan Fraud
• Aggressive solicitations to targeted neighborhoods. • Kickbacks to mortgage brokers (e.g., yield-spread premiums). • Racial steering to do business with high interest rate lenders. • Multi-level sales schemes targeting ethnic groups. • Purposely structuring loans with payments the borrower cannot afford. • Falsifying loan applications (particularly income levels). • Adding insincere co-signers. • Forging signatures on loan documents. • Mortgages in excess of 100 percent loan-to-value. • Changing the loan terms at closing. • Unlicensed mortgage brokers.	• Unusually high variable interest rates. • High points, or padded closing costs. • Padded recording fees. • Unexpected balloon payments. • Inflated appraisal costs. • Bogus broker fees (5 to 10 percent). • Unbundling (itemizing duplicate services and charging separately for them). • Forced-upon homeowners insurance.

Furthermore, after the closing of a home loan, predatory lenders weren't done with their prey. They would charge *daily* interest when the loan payments were late, use abusive collection practices, and apply excessive prepayment penalties. They would also fail to report any good payments on the borrower's credit reports, or provide the accurate loan balance and payoff amount.

The OC's Merchants of Misery

Orange County, California, (also known as "the OC") is a place of superficial beauty, vast private wealth, and shiny corporate buildings that has a history as a breeding ground for white-collar crime: late 1980s savings and loan frauds and big-time real estate scandals. That history made it an ideal setting for launching the subprime sector, which grew in large measure due to bait-and-switch salesmanship and garden-variety deception.[3] By the height of the nation's recent mortgage boom, Orange County was home to four of the nation's six biggest subprime lenders. Together, these four lenders—Ameriquest, Fremont Investment & Loan, New Century, and Option One Mortgage—accounted for nearly a third of the US subprime market.[4]

It's easy to understand why Orange County had become fertile ground for white-collar fraud. Long before TV shows such as *The OC* and *The Real Housewives of Orange County* introduced America to the region's exotic mix of beaches, mega-malls, and plastic surgery practices, Orange County embodied the high life—a new "la-la land" of hot money.

People with a staunch fervor for free enterprise found a welcoming home in Orange County. It had grown from some 130,000 residents at the start of World War II to a population of more than two million in the 1980s. It was a modern day version of the California gold rush—making Orange County the new frontier of the second half of the twentieth century.[5] The OC rush was led by a tight clan of ranchers-turned-developers, real estate speculators, and prosperity-gospel evangelists who heralded individual uplift and despised government intervention in the market.[6]

Former employees from Ameriquest described a system in which they were pushed to falsify documents on bad mortgages and then sell them to Wall Street investment banks eager to make quick-and-dirty profits. In 2007, lawyers for borrowers of Ameriquest mortgages, who are seeking to combine twenty lawsuits into one class-action suit, asserted in a filing that "assets of Ameriquest entities were transferred to Roland Arnall [the mortgage company's owner] with the intent to hinder, delay, or defraud the plaintiffs in this action."[7] The problems confronted by companies such as Ameriquest could be a contributing factor to the welcomed rise of Certified Mortgage Planners, experts that work with Certified Financial Planners who help consumers with their overall investment portfolios.

———

A study by the Joint Center for Housing Studies at Harvard University indicated that regulators (who didn't do much), coupled with too much money looking for something to invest in, combined to cause the boom—and then bust—of subprime mortgage lending in the United States.[8] The combination of predatory lending, an excess of global liquidity, low interest rates, high leverage, and regulatory laxity in the context of over-valued housing markets triggered staggering risk taking. Capital markets supplied credit through Wall Street in large volumes for dicey loans to risky borrowers and then multiplied these uncertainties by issuing screwed up derivatives that exposed investors to risks in amounts much larger than the face amount of all the loans. According to the Harvard study, the nation's mortgage meltdown has been felt the most in the Central Valley of California, a vast agricultural region that has no resemblance whatsoever to shiny Orange County.

Meltdown Valley

California gave the world the iPhone, the first satellite, and the skateboard. It is America's biggest economy and the home of innovation that created technology giants such as Google and Facebook. But despite its plentiful resources, creative thinkers, and entrepreneurial culture, the once-Golden State is in deep trouble. It has a budget deficit that stands at nearly $19 billion and it has yet to recover from the housing crisis.

———

The Central Valley is a large, flat area that dominates the central portion of California (see map 4-1). It's home to many of the state's most productive agricultural businesses and farms, as well as one of the highest concentrations of Hispanic (Latino) immigrants in the United States. The valley stretches approximately 500 miles from north to south. Its northern half is referred to as the Sacramento Valley and its southern half as the San Joaquin Valley.

Map 4-1: Meltdown Valley, California

Map 4-1: Meltdown Valley, California

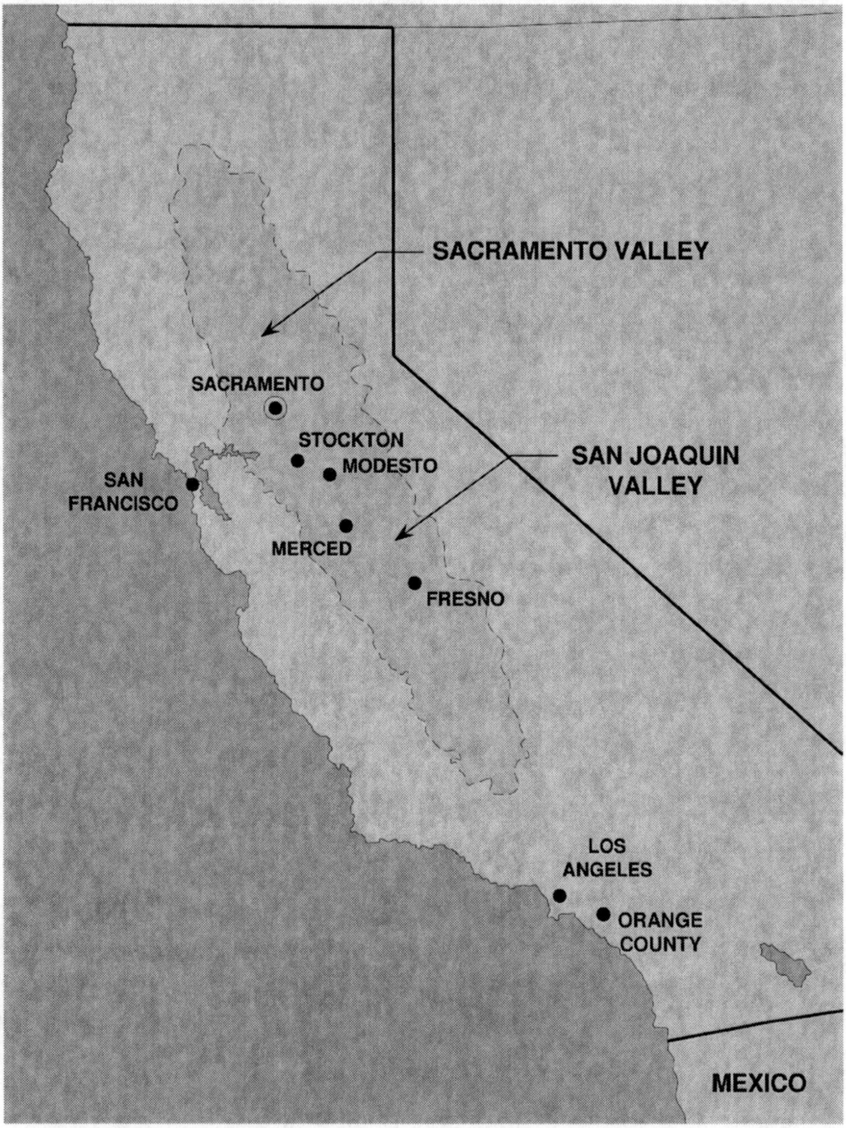

In recent years, seven of the ten least-affordable metro areas in the nation were located in California, a state that is typically a housing bellwether. At the peak of the housing crisis, the largest defaults in America as measured in dollar losses (number of defaults times loan size) came out of California's exurban fringe, namely the Central Valley, and at the height of the housing boom, California had only 10 percent of the nation's housing units— but in 2009, it had 34 percent of all the foreclosures in the country.[9] California was most vulnerable to foreclosures because the median value of owner-occupied housing was 8.3 times median family income, while the national average was only 3.2.[10]

Since the 1980s, the Central Valley cities of Modesto, Merced, and Stockton grew rapidly in both area and population, as housing values along the California Coast increased significantly. Many people from Los Angeles and the San Francisco Bay area relocated to the growing San Joaquin Valley in search of more affordable housing, while retaining employment outside the valley. Many immigrants from Mexico and Central America were also attracted to the region because of an abundance of agricultural jobs. About 6.5 million people live in the Central Valley today, comprising 17.5 percent of California's total population.

Fueled by sharp price reductions in many Central Valley communities due to high foreclosure rates and a deluge of supply, housing affordability soared in many parts of the state in 2008–10. But the bulk of those affordability gains were in communities most affected by the subprime mortgage and foreclosure fiascos— especially Central Valley cities such as Stockton.

Predatorville, USA

Stockton is the San Joaquin County seat, one of eighteen counties that comprise the vast Central Valley. Since the financial crisis began, the inland port city of Stockton, some eighty miles east of

San Francisco with a population of about 325,000, has had one of the worst foreclosure rates in the country. At the height of it, about one in ten houses fell to foreclosure. Houses that sold for more than $500,000 before the crash went for $200,000 in 2010. In some neighborhoods, fixer-uppers cost less than a new Honda Civic—under $25,000.

According to John Burns Real Estate Consulting, Stockton has one of the highest numbers of shadow inventory in terms of months of supply, estimated at twenty-seven months. Shadow inventory, also called "supply overhang," is based on the number of properties that are seriously delinquent (ninety days or more), in foreclosure, REO (bank real estate-owned/taken back due to foreclosure), or that are not currently listed on multiple listing services (MLSs).

The California real estate boom that began in the late 1990s significantly changed the San Joaquin Valley. Some three years after the financial crisis, Stockton is a completely changed place. Whole neighborhoods have been decimated by the mortgage disaster. The tax base has shrunken and city services and municipal jobs have been drastically cut. Unemployment hovers at around 18 percent, and economists are predicting that it will take years for Stockton to recover from the grinding crisis.

Housing developments built for commuters have been hit the hardest, since they were the ones to attract newcomers fleeing the huge spike in prices closer to the San Francisco Bay area. Those whose livelihoods depend on a healthy housing environment—real estate agents, contractors, day laborers—are barely making ends meet.

To visit Stockton, a generic city of bland single-family home neighborhoods edged by freeways, is to begin to understand the

calamitous effects of the nation's foreclosure crisis, which has dev-
astated so many communities.

Shattered Dreams

The high foreclosure rates in the Central Valley have mostly been
experienced by minorities and Hispanic immigrants, who were
the prime targets of predatory lenders. It has been documented by
the Center for Responsible Lending (CRL) that African-American
and Hispanic families disproportionately received the most expensive and dangerous types of loans during the heyday of subprime
lending.[11] According to an analysis of the Fed's Home Mortgage
Disclosure Act data, higher-rate mortgages were disproportionately distributed to borrowers of color between 2004 and 2008.[12]
For example, in 2006, among consumers who received mortgages
for single-family homes, roughly half of African-American and
Hispanic borrowers received a higher-rate mortgage compared to
about one-fifth of non-Hispanic, white borrowers.

In addition, a CRL study provided evidence that loans in
minority communities were more likely to carry prepayment penalties than loans in white communities.[13] It therefore stands to
reason that borrowers of color, who were deliberately targeted by
some subprime lenders and steered into the most abusive products, are disproportionately bearing the brunt of the ongoing
foreclosure crisis.

As shown in table 4-2, the vast majority of California foreclosures were on loans originated between 2005 and 2007. This is
not surprising for two reasons: First, most borrowers who received
their loans prior to 2005 likely would have built up enough equity

during the housing boom. This equity would have allowed these borrowers to sell or refinance into another loan if and when they faced economic hardship or "payment shocks." On the other hand, borrowers who received their loans closer to when housing prices peaked in 2006 built up little or no equity when prices fell and, therefore, were far less likely to have such options.[14]

Table 4-2: Distribution of California Foreclosures* by Mortgage Origination Year

Origination Year	No. of Foreclosures	Share of Total
2000–2003	23,600	2.7%
2004	50,900	5.8%
2005	246,500	28.1%
2006	364,300	41.5%
2007	172,400	19.7%
2008	19,500	2.2%

Source: Center for Responsible Lending's analysis of Foreclosure Radar data.

*September 2006 through October 2009. Number of foreclosures rounded.

The second reason that foreclosures were concentrated in the 2005–07 cohorts is that this was the period during which the high-risk and weakly underwritten subprime and Alt-A products were most aggressively structured, marketed, and sold as mortgage-backed securities.[15]

As shown in table 4-3, six of the top-ten California metropolitan statistical areas (MSAs) by foreclosure density—including the three highest—are located in the Central Valley. Since 2006, no

California community has experienced a higher percentage of housing units entering foreclosure than Modesto and Stockton.

Table 4-3: Top Ten California MSAs by Foreclosure Density*

Metropolitan Statistical Area	Foreclosure Density (Share of Housing Units Experiencing Foreclosure)
Modesto	16.1%
Merced	16.0%
Stockton	15.8%
Riverside-San Bernardino-Ontario	15.6%
Bakersfield	11.4%
Yuba City	11.1%
Madera-Chowchilla	11.0%
Vallejo-Fairfield	10.7%
Sacramento-Arden-Roseville	9.7%
El Centro	9.3%

Source: Foreclosure Radar, US Census. *September 2006 through October 2009.

As an example of how fast the housing bubble grew in this part of California, table 4-4 shows the area median home price-to-area income ratios. Between 2000 and 2008, the price of the median home compared to the average income nearly doubled in each of the indicated MSAs in the Central Valley. This may have been an important factor in the increased incentive for borrowers to enter into a risky mortgage and in the resulting volume of overextended borrowers entering foreclosure.[16] Table 4-4 also shows that these hardest hit MSAs have high concentrations of Hispanic borrowers, offering yet another explanation for the disproportionate impact of California's foreclosure crisis on this region.

Table 4-4: Area Median Home Price-to-Area Income (AMI)
Ratios—Central Valley

	Median Home Price-to-AMI Ratio		Proportion of Population Comprised of Hispanics	
MSA	**2000**	**2008**	**2000**	**2008**
Modesto	3.1	5.5	27.2%	34.5%
Merced	3.1	5.7	40.5%	48.0%
Stockton	3.3	5.8	27.0%	32.7%

Source: CRL calculations of American Community Survey data

The causes for the high concentrations of foreclosures in these areas are several, including a tendency by some first-generation immigrants to overspend on homes to show that they have "made it" in America, abuse by predatory lenders, low incomes, a lack of knowledge about basic real estate finance and borrowing, as well as a poor command of the English language. More important, however, is that the declining economic conditions in the region's agricultural centers have depressed communities and crushed surrounding property values. This, along with the threat of further foreclosures of subprime and Alt-A mortgages, poses serious adverse risks to California's economy, threatening both working-class and middle-class residents of a state already in economic distress.[17]

Rafael, the Strawberry Picker

On a hot afternoon in July 2005, Rafael Garcia was driving along Interstate 5 back to his small apartment after a long day of work in a strawberry field near Stockton. He wanted to freshen up a bit, so he decided to stop at a road side bar to have a beer. While sipping his chilled beverage, he glanced through a local newspaper and noticed an ad in Spanish that said: "Buy new with zero dollars down. The time has arrived. Stop throwing your money away and start building equity in your own home today! And with no money down, low monthly payments, and no private mortgage insurance needed, the American Dream is much closer than you realize!" For a moment Rafael thought that it sounded just too good to be true. But it *was* true. The offer was from a regional subprime lender, looking to reel in thousands of unqualified and ill-advised homebuyers, only to slap them with add-ons, fees, and variable rates. It was a teaser—a trick, but little did he know. In September 2005, Rafael took the bait and bought a new 2,400 square-foot house in Stockton financed by the subprime lender.

Rafael, 38, had moved to the Central Valley from Ciudad Juarez, Mexico, in 1999 with his wife Rosa and two children.[18] Despite making only $15,000 a year—and with dubious residency status—Rafael managed to buy his own slice of the American Dream. But his Stockton home came with a hefty price tag: $700,000. So how did Rafael, the strawberry picker with an annual income of just $15,000, purchase a $700,000 home in California without any money down? He had some shaky help. Although Rafael was the only one to sign the purchase agreement and the only one named on the loan documents, he bought the house with his wife Rosa (who worked as a house cleaner), along with their friends Antonio Delgado and his wife. But even in a good month, the two couples together didn't earn much more than $6,500.

With their combined incomes, the two couples estimated that they could only afford monthly payments of $3,000. For the

$700,000 home, the initial monthly payments were about $5,000, or a whopping 77 percent of their income. (As a rule of thumb, people shouldn't pay more than 28 percent of their gross monthly income on housing). However, Rafael and Rosa were brainwashed by their real estate agent, Maria, into believing that they could easily refinance their home in three to six months to an affordable interest rate.

Until then, Maria said she would plug in and pay for whatever they couldn't afford to help the two families buy the home they wanted. She also requested that the two couples pay her back as soon as they got their refinancing and cashed-in on their home equity. But in reality, Maria knew that Rafael could never afford the house, and she did the deal only to get the sale's commission. Nonetheless, Maria did supplement the mortgage payments on the Stockton home, paying about $2,000 per month for nine months. But the refinance never happened, and Maria stopped helping with the mortgage payments in May 2006. A year later, Rafael defaulted on his loan and the two couples tried desperately to offload the house before repossession by the predator lender. Three months went by and nobody wanted to buy their house as the subprime mortgage crisis was starting to mount. The inevitable happened: a foreclosure date was set for October 15, 2007.

The language barrier (Rafael, a native Spanish speaker, could barely speak English) also played a big role. Subprime mortgage brokers aggressively targeted non-English speakers and minorities. Nearly all mortgage advertisements in Spanish-language newspapers were from subprime brokers peddling loans for predatory lenders.

Conclusion

Most people are vulnerable when it comes to mortgages because the situation can be quite complex. But recent immigrants and people of color feel their choices are more limited, so they're much more vulnerable to financial abuse. Some claim that subprime loans got a bad rap, saying that those loans made it easier for many people, especially minorities, to purchase a home. But there are serious concerns and problems intrinsic to purchasing a home with almost no money down—with no skin in the game.

First and foremost, if the housing market declines by even a small amount, homeowners will go underwater immediately. If the price of the house falls by even a bit, they will owe more on the mortgage than the house is worth. If they need to sell it, they need to come up with extra cash to pay back the bank for the difference between the original loan and the new loan. And the fact that the victims of predatory lending only had several thousand dollars to put down in the first place implies that they didn't have much financial breathing room anyway.

The foreclosures in the Central Valley of California epitomized the widespread havoc caused by the mortgage crisis, especially its troubling social dimensions. The magnitude and nature of the crisis suggest three changes that are needed in the real estate sector (as will be further discussed in chapter 12): First, preventing avoidable foreclosures is critical, and for homeowners of every color. Second, steps must be taken to ameliorate the consequences of foreclosures for families and for neighborhoods directly affected. Third, policies should be put in place to help avert a similar crisis in the future.

———

True, we are all ethically challenged. Yet most of us try to resist a lust for money that is driven by avarice. Finance and banking used to be about stability, value, relationships, and maintaining a ratio of two-thirds assets to one-third loans. But now, the focus of the dog-eat-dog housing finance profession, dominated by bankers who are so cavalier with other people's savings and investments, is exclusively on making a lot of money as quickly as possible.

The subprime crisis was partially caused by arranging for low-income people to get mortgages they could not pay. It was also instigated by reckless lending practices and an incessant demand for risky loans by an overly leveraged secondary mortgage market ruled by nerds in windowless offices—in concert with old-time con-men on the ground—who securitized those perilous loans. The greedy predatory lenders were the tip of the proverbial iceberg of a corporate America that has an insatiate appetite for short-term profits.

Chapter 5: Wicked Incentives

As one digs deeper into the national character of
Americans, one sees that they have sought the value
of everything in this world only in the answer to this
single question: how much money will it bring in?
—Alexis De Tocqueville, historian

Like night follows day, misery follows greed. The Great Recession from which the United States is still trying to recover was caused by a number of interconnected factors, including excessive, unsustainable debt levels and the failures of checks and balances at many different levels. It was also caused by a pattern of behavior by some corporate leaders that was laced with excessive greed.

The excesses that we have been seeing in management behavior, such as large-scale fraud, and ostentatious remuneration (base salaries, cash bonuses, stock options, etc.) are to a large extent part of the US business environment itself and wildly exaggerated in investment banking. Greed is everywhere. It is part of human nature.

Greed (which shouldn't be confused with relentless ambition or self-interest) is responsible for the exorbitant salaries of CEOs in America. In the 1970s, the ratio of chief executive officers' compensation to average workers' compensation was approximately 35:1. Estimates put the US ratio today at 350:1. (In the UK the ratio is closer to 88:1).[1]

Ravenousness is also responsible for the endless stress and ruthless competition of the workplace, and along with them, the strains and tensions of professional-class marriages. Greed is responsible for outsourcing by US companies, and some of the CEO class seems oblivious to the fact that the employees who lose their jobs are also the consumers who sustain the American economy.

Of course, there are thousands of decent and visionary CEOs and senior managers in the United States. There are also many bankers who are—as are journalists, actors, and postmen—neither saintly nor evil. But it takes only a limited number of crooks and incompetents to bring an entire financial system to its knees.

Risk? What Risk?

Poor risk management, including deliberately hidden and, thus, insufficient data and incomplete performance metrics—coupled with a short-term focus by senior business managers—were indirect factors that contributed to the collapse of the US housing market. According to a study conducted by the University of Maryland and sponsored by the Mortgage Bankers Association, the combination of informational limitations on risk managers and a governance culture that tipped decisions in favor of business-driven strategies caused the unprecedented increase in risk taking that took place throughout the real estate sector.[2] That is, as home prices increased dramatically and capital sloshed into the US financial system, lenders were heavily pressured to put that money to work and offer "anything goes" loan products that would speed up home buying by low-income borrowers.

The resulting increase and expansion of risk layering (the tendency to accumulate high-risk), along with fundamental changes in borrower behavior, left managers unable to offer reliable estimates of uncertainty.[3] When market conditions changed, mortgage performance models proved highly unstable, with loans originated in 2006 defaulting at four times the rate of what a model prior to 2004 would have predicted.[4] For that reason, it is essential for the mortgage sector to develop early warning measures of the level of risk in new originations, with less reliance on imprecise historical performance of loan products.

In addition to limited information available for proper risk assessment, an American corporate culture obsessed with short-term earnings heavily influenced decision-making during the recent boom. The decline in senior management's loss aversion due to a euphoric period of high property prices and low defaults led to sloppy underwriting, complacency, and significantly higher levels of risk layering.

The Almighty Multiple

Share prices in a publicly traded company are determined by market demand and supply, and, therefore, depend heavily on the expectations of buyers and sellers. Among these expectations are the company's future and most recent performance, including potential growth as well as perceived risk which can be measured with the price-earnings (P/E) multiple.

By dividing the price of one share in a company by the profits earned per share, the P/E multiple (also known as the P/E ratio) is derived. If earnings per share (EPS) move proportionally with share prices, the ratio stays the same. But if share prices gain in value and earnings remain the same or go down, the P/E rises.

The problem with P/E multiples is that they are both specious *and* essential. While the measure has questionable predictive power, its ubiquity as a valuation benchmark makes it difficult to ignore. A P/E multiple is a tool for comparison. It must be placed next to corporate peers, the market, and a stock's own growth and valuation history. A P/E multiple of, say, fifteen means that the stock is selling for fifteen times earnings, or put another way, for every $1 of earnings an investor is willing to pay $15 to buy that $1 of earnings. (With an EPS of $2, the stock would be selling for $2 x 15 = $30 per share, and so on).

On the other hand, a capitalization rate (or cap rate) is the inverse of a P/E multiple, and is used pretty much exclusively in real estate.[5] The cap rate is generally defined as the first year's net operating income (NOI) divided by property value. The real estate profession's usage of cap rates reflects its historic linkage to the bond market, as real estate derives its income from promissory income streams. So just as the bond market commonly uses yield—as opposed to multiple—when valuing a bond, the property sector uses cap rates. But this difference in applied metrics can cause unnecessary confusion for investors and the general public. For example, in court cases where a real estate appraiser has to provide testimony, he or she has to speak in terms of P/E multiples so that the jury can easily follow the discussion.

The P/E multiple is a significant focus for senior management in most US companies and industries. This is because senior management is primarily paid with their company's stock—a form of payment that is supposed to align the interests of management with the interests of other stockholders—in order to increase the stock price. The stock price can increase in one of two ways: either through improved earnings or through an improved multiple that the market assigns to the earnings.

———

The remuneration of most CEOs in the US is based on such short-term winnings, and only a minority is rewarded for taking the long view. Publicly traded American corporations are obsessed with quarterly earnings that determine, in the short-term, how share prices move. To boost these earnings, corporate executives also routinely avoid investing in future growth and research and development (R&D) that create jobs. Instead of making these long-term commitments, some CEOs take myopic steps that quickly inflate their company's share price: they lay off thousands of employees, they fork out special dividends, and they plot mergers and acquisitions.[6] Such actions are used by companies to structure themselves to be perceived as commanding a higher P/E multiple and are designed to increase the stock price. Thus, maximizing the stock price easily acts as a "perverse incentive," and those sorts of short-term moves quickly translate into obscene bonuses for the executives who make them. In other words, the US economy is richly rewarding its most powerful players for their myopic view and speculation. Highly excessive bonuses for executives don't, in fact, just reward this short-termism—they invite it.[7]

A higher P/E multiple is the result of an apparent competitive advantage that's *perceived* by the market, allowing a company to grow earnings over time (i.e., investors pay for peace of mind or upside potential). Tactics by management to convince investors that their companies have a competitive advantage tend to have profound effects on P/E multiples. For example, the primary motivation for establishing for-profit corporations is to diversify earnings so that their net incomes increase steadily over time, often times regardless of the means involved to achieve that goal. If the primary motive of most US corporations is to increase earnings, then short-term measures such as layoffs and outsourcing are simply viewed as means to attain the Holy Grail of corporate finance—a high P/E multiple.

Some US companies tend to veil excess earnings in good years to cover for losses in bad years, a suspect accounting mechanism that's designed to create the perception that the company always (slowly but steadily) increases its profits, with the ultimate goal being the increase of the P/E multiple. In addition, companies can convince "Mr. Market" that they should command a higher multiple by closing down or selling off businesses just because they are perceived to be volatile, even though they produce profits. After all, in corporate finance perception *is* reality.

————

If corporate America is to avoid short-termism, regulators need to help to free money managers and senior company executives from the tyranny of quarterly results. Chief executives also need to step off the consensus earnings treadmill. At the same time, however, one cannot neglect the immense pressures related to taking a short-term perspective in the financial markets, and the often unintended collateral damage they can cause.[8] This problem is particularly evident in that other countries don't focus on the short-term nearly as much as is done in the United States. As a result, these pressures impede the pursuit of long-term strategies by American public companies, sometimes to their competitive disadvantage in the global marketplace.[9]

While some problems do indeed lie with money managers, one has to consider (and as noted above) the unrealistic pressures they face from their US clients (who are also obsessed with short-termism). The returns of most money managers are published quarterly and compared against all other managers in their peer groups. Most clients are tolerant of a bad quarter, but fewer have patience for a bad year. As a result, "rock star" money managers can attract a lot of capital very quickly, while struggling managers can face heavy redemptions (cash withdrawals by clients).[10]

But it's not just the money managers who cause the problems. Over half of the companies in the S&P 500 feed the short-term beast by projecting EPS for the next quarter.[11] When companies make projections of next quarter's earnings, they tend to take a short-term approach to corporate decisions. If the collateral damage of this focus was felt only by investors that would be one thing. But it's not. This short-termism directly impacts a firm's ability to innovate. In a survey by the National Bureau of Economic Research of some 400 senior financial executives, a whopping 80 percent said they were willing to forgo spending on R&D just to meet their quarterly projections.[12]

So why do CEOs in America keep churning out these quarterly projections despite the problems they cause? Many CEOs claim they are concerned that putting a halt to quarterly projections will hurt their stock price. But this concern is not supported by a McKinsey & Company study of 1,200 companies that compared those projecting quarterly earnings to those that did not.[13] The study found no statistically significant differences between the P/E multiples of the two sets of companies.

How Their Ways May be Made Straight

Top executives are supposed to answer to shareholders, but to a large extent they have been able to determine their own pay packages. "Say-on-pay" votes and other measures that empower shareholders and outside directors are meant to shift that balance of power, but they are seldom effective. Most shareholders knew (and still know today) that these executives were overpaid. Even CEOs with abysmal track records made the big bucks.

To pin the financial crisis on mortal flaws like greed and arrogance would be too simplistic. Rather, it was the failure to account for human weakness and error that is relevant to the financial meltdown.

In 2010, the US government began sweeping reform over CEO accountability and the compensation practices of corporate America through the Dodd-Frank Wall Street Reform and Consumer Protection Act. In addition to the disclosure of the annual compensation of CEOs, Dodd-Frank requires organizations with publicly held stock to disclose the median total annual compensation of all employees and the ratio comparing these two amounts. The intent is clear. It is to provide a periodic reminder to shareholders and others of the reasonableness of CEO compensation.

CEO compensation publicity should bring good reform because it would reveal the dirty secrets of the metrics and parameters of remuneration. This should also lead to more clarity and transparency about activities and levels of accountability carried out by CEOs in various companies. Comparison of pay on different rating measures should compel CEOs either to perform or perish. Moreover, compensation publicity should make them

more accountable toward shareholders. Transparency in pay levels, promotions, and career opportunities promote trust and leadership sustainability in organizations.

Chained but Untamed

Angelo Mozilo, the former CEO of Countrywide Financial—once
the nation's largest mortgage lender—epitomizes the questionable business practices of a number of CEOs in the real estate
finance arena who contributed to the housing bubble, the shady
financial machinations that surround it, and a disastrous lending spree that ultimately threatened to undermine the nation's
economy. He was the Johnny Appleseed of subprime mortgages
who spread toxic loans across the American landscape like wild
crabapples.

The slapdash Mozilo and two of his former colleagues were
accused of misrepresenting the company's declining lending
standards during 2006–07 and portraying themselves publicly as
"underwriters of high quality mortgages," even as they learned
that the company's loans were becoming increasingly risky. In
2010, Mozilo agreed to pay $22.5 million in a penalty and repara-
tions to investors and has been banned for life from serving as an
officer or a director of a public company.[14]

In addition, Lee Farkas, the former chairman of Taylor, Bean
& Whitaker Mortgage Corporation, was found guilty in April 2011
on fourteen charges stemming from a seven-year, multibillion-dol-
lar fraud scheme that led to the collapse of his firm and Colonial
Bank. Farkas, who owned airplanes, several homes, dozens of cars,

and personally pocketed $40 million, was sentenced in June 2011 to thirty years in prison.

Over nearly two decades, Farkas transformed his Florida-based firm into the largest non-bank mortgage lender in the country. At its height, it was the fifth largest originator of loans insured by the Federal Housing Administration (FHA) and was one of the top sellers of mortgages to Freddie Mac. The prosecutors alleged that he had fraudulently tried to obtain more than $550 million in bailout funds for Colonial Bank, a major lender to Taylor, Bean & Whitaker from the US government's Troubled Asset Relief Program Fund. No TARP funds were ultimately committed, and Colonial was placed into receivership by the Federal Deposit Insurance Corporation in 2009.

———

Some elements of the financial crisis were provoked not by irrational behavior but by rational responses to perverse incentives. There is plenty of evidence that the corporations deeply involved in the financial meltdown acted irresponsibly. But the fact that executives of major financial groups put their firms in harm's way is by no means baffling. There were immediate gains to be made, namely huge bonuses and the appreciating value of previously awarded stocks and stock options meant large fortunes to business executives, regardless of how their companies fared in the longer-term. In their view, this was a once in a lifetime opportunity that was just too good to pass up, and too many people were making too much money for the party to stop.

Fixing the BOD

The bad investment decisions, the magnitude of the exposure, and the lack of oversight by corporate boards at the company level also played a role in the financial crisis. The board of directors (BOD) is the strategic "body" of a firm and is formed to ensure that the value of the company is sustained and shareholder value is created by holding the company's management accountable.[15] It also approves all elements recommended by the compensation committee as it pertains to all stock options and cash awards, as well as in-kind benefits. Therefore, it is necessary—in light of the inconsistency of executive payouts during the recent crisis—that the BOD requires financial-pay consultants to sit on the compensation committees. This should achieve two goals: one is the addition of expertise to compensation committees, and second is the independence from the BOD, as sometimes the individuals on the committees incestuously come from the board itself.

In relation to the tools that are available to the BOD to ensure executive pay is more closely tied to long-term performance and aligned to shareholders interests, some of them need to be modified. These tools are: base salary, stock options, restricted stock, cash bonuses, and termination packages.[16] Compensation payouts can sometimes include all of these five components or some combination of them.

Starting with the basics, a base salary should be the smallest portion of an executive's total compensation relative to industry peers.[17] Stock options should be granted to the top-ten executives of the firm and be "out-of-the-money" with a maturity of at least two years. Restricted stock should also require executives to hold shares for longer periods of time, subject to a minimum three-year vesting period. If the executive retires, he or she should be required to continue holding the shares until the vesting period is completed.[18]

As to the cash bonus component, it should be divided into two parts: a regular year-end cash component and a deferred cash component that also vests over a three-year period, including a claw-back provision.[19] During this three-year deferment period, executives would have the choice of a variety of investment options to earn competitive returns for the deferred cash.

The cash compensation tends to be a big portion of the total package and, therefore, should be contingent on certain conditions. It should be tied directly to the firm's performance over a three-year period—with one third of this compensation tied to the firm's return on equity (ROE), a second third tied to the company's relative ROE versus its peers, and the last third tied to the total shareholders return on a relative basis.[20] Lastly, termination packages are where companies need to do lots of modifications. When a CEO retires or is terminated, it's usually because of either the result of a personal misconduct (i.e., bacchanalian romps) or poor company performance. In both cases, he or she should not be given any compensation on their way out and there should be no unvested equity granted upon employment termination.[21] Why should companies reward executives who have damaged the company's reputation or have destroyed shareholder value?

During financial crises, no stock options or cash bonus should be granted as part of a year-end compensation to any executives whose companies receive federal assistance. Compensation should be capped at, say, $750,000, severance payments barred, and cash awards be subject to a provision that would be triggered if the individual engages in conduct detrimental to the firm, or if financial reports are later proven to be materially inaccurate.[22]

————

As we well know, public pressure has been rising as many individuals have seen their savings fluctuate wildly over the last three years. They want to see more of the executives of mortgage companies, banks, and their BODs that contributed to the financial crisis be held accountable for the widespread economic destruction they caused.

But the problem is that the boards of directors don't seem to learn from past mistakes. For example, many companies take the same steps just as a cosmetic remedy to their current situation and to appease their shareholders. Admitting losses on their books, a BOD convenes "urgently," the chief executive officer is fired, and an interim CEO is announced until a search for a new one is complete. That was the typical scenario at almost every financial institution that was affected by the crisis. It seemed that the BOD just wanted to show that they were taking some kind of action, and addressing the situation for the sake of taking action. In other words, "a smoke and mirrors" approach in which they're always *reactive*, not proactive.[23]

The financial crisis reaffirmed that the incentives of CEOs and the reactive approaches of BODs led to system-destabilizing events, and that the destabilization inevitably spills over into the lives of millions of people, something about which the US media failed to adequately forewarn the public.

All the News That Should be fit to Print

The US media has repeatedly failed to warn the public about huge, visible risks. The media was grossly deficient when it came to covering the reckless behavior, sleaze, and willful ignorance (much of which was reasonably obvious to anyone who was paying attention) that inflated the housing balloon. Their frequent cheerleading for bad practices—and near-total failure to warn us relentlessly of what was building—made a bad situation worse.

In Florida, Arizona, Nevada, and California, among other centers of the housing bubble, newspapers might have told their readers the inconvenient truth. They could have explained that the housing bubble would inevitably lead to personal financial disaster for many in their regions, not to mention fiscal misery for local and state governments. But the media didn't do this, most probably because of its reliance on advertising from those who profited from the crazy housing binge (i.e., homebuilders and lenders). That is, objective journalism was overwhelmed by herd coverage, usually peppered with overly optimistic quotes from people who stood to benefit from the balloon's continued inflation.

We saw endless, glamorized stories about "fearless" home-loan borrowers, about "shrewd" people who flipped homes for big profits, and about the way home values kept rising in unprecedented ways. We saw few cautionary accounts about what happens when bubbles burst—how families and economies can face swift ruin.

I was visiting family in Los Angeles for Thanksgiving in 2005 as the US economy was throbbing on Viagra. After shopping on the Friday after Thanksgiving at a large department store with hundreds of customers waiting in long check-out lines, I remember buying a copy of a leading local newspaper that had a front page article with a title saying something like, "Black Friday retail sales are up 8 percent compared to last year—but will it last?" The paper had another story right below about the dining choices in a particular Los Angeles neighborhood, with a large photo of a completely empty restaurant. As an average consumer, I had to only guess that, given the respected newspaper's tone, perhaps something grisly was going to happen to the US economy. This should have been done more often by the national media.

Moreover, the business press often referred to the "real estate market" without making any distinctions. In other words, which specific elements of it were deteriorating, and which, if any, were showing resiliency? As we know, the subprime mortgages that experienced the weakest credit performance were a sub-segment of this market—one with the highest layering of underwriting risk.[24] This risk layering in underwriting subprime mortgages was unprecedented but was not objectively exposed by the media pundits.

The media in America, like in many other countries, thrives on controversy, sensationalism, and sheer shock value just to sell newspapers, increase viewership, and to spike short-term earnings. This includes slapping attention-grabbing headlines on front pages which, in a most subtle way, can cause consumers and investors to second-guess themselves.

The crisis has made it obvious that when things get frothy, banks find it difficult to hold back. US regulators who issued warnings were disregarded. Some academics, analysts, and whistleblowers inside banks fared little better. An ex-employee of Countrywide, the once gung-ho American lender, recalls presenting a forecast of a flat housing market to a meeting at the bank in 2006 and being shouted down by salespeople who argued that if they priced for credit risk on that basis they would be out of business.[25]

Although this was the general tenor of the US media, there were several observers who tried to send out warnings, but were mostly scoffed and ignored by the mass media machine. Five of the most notable contrarians who predicted that the housing boom of 2004–06 wouldn't last were Michael Burry, founder of the now-liquidated Scion Capital hedge fund, Raghuram Rajan of the University of Chicago, Ken Rosen of Berkeley, Nouriel Roubini of New York University, and Robert Shiller of Yale.[26] Others who were trying to send warnings about the impending economic crisis but were not given a platform included the authors of several books published between 2003 and 2005: *America the Broke* by Gerald Swanson, *The Coming Crash in the Housing Market* by John Talbott, and *The Second Great Depression* by Warren Brussee. As such, going forward it would be wise if the US media gave more attention to such brilliant (or just plain lucky) Cassandras.

Conclusion

An obsession with maximizing shareholder value continues to blight American capitalism. By straining to hit quarterly targets, chief executives are not only short-changing their clients, they are losing touch with the real reasons for being in business.

There is nothing wrong with large corporations making large profits. Yet the news from Wall Street continues to attract the ire of Main Street, which continued to struggle in 2011.[27] Based on what we've just been through, one can sadly say that there has been, and perhaps continues to be, far too much emphasis on short-term projections and performance in corporate America.

The media and the investment community exert enormous influence on the publication of quarterly results, and the over analysis of these imperfect metrics is one of the sources of confusion in the financial markets—whether the analysis is for the real estate sector, high-tech, or consumer products. But sell-side analysts desperately need it, and many companies still rely on the sell-side to market their stock to lay investors and to their preferred clients who are also short-term players. In addition, in these days of twenty-four-hour news and endless reports on all manner of hand-held electronic devices, business news has become like sports-talk radio and TV—constant analysis, constant blabber, and always conflict—often concocted for the sake of the story between ultimate winners and losers. After all, a business news telecast would be quite boring without the quarterly excitement of beating or missing earnings estimates.

Another reason is compensation. With senior management pay being largely equity-based and tenure being generally short-term, it is to be expected that incentives are short-term in nature, with corresponding myopic actions that follow. The CEOs who claim that "the-devil-made-me-do-it" is pretty thin for people as well compensated as they are. Most CEOs are concerned about their stock price because it has an immediate impact on their personal wealth on paper. They don't lose too much sleep over the value of their company's stock in five or ten years.

Greed and arrogance are traits that have always challenged humankind; they didn't just appear in the recent past. The majority of us are good people who have to fight for what is right and fair, and most business people are like most people everywhere: wanting to do the "right thing" but at times confused about what the right thing is in a messy, complex world.

I don't want to join the soppy chorus of calls for business to simply be more "moral." Corporate America does indeed need to be more moral than it often is. But much debate on business and general morality is too sentimentalist to be useful. What's needed is more hard-headed thinking, coupled with the ingraining of a new American business culture that values moral virtue *along with* making money and better risk management. We need free markets, but we need them to be principled. With new regulations set in motion we can only hope that greed in corporate America might be more discreet and perverse CEO incentives more sized-up, positively affecting sectors such as real estate and its grassroots level employees—real estate agents, mortgage brokers, loan officers, and appraisers.

Chapter 6: Cheese, Sleaze, and Filling in the Boxes

I detest that man, who hides one thing in the depths
of his heart, and speaks forth another.

—Homer, poet

The vast majority of residential real estate agents, mortgage brokers, loan officers, and appraisers are—without any doubt—hardworking, highly intelligent, honest, and take their duty to represent their clients' interests very seriously. Some of them, unfortunately, engage in highly questionable practices that can lead to homes selling for more than what they're worth, resulting in homeowners quickly finding that they're underwater. But in any sector where large sums of money are at stake, some people are bound to be less than honest.

———

Before the financial crisis, I had a meeting in San Francisco with a managing director of a private equity firm who was considering investing in luxury hotels. He was brilliant yet full of hubris. He knew that property was a good sector to be in, but toward the end of the meeting he mentioned with a grin that, "people who work in real estate are at the bottom of the food chain of finance-related professions."

Walking back to my office after the meeting, I thought about his rather blunt comment and why he might have said it. Is it because real estate and its bricks and mortar livelihood is slow-moving compared to the panache of lightning-fast trading, global arbitrage, and interest rate swaps? Is it because every profession has to have a pecking order where some have the need to look down on others just to feel superior? Or is it because the prosaic world of square feet is familiar to most people and familiarity breeds contempt?

Outsiders may not understand exactly what happens on a bond trading floor or in a hedge fund, but they *perceive* it as intellectually complicated. On the other hand, with real estate—which is more common sense than rocket science—practically everyone has been into a single-family home, an office building, shopping mall, apartment complex, or hotel.

Although the answers to the questions above lean toward the affirmative, those like the managing director probably have a bad impression of the real estate profession because it has caused so much damage to the US economy. Over the last twenty years or so, the United States has experienced financial meltdowns with decimating effects that were directly caused by the property sector, namely the savings and loan (S&L) crisis of the late 1980s, and, of course, the subprime fiasco of the late 2000s.

The S&L crisis created the greatest banking collapse since the Great Depression. Between 1985 and 1994, more than one thousand banks with combined assets of over $500 billion failed. By 1999, the lengthy aftermath of the crisis cost a total of $153 billion, with taxpayers footing the bill for $124 billion and the S&L

sector paying the rest. The subprime crisis, which is still unleashing the tail-end of its wrath, has cost the US trillions of dollars, not to mention the global financial chaos and the long-term social impacts of unemployment, bankruptcies, and foreclosures.

I'm not inferring that some real estate professionals intentionally caused these crises, or that those (including myself) who earn their living in the property sector have champagne bubbles in their heads. What I'm inferring is that Wall Street and state and federal regulators have not been paying enough attention to the risky real estate sector, especially at the grassroots level—the day-to-day functioning of real estate agents, mortgage brokers, loan officers, and appraisers.

I appraise properties and also hold a real estate salesperson license. It breaks my heart when I hear about appraisal fraud or agents who deliberately mislead their clients just to get a commission. By no means do I intend to simply grumble about property appraisers, agents, mortgage brokers, or loan officers—I am one of them and of the same cloth. To the contrary, my intention is to provide constructive suggestions for the betterment of the overall real estate profession—a profession that has been impacted by a few incompetent and greedy practitioners.

Risky Business

So why is the real estate sector so risky? One evident answer is the sheer size of the asset class. The aggregate value of property held by American households in the peak year of 2006 was $20.1 trillion, the biggest single asset by a wide margin (pension-fund reserves were next, at $12.8 trillion).[1] Real estate is so big and takes so long to transact that when credit conditions loosen it is likely to absorb a lot of the extra liquidity. And when something goes wrong, the effects can be calamitous.

A second reason is the absolute amount of debt it involves. Most people don't borrow to buy shares and bonds, and if they do, the degree of leverage usually hovers around 50 percent of the value of the investment.[2] Moreover, when stock prices fall, borrowers can usually get their loan-to-value ratios back into balance by selling some of the shares. Meanwhile, in the pre-crisis US housing markets buyers often took out loans worth 90 percent or more of the value of their properties. Most had no way of bringing down their debt, short of selling the whole house. Leverage in commercial real estate was lower, but in the boom years it still reached 80 to 85 percent. With little skin in the game to protect them, many owners were quickly pushed into negative equity when property values fell. As borrowers defaulted, the banks' losses started to erode their own thin layers of capital. Banks are leveraged and property is leveraged, so there is double leverage. That is why a real estate crash is such a huge problem for banks.[3]

A third reason is the systemic effect of the feedback-loop between asset prices and the availability of credit. In a boom, rising property prices increase the value of the collateral held by banks, which makes them more willing to extend credit. Easier credit means that property can sell for more, driving up prices further. Expectations of higher prices also explain why bubble-era buyers were more willing to buy risky mortgage products and take on ever greater quantities of debt. The loop operates in reverse too. As prices fall, lenders tighten their standards, forcing struggling borrowers to sell and speeding up the decline in prices. Since property accounts for so much of the financial system's aggregate balance sheet, losses from real estate busts are meshed across banks.[4]

A fourth reason is the lack of transparency in real estate markets. In general, property markets are opaque and dysfunctional, and there is an overall culture of secrecy supported by landlords, tenants, and agents. Unlike stock and bond markets, there is no free and easily accessible source of instant information on transaction prices. While this situation is improving with web-based services, the data is usually quite expensive to obtain. In the absence of information there is always the potential to ask, "Is this the best price for the property I'm selling?"

A fifth reason is "maturity transformation." That is, a bank could have substantial long-term assets (such as fixed rate mortgages) but short-term liabilities, such as deposits. This is also called "maturity mismatch" which can be measured by the duration gap (the difference between the duration of assets and liabilities held by a lender). Alternatively, a bank could have all of its liabilities as floating interest rate bonds, but assets in fixed-rate instruments.

However, this creates problems because banks are lending money that they don't own or control. If the bank only controls the money for, say, six months, lending it for a twenty-year term is risky. The depositor is also in a potentially risky position. He has lent his money to the bank for six months. The bank has taken this money and lent it to someone for twenty years. It has taken this action knowing that it will not get the money back from the borrower (i.e., when the term-deposit is due to be repaid in six months). Unless the bank has other mortgages that will be repaid at that time, it will have to obtain the money to repay the depositor from some other source, thus potentially creating a fragile house of cards.

To further explain, the bank is making a commitment to return the depositor's money at the time when the term is complete, without knowing where or how it will obtain the money to fulfill this commitment. Most of this risk rests with the bank. It should normally be able to get the financing from another source, but it doesn't know what the future holds.

Economic conditions can change dramatically by the time the term-deposit matures. If economic conditions deteriorate, the bank might have to offer a much higher interest rate to attract the financing it needs. That is why the key goal is to ensure that banks always retain sufficient net equity to be able to weather financial storms.

What happened before the financial crisis was that a variety of shadow banking institutions (i.e., hedge funds, foreign investment banks, conduits, and structured investment vehicles) evolved that played a similar role to that of traditional banks, but that were outside the regulatory structure. Rather than acquire funds from depositors, these financial intermediaries got their funds by issuing short-term commercial paper. Instead of lending directly, these institutions bought murky assets such as mortgage-backed securities, paying the holder a certain subset of the receipts on a larger collection of mortgages that were held by the issuer.

With stronger credit quality than most other borrowers, banks can minimize maturity transformation (mismatch) by aggregating issues (accepting deposits and issuing banknotes) and redemptions (customer withdrawals). They can also maintain reserves of cash, invest in marketable securities that can be readily converted to cash if needed, and raise replacement funding as needed from various sources such as wholesale cash markets and securities markets. This sounds good on paper but, unfortunately, reality more often than not turns out to be very different.

Lastly, real estate is not a commodity that is freely interchangeable. One corner location is more valuable than another corner location. Therefore, it's very difficult to create an apples-to-apples comparison between one location and another.

On the other hand, when asset-managed properly, real estate can provide numerous benefits to investors. For example, property is one of few asset classes that are locally priced so investors get genuine risk diversification, whereas equities and bonds are inter-linked. Property yields can deliver steady returns that are higher than equities and much higher than short-term inflation-protected bonds. There is also a contractual obligation by tenants to pay their rent, which ranks ahead of their obligation to bond and equity holders. In addition, even if a tenant was to default on its lease, the property owner still has a building it can let to another client, albeit potentially for a lower rent. In contrast, equity and bondholders can lose all their investment.

Unlike many types of bonds, property is also seen as a useful hedge against inflation because rental agreements can be renegotiated with tenants to reflect rising prices. So while real estate is viewed by some investors as being the most dangerous of all asset classes, it can provide attractive returns to compensate for the risks involved.

Sultans of Slither

Real estate brokers/realtors and their salespersons are also called "real estate agents." This book refers to them simply as "agents" who specialize in the buying and selling of residential or commercial property.

When I first started working in the United States, a seasoned principal with the firm I was with told me that agents basically come in two types: those who are cheesy and sleazy, and those who are honest and trustworthy. At the risk of generalizing, I have found that to be true, both in the United States and internationally. Those who are dishonest are quickly identifiable. They are shallow, manipulative, transparently self-interested and self-promotional, and are usually new to the business.

When I was involved in real estate brokerage, it would be quite amusing to listen to insecure agents on conference calls that would often turn out to be mega-ego feasts between predominately white, Alpha-type males who were desperately trying to one-up each other in front of their peers.

On the other hand, dealing with highly intelligent, confident, and honest real estate agents—of which of course there are many in the profession—is both a treat and a privilege. Successful real estate agents have complete knowledge of the markets in which they sell property. They know exactly how to answer the myriad of questions asked by prospective investors in helping them to identify the assets that best meet their needs and risk-tolerance levels.

Unfortunately, the real estate agent profession has come by its reputation much the same way as any other commission-based pay positions, such as automobile salespeople. Pay that is based on the cost of the item purchased can easily initiate selfish advice and scheming tactics on the part of the salesperson. This, combined with the potential complexity of transactions and the emotional involvement of clients, leads to the general perception of dishonesty. In addition, any business in which you can sell a product (i.e., a house or an office building) and make money without having to worry how the product performs is going to attract some cheesy people. Probably the best depiction of the shenanigans of shady real estate agents, who are the minority in the business, is the 1992 movie *Glengarry Glen Ross*, starring Alec Baldwin, Jack Lemon, and Al Pacino.

———

Most homeowners in the United States have probably experienced the following scenario. After attending an open house and express-ing some interest in a home for sale, in less than twenty-four hours the flashy real estate agent driving a leased Mercedes-Benz will call and frantically inform you that someone else is getting ready to put an offer on the house. Or maybe the agent will claim that they already have, so you better make an offer really quick—preferably a high one—or else you'll lose your "dream house" forever. Nine times out of ten, no one else is interested in the house. The agent is simply trying to create a false sense of urgency.

Some agents can also convince sellers to take their property off the market and then relist it for sale. They do this because they'd rather tell a potential buyer that the house has only been on the market for five days and will probably go fast. The reality is the property has probably been for sale for months and the seller is just getting desperate.

Crystal Balls

Some residential real estate agents lose credibility in the eyes of homebuyers because they can often indulge in mountains of hype. Let's take an example of a "state of the market" letter from a Phoenix, Arizona agent written in 2005, which provides some bold predictions for a market that, in hindsight, has only recently hit bottom:[5]

September 2005—Phoenix, Arizona
How rich would you like to be?
In the twelve months leading up to August 1, 2005, single-family residences in the metropolitan Phoenix/Scottsdale market appreciated by an average of 47 percent. That's the average, and it includes challenged neighborhoods and cities as remote as to qualify as rural.

If you look at just the sweet spot, the middle of the bell curve, Phoenix/Scottsdale area homes appreciated by 60 percent, 80 percent, over 100 percent in some areas.

Price pressure has not slowed down, and there are good reasons to believe that appreciation over the next twelve months will be 20 percent or more, possibly a lot more.

We have a built-in baseline demand from the Great Lakes and other snowy regions. And we seem to be experiencing a steady increase in our long-term immigration from California.

Our best estimate right now is that annual appreciation over the next seven or eight years should average out to around 11 percent.

If you can make that down payment, or if you can absorb a negative cash flow from other sources of income or with a negatively amortized loan, your ability to build long-term wealth in the Phoenix residential real estate market is tough to beat.

Now take a look at figure 6-1, which shows how the Phoenix/ Scottsdale area residential market actually performed.

Figure 6-1: Median Home Prices in Phoenix/Scottsdale

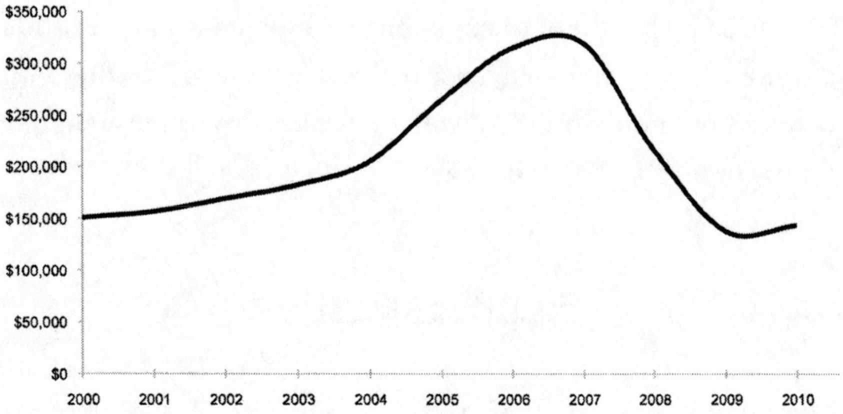

Source: Arizona State University

Hindsight, of course, is 20/20, and it's easy to critique this agent for his letter today. When the agent made these statements in 2005, he was probably confident that the bottom was never going to fall out of his market, and to suggest that he intentionally misled his clients would be a stretch. If they are to retain any credibility, such agents should only share their *opinions* and should not make bold public *predictions* on the direction of a market, leaving forecasts to savvy economists.

One can only read with amazement the predictions by some agents about a specific market and wonder how they can be qualified to make such sure statements about the future. It's dangerous to make these forecasts in the public arena because some naïve homebuyers assume that they are accurate and can act on them.

But why do some feel they have a crystal ball and are in a position to make such predictions? It's because some in the real estate profession start to believe their own hype and their egos begin to take over. They become so immersed in their markets that it sometimes becomes difficult to step back and imagine anything different than what they are experiencing on a daily basis. Further, anyone who has experienced a real estate cycle knows there will be wild ups and downs. So if you see broker projections that only forecast growth, trash them away.

Pssst! Want a Killer Loan?

The number of mortgage brokers in the United States increased from approximately 30,000 in 1990 to 147,000 at its peak in early 2006. (In 2011, the number was back down to 43,000).[6] As commission-based contractors, mortgage brokers are a highly cost-effective field force for lenders. The huge rise in the number of brokers made the mid-2000s an especially competitive era. To make a living in such an environment, most brokers were incentivized to originate a large number of deals and to push toward the highest possible loan amount.[7] This set of incentives made them behave in ways that may have differed from the behavior of salaried employees within financial institutions.

In the past, the general view of the mortgage broker's function was that he or she worked to find the lowest interest rate on the "best" type of loan for the client's financial and lifestyle circumstances. Unfortunately, some mortgage brokers viewed their job as extracting the highest commission possible from their clients, putting them into a loan product that would have them needing to refinance in two to five years. They had turned into a shyster army peddling tricky mortgages.

For example, a heavily marketed loan before the financial crisis was the infamous ARM, in which the homeowner made interest-only payments at a low rate—say 5 percent for two or three years—and then started making regular payments at a rate of around 9 percent. As a result, payments on a $200,000 mortgage could quickly go from about $800 a month to over $1,600. Such products were, amazingly, being peddled by mortgage brokers who weren't even licensed or qualified in the basics of real estate finance. It was a free-for-all that attracted the lower ranks of people who lacked a professional conscience.

However, in a positive attempt to restrain the deceptive lending in the home financing business, mortgage brokers now have to be fingerprinted for background checks and sign up with a central registry to do business, according to rules issued by the Fed and other regulators. The rules are part of the Secure and Fair Enforcement for Mortgage Licensing Act (known as the SAFE Act).[8] Since 2008, thousands of mortgage brokers have gone through mandatory background checks, education, testing, and licensing requirements in order to retain the right to handle mortgage originations. The process has thinned the ranks of mortgage brokers, which may be even fewer in the future given a reported 30 percent fail rate on testing. The goal has been to clean house and get rid of the riffraff.

———

Another prudent effort by regulators to minimize the sleaze factor in the home mortgage business is related to yield-spread premiums (YSPs). Pre-crisis YSPs were basically kickbacks that mortgage brokers received from a lender for bringing in borrowers with high-interest loans. These loans, often subprime, were what lenders coveted the most as they raced to rake in the profits in the lead up to the subprime collapse.

YSPs were widely blamed for helping cause the mortgage crisis and have been banned by new rules adopted by the Fed. The new rules, which were announced in 2010, are designed to protect borrowers from unfair, abusive, or deceptive lending that can arise from lender compensation practices. They apply to mortgage brokers and their employers, as well as loan officers employed by depository institutions. The new rules should prevent loan originators from increasing their own compensation by raising borrowers' loan costs, such as increasing the interest rate or points (each mortgage point is a fee based on 1 percent of the total amount of the loan). Nevertheless, loan originators can continue to receive compensation based on a percentage of the loan amount, which has been common practice.

To prevent mortgage originators from steering a buyer into a loan that offers unfavorable terms, the new rules also state that the borrower must be provided with competing choices, including the lowest qualifying interest rate, the lowest points and origination fees, and the lowest qualifying rate without risky features such as prepayment penalties.

It should be noted that, with the Fed's new rules placing compensation restrictions on mortgage brokers and loan officers, lenders are looking at ways to restructure how their associates are paid—a move that could shake up the sector. Mortgage brokers and loan officers had typically been paid commissions on top of yield-spread premiums. But with the new Fed rules, and lenders

no longer paying brokers YSP fees, the way that long-term compensation for originators is going to be handled is still unraveling.

Mortgage lenders are already looking into alternatives that
could range from paying brokers and loan officers a flat fee per
loan, to a policy that could place higher upfront fees on borrowers to cover the commission costs. This could result in higher
interest rates or higher percentage points charged to homebuyers for origination fees. What is currently the standard upfront
fee of 1 percent could double to 2 percent. The Dodd-Frank Wall
Street Reform and Consumer Protection Act, coupled with oversight from the newly established Consumer Financial Protection
Bureau, caps the amount a broker or loan officer can receive on
the sale of a high-cost mortgage at 3 percent.

Filling in the Boxes

An appraiser is basically one who decides a value for a property.
Similar to agents, real estate appraisers come in two types: those
who just fill in boxes on standardized appraisal forms and those
who are true advocates of their estimates of market value.

In the early to mid-twentieth century, property appraisers used
to be like plumbers, tradesmen who learned the art at the hands of
their fathers. But after appraisers got caught signing off on some
of the most preposterous adventures of the S&L crisis, reformers
decided to open the profession to new blood.[9] Unfortunately, not
all new appraisers who entered the business were honest.

Decent appraisers take well-deserved pride in the dignity
and honesty of their profession and Members of the Appraisal
Institute (MAIs)—who value all property types—are highly

regarded because of their organization's superior ethical and educational standards. But, sadly, the real estate sector is not without its appraisers of easy virtue. They are often referred to as "tame" appraisers who will value a property for whatever it is listed at, or based on "three comparables and a cloud of dust," just so the sale can go through and the appraiser continues to be hired by lenders because he or she knows how to come up with the "right number."

For a long time, banks were able to get appraisals in which everyone involved knew that the appraised value was way too high. As a result, tame appraisals led to homes selling for more than they were really worth and, depending on the percentage of the financed home's value, caused many homeowners to be underwater today.

———

Let's assume a pre-crisis scenario in which you wanted to buy a house. If there was a bank involved, you would be asked to have an appraisal done. It would be your responsibility to pay the lender for it. When that appraiser accepted the check, he or she would be bound by a "fiduciary responsibility" to give the lender an accurate and objective appraisal. Even if the appraiser wasn't highly trained or licensed, he or she would still be obliged to follow national guidelines known as the Uniform Standards of Professional Appraisal Practice (USPAP), established by the Appraisal Foundation in the 1980s.[10]

Once the valuation report was complete, the bank would most likely lend according to the appraisal, assuming it was the number they were looking for. Even if the bank lent 100 percent of the estimated market value, it was only on the hook for 80 percent because a mortgage insurance company would guarantee the other 20 percent. Up to that point the system was working, and if the appraiser had done his or her job correctly, the bank couldn't get hurt because there still was no shock to the system, so the value couldn't have fallen more than 20 percent. However, before the financial crisis, this utopian scenario (of course) wasn't happening. Some appraisers knowingly breached their fiduciary responsibility by inflating values.

By ignoring fundamental values and common sense, prices increased drastically sale after sale—up and up into a huge speculative balloon. Had there been a more effective system of checks and balances in place, everyone would have done their job to the best of their ability. But, unfortunately, that wasn't the case. It was a grand financial bordello where many were drunk on euphoria and doing hazy math.

For instance, after the failure of Independent National Mortgage Corporation (IndyMac), the Treasury's Office of Inspector General (OIG) conducted a material loss review. According to the OIG report, "IndyMac's business model was to produce as many loans as possible and sell them in the secondary market. To facilitate this level of production, it was found that IndyMac often did not perform adequate underwriting."[11] The Office of Inspector General reviewed a sample of twenty-two delinquent loans from the lender's vast portfolio. For these loans, the OIG found:

> Little, if any, review of borrower qualifications, including income, assets, and employment. We also found weaknesses with property appraisals obtained to support the collateral on the loans. For example, among other things, we noted instances where IndyMac officials accepted appraisals that

were not in compliance with the Uniform Standards of Professional Appraisal Practice. We also found instances where IndyMac appraisals on a property had vastly different values. There was no evidence to support, or explain, why different values were determined. In other instances, IndyMac allowed the borrowers to select the appraisers.[12]

In addition, lenders' salespeople were also finessing the official mortgage paperwork with a variety of misrepresentations, exaggerating borrowers' incomes and their home values. One former loan officer and branch manager testified that inflating property appraisals served the "dual purpose of both making sure the loan was approved by the home office as well as making the loan more attractive to sell to investors."[13]

Some loan officers also pressured appraisers to inflate valuations by $20,000 or $30,000—sometimes by more than $100,000—and to lie on their reports about the appraised properties' defects. In one instance, a loan officer demanded a $500,000 valuation in a town where the most expensive house was worth no more than $425,000.[14] Other lenders asked for higher values, too, but they'd simply take the appraiser off their list if he or she didn't cooperate and find somebody else who would hit the numbers needed. In other words, many hard-working appraisers were between a rock and a hard place.

One of the issues at the foundation of the ongoing economic weakness in America is that investors and lenders still don't believe in the estimated value of properties—and that is a crisis of competency for the appraisal profession.[15] Investors have to have faith that someone is telling them the truth about a property's value. A lot of the critical skills and tools used by appraisers in prior recessions have not been required by lenders in nearly two decades but are once again needed. That's because some appraisers got lazy and lenders didn't have decent appraisal-review programs.

According to the Appraisal Foundation, of the 92,000 licensed appraisers in the United States, only about 30 percent are members of any professional appraisal organization. Without a group affiliation, such appraisers have little exposure to innovations in their profession, and where they get their sense of what's going on in appraisal land isn't clear. In other words, complacency isn't an option for appraisers in today's environment.

The market is now searching for a viable mechanism to assist in determining value during periods of financial distress. Appraisers have to get back to the business of doing solid analysis, looking at real estate market-by-market and property-by-property, and relying less on automated valuation models (AVMs).[16] For example, all real estate is not distressed, yet in a declining market all property appears to be painted that way with the same broad brush.

There's plenty of blame to go around, but appraisers did have a fiduciary responsibility and a legal obligation to perform to the best of their ability. As such, some residential real estate appraisers were among the main culprits in the financial crisis. Of course, those appraisers didn't directly cause values to decline, and they weren't the catalyst for homeowners ceasing to pay their mortgages. But some of them did help create fictitious equity and were complicit in facilitating trillions of dollars of loans that never should have been made.[17]

As discussed earlier, there were varying degrees of valuation-inflation performed by some appraisers (see figure 6-2). On the light side, there were appraisers who hit the *highest* possible value as opposed to the most *probable* value. On the dark side, there was blatant fraud. And then somewhere in the middle, there was the failure of some appraisers to recognize an overheated market and to objectively report the most pertinent trends and risks to their clients. The appraisers who had inferior skill sets were used to producing inaccurate reports and were probably geographically incompetent (had no local experience).

Figure 6-2: Appraisal Fraud and Misrepresentation

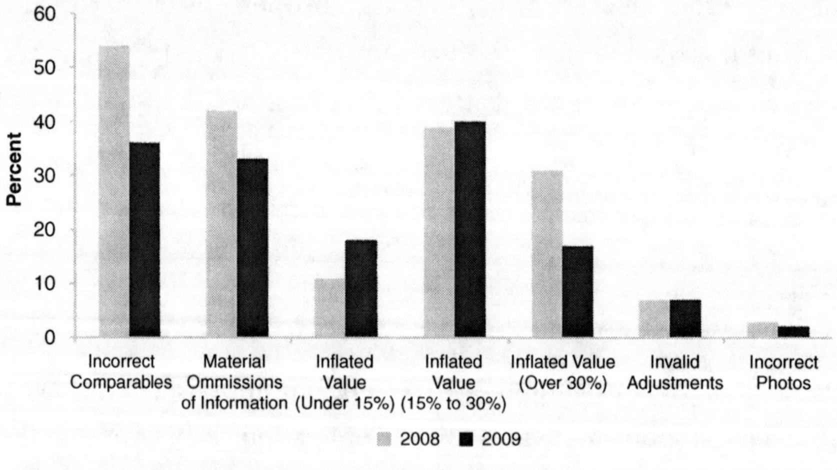

Source: Appraisal World

But the purpose of this book is *not* to dwell on the past or to point fingers at a specific profession. What matters is that we identify the parts of the real estate valuation process that should be re-engineered; those appraisal practices that helped promote the boom and bust by relying on only one input—the latest prices in a runaway Wild-Wild-West market.

During a boom period, increasing property values are supported with great ease, because comparable sales and rentals tend to be readily available. In short, increasing values are effortlessly supported by the most recent comparable sales and rentals, which can make some appraisers lazy in their due diligence.

––––––

When large sums of money are lost and disaster is at the door, what's the natural response in the United States? File a lawsuit. The majority of legal claims against appraisers today are based on allegations of erroneous property valuations. The huge increase in foreclosures has put residential appraisals in the limelight, and many claims are being filed for valuations that were done several years ago when property values were at a peak. For instance: a buyer defaults on a mortgage and the lender goes back to the appraiser for damages, stating that the estimated market value of the home was too high.

Another ugly litigation scenario occurs when the buyer, after having acquired at the top of the market, tries to sell after prices have fallen and cannot regain his investment, suing the appraiser for over-valuation. To make things worse, many claims today are also alleging that a property was *under-valued*. Appraisals done during the current market are obviously showing much lower valuations, and a growing number of claims are being made against these "low ball" appraisals, as homeowners have difficulty refinancing. An even more recent concern is the notorious strategic default, which occurs when a homeowner calculates the so-called financial benefit of simply walking away from the property, leaving the lender high and dry, which is more bait with which to catch an innocent appraiser.

Unfortunately, real estate appraisal issues are rarely inserted in the conversations of the national media, the Treasury, the Fed, and other high-finance influentials. It seems that bank regulators haven't been paying enough attention to this honorable yet underappreciated and overlooked profession. Also, some lenders treat appraisers as mere providers of a cheap commodity—voluminous valuation reports that hardly ever get read, ending up as "file fillers" in the cabinets of bank credit departments.

At the same time, the residential mortgage-backed securities market has diminished significantly because of a lack of trust and confidence. If all residential appraisers had credibly valued the underlying housing collateral, there could have been an active residential mortgage-backed security market today, but that market is hesitant, in part because no one really knew (or knows) what the underlying collateral is really worth during these times of financial uncertainty.

In addition, downward fee pressure, coupled with the prevalence of appraisal management company (AMC) business and fee-split arrangements, created an environment in which the gross fees paid to appraisers declined considerably over the past decade. (AMCs put together pools of residential appraisers and then assign them to individual single-family housing transactions).

The decline in the fee structure and the favoring of speed of delivery over quality created a dismal environment for residential appraisers. For the most part, the repression of fees was maintained under the pretext of homebuyer sensitivity to origination costs. In the end, it was the homebuyer who paid for the tremendous losses in this housing market depression. We tripped over trillions just to save a few hundred dollars on each appraisal.

Game Change

At a time when the US economy is still trying to get back on its feet, the Dodd-Frank Wall Street Reform and Consumer Protection Act of 2010 is an attempt to prevent future economic catastrophes. As will be discussed in chapter 9, the legislative origins of the Dodd-Frank act are rooted in modernizing bank regulations.

With the progression of time and the cumbersome legislative process, Dodd-Frank has morphed into one of the most significant financial pieces of legislation in US history. The overarching themes to this law are consumer protection and accountability for Wall Street and banks. While consumer protection and corporate accountability are at the forefront of the act, the real estate sector will also be impacted.

The act changes the dynamics of some existing financial regulatory bodies, while creating entirely new rule-making entities. Although some of the specific rules were ironed out in 2011, and while the comment period for some of the rules has already started, the final rule-making period continues through 2012 and beyond.[18]

On the legislative and regulatory front, the Appraisal Institute has been involved in what could be the largest overhaul of US appraisal regulation in twenty years with the passage of Title

XIV of the Dodd-Frank act. The specifics of this major overhaul include:[19]

- Enhanced considerations for appraisal designations.
- Ensuring that residential real estate appraisers are free to use their independent judgment in valuing homes without influence or pressure from parties with financial interests in the transaction.
- Prohibitions on using broker price opinions (BPOs) in mortgage origination.
- Helping to secure sound risk management practices in real estate lending while promoting a return to basics and common sense approaches to collateral valuation.
- At the state level, twenty states have passed laws regulating AMCs based on a bill developed by the Appraisal Institute.

Additional suggestions and possible solutions to the unresolved problems inherent in residential property appraisals include:[20]

- A self-regulating organization needs to be established by Congress to include *all* parties touching collateral valuation for the US home mortgage sector—appraisers, appraisal management companies, credit rating agencies, loan officers, mortgage brokers, Main Street banks, and Wall Street. Such an organization would be the appraisal profession's all-encompassing standards bearer.[21] Such an organization could be the Appraisal Institute or a completely new entity.
- Appraisers should be required to present home values that reflect the potential for a down market through the application of scenario analysis. This would help lenders con-

trol downside collateral risk and to better assess how likely home value decreases could impact their balance sheets.

- Require that residential appraisers who are not working for a lender underwriting to be state certified. This would considerably increase professional standards.

- Any real estate agent who wants to engage in valuation services outside of the real estate listing process must also be a state certified appraiser.

- Due to potential conflicts of interest between real estate agents and lenders, prohibit the use of BPOs related to the Home Affordable Modification Program to determine if loans qualify for modifications, or for the Home Affordable Foreclosure Alternatives program. In addition, broker price opinions should not be used for the valuation of lender real estate-owned properties, short-sales, the establishing of home-equity lines of credit in connection with loss mitigation and collection efforts, or for refinancings. (BPOs are best suited for the valuation of distressed notes that are either already in default, under bankruptcy protection, or in distress and heading toward such a situation).

- Compensation methodologies for appraisers should support independence and the integrity of the valuation process.

- Offer training for appraisers in the valuation of complex mortgage-related bonds.

Conclusion

Wall Street, regulators, rating agencies, lenders, mortgage brokers, and appraisers all played a role in the financial crisis in varying degrees. Appropriate fail-safes of any one of these segments could have prevented, or at least moderated, the spectacular collapse of the US housing market.

Many mortgages rested on multiple scams by some real estate "professionals." The commissions of mortgage brokers and the bonuses of loan officers led them to advise to file fraudulent applications and caused them to ensure that the appraisers who were picked would inflate market values "as instructed." In their excessive enthusiasm to catch more borrowers, some of these real estate employees gave the impression that there was no risk to these mortgages and that the costs weren't really that high. Therefore, many borrowers simply assumed debt that they couldn't afford.

While some real estate professionals are to blame for the financial crisis, one cannot ignore the "I-want-it-all-*now*" homebuyers who were playing an extremely risky game by acquiring houses they shouldn't have bought. They were able to make these purchases with mortgages that offered low introductory rates and no down payment. Their hope lay in ever-lasting price appreciation, which—in principle—would have allowed them to refinance at lower rates and take the equity out of the home for use in other rapacious spending. Instead of continued appreciation, the housing bubble, of course, burst and home prices dropped dramatically. It is safe to say that, had they not made such an aggressive purchase and assumed a less risky mortgage with more skin in the game, the overall impacts would have been much more manageable.

It can also be argued that the role of mortgage brokers was not a direct contributing factor to the financial crisis but a "normal" human behavioral observation as seen in all mad bubbles. That is, one of many expected human behavioral observations rooted from the main causes of the real estate mortgage crisis. This infers that an appropriate system of checks and balances needs to be implemented to manage such behavior.

The missed assessment of real estate debt risk by the credit rating agencies and regulators was among the main causes of the financial meltdown because it enabled the credit markets to provide high-risk mortgage products to flourish when the market risk of probable loss was accumulating. All financial intermediaries in this loan origination process were "doing their best" to keep the loan origination pipeline full.

As discussed earlier, there were willing participants who wanted to buy a home, obtain a lower interest rate, cash-out money from their home to pay off credit card debt, or just to spend more. Some of these borrowers may indeed have been "victimized," but it is doubtful that they would have said they were being victimized when home prices were consistently increasing year after year. Many homeowners were speculating that if the mortgage could not be paid, they could either refinance or sell their homes. In that kind of a market, there are no victims—only partners in crime.[22]

Today, we are faced with the implications of the biggest missed assessment of real estate debt risk in our lifetime. The last time this occurred in large scale for single-family residential was during the Great Depression of the 1930s.

There is also a big distortion that the real estate market is just "old news." Unfortunately, real estate capital markets are chaotic just like the stock market, and there will likely be a continuation of the distortion of a stabilized outlook compared to a reality of more bad news to come down the road, as large amounts of foreclosures continue to flood the market over the next few years.

Although not insurmountable, the US commercial real estate sector has several unresolved problems. For example, the commercial property sector has close to $1.15 trillion in debt maturities that are coming due between 2012 and 2015. These pending maturities have been labeled by naysayers as a so-called "debt tsunami"[23] because nobody really knows how they might be paid off or refinanced in light of weak property values, among other factors that are discussed in the next chapter.

Chapter 7: Mixed Signals

The market won't recover until 2020...
maybe never.
—Kenneth Riggs, CEO of RERC

We're very bullish on the commercial asset class.
—Frederick Crawford, CFO, Lincoln National

The commercial real estate sector, which primarily includes office, retail, industrial, apartment, hotel, and vacant land properties, was not the cause of the financial crisis. The meltdown was instigated by the residential sector, which is a completely different animal. Nonetheless, it's important to realize the impact of the residential market's folly on US commercial property, which can be described as "guilt by association."

———

Contradictions create confusion, which causes more distortions. The commercial real estate investment environment seems to be more confusing than normal, but perhaps investor confusion is a response to all the overload of contradictory economic data. Are jobs being created or not? Is the consumer coming back, or is any improvement in retail sales merely a blip on the screen? On the surface, banks are healthier based on their opaque balance sheets, but will they lend to smaller companies? Real estate investors and corporate executives always live with uncertainties, but in 2012 the overall outlook is still hazy, making it difficult to make decisions, including formulating long-term capital allocation strategies.

Some pessimists still believe that commercial real estate could be a ticking bomb with its explosive material comprised of loan defaults.[1] They fear that a significant wave of commercial defaults could trigger economic damage from decreased property values that translate into lower tax revenues; lost jobs from foreclosed retail stores and hotels; and at-risk banks becoming even more reluctant to lend.[2]

Real estate is hardly the only asset class to experience booms and busts; stock markets do it all the time. But when property markets experience these extremes, the knock-on effects appear more damaging to the wider economy than for any other asset class. The bursting of the dot-com bubble in 2000–02, for example, did not produce anything like the Great Recession of 2007–09. And it was not just housing where the property sector balloon popped. Commercial real estate also followed the trend.

The commercial property sector (which had an aggregate value of $10.1 trillion in 2006) is significant to the broader US economy because of several factors. For one, it's a unit of production. That is, the price of real estate is an important factor in determining relative productivity costs across all markets, but the single most important reason why commercial property prices matter is because of their ability to send shockwaves through the "credit channel."

Commercial property is typically heavily leveraged. Even when cash-rich investors acquire real estate, they generally do so using money borrowed from banks to increase their internal rates of return.[3] So how does the credit channel fit in? As property prices fall, recorded loan-to-value (LTV) ratios rise. This, in turn, requires banks to set aside higher reserves against those loans (known as loan loss reserves), even if borrowers are still paying principal and interest. Lenders then become more cautious about extending loans to new borrowers and the pool of available investors begins to shrink.

———

To explain the relationship between bank capital and loan loss reserves, assume that in May 2009 a bank chose to acknowledge the current market value of an asset, which in the case of a bank is a loan to a borrower. If the original loan was for $10 million and now is only worth $6 million, the bank would need to write-down the loan to the market value and take the loss on its income statement of $4 million. Otherwise, the write-down could come from its loan loss reserves, with the money coming from either profits or capital. A sensible bank will have sufficient loss reserves set aside from its earnings to handle bad loans. But a bank whose loan portfolio is struggling will often have no profit to support making additional deposits into its loan loss reserve, so any additional write-downs must be offset with a reduction in the bank's capital. The problem here is that although the bank may have plenty of money, it is depositors' money, which is considered as a liability of the bank and must be repaid.

Is the Glass Half Empty?

Speculative borrowing between 2003 and 2007 contributed to unprecedented rising debt levels and the eventual cratering of commercial asset values. Although the real estate meltdown has focused on the residential mortgage fiasco, approximately $1.15 trillion in loans to commercial properties are coming due between 2012 and 2015 (see figure 7-1).

Figure 7-1: US Commercial Real Estate Debt Maturities

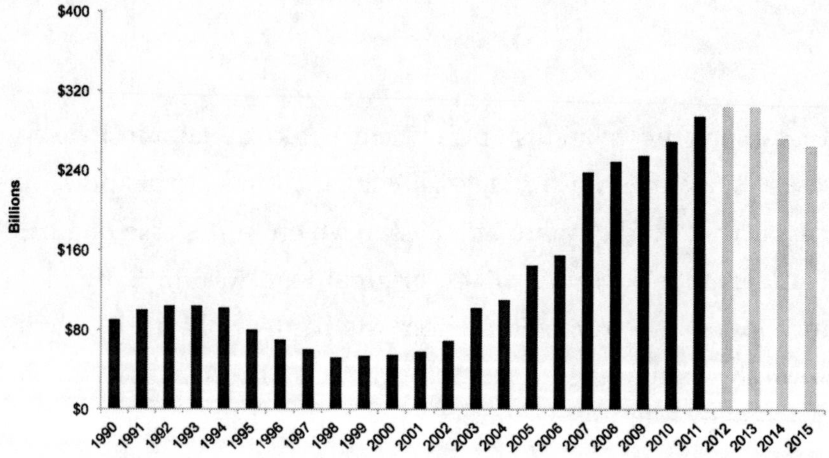

Source: Deutsche Bank, Foresight Analytics. Data includes the debt of banks, CMBSs, life companies, and others.

It can be estimated that at least half the loans—and two-thirds of those packaged and resold as bonds—might not qualify for refinancing.[1] As a result, borrowers may default, leading to losses on securitized mortgages and commercial real estate loans. Most mortgages for commercial property are structured as five-year loans. After that, the loan is normally refinanced, but the Great Recession eroded the fundamentals of many good refinancing candidates.

In 2011 vacancies were still increasing in some markets, cutting potential income that properties need to make on their debt service payments (see figure 7-2). Just as the residential market decline started with subprime loan failures and careless lending standards—conditions that ultimately eroded home values—commercial property owners have been impacted as well.

Figure 7-2: Vacancy Rates by Property Type

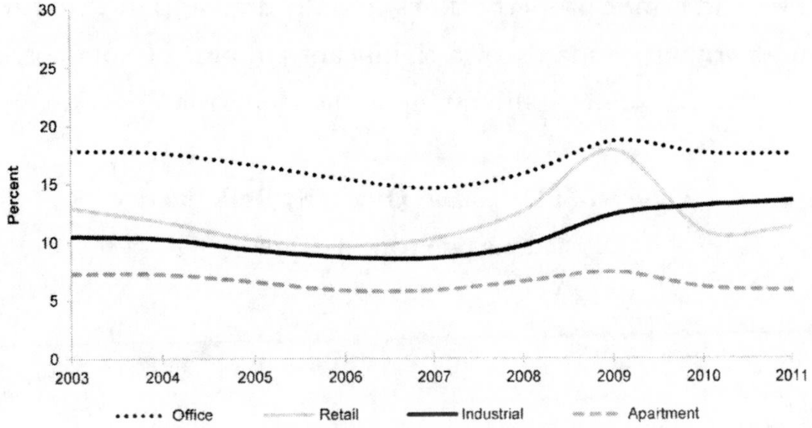

Source: Property and Portfolio Research, REIS, PwC, CBRE, National Association of Realtors. Hotel vacancy rates are much higher as hotels offer nightly rentals; therefore, they are not shown.

It is doubtful that many banks would want to own commercial properties that are empty. In turn, underwriting standards have significantly tightened since the commercial sector's boom years of 2005–07, when banks granted loans of up to 95 percent of a property's appraised value. Today, average LTV ratios on senior debt have dropped to close to 65 percent, and lenders are requiring more in the way of recourse, which means that only the best properties can really attract financing. As such, a large percentage of outstanding loans might not qualify for refinancing.

Although relatively few troubled loans came due in 2005–08, commercial mortgage-backed security (CMBS) loan delinquency rates continue to be high, especially for hotels and apartments, with an average of approximately 14 percent (see figure 7-3). There are two main reasons for the commercial property sector's difficulties: (1) The economic downturn that resulted in the significant deterioration of commercial real estate fundamentals such as high vacancies, falling rental prices, the decrease in cash flows, and erratic property values; and (2) dramatically weakened underwriting standards of a significant amount of commercial property loans during the run-up to the meltdown.[5]

Figure 7-3: US CMBS Quarterly Delinquency Rates by Property Type

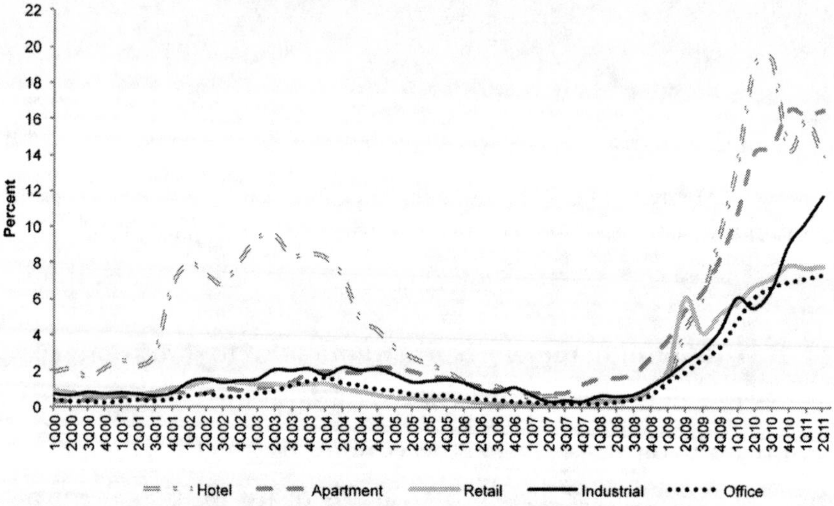

Source: CRE Finance Council, Trepp LLC

It appears that the ultimate impact of the commercial real estate whole-loan (an original mortgage as compared to a pass-through security) problem could fall disproportionately on smaller regional and community banks that have higher concentrations of and exposure to such loans than larger national or money center banks.[6]

———

National commercial property prices declined significantly between October 2007 and October 2009, falling nearly 44 percent as troubled loans mounted.[7] As indicated in figure 7-4, the Moody's/REAL monthly Commercial Property Price Index (CPPI) has demonstrated an erratic trend since October 2009, impacting investor confidence in a sustainable recovery. This type of volatility largely reflects what is actually going on in the US commercial property market, as asset markets typically display greater volatility during periods of fundamental uncertainty and rapid economic, regulatory, and political change.

**Figure 7-4: Moody's/REAL Monthly Commercial
Property Price Index**

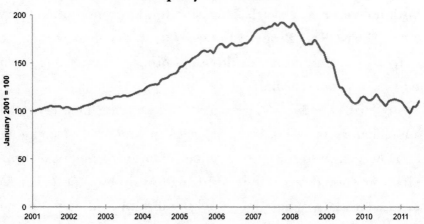

Source: MIT, Moody's, Real Capital Analytics. Measures price changes on completed sales of apartment, office, industrial, and retail properties.

Or Is the Glass Half Full?

Doom-laden warnings issued in 2008–09 that commercial real estate would be the next economic shoe to drop have not come to pass. That is because commercial space was not at the heart of the financial crisis—the residential sector was the culprit.

As indicated earlier, commercial property prices fell by approximately 44 percent from the peak in October 2007 to October 2009. The price decline was steep and swift, in contrast to previous recessions when write-downs dragged on for several years. Although it's impossible to predict an exact recovery timeline, some real estate executives believed in 2011 that we were already in an upturn, albeit mainly for well-occupied properties in primary markets (trophy assets).

———

The National Council of Real Estate Investment Fiduciaries (NCREIF) has been tracking returns for properties owned by institutional investors such as pension funds for more than thirty years. The NCREIF Property Index (NPI) tracks the performance of returns for more than six thousand properties, breaking down returns by property type.

In 2010–11, the NPI registered an increase in the overall appreciation return for the first time since mid-2007 (see figure 7-5). As such, the declines in value for most commercial property types should be behind us. Pricing for trophy assets (Class-A) in gateway markets have increased significantly, although pricing for most Class-B and Class-C properties in tertiary markets (often referred to as "dogs" in real estate parlance) continues to decline, but at a much slower rate than before.

Figure 7-5: NCREIF Property Index Returns by Property Type

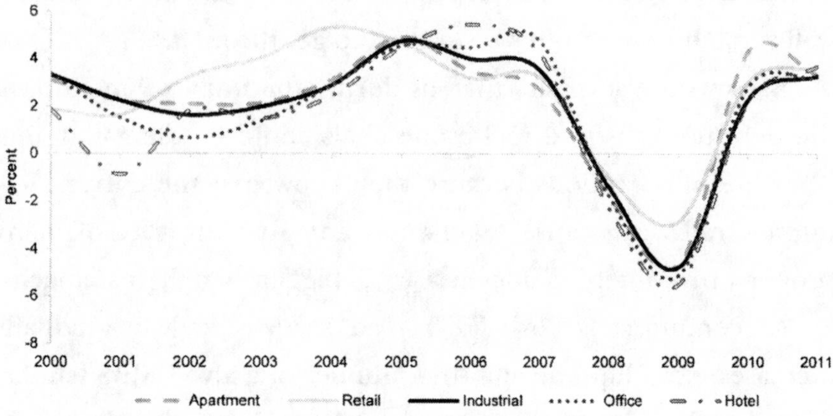

Source: National Council of Real Estate Investment Fiduciaries (NCREIF)

Notwithstanding the slow and uneven progress in the general economy, real estate capital markets improved in 2011. Lenders, especially life insurers, reentered the commercial loan sector. Increased competition among lenders led to lower loan interest rates and the added liquidity helped increase transaction volumes for core (prime location) properties. With vacancy rates still high, construction financing, however, is limited, and with rents below the levels necessary to justify new construction, supply pipelines are also far below long-term averages. As a result, 2012 should see a limited amount of new inventory, which will be a big benefit for owners.

The End of Casino Banking

One of the main reasons that the commercial real estate sector is sending mixed signals is directly related to financing. Getting financing from banks today isn't easy, and the impacts of the Great Recession have been so prolonged and severe that, unless you're a well-capitalized entity, it's been hard to get through.

Bankers are still wary that, as during the financial meltdown, the debt used to fund real estate deals could be their undoing. They are also cautious because they know that the current low interest rates can cause temptation and that the eyes of many property investment managers are still bigger than their stomachs.

As commercial mortgage-backed security activity gradually increases, both liquidity and the number of active CMBS lenders in the market should ramp up in tandem. However, today's market for bank debt remains challenging. The limited availability of active lenders, conservative underwriting, and the zero tolerance for risk—which are all positive changes—have lengthened the approval and closing processes of the vast majority of banks. Sponsors should, therefore, be aware of these challenges before entering into purchase agreements and should take the following precautions to ensure that their deals get financed.[8]

Sponsors should expand their banking relationships to include at least three lenders, if not more. Many banks are still not lending on commercial real estate, and if they are, their parameters have changed significantly. Sponsors should reevaluate their existing banking relationships to see if they still fit with their lending needs. Even if they do, it's still prudent to have at least three backups in the current environment, especially developers who are in need of construction financing.[9]

Banks are proceeding with caution and are able to be more selective in choosing the deals they lend against. The deals that are getting bank financing have the most clear-cut business plans and can have only *one* risk variable associated with them, whether it be sponsorship, lease-up, or construction risk.

A good way for a sponsor to improve the chance of qualifying for financing is to mitigate the deal variables before approaching a lender. Once the lender is approached, a sponsor should expect at least sixty days to arrange the financing—especially when dealing with banks.[10] Therefore, being patient with the lender will help get financing done.

In addition, borrowers should expect to use much more equity. The days of 80 percent to 90 percent leverage from banks are over. In 2011, the average loan-to-value ratio for senior loans originated by regional and national banks was in the 65 percent range (for portfolio loans, it was approximately 50 percent).

The combination of increased pressure from regulatory examiners and banks' aversion to risk have lowered the amount of proceeds available for most deals.[11] Banks are being very selective not only about the properties on which they lend but also the sponsors with whom they deal. Lastly, it's important for borrowers to have a track record of success and a solid balance sheet when seeking bank financing. If these aren't readily available, the sponsors should find a partner that brings both into the game.

Putting Lipstick on the Pig

Post-crisis real estate investors assumed that the vast number of distressed assets would mean a flood of properties coming onto the market, as owners tried to offload their buildings and borrowers breached their debt covenants. Yet there is still a gap between the prices that owners want and what bargain-hunters are prepared to pay, which has been holding up some large deals. There has also been a wide price gap between fully leased and non-stabilized assets, which mostly has to do with the lack of financing for the latter, causing non-stabilized property owners to hold out and attempt to lease their space.

Many banks have been willing to roll loans over and ignore breaches of loan-to-value covenants caused by falling values (a practice known as "extend-and-pretend" or "delay-and-pray," depending on which banker you speak to) rather than force a sale. Selling assets forces banks to recognize their losses; not selling them allows them to pretend that the assets haven't deteriorated in value. In addition, banks aren't foreclosing on commercial real estate because owner-managed properties sell for some 20 percent more than bank-owned properties, and cost the banks less to hold.

A senior banker I spoke with about the extend-and-pretend maneuver insisted that the word "pretend" is a myth. He indicated that bankers know of the loss potential but hope like all other people who do a deal that their investment will be safe and sound as the economy picks up again. The banker also noted that, "There is no pretending. We know our loss potential today but the loans are due sometime in the future. So why take a hit now in poor market conditions when the position in an investment to become whole again could change in the future? It's not pretending—it's optimism!"

———

Low interest rates have certainly helped borrowers keep up with their extended loan payments just to stay alive and lenders to forbear, albeit with little prospect of a strong recovery in values. Without a strong increase in overall property values, the nearly $1.15 trillion of commercial real estate debt maturities coming due nationwide in 2012 through 2015 could force borrowers to refinance or default on their obligations, potentially putting a damper on any nascent confidence in commercial space. But refinancing debt might be very tricky, as banks are still under pressure to bring down the debt on their balance sheets.

Following the financial crisis, lenders in a big way applied the extend-and-pretend tactic, in which they extended the loan terms and pretended that everything was peachy in the hopes that underwater loans would be salvageable once the economy bounced back. The extend-and-pretend practice delays foreclosures by altering the terms of payments or extending the time a borrower has to pay-down a loan. While often criticized for delaying inevitable foreclosures, or promoting a "living-in-denial" attitude by the parties involved, the practice has, nonetheless, been helpful for the commercial real estate sector's slow recovery by offering loan modification or restructuring opportunities, such as discounted payoffs and new principal guarantees.

Most often, loans are extended as they near their maturity, as all parties involved understand that the loans cannot be paid off today. While stretching out the payments on a loan may well save the borrower, the practice can also delay the pain. In other words, a lot of loans that mature today or tomorrow are being extended out, sort of pushing the can down the road. While extending and pretending has kept many properties out of foreclosure, other borrowers are surviving on savings or loans with low interest rates. However, all that could change when interest rates increase, making loan payments higher, which could force distressed properties to be put on the market.

On the other hand, some argue that the restructuring of commercial property loans around current cash flows and interest rates is preferable to foreclosures and forced sales of distressed properties. In most cases it is more advantageous for both the borrower and lender to restructure in order to yield the highest return as opposed to allowing a property to go into the abyss of foreclosure. Moreover, lenders don't want to take over properties and become landlords because the last thing they want to do is be in the real estate ownership business.

Commercial lenders avoid foreclosure if at all possible because in almost all states the process is often long and burdensome. The time element is the most costly of all, since much can happen to the value of the property while the foreclosure grinds toward the eventual sale or redemption of equity. At best, it's not a simple event. At worst, a year can pass before the final document is filed and title is granted to the winning bidder at the foreclosure sale. Most commercial lenders are also loath to foreclose on a property because it requires writing-down the value of the asset on their books, which forces them to raise additional capital to meet regulatory capital requirements.

———

The historic Washington, DC, Renaissance Mayflower Hotel is one of the high-profile properties that have benefited from extending-and-pretending. Royalty, high-powered politicians, and celebrities have been guests of the Mayflower, including Queen Elizabeth II, President Harry Truman, and John Wayne, among many glamorous others.

Rockwood Capital acquired the 544-room hotel for $260 million (or approximately $478,000 per room) in March 2007, with some $200 million in debt (a 77 percent LTV ratio). By August of that year, credit agency Realpoint valued the property at $128 million ($235,000 per room), or a 51 percent decrease in value even after a $21 million renovation. The Mayflower's CMBS loan was underwater, but rather than refinance or default, the special servicer extended the loan's due date by a year, to 2013. In return, and according to Standard & Poor's, Rockwood Capital recapitalized the loan by putting up $11 million of additional cash. The deadline could even be pushed to 2014, but only if Rockwood meets specific performance benchmarks.

It's quite amazing that Rockwood put up $11 million for a deal that was $132 million underwater ($260 million less $128) just to get an initial one-year extension. It could be that Rockwood was in a position where it had to protect its reputation on the street and hold on to the high-profile asset.

———

The extend-and-pretend tactic is bound to end as foreclosed activity picks up due to market pressures. In addition, extend-and-pretend is no longer a freebee from lenders, as they are now requiring cash flow "sweeps." (A cash flow sweep is a requirement of certain debt covenants to pay-down any outstanding debt with available cash flow).

When extend-and-pretend does end, many property owners could be forced to sell or hand the real estate back to the lender and the flow of distressed properties for sale could increase, which would help the commercial real estate transactions market clear itself out via the basic laws of supply and demand.

Conclusion

Commercial real estate markets in the US have been a source of strength during recent recoveries, but this time it's obviously different. There are still several threats to the fragile stabilization of the commercial property sector. First, delinquency rates on CMBSs have reached record highs. Second, massive amounts of commercial real estate debt will be coming due by 2015. Third, refinancing options are still limited, despite historically low interest rates, because many of these loans are higher than the original balances. Fourth, renewed strain on credit conditions may materialize from loan losses due to delinquencies, forming higher capital and liquidity requirements in the context of new international banking regulations.[12]

The "glass is half empty" view is that the US commercial real estate sector could dip again. Although capital markets—the lifeblood of real estate—remain timid, US banks have made progress in rebuilding their capital. However, important risks continue to revolve around the exposure of financial institutions to commercial real estate, especially by small and mid-size banks, which are major providers of credit to small and medium-size property owners. In addition, continuing weakness in private-label securitization markets is limiting the ability of banks to offload commercial property debt risk from their balance sheets.

In other words, and given the mixed signals emanating from the markets, the commercial real estate sector is not out of the woods yet. With approximately $1.15 trillion in commercial debt due to mature by 2015, thousands of owners and developers across the country may find themselves with limited choices when their loans mature. With property values less than the original debt, owners and developers may have no choice but to sell their properties at a loss, or face foreclosure when their loans mature (depending to which extent the extend-and-pretend approach continues to be applied by lenders).

In turn, in the "glass is half full" view—of which I'm a proponent—there are varying signs of life in each of the main commercial real estate segments. There is light at the end of the tunnel for commercial space, although the sector's recovery is likely to play out in an "era of less."[13] That is, every property type will continue to be affected by the major economic transformations that are taking place in the country. As a result, the conditions that caused commercial real estate values to surge to euphoric heights in 2007 are not likely to materialize any time soon. In addition, scaling back will mean fewer cars, smaller offices, fewer vacations, and fewer trade distribution links. Therefore, most commercial property segments still face some continued scaling back rather than any substantial increase in demand for new space. It could be the new reality, at least in the short-term.

————

The outlook for US commercial space has clearly improved, but any enthusiasm should be restrained by the challenges that remain. What is most frustrating for commercial property is that its future is not entirely within its control. That is because debt is the overriding predicament. As I discuss in the next chapter, the fundamental problem has been the excessive use of leverage, unsustainable property debt growth, and the misalignment of real estate debt risk to capital, which could take several years to fix.

Chapter 8: Violating the Law of the Lever

What can be added to the happiness of a man who is
in health, out of debt, and has a clear conscience?
—Adam Smith, pioneer of political economics

This chapter emphasizes the dangers of debt, the "cocaine" of real estate investors. Wall Street executives have blamed everything from sloppy errors and ignorance to government incompetence and an outbreak of industry-wide folly. But in my view, one of the most important factors that contributed to the financial crisis was the misalignment of real estate debt risk to capital.

The Law of the Lever

In very basic terms, a lever is a tool supported by a fulcrum (the support around which a lever turns) that can be used to lift heavy objects. Archimedes, the ancient Greek mathematician and physicist, calculated the Law of the Lever. He is reported to have said that if he had a lever long enough and a fulcrum large enough, he could lift the whole world.[1]

When applied to real estate, the principle of leverage enables investors to purchase properties they would not otherwise be capable of acquiring with all-cash equity—the gold standard of capital. Applying leverage (borrowing money to increase the wallop of your bet) to the various financing mechanisms available can potentially allow individuals and firms to increase the return on their commercial property investments in a stable or rising market. In the case of single-family residential, most people would not be able to acquire a home without leverage since they can barely save enough money to make a small down payment.

Investors use the basic law of leverage to help them "lever-up" the returns on their holdings. The application of this law suggests that investors will use a lever, which is supported by a fulcrum, to lift something that they would otherwise not be able to lift. In this analogy, the fulcrum can be moved closer to the property purchase price, or farther away from it. The debt can be increased by moving the fulcrum toward the property investment price, since moving the fulcrum closer to real estate increases leverage force, requiring less equity-weight to lift the property investment.

On one end of the lever is an investor's initial capital outlay, and on the other end of the lever is the real estate being financed. The fulcrum, therefore, enables investors to apply Archimedes' Law of the Lever with a sufficient amount of debt relative to the equity contributed.

The principle of leverage as it relates to real estate rests on the premise that the cost of debt must be less than the overall expected return on the asset being acquired. For example, if an investor borrows from a bank, the cost of borrowing money must be less than the return on the asset it's invested in. If it isn't, then the cost of debt would decrease the expected rate of return on the property acquired.

Leverage Can Kill

Although there are multiple reasons why debt increases the value of real estate, this doesn't imply that borrowing, for example, $65 million on a $100 million office building automatically increases the value of the property. If it did, then all investors would acquire properties using leverage. So, there is more to leverage than meets the eye, especially due to operational issues at the property level.

The availability of debt, weak or tight underwriting, and interest rates are all major factors affecting the amount of debt and equity that can be raised to finance a property, thus impacting its value. With the equity yield expectation remaining fairly constant, the lower cost of debt coupled with the movement in the fulcrum mentioned above, can also dramatically affect property value at any point in time. Naturally, a 5 percent long-term loan in a 7 percent market does add relative value, but that relative value is derived from below-market financing and not from the decision to use debt per se.[2]

———

The tax basis in a property is defined as the purchase price plus any costs for improvements, less any taken depreciation as scheduled by the federal tax code. Debt has actually no impact on the tax basis; however, when a property owner uses debt, the interest payments are a tax deduction. But the most obvious use of debt financing is the reduction of the minimum equity investment necessary in any given real estate acquisition. Because many investors generally have limited capital resources, a reduced minimum equity investment in one transaction allows them to spread their wealth over several deals.

Combining financing possibilities with various forms of ownership, the decision maker can create new risk-return opportunities—meaning that new investments fit specific investor criteria. As such, the flexibility to tailor the investment to suit the needs of specific real estate investors is an additional benefit of using leverage. On the other hand, a chief disadvantage of debt is when it becomes too costly and reduces the return on equity (ROE) below the overall return of an investor's assets. In addition, investors who are highly leveraged might find it difficult to make payments on their debt and might also experience resistance in obtaining additional replacement-debt from lenders. Most debt is secured by real assets and, when asset prices fall, lenders worry about being repaid. But borrowers are not off the hook. They still have to repay their debt. A summary of the advantages and disadvantages of leverage are presented in table 8-1.

Table 8-1: Advantages and Disadvantages of Leverage

Advantages	Disadvantages
• Higher return on equity (ROE) for a property with right-sized debt over an investment period. • If the interest rate on a loan is less than the required equity return, then the lower cost of debt will increase the ROE.	• Risk of loss of initial equity investment if debt amount is too high for a property. • Negative financial intermediary market conditions can change loan underwriting requirements from being accretive to the equity to being a loss on the equity.

(Table continued on next page...)

Advantages	Disadvantages
• Debt is an "enabling tool" that allows investors to tap into capital that would otherwise be unattainable all-cash. • Debt uses other entities' capital while allowing maximum control over the business by its investors. • With an increasing property value, the fixed amount of the initial debt at acquisition can significantly increase equity levels upon sale and turbo charge the ROE.	• High debt levels impose a higher risk of default and equity loss-potential. • Requires regular monthly payments of principal and interest (debt service). Investors often experience shortages in cash flow that may make such regular payments difficult. Most lenders apply severe penalties for late or missed payments, which may include charging late fees, taking possession of collateral, or calling the loan-due early. • Debt can be worked off only slowly, while interest rates can rise suddenly. • Real estate borrowers are constantly vulnerable to potentially severe and rapid credit deterioration. • Floating-rate mortgages expose borrowers to the risk of significant "payment shocks" as interest rates rise. • High debt really limits your options when economic difficulties arise.

To demonstrate the basic principle of leverage, suppose that an urban hotel is acquired for $30 million and the revenue is $10 million, while total operating expenses and fixed charges are $7 million. Table 8-2 shows the investor's ROE if the hotel is purchased with no debt (unleveraged), and if it is 65 percent financed with a 7.5 percent, twenty-five-year amortization period, monthly-payment conventional loan (ignoring the impacts of principal repayment, physical depreciation, and income taxes).

Table 8-2: The Basic Principle of Leverage

	Without Leverage	**With Leverage**
Acquisition Value	$30,000,000	$30,000,000
Less Loan Amount	$0	$19,500,000
Equity Value	$30,000,000	$10,500,000
Loan-to-Value Ratio	0.0%	65.0%
Total Revenue	**$10,000,000**	**$10,000,000**
Less Operating Expenses	$7,000,000	$7,000,000
Net Operating Income	$3,000,000	$3,000,000
Less Interest Expense	$0	$1,450,000
Cash Flow Before Tax	**$3,000,000**	**$1,550,000**
Return on Equity (ROE) Before Tax*	**10.0%**	**14.8%**

*Cash flow before tax divided by equity value.

A real estate investor will borrow because the interest tax shield is valuable. At relatively low debt levels, the probability of financial distress is low and the benefit from debt outweighs the cost. At very high debt levels, however, the possibility of financial distress is a chronic, ongoing problem for a property, so the benefits from debt financing may be more than offset by the costs of financial distress. In other words, the Achilles heel of real estate is too much debt, and a delicate balance between these extremes needs to be attained.[3]

Table 8-3: The Destructive Power of Leverage

	Without Leverage	With Leverage
Acquisition Value	$30,000,000	$30,000,000
Less Loan Amount	$0	$19,500,000
Equity Value	$30,000,000	$10,500,000
Loan-to-Value Ratio	0.0%	65.0%
Reduced Property Value*	$18,000,000	$18,000,000
Less Loan Amount	$0	$19,500,000
Reduced Equity Value	$12,000,000	$10,500,000
Total Revenue**	**$7,500,000**	**$7,500,000**
Less Operating Expenses	$5,950,000	$5,950,000
Net Operating Income	$1,550,000	$1,550,000
Less Interest Expense	$0	$1,450,000
Cash Flow Before Tax	**$1,550,000**	**$100,000**
Percentage Change in Cash Flow Before Tax	-48.3%	-93.5%
Return on Equity (ROE) Before Tax**	8.6%	1.0%

*Assumes a 40 percent decline in property value.

**Assumes a 25 percent decline in total revenue.

***Cash flow before tax divided by the reduced property/equity value.

Table 8-3 shows the destructive power of leverage when a property's value declines, completely wiping out an investor's created equity. As highlighted, the ROE of the same leveraged investor declines significantly from a respectable 14.8 percent (table 8-2) down to just 1 percent (table 8-3). The unleveraged investor, while also experiencing a decline in ROE, benefits from a positive cash flow before tax of $1,550,000, while the leveraged investor has to contend with a measly $100,000 because he has no "shock absorber."

According to the above scenarios, it's important to keep in mind that a strategy of investing the minimum amount of equity by maximizing the amount of leverage in a property with a positive debt service is only a wise strategy if the following five conditions/principles apply:

- The market and the value of the property are rising.
- The loan is non-recourse to the investor.
- If the property or market goes in decline, as long as the investment is non-recourse, the amount of equity lost on a real estate investment is capped by the initial amount invested, and no more. In other words, default *may* be an option to avoid more new equity contributions to try to save the lost invested equity. With recourse (or guaranteed debt), the risk of investing additional equity in a property with potentially reduced investment yields is much higher than if the debt is non-recourse (non-guaranteed) for repayment.
- If you have no debt, the amount of equity lost can be greater than if capped in a non-recourse loan. In table 8-3, the

reduced equity value is $12 million (without leverage). With leverage, the invested capital is capped at $10.5 million.

- Leverage spreads the same amount of 100 percent equity over several properties with the same size of deal, thus diversifying investment risk. Unless debt risk raises its ugly head—stranding all boats at low tide after the boats were loaded at high tide with excessive debt—the equity yield is higher for the investor with the conservatively leveraged strategy.

———

As shown above, leverage can be an easy way to increase profits. To give a different example, if you invest, say, $100 of your money at a 10 percent return, you will gain $10 in profits; but if you invest $100 of your money and $900 of borrowed money at a 10 percent return, your profits will be $100.

In turn, leverage significantly *increases* the chances that you will be wiped out. That is, a 10 percent loss on $100 of your own money is only $10, but a 10 percent loss on $100 of your money and $900 of borrowed money leaves you high and dry.

This is why regulators set limits on the amount of debt a bank can take on in the form of minimum capital requirements. Capital is the amount of money put up by the bank's owners (shareholders) and acts as a safety cushion in times of stress. The more the capital, the more money the bank can lose before it becomes unable to return money to its depositors and repay its debts.[4]

———

One motivation for securitization was to exploit a loophole in existing regulatory capital requirements. The amount of capital a bank had to hold depended on the type of assets it held. In essence, the riskier the asset, the more capital was required.[5] The loophole was that these requirements were set somewhat arbitrarily—4 percent for home mortgages, 8 percent for unsecured commercial loans, and so on.[6] As a result, a bank could take $100 of assets that required, say, $8 in capital; put them into a securitization pool; and through the alchemy of structured finance convert them into $100 of new securities that were treated differently by capital regulations and, thus, required only $5 in capital. The true risk of the assets hadn't changed, since the probability of default hadn't changed.[7]

But because financial "quant jocks" could create securities with just the right characteristics needed to get the right credit ratings (i.e., AAA), they could control the amount of capital that was required. So a bank could use securitization while reducing its capital requirements (meaning it could go and make more loans and have very little skin in the game).

Shifting Gears

Compared to leverage, *over-leverage* is the imprudent borrowing of too much money in order to minimize equity contribution in an investment in an attempt to maximize ROE. Most large-scale financial busts involve over-leveraging and the carrying of too much debt risk. For the most part, the US government has failed in curbing the problem of over-leverage secured by real estate. The Fed is supposed to tighten the money supply and sufficiently raise interest rates when the economy is over-expanding with high asset-price inflation, but the Fed ignored the signs of excessive debt during the gung-ho years of the mid-2000s, disregarding the inflated prices of real estate.

On the other hand, to *de-leverage* (or debt-shedding) is to reduce borrowed funds that were used to finance an investment. This is usually done when an investment goes bad, or the market goes south. Artificially cheap credit caused over-expansion, excessive risk taking, inflation, and a destructive asset-price bubble.

The "hangover effect" of the debt-fuelled, house-buying and consumption binge that started to unravel in 2007, of course, has been taking its toll.[8] People today are no longer able to borrow unless they have a good credit history. In any event, many people may not necessarily want to borrow in today's market. They are focused instead on reducing the debts they have taken through the process of de-leveraging—either by choice or because they cannot roll over debts with new loans.[9]

———

In advanced economies, a feature of the real estate cycle over the past decade that differs sharply from past cycles is the excessive access to credit.[10] Easy monetary conditions and so-called financial innovation gave households greater access to credit and spending, leading to a massive buildup of unsustainable real estate debt. In what can be described as a dilemma since the objective should be to *decrease* debt levels, the process of de-leveraging could make the long-term macroeconomic impact of this housing bust much greater than in the past.[11]

Household sector de-leveraging proceeds at a much slower pace than corporate or financial sector de-leveraging. This is because the largest portion of household balance sheets (on both the asset and the liability side) tends to be real estate, which is more difficult to sell in a fire-sale than bonds or stocks. Therefore, the US recovery is likely to be much slower than in previous recessions that were triggered by problems directly related to corporate balance sheets.[12] In addition, with a huge overhang of debt, real estate isn't likely to lead the nation's economy out of this period of uncertainty, with both the housing and commercial property markets continuing to act as a drag on the US economic recovery for the next few years.

The Land of the Rising Debt

In 2004, the Security and Exchange Commission's (SEC) decision to deregulate the big investment banks loosened up the rules pertaining to debt, yet many of the banks that lobbied for this new rule failed a few years later. Between 2004 and 2007, the promiscuous US financial system was a house of cards built on nothing but financial leverage, excessive credit, and rampant speculation. That is why the Great Recession of 2007–09 was unusually severe and long, with its impacts still being felt in 2012 despite officially ending in June 2009. The length and severity of recessions depend on the magnitude of the dislocations and imbalances that have accumulated in the economy during the preceding boom. As such, the US economy was in for a very hard landing, and the excessive monetary looseness had only postponed the inevitable crisis.

Furthermore, disillusionment with the economy has risen following the Great Recession. The huge capital inflows were the US financial markets' most paramount crutch. That crutch was taken away and the capital markets instantly collapsed with devastating effects for the US economy, turning quickly into a vicious credit crunch.

The share of real estate loans in all bank lending rose sharply from 39 percent in early 2001 to 56 percent in early 2002, due to the dot-com crash and anxious money chasing the higher and riskier real estate yields. Ever since, mortgages have been by far the largest category of debt outstanding in the American financial system.

As shown in figure 8-1, total US national debt in 2011 was projected to balloon to a jaw-dropping $14.5 trillion (and counting). That's about $126,000 in debt for every household in the US. In addition, the US is now in a position where it must borrow more to continue to function properly and to pay its bills. This has been impacting every level of the American economy.

Figure 8-1: Total US National Debt (Inflation Adjusted Dollars)

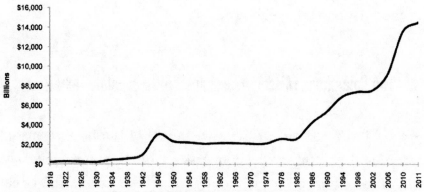

Source: Bureau of Economic Analysis

No country can continue to exist on debt when there is very little probability of repaying it. How can the United States continue to function fiscally when its standard of living and strength is dependent on ever-increasing imports and endless consumption, or when its whole economy can only be temporarily sustained by ever-rising debts?

―――――

Moreover, and as discussed in chapter 7, the commercial real estate sector has close to $1.15 trillion in debt maturities due between 2012 and 2015. The greatest concern is that nobody really knows whether they will be paid off or refinanced in light of weak net operating incomes caused by weakened demand.

Chapter 1 presented the excessive debt culture and consumerism inherent in American society, which morphed into a gigantic financial disaster. But what could have been done to prevent, or at least minimize, the massive financial destruction caused by the over-leveraged US economy? The following section sheds light on the warning signs that were ignored by regulators and financiers in the run-up to the meltdown.

The Calamitous Missed Assessment of Real Estate Debt Risk

We are faced today with the after-shocks of the biggest missed assessment of real estate debt risk in our lifetimes. The last time this occurred on such a large scale was during the Great Depression. The property mortgage defaults that we're experiencing today will continue to be a major drag on the US economy for several years. At the same time, it's important to keep in mind that the modification of problem mortgages and home loan foreclosures doesn't create wealth—it creates financial *losses.*

According to 2011 estimates from the Mortgage Bankers Association, approximately 4.1 million borrowers are in foreclosure or near it, the latter being borrowers who are more than ninety days delinquent on their mortgages. Many of the homes under these mortgages are likely to be repossessed by lenders and resold, known as shadow inventory. How much these homes will affect the broader housing market depends on when they actually become available for sale and how long they remain on the market. Some analysts are concerned that a surge in the availability of repossessed or bank real estate-owned properties—or a persistently high level of them—could put downward pressure on prices. This could, in turn, induce additional foreclosures in an already fragile housing market.[13]

Debt risk is the rising of residential and commercial leverage to unsustainable levels; therefore, the assessment of real estate aggregate debt risk in the US economy is paramount. Subprime mortgage and derivative losses were caused by this calamitous risk, such as the screwed up morass of collateralized debt obligations (CDOs) and credit-default swaps (CDSs), which were merely a subset of this risk. If aggregate real estate debt risk was appropriately assessed and priced with higher interest rates as the property bubble was beginning, it would not have occurred as a gargantuan systemic threat.[14]

Excessive Debt Growth of Commercial Real Estate

The growth in aggregate debt for all income-producing property (including apartments) was 123 percent from 2000 to 2008, versus 29 percent from 1990 to 1999.[15] There appears to be no question that the cause for the high aggregate debt growth in income property since 2000 was due to the high escalation of a then-relatively new entrant in the marketplace. After reviewing the Mortgage Bankers Association *Data Books*,[16] it is clear that the cause for excessive aggregate debt in the United States was high commercial mortgage-backed security loan originations (see figure 8-2).

Figure 8-2: US Commercial Debt Outstanding Growth, 2000–2008

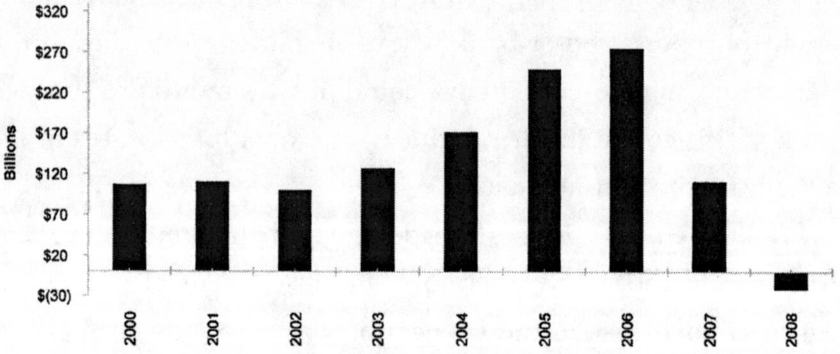

Source: Flow of Funds Accounts, Federal Reserve Board, MBA *Data Book*. Represents change in debt outstanding from 2000 to 2008, including CMBSs.

In the S&L crisis of the late 1980s, a similar change in the amount of debt outstanding occurred (figure 8-3). The aggregate growth rate in income property loans in the US at the time was 127 percent. This level of loan growth over a decade is similar to the 123 percent aggregate income property loan growth rate from 2000 to 2008.[17]

Figure 8-3: US Commercial Debt Outstanding Growth, 1985–1994

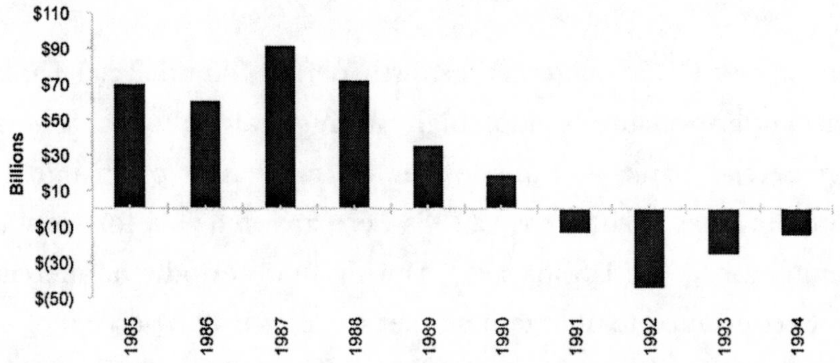

Source: Flow of Funds Accounts, Federal Reserve Board, MBA *Data Book*. Represents change in debt outstanding from 1985 to 1994.

The growth rate in commercial mortgage-backed securities (CMBSs) was likened to what was observed during the S&L crisis. Instead of the S&Ls, it was the CMBS market that was providing easy credit—supporting significant speculative behavior in income property investments. From 2004 to 2007, CMBS loans outstanding more than doubled, from $383.3 to $820.9 billion. Figure 8-4 provides net annual CMBS issuance growth from 2000 to 2008.

Figure 8-4: US CMBS Net Annual Issuance Growth, 2000–2008

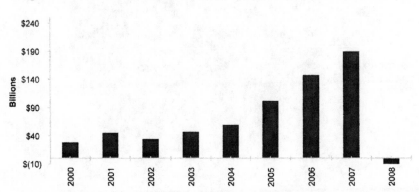

Source: Wachovia Capital Markets, Index Solutions, MBA *Data Book*. Represents change in outstandings from 2000 to 2008.

Impact of the Commercial Banking Sector

During the CMBS aggregate growth period, commercial banks were under pressure to book high-earning real estate loans. Most commercial banks became extremely aggressive over time to maintain market share, as CMBSs were growing as a formidable competitor in the US market.[18] During that period, commercial banks continued to maintain market share with 42.8 percent of all commercial real estate loans in 2004 compared to a 44.8 percent share in 2009.[19] Figure 8-5 highlights the continuing dominance of commercial banks in terms of debt supply at 45 percent.

Figure 8-5: US Commercial Mortgage Debt Outstanding

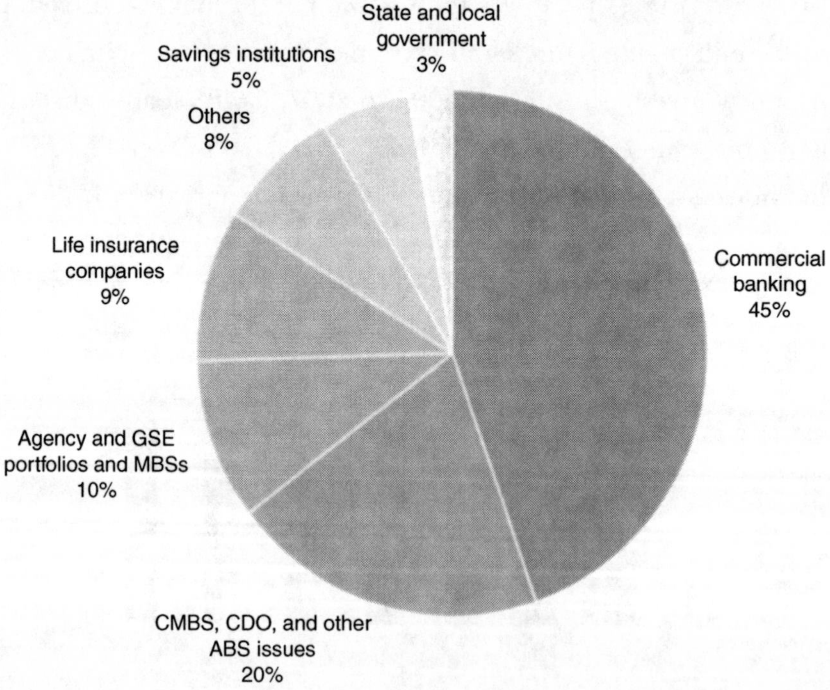

Source: Mortgage Bankers Association, Federal Reserve Board. By investor group, including the apartment segment (2010 data).

As did credit rating agencies, commercial bank regulators completely missed the assessment of real estate debt risk during this
high debt-growth period. According to Bloomberg.com in an
October 2009 article, the FDIC failed to limit the amount of commercial real estate loans as a percentage of capital within banks.[20]
The FDIC regulations indicated a maximum guidance amount of
commercial property loans to be no more than 300 percent of capital.[21] One bank referred to in the Bloomberg article was Security
Pacific Bank in Los Angeles, which had, as of September 2008, a
ratio of nearly 1,400 percent in commercial real estate loans-to-
capital.[22] The bank was closed two months later by the FDIC. In
addition, according to Chip MacDonald, a partner specializing in
financial services at Atlanta-based law firm Jones Day, "of ninety-
five US bank failures before September 2009, seventy-one were
caused by non-performing commercial real estate loans."[23]

Although there was a rising concern by many FDIC regulators during the period of 2005–07, they seemed to have difficulty
enforcing their own regulations. When economic times are considered favorable, commercial bank regulators complete audit
reviews assessing very low risk of probable loss as supported by
a high debt service coverage ratio (a measure of whether there's
enough income to cover debt payments), or as supported by
recent comparable property sales of the collateralized real estate
loans.[24] Unless all financial intermediaries in the market deploy
a uniform aggregate property risk assessment methodology, dis-
crepancies in risk taking will impact the overall lending behavior
of competing financial institutions in their attempt to maintain
earnings growth and market share.

Extreme Debt Growth in the Residential Market

To better understand the capital markets, it's necessary to study the risks associated with the much larger single-family residential mortgage-backed security markets. Applying the same risk assessment to single-family markets, it is clear that the highest risk in the US economy resided in the excesses in aggregate debt growth in the single-family loan sector. This aggregate debt grew by an enormous 107 percent from 2000 to 2008.[25]

The single-family residential debt market is significant as it relates to the overall US economy, owing to its large scale as compared to annual GDP. In 2000, the US single-family aggregate debt relative to GDP was 50 percent. In 2008, it rose to 93 percent. It's not likely that households can "grow" the economy to outpace aggregate single-family debt growth when consumer spending comprises close to 70 percent of GDP.

————

If consumers are burdened with home mortgages, they are less able to contribute to the consumption of products and services which, for better or for worse, are major drivers of the US economy. In addition, the mounting losses in single-family mortgages are likely to continue for years, keeping housing prices at relatively low levels compared to the value of mortgages collateralized by single-family homes.

The largest percentage of aggregate single-family residential debt growth and price appreciation began in 2003. With residential prices (excluding condos)[26] falling from their height in 2007 back to 2000–03 price levels, the collateral values for single-family residential debt originated since 2003 no longer support the huge amounts of residential mortgages outstanding. As such, it could take between five and ten years to work through the massive amount of over-leveraged homes in the country.

By applying an aggregate debt risk assessment, one can estimate loan loss probability on the single-family mortgage market to be in the trillions of dollars over the next ten years. With single-family housing prices still falling to 2000–03 prices in many distressed markets, the single-family appreciation rates that supported the growth in home mortgages are no longer sustaining the aggregate amount of debt in the single-family marketplace.[27]

How Unsustainable Debt Risk Could Have Been Controlled

The sleepwalking credit rating agencies didn't realize they were flawed in their assessment of risk in CMBS issuances as the actual risk of probable loss was increasing from 2005 to 2007. If the agencies had appropriately assessed probable loss risk as increasing each year, the percentage of CMBS AAA-rated tranches would have decreased during this period, with a corresponding increase in mezzanine and B-piece tranches. Had any of the credit rating agencies known about aggregate debt risk and chosen not to assess risk correctly because of a reason as yet undisclosed, they may be liable to the investment public they serve.[28]

In addition, commercial banks would likely have been more conservative in their lending. A uniform risk assessment methodology employed by credit rating agencies and bank regulators would have increased interest rates on the CMBS issuances and commercial bank property loans. The higher interest rates would, in turn, lower the qualifying amounts for loans, and the adoption of this recommendation would result in the correct alignment of debt risk assessment models backed by real estate mortgages with AAA credit risks.[29]

Had this aggregate risk measurement methodology (developed by banker Marc Thompson and presented in his 2010 research titled "A Missed Assessment of Real Estate Debt Risk") been applied to residential mortgages, the home loan debacle would have been less severe, and the financial meltdown and many other negative, unintended consequences probably wouldn't have occurred. As such, the missed assessment and misalignment of real estate debt risk were the root causes of both the S&L crisis and the recent financial meltdown.

Thompson's methodology infers that a high risk of probable default developed as aggregate debt increased above the annual average increases in both GDP and consumer price index (CPI) measures over a number of years. In addition, his calculations assess how the probable risk of default increases each year when the loan aggregate growth rate is *higher* than the average rate of GDP and CPI, explaining why the loan issuance years of 2005–08 have such a high risk of probable default. In other words, the financial crisis would not have occurred if the credit rating agencies and commercial bank regulators had developed and implemented an aggregate debt growth risk assessment methodology no later than the year 2000.[30]

Keep Hope Alive

Despite the calamitous missed assessment of real estate debt risk by banks, credit rating agencies, and regulators, there has been an improvement in loan underwriting standards. As discussed in chapter 7, many banks have been restricting their lending on property because they already have so many non-performing property loans on their books.

Another tactic applied by banks today is to accept as loan collateral only those assets that produce *current* cash flow, rather than those with no cash flow but supposedly high market values. For example, vacant land is considered of zero value if it produces no current cash flow, no matter how valuable it may seem in some markets.

According to the Urban Land Institute lenders have become more active compared to 2009 and 2010, citing pressure to put money out for strong sponsors with quality real estate. There is a broader appetite for high quality, cash-flowing assets across most major property classes.[31] There is also an active market for financing mortgage (note) purchases.

———

Fundamental real estate analysis is in vogue again, with lenders focusing on "basis" (the original cost of a property adjusted for factors such as physical depreciation). Lenders are also much more focused on the prudent underwriting of tenancy, market rents, occupancies, lease rollovers, as well as debt yield (the ratio of verifiable net operating income divided by the loan's principal balance). CMBS loan sizing is now based almost exclusively on real performance history—on in-place trailing twelve-month debt yield and the debt service coverage ratio.

In addition, there is a significant amount of private capital available on the sidelines to support the debt markets, as life insurance companies have become more active, continuing to focus on high quality assets in primary markets. Moreover, domestic money center banks are focused on institutional quality and stable properties in major markets with best-in-class sponsors, while community banks are more focused on smaller loan balances with existing clients for cash-flowing assets.[32] Lastly, US banks are now seeking some level of recourse, which means that banks are finally going back to basics.

Conclusion

If there is one big lesson from the recent crisis, it is that leverage can be lethal. Increasing the amount of equity that banks have to hold is one way of keeping down the amount of debt that finds its way into real estate, but this is still an asset class that is privileged, not completely imprisoned, by the capital regime.[33]

The best way to limit the damage from a property bust is to exercise more direct control over the amount of debt available to property owners and developers, whether through discretionary interventions or standing rules. For capitalism to function and interact properly with real estate, credit must be rationed on the basis of balance-sheet soundness.

In his 1934 classic *Security Analysis*, Benjamin Graham wrote about how leverage results in increased corporate profits, but he also warned that leverage results in an increased chance of bankruptcy.[34] Debt in modest quantities does, of course, improve the rate of growth of an economy and does create higher standards of living. But in excess, leverage creates disastrous effects as we have so miserably experienced recently. In other words, debt can be your friend in good times, but an unforgiving enemy in bad times.

———

When economies accumulate too much debt, there is the risk that they stop responding to monetary policy in the usual way.[35] It is this predicament that has dogged Japan for the past twenty years. Could this Japan-risk be possible in the United States? Excessive debt helps explain why Japan went bust in the 1980s, companies at the end of the 1990s, and American banks over the last three years (see figure 8-6).

Figure 8-6: US Bank Failures

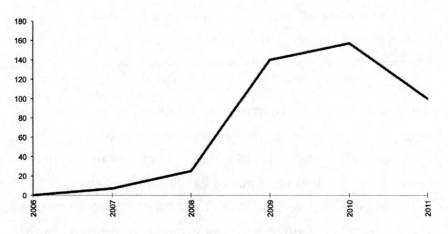

Source: Foresight Analytics, FDIC

The build-up of debts should send warning signals, because they are unsustainable. Therefore, it should be relatively easy to see when the next bubble will be forming—it is whichever sector is accumulating the most debt. Until debt is reduced to much more sustainable levels, economic activity in the United States will remain weak (see figure 8-7).

Figure 8-7: US Household Debt as Percent of GDP

Source: Federal Reserve Board *Flow of Funds Report*

Some bank bosses shriek that leverage limits are "anti-American." However, banks could support job creation with far less debt and far more equity, or skin in the game. A lender's capacity to hold assets is independent of its mix of liabilities. For example, a bank that wants to lend $100 can do so by raising $1 of equity and $99 of debt, putting the entire economy in jeopardy, or it can raise $15 of equity and $85 of debt, sparing taxpayers the risk of a bailout. In other words, when bankers say that they can't operate without that wacky leverage, they are making stuff up.[36]

So if banks could do their work with much less borrowing, why do they claim otherwise? Banks gorge on debt because of government distortions. The implicit promise of a bailout constitutes a subsidy for reckless borrowers, and the US tax code obliquely favors leverage by taxing equity more heavily than debt.

———

The American capital markets are not dissimilar to a random walk down a road filled with chaos, dilemmas, and risk, switching direction with very little notice. A way to minimize such uncertainties is to apply the previously discussed risk assessment methodology, which would help lenders, borrowers, regulators, and the US government to make better decisions going forward. This risk assessment methodology is recommended to be added to other probability of loan loss risk factors, such as property type and loan underwriting credit quality in a specific origination.

Aggregate debt risk assessment can be applied to both income-producing property and single-family markets in similar ways. More specifically, in the risk assessment of mortgage-backed-security issuances compared year over year. In sum, the risk assessment methodology should be applied to correctly measure mortgage-backed issuances and other financial institution loan originations, so that the alignment of real estate debt risk to capital is not heavily skewed again in such a way that the US financial system is brought to its knees.

The next chapter ventures into the tedium of government fiddling with the real estate sector, including its ongoing attempts to address the ubiquitous problem of no skin in the game.

Chapter 9: Fiddling With the System

Government has no other end, but the preservation of property.

—John Locke, philosopher

To a large extent, the US real estate sector suffers from a lack of confidence borne of confusion on new regulatory expectations. Many Americans today question the ability of the federal government to effectively reconstruct the economy after the recent debacle that has caused millions of property foreclosures and vanishing home equity.

Though far from a stellar performance, the US government should at least be given some credit for trying to preserve the property sector, especially given the depth and complexity of the issues at hand. It's safe to assume that no matter where the next shock may come from, there is a reasonable expectation the financial system should be more resilient. The problem, of course, is that so much of the structure of regulation is being changed in one go that the implementation risks remain formidable.

―――

Over the decades, US government officials have had a remarkable track record of making both a positive and negative impact on housing in America (see figure 9-1). The series of policies that

Figure 9-1: History of Government Intervention in US Housing

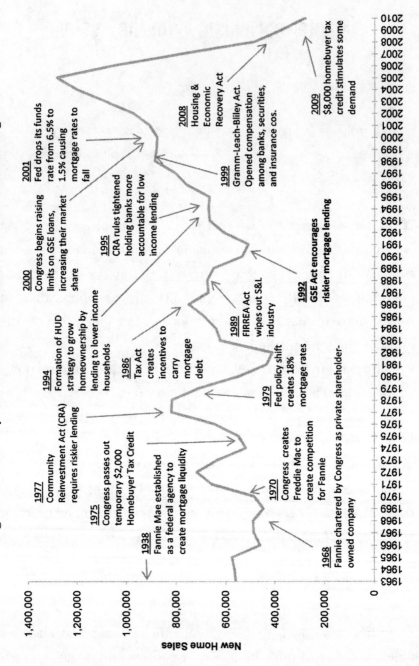

Source: US Census Bureau, John Burns Real Estate Consulting

culminated in the greatest housing market collapse in more than seventy-five years essentially started with the Federal Housing Enterprises Financial Safety and Soundness Act of 1992 (commonly known as the Government-Sponsored Enterprise Act). The "GSE" act mandated that Fannie Mae, Freddie Mac, and the twelve Federal Home Loan Banks promote credit access (read: lending to ever-dodgier types) for low-income households in minority neighborhoods. It was when high-finance first met lower middle-class America.

The driving forces behind the financial crisis were a complex array of interlaced causes and players, including the missed assessment of real estate debt risk, a lack of regulation, and the inability of the free market to self-regulate, as well as banks giving out far too many bad loans to people who couldn't afford them. As a result, the government has had to intervene aggressively to prevent a massive meltdown in the US financial system.

Debt-ridden banks became greedy during the real estate bubble, thinking that home values were going to keep rising and make everyone rich, especially the bankers themselves. They didn't really care if the housing market was going to fail because they were counting on homeowners paying back their loans. And if they didn't pay, the government would come running to the rescue with all its largesse.

Bailing Out the Herds

As discussed in chapter 1, financial crises of varying severity have been a recurring historical phenomenon. While each crisis has had its distinct characteristics, there are a number of similarities among them. One of the more prominent and consistently recurrent features is what the relatively new field of behavioral economics refers to as "herding behavior," or following the trend—actions that, although individually rational, produce group behavior that is irrational.[1] This herd-like behavior is said to arise from an "information cascade" that occurs when people observe the actions of others and then make the same choice that the others have made, independent of their own private information signals.[2] It has been seen in the vicissitudes of the 2004–06 housing market, the dot-com euphoria of the late 1990s, and the stock market crash of 1987, among others.[3]

The trouble usually begins within a good economic environment in which people have a surplus of disposable income and are in search of investments—a search in which the investors seem to concentrate on trendy, sexy assets. The model implies that under some conditions investors will focus only on a subset of assets (herding), while neglecting other possibilities that lie outside their narrow field of vision.[4]

The financial crisis was partly a result of the "cops not being on the beat." Mistakes that were previously made in the run-up to the S&L crisis, such as irrational herding, were repeated. In the case of the recent meltdown the herd element was seen in the surge of unprecedented borrowing levels, housing demand, and investments in sliced-and-diced mortgage securities. Frequently, and as the herd grows larger, a criminal element may seek to take advantage of the situation. Then after the inevitable crash, the government steps in to mitigate the magnitude of the disaster—to bailout failure and incompetence.

Although not entirely effective, the US government has implemented massive interventions to help stave off a collapse in the economy. If there was no intervention, the sovereign prestige of America would have been severely impacted. In other words, it was a dire situation in which the US government would be "damned if it did and damned if it didn't." (Appendix B provides a summary of the government's intervention during and after the financial crisis).

Good Fiddling

Today, real estate investors should take advantage of some of the good that comes from government intervention. They should lock in as much low-interest, long-term, fixed-rate debt as possible before interest rates go back up (as will be discussed later). When the numerous reforms eventually trigger inflation, property owners should also be able to ride a wave of rent increases. Real estate investors like inflation because they are holding a hard asset with variable rents, so when inflation hits they can charge more. When the money supply is increased by more hundreds of billions of dollars, it can only lead to inflation. It might be a year or so out, but inflation in the United States is inevitable.

The Fed's plan to stimulate growth by suppressing long-term interest rates has strengthened the bottom-line of many real estate investors, and today's low mortgage rates are a result of positive government intervention. There are indirect benefits as well. Rising asset prices should increase the confidence of US consumers, spurring purchaser spending, and boosting fundamentals across the real estate space. If low interest rates lead to increased demand for alternative higher-yielding and riskier investments, property investors may also gain wider borrowing options as lender appetite for risk opens up concurrently.

Some believe that many of the recent reforms by the US government can be likened to giving methadone to a heroin addict. That is, Fed tools that led to the financial crisis, such as extremely low interest rates, are being applied once again. My response to them is that the Fed's low interest rate policy is designed to prevent an uncontrolled collapse of the mountain of debt into mass bankruptcies and, instead, allows debt to be paid down and the financial system to return to health more gradually. With higher interest rates in the current environment, house prices would fall further, unemployment would rise, more loans would default, and banks would fall back into a dark swamp. The key is to get the timing of interest rate hikes and cuts right.

The arduous task of the US government is to cure the ills bequeathed by the recent meltdown without creating either a depression or more unforeseen bubbles. Has the US government been doing a good job? Yes and no, but it could be much worse. The government's role is to maintain a healthy financial system, not a utopian economy.

Not-So-Good Fiddling

It's accepted that regulatory failures allowed the US financial markets to chase higher returns through excessive leverage and risk taking. Specifically, such regulatory lapses included the failure to:

1. Introduce tougher rules on lending in the run-up to the crisis;
2. Closely supervise non-bank financial intermediaries;

3. Prevent unprecedented layering of risk in mortgage underwriting;

4. Adequately supervise the credit rating agencies; and

5. Impose stiff enough counterparty risk controls, such as insisting on greater transparency in the capital markets and requiring higher reserves against debt risk.

On the other hand, it's hoped that the litany of new regulations enshrined in the Dodd–Frank Wall Street Reform and Consumer Protection Act will fix some of the regulatory failures mentioned above. That is, a new era of tougher regulation and oversight and less accommodating markets probably beckons in post-crisis America, depending, of course, on how many loopholes will be discovered by Wall Street bankers.

———

Both failed government regulation and deregulation indirectly contributed to the financial crisis. In fact, in a testimony before Congress in September 2008 both the SEC and the previous Fed chairman Alan Greenspan conceded failure in allowing the self-regulation of investment banks.[5]

Whether it was for political reasons or because of special interest groups, the US government was complicit in easy lending standards and a lack of regulation in driving up the huge housing bubble. Fannie Mae and Freddie Mac failed due to a toxic combination of perceived government guarantees and ineffective oversight. While they weren't the sole cause of the housing bust, they made the crisis significantly worse.

———

As background, the Glass-Steagall Act became part of the law in 1933, during the Great Depression. It separated commercial banks and investment banks, in part to avoid potential conflicts of interest between the lending activities of the former and the rating activities of the latter. Glass-Steagall remained in place until 1999 when Congress repealed it by passing the Gramm-Leach-Bliley Act (also known as the Financial Services Modernization Act), which allowed commercial banks, investment banks, and insurance companies to merge and interact—or more directly stated, to be in cahoots.

For example, the passage of Gramm-Leach-Bliley freed Bank of America, Citigroup, JPMorgan, and Wells Fargo—as well as the other banks that were created by a merger wave—to plunge headlong into the business of buying, securitizing, selling, and trading mortgages and mortgage-backed securities.[6] Because there was no way to seal off the banks' securities operations from their ordinary banking operations, this meant that the government guarantee of the banking system (in place since the 1930s) was effectively extended to investment banking. Deposits that were insured by the FDIC could be invested in risky assets with the assurance that any losses would be made up by the FDIC.

———

The larger the bank, the stronger its government guarantee. In 1984, when Continental Illinois was bailed out, the Office of the Comptroller of the Currency (OCC) said that the top eleven banks were "too big to fail." By 2001, there were twenty banks that were as big relative to the economy as the eleventh-largest bank had been in 1984.[7] As in any capitalist system, bank employees and shareholders would enjoy the profits from their increasingly risky activities. But at that time, the federal government was already on the hook for potential losses.[8]

Economist Joseph Stiglitz believes the replacement of Glass-Steagall with Gramm-Leach-Bliley contributed to the financial meltdown because the risk taking culture of investment banking dominated the more conservative commercial banks, leading to increased levels of risk taking and leverage during the boom period.[9] Many in the banking and business communities also opposed the repeal of Glass-Steagall with concerns that the intermingling of various financial entities with commercial banks would eventually cause a crisis. Their concerns, of course, became reality with the interrelated and murky transactions between merged financial behemoths.

Had the Glass-Steagall Act been in place, its laws would have prevented many of the elements that caused the financial meltdown, such as toxic assets and subprime lending based on out-of-control mortgage-backed securities. This isn't to say that some financial firms wouldn't have violated the law established by the act, but in all likelihood the financial crisis wouldn't have been so severe.[10]

Government Distortions

If most Americans had made their mortgage payments there would have been no collapse. But lenders made many bad loans. That's because US government policy inadvertently distorted the data used to measure risk so that loans appeared to be less risky than they really were. Like school children tallying rolls of the dice, investment risk managers compile a record of historical price changes and plot the probability of large future shifts.[11] Lenders, securities underwriters, rating agencies, and regulators also relied on some variation of this technique to help measure risk. They all analyzed the same historical data to project housing prices and estimate future defaults on home mortgages.[12] Pre-crisis default rates were low, making mortgages look like low-risk investments to portfolio managers, their federal regulators at the Office of Thrift Supervision, and many others. That historical data, though, was becoming increasingly skewed by federal policies.

Legislation and regulation encouraged mortgages for underserved borrowers. Following the introduction of the GSE act in 1992, the largest mortgage investors, Fannie Mae and Freddie Mac, were given "affordable housing goals" by Congress. Those policies significantly increased the number of home loans made and houses purchased, and US regulators allowed financial groups to make loans with very little skin in the game—using less capital and more borrowed money than they required for other loans.

As demand for housing rose, so did home prices. As government policy pumped up home prices, the rate of mortgage defaults was artificially suppressed because distressed borrowers had no need to default. And as the bubble grew, they could sell the home at a profit and pay off the mortgage, or simply refinance.[13]

Federal policies to promote homeownership were, therefore, distorting the default data. It was as if the school children were tallying data from crooked dice.[14] It all began to unravel as lending standards softened until loans were extended to borrowers so marginal that they defaulted before their home values increased. This suggests that the financial crisis was not only an unregulated market failure—it was also a failure driven by a public policy that was pushing Americans into homes that they shouldn't have bought.

Greenspan Double-Speak

In addition to the government's failures mentioned above, the interest rate policy during the early 2000s, under the direction of Alan Greenspan, was misguided, leading to a monetary policy that indirectly contributed to the housing bubble.

Greenspan mesmerized nearly everyone when the good times were rolling. I used to be fascinated by his intricate language and gnome-like intellectual demeanor. But the more I heard him speak, which was nearly always in incomplete sentences and double negatives, the more I felt that he preferred to wax poetic rather than convey the hard facts. For example: "I guess I should warn you, if I turn out to be particularly clear, you've probably misunderstood what I've said."[15]

I also sensed that his goal could actually have been to confuse people into inaction with his impressive-sounding gobbledygook. After all, complexity is the handmaiden of deception. Here is another example of classic Greenspan double-speak:

Derivatives have been an extraordinarily useful vehicle to transfer risk from those who shouldn't be taking it to those who are willing to and are capable of doing so…The vast increase in the size of the over-the-counter derivatives markets is the result of the market finding them a very useful vehicle.[16]

Like many others, I was led to believe that Greenspan was an invincible soothsayer because he had an army of economists and analysts who calculated abstruse data series and ran econometric models all the time, trying to figure out what the economy would do next. But given what happened in 2008, were their statistical details, data mines, syllogisms, and algebra just a great fantasyland?

Of course, Greenspan isn't at fault for all of today's financial woes. Nonetheless, he did lead the Fed down an interest-rate-cutting path that created the cheap money that resulted in the housing bubble as a knee-jerk reaction to a relatively soft recession after the 2000–02 dot-com implosion and the 9/11 terrorist attacks. Although the US economy did recover, its growth was built on a housing boom—a boom that ultimately became a massive bubble.[17] Greenspan had expected the housing boom, but he hadn't counted on the bubble—and he certainly didn't expect the economic cataclysm that came afterward.

To this day, he rejects the notion that his aggressive lowering of interest rates in the early 2000s helped contribute to the subprime mortgage crisis.[18] Indeed, it is reasonable to argue that, based on the apparent threat of deflation at the time, it was necessary for the Fed to act forcefully. It is even understandable why he felt that the most efficient way to lift the broader economy was through a booming housing market. It is wrong, however, to argue that these policies did not contribute to the crisis that subsequently ensued. They did.[19]

Fat Fannie and Happy Freddie

As mentioned earlier, government regulations through the GSE act of 1992 encouraged homeowners to over-leverage in order to put more minorities into homes, since requiring a down payment was considered by politicians to be unfair to minorities.

The GSE act established the Office of Federal Housing Enterprise Oversight (OFHEO) within the Department of Housing and Urban Development (HUD). It also mandated that HUD set specific goals for government-sponsored enterprises Fannie Mae and Freddie Mac with regard to low-income and underserved housing areas.

Starting in 1993, HUD authorized that a certain percentage of Fannie and Freddie business be aimed at improving homeownership of low- and middle-income families and underserved areas through "special affordable methods" such as the ability to obtain a thirty-year fixed-rate mortgage with a very low down payment, as well as the continuous availability of mortgage credit under a wide range of economic conditions.[20] In other words, the GSEs were forced to buy subprime loans in huge numbers, which ended up feeding an insatiable securitization food chain.

Prior to 1992 and the passage of the GSE act, if a lending institution wrote a subprime loan it essentially had to accept the risk of making that loan, whether or not it would be repaid. Fannie and Freddie wouldn't purchase such a loan because subprimes didn't meet their guidelines at the time. Therefore, not many subprime mortgages were written. But with the passage of the GSE act, and the resultant lowering of Fannie and Freddie guidelines to purchase subprimes, these mega-debt dealers could purchase mortgages and securities backed by subprimes with great ease. Fannie and Freddie were also given government tax incentives to purchase many of these dicey mortgages.

Lending institutions could make their money on origination fees and other charges, while pushing the repayment risk of the loan onto Fannie and Freddie. Many applauded the massive increase in the number of low- and moderate-income homeowners, but very few noticed the looming risks to Fannie and Freddie—and the entire US financial system.

Then in 2004, the housing bubble began. The market shifted away from regulated GSEs and moved radically toward mortgage-backed securities issued by unregulated (private-label) securitization conduits, typically operated by investment banks.

The shift occurred as financial institutions sought to maintain earnings levels that had been elevated during 2003–04 by an unprecedented refinancing boom due to historically low interest rates.

Earnings depended on volume, so maintaining elevated earnings levels necessitated expanding the borrower pool using lower underwriting standards and new products that the GSEs would not (initially) securitize. Thus, the shift away from GSE securitization to private-label securitization (PLS) also corresponded with a shift in mortgage-product type—from prime, fixed-rate mortgages (FRMs) to subprime, structurally riskier, adjustable-rate mortgages (ARMs)—which started a sharp deterioration in underwriting standards. The growth of private-label securitization, however, forced the government-sponsored enterprises to lower their underwriting standards in an attempt to reclaim lost market share in order to appease their private shareholders. In other words, shareholder pressure pushed the GSEs into competition with PLS for market presence, and the GSEs significantly loosened their mortgage-guarantee underwriting standards in order to compete as if they were Wall Street investment banks.

The growth of private-label securitization and the lack of regulation in this segment of the market resulted in the oversupply of underpriced housing finance that led to an increasing number of borrowers. By 2008, these borrowers, usually with poor credit, were unable to pay their mortgages (particularly ARMs), causing a dangerous increase in home delinquencies and foreclosures. As a result, home prices declined significantly. In 2009 and 2010, the percentage of subprime mortgages in delinquency (ninety days or more) ballooned dramatically (see figure 9-2).

Figure 9-2: Share of Subprime Mortgages in Delinquency

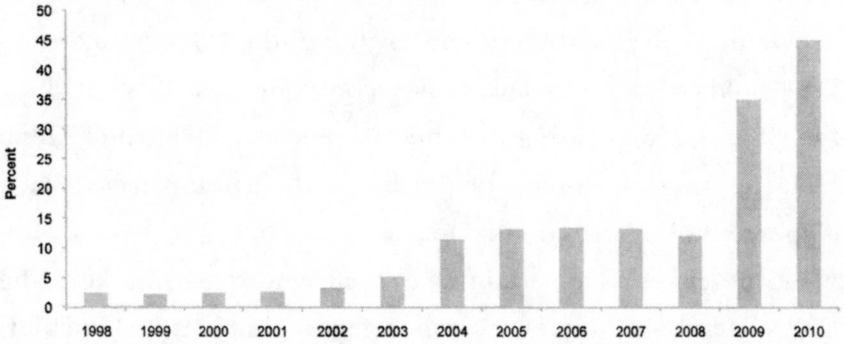

Source: Mortgage Bankers Association, Bank of America Merrill Lynch

Reinventing the Fallen

Given the big mess the GSEs got themselves into, the Obama administration's long-term working plans to reinvent fallen mortgage goliaths Fannie Mae and Freddie Mac—and the entire mortgage finance system—include a phased-out role for government. The mortgage finance debate is highly contentious because it requires a complete reexamination of whether the government should subsidize homeownership in America. The debate is basically whether the United States should continue to promote a low-cost, thirty-year, fixed-rate mortgage, which often requires some type of government guarantee (subsidy) to make investors buy mortgage-backed securities.[21]

Such long-term, prime loans have always been popular with consumers, and it's possible that the rates on mortgages would be higher if it weren't for government backing. The administration's massive support for a government guarantee underscores its preference for a housing finance system where thirty-year fixed-rate loans are readily available.

Getting the government entirely out of the US mortgage market would, of course, have major consequences. If we include the GSEs together with government agencies such as the Federal Housing Administration, the government currently backs nearly 90 percent of new residential loans.

Another key issue pertaining to the US mortgage market is the GSE's defaults on single-family mortgages. That is, if such defaults stabilize, Fannie and Freddie would post fewer reserves and could see their losses decline, making it easier and quicker for the government to phase-out these outdated mortgage behemoths (see figure 9-3).

Figure 9-3: Fannie Mae and Freddie Mac Single-Family Non-performing Assets

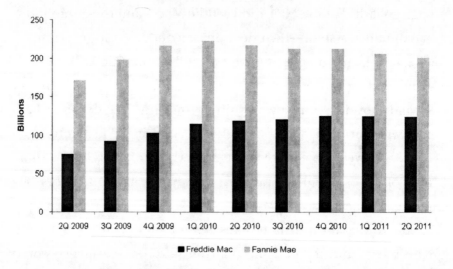

Source: Fannie Mae and Freddie Mac

Chris and Barney Do Washington

When Congress passed the monstrous Dodd-Frank Wall Street Reform and Consumer Protection Act in the summer of 2010, it was clear that surprises were lurking in its 848 pages. It could be years before the real estate sector feels the full impact of its across-the-board financial reforms as federal regulators transform the lengthy law into specific, workable standards and regulations. But these things don't happen overnight because there are so many different interests to consider. I would also like to point out that Dodd-Frank, which entails launching 122 oversight panels and offices, is very much a moving target, and in 2011 many of its measures were still being modified. In addition, with a Republican-majority House of Representatives, portions of the sweeping Dodd-Frank act may even be rolled back.

The measure, proposed by then-Senate Banking Committee chairman Chris Dodd and Congressman Barney Frank, is intended to correct a slew of conditions that contributed to the financial crisis, including systemic risk in the banking system, predatory lending, and the risk retention requirements for securitized lending related to mortgage-backed securities (MBSs). Dodd-Frank's crucial innovation was to recognize the shadow banking system (discussed in chapter 2) as an enormous source of systemic risk, and to provide regulatory tools to mitigate the problem. Without doubt, Dodd-Frank could prompt extensive changes to the control structures of financial institutions for some time.

In 2011, federal banking agencies and the SEC proposed regulations requiring issuers of MBSs (or in certain cases the originators of the underlying debt) to retain an economic interest in the credit risk for securitized assets. Although the final regulations should become effective in 2013, securitized loan documentation has already begun to reflect some of the new requirements.[22]

More specifically, the Dodd-Frank act requires loan securitizers and originators to retain not less than 5 percent of the credit risk for an underlying asset, or less than 5 percent if the originator meets stipulated underwriting standards (with exceptions). As I discuss in detail in chapter 10, the new "5 percent rule" is intended to promote improved underwriting and to better align the risks of the investor and the debt originator. In other words, if the originator is required to hold a portion of the debt, it can be assumed that the originator will look more closely at the underwriting—a good thing compared to what was going on in the run-up to the crisis. In addition, if the asset does not perform, the originator's return (like that of the securitization investor) will be adversely affected, thus assuring an alignment of interests. As such, the risk retention mandate, commonly known as skin in the game, is a vital component of Dodd-Frank and an urgently needed directive for the US financial system. Like many of the new law's provisions, however, the risk retention mandate must still be worked into a set of rules before it can be implemented.

———

A new Office of Credit Ratings, planned to be created within the SEC through Dodd-Frank but put on hold in 2011, was intended to promote greater transparency and reduce conflicts of interest among rating agencies. Therefore, the market unfortunately continues to remain wholly dependent on the idiocy of credit ratings. Absent pre-crisis active regulation, the rating agencies had, of course, misrated residential mortgaged-backed securities en masse.

Regrettably, the license of the SEC-approved Nationally Recognized Statistical Rating Organizations still grants the credit raters a carte blanche of government-approved oligopolistic power. Without an Office of Credit Ratings, they continue to operate under only the lightest of regulation and are exposed to only negligible legal liability for any further damages that they cause.

For trust to return, the US market needs to be sure it's relying on objective rating sources. After such a shock to the system, it may require active regulation and supervision of rating processes to encourage confidence that ratings are no longer being inflated. This is a serious fallacy in the US financial system that has yet to be fully addressed by regulators. The change that would help is to assist the rating agencies to actually become independent. That would entail ending the model whereby they are compensated by companies to rate their instruments and by clients to access the research. Either the rating agencies continue to be paid to generate ratings but the research is then made freely to *all*, or they are not paid to generate the research but live from the sale of the research to end-users.

Lastly, under the so-called Volcker rule, adopted as part of the Dodd-Frank act, federally insured banks are barred from speculating with their own money, with certain key exceptions.[23]

There is no doubt that these new rules could change the US regulatory landscape and affect the real estate sector. However, critics note that Dodd-Frank doesn't do enough to address systemic risk in the financial system, and that it penalizes *all* financial institutions for the mistakes of a few who were greedy and/or incompetent. According to a survey conducted by the Chartered Financial Analyst (CFA) Institute—the body that controls access to the upper echelons of fund management—75 percent of its members indicated that the Dodd-Frank act wouldn't help prevent another full-blown crisis, noting that the legislation relies entirely on existing regulators to recognize and then fix threats to the system, something they failed to do in the lead-up to the financial meltdown.[24]

Although Dodd-Frank does a pretty good job of addressing some important issues that didn't lead to the financial crisis, like proxy access (giving shareholders a meaningful voice in corporate board elections), a number of CFA Institute members believe that it falls short of what's needed to effectively supervise and regulate the US financial system. For example, it doesn't address the government-sponsored enterprises Fannie Mae and Freddie Mac, which, according to 57 percent of the survey's respondents, is a significant weakness.[25]

———

The meltdown exposed obvious failures in the previous regulatory framework of the US financial system—notably the lack of a formal "resolution authority" allowing regulators to wind down systemically dangerous firms in an orderly way. Although the newly established Financial Stability Oversight Council now has the power to wind down financial firms and any other companies deemed systemically "relevant," critics note that it's led by the US Treasury and lacks political independence. Moreover, the extent of the authority of the Fed and the Treasury in guaranteeing the assets and liabilities of failing institutions is unclear, which leaves open the whole issue of "too big to fail."[26]

New systemic risks will always develop, so "Mr. Market" can't be relied on to control all the risks. The US financial system needs a new regulatory body to gather information and decide where it is in the cycle and where risk is brewing. The Fed is supposed to manage systemic risk, but it's also expected to stimulate the economy, two mandates that are fundamentally conflicted.

The United States needs to create a new federal agency similar to the National Transportation Safety Board, which has no regulatory responsibility. Rather, it would sift through the "crash site" and can openly criticize, while not being obliged to any entity.[27] My hope is that the newly created Office of Financial Research has the potential to greatly improve the ability to identify and monitor mounting systemic bubbles. But to be truly effective, such an agency must be populated with individuals with unrestrained authority to investigate and make recommendations they deem appropriate, and who are completely independent of the all-powerful political-financial complex—Wall Street, the Fed, Congress, and the White House.

———

In sum, investor uncertainty could be replaced by regulations that are unrealistic in their execution. The United States is in for a long, slow recovery as mortgage liquidity in the property sector crawls along with moderate growth. But above all, financial regulators and policymakers must ensure that the new rules provide a framework for a lasting real estate recovery—not just a hodgepodge of rules that cause confusion in the marketplace.

Quantitative Laxatives

Quantitative easing, pumping big-time money into the economy through the purchase of Treasuries, provides a method for the Fed to increase the monetary supply, drive down long-term interest rates to support economic growth, and combat deflationary forces.

The first round of quantitative easing, nicknamed QE1, covered the period from January 2009 to March 2010, and involved the purchase of approximately $1.4 trillion of mortgage-backed securities and Treasuries.[28] (This didn't include the Troubled Asset Relief Program, or TARP, stimulus package, which amounted to $2 trillion). To give credit where it's due, these massive stimulus efforts did hold off a collapse of the US economy and had the visible impact of improving stock prices as well as reducing the borrowing rates for homeowners and commercial property investors.

In November 2010, the Federal Open Market Committee announced plans for a second round of quantitative easing, or QE2, which called for the repurchase of an additional $600 billion of long-term Treasuries that ended in June 2011. The result from this move was that interest rates have continued their low levels, just as they did following QE1. One reason for that is sustained demand from foreign investors led by central banks of countries including China with large trade surpluses that want to recycle their foreign currency holdings into US Treasuries. As long as the growth in their reserves continues, then foreign sponsorship of Treasuries is likely to last.

The Inflation Game

The current low interest rate environment, which won't last for long, should help real estate owners refinance and to increase their property returns at a time when rents continue to decrease with lease expirations due to the ongoing weakness in office and retail segment fundamentals.

The goal of QE1 and QE2 was to manage inflation. In fact, the consumer price index was forecast to increase by 3 percent in 2011, which is slightly above the Fed's target rate of 2 percent because of high food and gas prices.

Another benefit from inflation is that it should help the net operating incomes of real estate assets to recover, which will be good for both performing and underwater properties. It may also help lenders sell their problem loans at close to par value, taking more real estate out of the extend-and-pretend bog (discussed in chapter 7), which tends to make it difficult for players at all ends of the investment spectrum to reconcile where property values actually lie.

As shown in figure 9-4, the US monetary base (the sum of currency in circulation plus reserve balances held by the Fed) has been exhibiting an unprecedented increase due to the government's huge stimulus efforts. This massive increase in money supply will, sooner or later, increase the inflation rate.

Figure 9-4: US Monetary Base

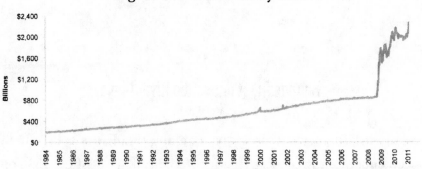

Source: Federal Reserve Bank of St. Louis

However, dousing the system with liquidity and printing money for stimulus programs will not put the US economy back on track. There needs to be sustained economic growth and a return to pre-2008 consumer confidence levels (see figure 9-5) to fill vacant property space and make the cash registers ring again. Owners of office, retail, and hotel properties draw upon both consumers and businesses as their customers. The businesses that occupy office buildings and book rooms in hotels, as well as retailers, in turn, depend upon consumers whose spending accounts for close to 70 percent of GDP. One way or another, American real estate is heavily dependent on consumers.

Figure 9-5: US Consumer Confidence Index

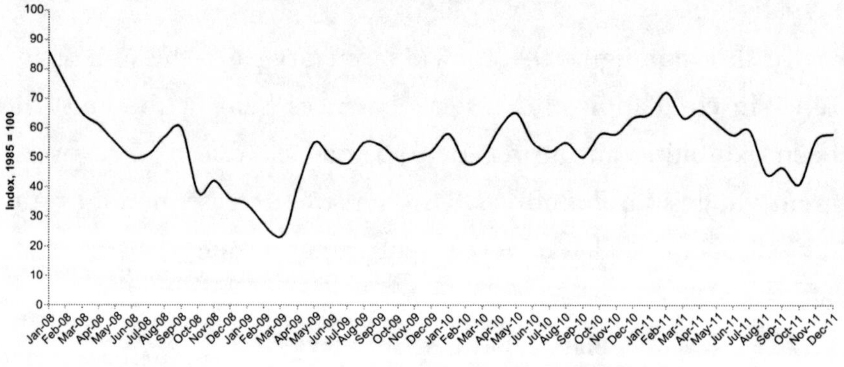

Source: The Conference Board

Hammering it out on the River Rhine

Before the financial crisis, global banking regulators had actually been encouraging banks to securitize their loans, pushing risks off their balance sheets.[29] This attitude was also codified in a series of agreements known as the Basel Accords, named for the Swiss city located on the River Rhine in which they were first hammered out.[30] For centuries, Basel has been the site of peace negotiations and international meetings. Banking is also extremely important to this sophisticated city; Union Bank of Switzerland (UBS) maintains its central offices in Basel, giving finance a pivotal role in the local economy. In addition, the Bank for International Settlements (BIS), known as the "central banker's bank," is located there. The BIS is composed of the elite central bankers of eleven different industrialized countries (the US, UK, Belgium, Canada, France, Germany, Italy, Japan, the Netherlands, Sweden, and Switzerland).

The first Basel Accord on minimum capital standards for banks was reached in 1988 and implemented globally during the 1990s. Later on, Basel II provided much more comprehensive guidelines and was implemented during the early 2000s.[31] In response to the financial crisis of 2008, which pushed several institutions to the verge of collapse (and a handful beyond), new rules have been drawn up by global financial regulators to improve the stability of banks and, therefore, prevent a rerun of the meltdown.

Where regulation of banking is concerned, the devil is always in the detail. Under the conditions of Basel III, the biggest banks will have to hold 9.5 percent of their capital as equity reserves, instead of holding "insurance" equivalent to just 2 percent of their risk-bearing assets as was mandated under Basel II, which to date has allowed banks to hold nearly fifty times more in riskier assets than their core Tier 1 capital ratio.[32]

As noted, institutions deemed "systematically important" will be forced to hold up to 9.5 percent in capital reserves.[33] The new capital reserve rules—to be rolled out in stages between 2013 and 2019—should cushion the banking sector from another meltdown and require lenders to have more skin in the game. But time will tell if Basel III actually delivers what it promises.

Conclusion

Part of the Fed's mandate is to foster maximum employment and price stability, so doing nothing would be incompatible with this thorny obligation. But going overboard with intervention programs and bailouts contributes to the already-astronomical national debt. In other words, government intervention isn't a bad thing, but it should not be excessive.

The missed assessment of real estate debt risk in the period leading up to the recent crisis stemmed, in part, from antici-pated government or central bank intervention in markets, like a spoiled rotten kid who knows that daddy will always give him more money to spend even when the kid screws up. Market opera-tors who become overly dependent on the government's largesse breed complacency, incompetence, and mediocrity.

———

All financial crises are caused by too much leverage. It appears that the US financial system has a very short-term memory and doesn't learn much from its previous colossal mistakes. For example, the recent crisis had many similarities to the S&L fiasco of the late 1980s, in which a banking system welcoming deregulation decided to capi-talize on a massive, debt-financed real estate boom without much concern about the downside. That's because the players expected the government to intervene when financial hell broke loose.

S&Ls made far too many risky commercial real estate loans that were backed by unqualified assets. Another major issue was banks and thrifts loading up on "junk bonds" that were rated much too high. This is similar to the rating agencies completely missing the boat on the recent financial crisis, labeling collateralized debt obligations (CDOs) with halcyon AAA ratings.

The essence of free-enterprise capitalism is the freedom to fail as well as to succeed, not a system that depends on government backstops to automatically bailout greed and incompetence in an orgy of risk taking.[34] Ideas about new regulations are usually popular in the aftermath of a crisis but tend to be whittled away as the memories of the crisis fade. So it is better to implement strict, long-term regulations and get it right once and for all than to err again and again.[35]

One can view the history of American capital markets as a never-ending search for an elixir that insulates financial services institutions from the risk of instability. But dysfunctional, destructive market behavior is unavoidable because it's part of human nature. For every regulatory action, there is an equally opposite reaction by most market participants. The high-risk behavior doesn't go away, it just goes somewhere else.

If we look closely at the cunning financial products that were created by some very smart people—CDOs, CDSs, and so on—a defining feature was that they were intended to exploit loopholes in the US legal system. "Innovation" was therefore about dancing on the edge of laws, regulations, and ratings—but probably not *breaking* any laws. Indeed, the biggest banks typically hired armies of lawyers to ensure that the letter of the law was respected, even as the spirit was perverted in the most creative of ways.[36] Therefore, the US has to aim for a system that tightens such loopholes—in which no private institution has implicit or explicit protections provided by the government, one in which every private institution that makes serious mistakes knows it will have to bear the full financial costs of those mistakes.[37] We may not be able to predict the future, but we should incentivize caution as a general matter.

Despite the trillions of dollars injected by the government into the financial system, the economy continues to be dangerously over-leveraged and suffers from an anxious financial sector with hardly any skin in the game. The US economy still needs to fully escape from the swamp that is the burst mortgage bubble that created a number of unresolved problems for post-crisis real estate in America. These unresolved problems are the focus of the next chapters.

Chapter 10: The Seeds of Risk

*All parties need to have skin in the game. If mortgage
originators don't have a financial interest in the loan, they
will have less concern for its quality, and poor lending decisions
will happen and be passed along to investors.*
—John Stumpf, CEO, Wells Fargo

In real estate finance, skin in the game holds that lending quality is improved when those who offer mortgages must have a loss risk on the loan products they sell to investors. In turn, requiring the borrower to have skin in the game (equity capital) reduces the risk for the lender. Retention of even modest loss exposure by loan originators also reduces moral hazard, or the change in incentives that arises when individuals or institutions don't bear the full consequences of—or the responsibility for—their actions.

Before the financial crisis, originators of acquisition and development loans for apartments had been taking 5 percent first-loss positions for years. In addition, banks that originated non-recourse loans on their balance sheets took on all the loss risk for their mortgages. Only single-family residential and mortgage-backed security (MBS) loan originators, who were at the epicenter of the financial maelstrom, were not taking any. That tells us that skin in the game is a necessity for the long-term success and stability of the US financial markets.

The shifting of first-loss risk to loan originators would have made them much more risk averse in the recent go-go period of hyper-increasing real estate prices. Moreover, and in what was an iterative frenzy, low credit-quality borrowers would not have participated in the last boom and bust cycle if first-loss exposures to originators of single-family residential loans and MBSs were in place.

———

One of the main reasons that subprime and Alt-A loans proliferated was because of the very low default and loss rates on these loans from 2003 to 2006, propped by artificially high housing prices. Further, investors in these mortgages originally speculated that prices would continue to either increase or stay the same as when originated, keeping default and loss rates initially low on such poor credit-quality mortgages. Lending standards on subprime mortgages were weak because subprime lending standards were lax to start with. Put another way, poor credit quality begets poor loan performance, which begets high default rates.

When prices became unsustainable and began to fall for single-family homes in August 2006, subprime and Alt-A mortgages later collapsed because high loan-to-value ratios were excessively relied upon to support such debt instruments, not just because of the credit weakness of borrowers. Most subprime and Alt-A borrowers assumed that in the event they couldn't afford their home, they could just sell it and participate in the upside equity created.

The Origin of the Species

The dangers of unbridled capitalism are deeply embedded in the American no-skin-in-the-game way of doing business, which proliferated during the 1980s era of "greed is good" and insatiable lust for leveraged buyouts (LBOs).

The scene in the 1987 film *Wall Street*, when Lou Mannheim (played by Hal Holbrook) offers a warning to the young Bud Fox (Charlie Sheen), epitomizes the dangers of LBOs: "The main thing about money, Bud—it makes you do things you don't want to do."

LBOs also remind me of the 1993 movie *Barbarians at the Gate*, based on the true story when CEO Ross Johnson made plans in 1988 to buy out the rest of RJR Nabisco after seeing the results of the failure of Premier, the company's smokeless cigarette. The drama unfolds as Johnson's character initially discusses doing the LBO with Kohlberg Kravis Roberts & Company (KKR), but attempts to use Shearson Lehman Hutton instead. In this case, excessive pride and greed was involved and the drama ends with an inflated buyout price ($25 billion) and an incredible debt load.

———

Novelist Tom Wolfe coined the term "Me decade" in his article "The 'Me Decade' and the Third Great Awakening," published by *New York* magazine in 1976 referring to the 1970s. The term described a new attitude of Americans toward "atomized individualism" and away from "communitarianism," in clear contrast with the swinging 1960s.

The seeds of modern-day LBOs were sown in the 1970s, when Michael Milken, the infamous trader at Drexel Burnham Lambert, had the insight that junk bonds—debt instruments that were rated below investment-grade by the rating agencies and later sugar coated as "high-yield" bonds—were generally underpriced, either because investors had an irrational aversion to them or because they lacked a liquid market in which to trade.[1]

Milken capitalized on that market inefficiency, building an operation that dominated the trading and sales of junk bonds. By creating a large, liquid market for junk bonds—which grew from $6 billion in 1970 to $210 billion in 1989—he made it much easier for companies to raise money and opened up new ways for investment banks to generate profits by underwriting, trading, and selling these formerly neglected instruments.[2] Equally important, investor demand for higher-yield, higher-risk bonds remained strong—ultimately driving the recent boom in mortgage-backed securities, especially as returns on Treasuries fell to historic lows in the past decade.[3]

In addition, by making it easy to raise large amounts of money quickly, junk bonds made the LBO craze of the 1980s possible, in which vigilante buyers would pay for acquisitions by issuing large amounts of new debt. Those acquisitions, in turn, generated huge fees for the investment banks that advised the companies engaged in such transactions and underwrote and sold the necessary debt. They also left companies struggling with huge debt burdens, often requiring painful restructuring that oftentimes led to bankruptcy.[4]

The LBO boom of the 1980s was fuelled by a number of über-aggressive corporate raiders, most notably Jerome Kohlberg, and later his protégé Henry Kravis. Working for Bear Stearns at the time, Kohlberg and Kravis, along with Kravis' cousin George Roberts (who together founded KKR in 1976) began a series of what they described as "bootstrap" investments, a collection of methods used to minimize the amounts of equity needed from outside investors. Many of the targeted companies lacked a viable or attractive exit for their founders, as they were too small to be taken public and the founders were reluctant to sell out to competitors. Therefore, a sale to a financial buyer proved very attractive.

Several LBOs in the 1980s and later in the 1990s resulted in corporate bankruptcies. In 1990, Federated Department Stores, which at the time was under the control of Canadian financier Robert Campeau, went bankrupt after its hostile takeover of Allied Stores. Federated emerged from bankruptcy after the ouster of Campeau in 1992 as a new company and took over Macy's in 1994. The failure of the Federated buyout was a result of excessive debt financing, comprising about 97 percent of the total acquisition price, which led to large interest payments exceeding the company's operating cash flow. In response to the threat of LBOs, some companies adopted a number of techniques such as the "poison pill" to protect themselves against hostile takeovers by effectively self-destructing if taken over.

More recently, Blackstone Group bought Equity Office Properties Trust in 2007 for $39 billion, the largest LBO deal ever done by a single firm. Blackstone immediately flipped most of Equity Office's buildings to other buyers (who borrowed as much as 90 percent of the purchase price), many of whom took significant losses as the commercial real estate market cratered in 2008.[5]

———

An LBO is basically a transaction in which a publicly held company's stock is purchased by a group of investors through a negotiated deal or a tender offer. The company is then no longer publicly traded, but becomes a private or "closely held" firm owned by investors who are frequently the firm's management. The investor group gets the money to buy the stock by contributing a very small amount of their own equity and borrowing the rest (no skin in the game). The amount borrowed can turn out to be more than 95 percent of capital; hence, the term "leveraged" buyout. The borrowed funds usually come from asset-based financing, meaning that the loans are secured by a firm's own assets. Some courts have found that LBO debt constitutes a fraudulent transfer under US insolvency law if it is determined to be the cause of the acquired firm's failure.[6]

LBOs are risky because of the high debt burden placed on the firm after the change in ownership. For example, a firm has no debt but has $100 million in equity and whose stock is selling at book value (the value of an asset according to the balance sheet). Suppose that the management team purchases the stock at book value, contributing only $5 million of its own money and borrowing the rest. The firm's capital structure before and after the LBO would be as follows:

Table 10-1: LBO Capital Structure (in millions)

Source of Capital	Before LBO	After LBO
Debt	$0	$95
Equity	$100	$5
Total	**$100**	**$100**

It's important to realize that in such a scenario nothing has changed with respect to the operating ability of the company to generate money. However, the post-LBO firm has to pay interest on the debt of $95 million, making it high-risk. In such a case, the LBO is a takeover and not a merger. The company has been taken over by a group of investors but it hasn't been merged with anything. This is often a characteristic weakness of LBOs: no cushion. In other words, highly leveraged companies need realistic alternatives and more skin in the game should things take a turn for the worse.

LBOs have been criticized as ruthless profit-driven manipulations that can destroy sound companies.[7] Table 10-1 gave an indication of what is meant by this accusation. Before the LBO, the company was a conservatively financed firm, presumably with good operating prospects (otherwise the acquiring group wouldn't have been interested). After the LBO, the same firm was in serious danger of collapse under the weight of its excess debt.

Bad timing can also be deadly for LBOs. You can have a good business with a strong franchise, but if your timing isn't good, it may not matter. This lesson can be especially clear to companies in more cyclical businesses, such as retailers and hotel companies.

Another problem with LBOs is that the acquiring companies often think they'll always have access to even *more* debt, or that they'll grow beyond their current debt load. But US companies must always remember that the economy can worsen, and capital markets can quickly become frozen as we saw in 2008–09. Bottom line: it takes more than self-perceived infallibility and wishful thinking to get an LBO through such difficult periods.

History has taught that fixing a problem company by taking it private through an LBO is not a sure thing. Going private may rid a public company of those annoying shareholders who never seem to be satisfied, but dealing with a huge debt burden when a company isn't firing on all cylinders can be a much bigger issue.[8] History has also shown that adding piles of debt to a troubled company without any skin in the game is an easy way to go bankrupt.

———

In addition to LBOs, another factor that instilled the no-skin-in-the-game way of doing business was the Garn-St. Germain Depository Institutions Act, which Congress passed in 1982 during the pro-deregulation Reagan administration. Garn-St. Germain lifted many regulations on the S&L sector, allowing it to expand further into new businesses, such as commercial lending and investing in high-risk corporate bonds, namely junk bonds.

The bill also authorized state-chartered banks to offer mortgages with adjustable rates—a central feature of the last twenty-five years of change in US residential lending—and relaxed other constraints on mortgage lending for national banks.

In the early 1980s, and acting under the authorization granted by Garn-St. Germain, the Office of the Comptroller of the Currency lifted all restrictions on loan-to-value ratios (the percentage of a house's appraised value that could be borrowed), maturities (fifteen years, thirty years, etc.), and amortization schedules (meaning that banks could even offer mortgages where the principal balance went *up* and not down over time).[9]

As such, it's safe to assume that no skin in the game—originating through LBOs, the rise of Wall Street's powerful investment banks, as well as the deregulation of the US banking sector—indirectly led to the late 1980s S&L crisis and the 2008 financial meltdown.

Securitization and No Skin in the Game

The risk of exposure by subprime and Alt-A borrowers was not high after many consecutive years of house price increases. But what were subsidized mortgages for low-income owners, and which were only produced by the Federal Housing Administration (FHA), became mortgages for speculative homeowners with poor credit quality, fuelling unsustainable price increases. It's also important to remember at this juncture that the mortgage crisis was partly caused by excessive speculation risk fostered by no skin in the game and moral hazard inherent in securitization.

————

During the housing boom of the mid-2000s, the widespread securitization of residential mortgages fundamentally altered the incentives of key players in the loan origination and funding business.[10] A basic problem with the originate-to-distribute model of lending is that mortgage originators and the sponsors of MBSs had too little skin in the game.

The wave of mortgage securitizations in 2005 through 2007 is seen as one of the key culprits of the housing crisis because banks created and then sold billions of dollars of securities without conducting proper due diligence on individual loans embedded in the labyrinthine MBS pools. Banks fulfilled the obligations of the requirements of loan originators for the mortgage products sold, but the problem was the low requirements and poor credit-quality thresholds. Because of high origination volumes, the standard error rate was high and mortgage audits only became acute when losses were a significant issue. That is, too little too late.

As a result, several recent policy moves have attempted to get more securitizer skin in the game to ensure that someone is actually taking responsibility for diligent loan underwriting and monitoring. In many cases, securitization product issuers were poorly incentivized to conduct the appropriate due diligence on loan originators, including the review of financial statements, underwriting guidelines, and background checks because they had no skin in the game. In addition, they relied on the originators' own representations and warranties regarding the quality of the loans and the underwriting processes that turned out to be disastrous because the originators lacked the capital and liquidity to make good on their warranties.

According to the representations and warranties sections of MBS contracts, investors have the right to "put back" loans that fall short. That is, to obtain a refund. These "reps and warranties" have turned out to be ineffective safeguards as many investors are facing legal and procedural obstacles when analyzing original loan information to find out whether terms were breached.

Despite its shortfalls, securitization is a powerful financial tool. When properly used, it is an efficient and effective way to allocate capital to sectors of the economy that otherwise would be shut off. It also lowers the cost of capital for many investors, including homeowners. However, a lack of appropriate regulations and a lack of transparency allowed financial institutions to seriously abuse the loopholes in the system.

Single-family residential and MBS loan originators who issued mortgage loans and then sold them off had no skin in the game. They had no incentive to originate good loans, giving out bad ones instead to borrowers who were not creditworthy as long as there were eager investors ready to buy them. Banks originated MBS loans just to sell them in the securitization food chain as much and as quickly as possible—they had to feed the beast. It was the credit rating agencies that allowed this proliferation of poor quality loans, as well as the credit rating-reliant investors who continued to purchase them because of higher returns.

But why did investors buy bad loans in the first place? This is where a lack of transparency helped create the crisis of 2008. By creating opaque structures such as collateralized debt obligations (CDOs) and sick and twisted derivatives such as mezzanine CDOs and CDOs-squared, investment banks like Lehman Brothers were able to disguise the true quality of the underlying loan portfolios.

Most investors were just not sophisticated enough to evaluate these complex securities properly. Investors also bought them in large quantities out of what had to have been pure hubris and an overabundance of greed. Moreover, the rating agencies failed to conduct adequate due diligence in assessing these complicated structures, essentially misleading investors.

———

One of the biggest lessons from the US mortgage debacle is to ensure that financial intermediaries that originate loans be required to have skin in the game, meaning that they must share in future losses if those loans go bad. That is the only discipline and restraint that will ensure that financial intermediaries conduct proper due diligence on their borrowers *before* giving out loans. Furthermore, reporting and credit rating requirements must be strengthened, bringing more transparency to the US securitization food chain. Lastly, extreme complexity should be avoided in designing financial instruments, as there is almost never an economic rationale for an unnecessarily complicated financial product. The mere existence of such "smoke and mirrors" instruments should have triggered suspicion and inquiry by regulators.

As we know, many billions of dollars of losses on securities backed by subprime mortgages were at the heart of the financial crisis, as mortgage-backed bonds with AAA (or "best") ratings proved much riskier than expected and defaults soared. The losses have prompted regulators to seek to improve loan underwriting standards by forcing investors (who repackage the loans by selling them in the securitization markets) to retain skin in the game and share in any losses.

In its current form, Title IX of the Dodd-Frank Wall Street Reform and Consumer Protection Act requires securitizers to retain at least 5 percent of the credit risk associated with the loans sausaged into residential mortgage-backed securities. In addition, the legislation—which is expected to be implemented in 2013—prohibits securitizers from hedging or transferring that credit risk, although certain residential mortgages would be exempt from risk retention requirements. For example, for assets that meet new regulatory underwriting standards, the level can be below 5 percent. The new regulation could also prohibit the direct or indirect hedging of the risk required to be retained. The new rule might impose minimum risk retention periods as well, despite opposition from securitization market players.[11]

In 2011, Congress had left the risk retention mandate open to fine-tuning by regulators due to the urging of real estate sector participants who have stressed the need for flexibility in restructuring loan securitizations. The key is that there should be an alignment of interests with the sponsors of mortgage-backed securities and the buyers of bonds. There is no disagreement on that issue, but *how* that alignment exists has been the subject of much discussion and debate. Real estate lenders will wait to see the impact of the new rule before they consider easing the purse strings on new debt financing. But whatever the proposed Dodd-Frank risk retention rule ends up being, care must be taken to ensure that the rule would not impair the functioning of the US securitization markets as viable funding and capital management tools (i.e., the duplication of or conflict with risk retention requirements in other jurisdictions). Moreover, retention should only be required where necessary and appropriate, and not applied in a uniform way. Risk retention requirements should also focus on problematic asset classes and not take a one-size-fits-all approach. In this still-weak economic environment, credit should not be arbitrarily denied in *all* sectors of the securitization markets because of the excesses in limited sectors. It is hoped, of course, that the end result is more skin in the game and that more will have changed than will have stayed the same.

Affordable Disadvantage

"Buy new with $1,000 down," the advertisement says. "The time has come. Stop wasting rent check after rent check and start building equity in your own home *now*. And with only $1,000 down, affordable monthly payments and no private mortgage insurance required, the dream is closer than you think!"[12]

It sounds too good to be true in the post-crisis US housing market, but it *is* true. The advertisement references a program that was initiated by the National Council of State Housing Agencies (NCSHA) and Fannie Mae, the taxpayer-backed government-sponsored enterprise. The program was misleadingly called "Affordable Advantage" and it was officially adopted by several states, including Idaho, Massachusetts, Minnesota, and Wisconsin.

Given the proven dangers of these types of mortgages and the ghost of the financial crisis when unconventional loans wreaked disaster, it's worrying to see such programs surface once again.

There are major concerns and problems related to purchasing a home with almost no money down. Foremost, if the housing market turns negative even a small amount, the homeowner will go underwater immediately, owing more on the mortgage than the house is worth. If he needs to sell it, he needs to come up with extra cash to pay the bank back.

Although discontinued by Fannie Mae in March 2011, the program seemed contradictory in its fundamental premise. The buyers in the Affordable Advantage program had no skin in the game from the start and no guarantee that their homes wouldn't have lost value over the first year. Didn't the regulators learn from the recent crisis? What were they thinking?

Our Big Fat FHA Dilemma

With US banks reluctant to make loans to riskier homebuyers, the government is using the FHA to make home mortgages more accessible. However, in doing so, the government is insuring billions upon billions of additional housing debt with potentially disastrous effects.

Created by the National Housing Act of 1934, the FHA insures private mortgage lenders against borrower default on residential real estate loans (the FHA doesn't actually issue mortgages). Its current allure is that it opens the door to prospective homebuyers who almost certainly wouldn't qualify for a conventional home mortgage. These are buyers with no credit history, a history of credit problems, or not enough cash to cover a sufficient down payment.

The FHA is the largest insurer of loans for first-time buying of existing and new homes in the world, and it insures 30 percent of all US home mortgages.[13] In fiscal year 2010, the FHA insured nearly 1.7 million single-family mortgages totaling more than $329 billion.

Loan applications must meet certain requirements to qualify for FHA mortgage insurance. The insurance reduces the lender's risk by protecting the lender against losses that could result from defaults by homeowners. Homeowners pay a mortgage insurance premium into the FHA Mutual Mortgage Insurance Fund, and the US Department of Housing and Urban Development—which oversees the FHA—uses those premiums to operate the program. The FHA fund pays claims to lenders in the event of a homeowner default on the mortgage.

Loans that are FHA-insured are pooled and packaged into mortgage-backed securities by the Government National Mortgage Association (Ginnie Mae). A handmaiden of the FHA, Ginnie Mae insures the actual MBS pools composed of FHA loans. Its securities are the only MBSs backed by the full faith and credit (read: largesse) of the US government.

Because Fannie Mae and Freddie Mac securities are only *implicitly* guaranteed, banks that hold these securities as assets on their balance sheets must "haircut"—or set aside any reserves—based on a 20 percent risk weighting assigned to the value of those holdings. On the other hand, because Ginnie Maes are *explicitly* 100 percent guaranteed, they are considered "risk-free," on par with US Treasury bonds. However, there is no reserve requirement (haircut) on Ginnie Mae securities. By replacing their asset mix and holding Ginnie Maes, banks don't have to set aside any reserves. They can use the money they otherwise would have set aside to actually lever-up their balance sheets. On top of that, they are buying even more Ginnie Maes.

The effect of such an "asset swap"—basically one toxic pool for a replacement that's not much better—creates the illusion that banks have healthier balance sheets and that they're meeting their reserve requirements. But it's all a façade.[14] Capital ratios are being manipulated and banks that are over-leveraged and over-stuffed with junk debt are basically being propped.

The danger of relying on the FHA to prop the shaky housing market by facilitating mortgage originations, modifications, and refinancings to less-than-stellar borrowers will only result in more subprime loans being stockpiled on the Fed's balance sheet. Eventually, delinquencies could overwhelm the FHA and the hoped-for floor in residential real estate pricing could be prolonged.

American taxpayers, always the lowly minstrels holding the spit buckets, are already in place with the safety nets. Taxpayers will catch the FHA loans because they insure private lenders against low credit-quality borrowers with no skin in the game. In addition, taxpayers will also have to catch the buyers of Ginnie Maes because they guarantee MBSs in what can be described as a gigantic debt-binging loop.

———

Fannie Mae and Freddie Mac, which extend the vast majority of their loans to investors in the apartment segment, borrow guaranteed funds from the US government on the cheap through the Community Reinvestment Act mandate, and then spend it on buying mortgages in the secondary market. Along with the FHA, they guarantee more than 90 percent of new home loans in the United States. The dilemma is that the market is so dependent on the housing finance agencies that the government cannot quickly withdraw its massive support (which is one reason to expect the proposed winding down of Fannie and Freddie to be slow).

The FHA was essentially a non-factor in causing the housing boom, but its standards for providing mortgage insurance have recently been extremely slack. When the housing market finally seized up in 2007, the FHA made a determined effort to keep mortgage lending from completely drying up (see figure 10-1). In fiscal 2010, there were close to 550,000 FHA-insured homes that were delinquent ninety days or more, a figure that has been rising steadily for three years.[15] However, a report issued jointly by the Office of the Comptroller of the Currency and the Office of Thrift Supervision revealed that 67 percent of those modified FHA mortgages were in default *again* within twelve months.[16] Sooner or later, US taxpayers will be fully at risk with more than $898 billion in FHA-insured mortgages. In addition, banks will have to foreclose and convey to the FHA the hundreds of thousands of homes that are currently seriously delinquent.[17]

Figure 10-1: FHA's Percent Share of 1-to 4-Family Home Mortgage Originations

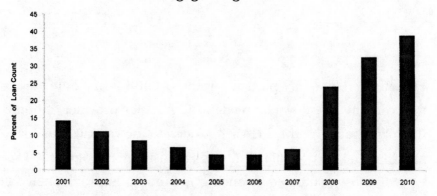

Source: US Department of Housing and Urban Development (HUD), Federal Housing Administration (FHA)

The FHA's $898 billion (and counting) insured-loan portfolio has been mostly packaged and securitized by Ginnie Mae, the wholly owned US government corporation. According to Lender Processing Services, the "cure rate" for such seriously delinquent mortgages has plunged to 1 percent, meaning that *99 percent* of these delinquent mortgages are headed for default and likely to be followed by a foreclosure (see figure 10-2).

Figure 10-2: Cure Rate of Seriously Delinquent FHA-Insured Mortgages

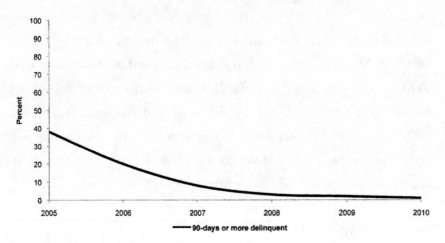

Source: Lender Processing Services (LPS), Amherst Securities Group

---

FHA-insured loans are particularly important for first-time buyers who can only put down a tiny deposit. A major provider of home financing today is the FHA's 3.5 percent down payment loan, known as the Section 203(b) Mortgage Insurance Program.[18] This type of thirty-year fixed financing is funding approximately 23 percent of all FHA-insured, single-family loans in the US today.

So first-time buyers in the US can purchase homes with FHA-backed loans with very little down. It sounds great, but is this really a smart idea? Isn't the lack of down payments one of the reasons we have so many owners being foreclosed upon today? Buying with practically nothing down is not good public policy, is not good for lenders, is dangerous for mortgage investors, and is very risky for borrowers. Should Americans worry about FHA loans with little down? Yes, of course they should worry because buying with hardly anything down does not suggest dealing with purchasers who have good financial capacity. If something goes wrong, such buyers can quickly be underwater. Moreover, when there's little or no equity, the option of selling without a loss is gone.

Borrowers applying for an FHA-insured mortgage with a minimum 3.5 percent down payment are required to have a FICO score of only 580 (even though 580 is considered high-risk).[19] Common sense dictates that the FHA is enabling too many people with shaky finances to get loans and in effect indirectly contributing to a potential repeat of the errors that caused the financial crisis.

Granted, the FHA program is important to the housing market because it enables people with modest incomes to buy homes—people who otherwise would probably be turned away by banks. Further support for that argument is that if loan originators were required to take a first–loss position on these mortgages, these products would not be available today, which would create instability in the single-family residential sector. It can also be argued that job losses and broader economic deterioration that made borrowers more vulnerable are primarily responsible for rising defaults. However, because their initial investment is so modest these borrowers have little incentive to stay in their homes if they are hit by a job loss or by a further drop in home values. One has to ask: Have we not figured out what got us here in the first place, and are we going to make sure we don't replicate a failed system?

Figure 10-3 shows the percentage of loans that were current at the beginning of 2007, 2008, 2009, and 2010, and ninety or more days delinquent or in foreclosure at the end of January of each of the four years (by type of loan). As indicated, the percentage of FHA-backed loans is the highest, increasing from approximately 3 percent in 2007 to nearly 8.4 percent (and counting) in 2010.

Figure 10-3: Percent of Seriously Delinquent Loans by Type

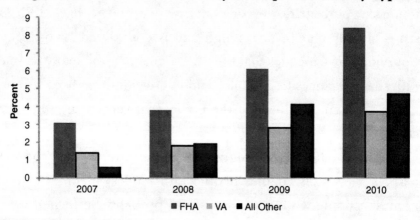

Source: Lender Processing Services (LPS)

———

Analysts often track loans made in a particular year, or "vintage," to better gauge the future performance of an entire product type

of mortgages. FHA-backed loans (including refinancings) that
had been originated thirty-five months from their origination at
the beginning of 2006 had a serious delinquency rate of close to
15 percent, while in 2007 the loans that were originated thirty-five
months prior had a much higher serious delinquency rate of close
to 22 percent (see figure 10-4). In 2008, the delinquency metric
increased to 23 percent after thirty-five months from origination.
The 2009 vintage of FHA-backed loans had a serious delinquency
rate of close to 7 percent, but indicated a sharp upward curve after
just twenty months from origination, while 2010 vintage loans
exhibited an upward curve after just eight months of origination.

Figure 10-4: FHA Serious Delinquency Rate by Vintage (All Loans)

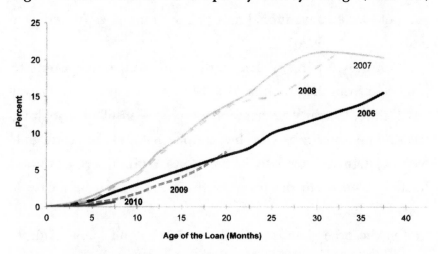

Source: US Department of Housing and Urban Development (HUD)

It's worth noting that FHA loans that are seriously delinquent
do not necessarily all head into foreclosure, with data pointing
that approximately 40 percent of all such delinquent loans actually get foreclosed.[20] Regardless, these are indications that FHA-
backed mortgages are high-risk, especially those involving 3.5

percent down payments. Moreover, the rising delinquency rates illustrate the challenges that face the FHA as one of the last backers of mortgages with extremely low down payments. It seems that the FHA is caught up in a time warp and is still infatuated with the go-go mid-2000s.

One proposed solution to the agency's troubles backed by Republican New Jersey Congressman Scott Garrett and others is to raise the minimum down payment on FHA loans to 5 percent. Backers believe that would encourage borrowers to stay in their homes and not let them fall into foreclosure. But even 5 percent is way too low as a down payment. Another insufficient effort to support lending and "sustainable homeownership" is Freddie Mac's reduction of the maximum loan-to-value ratio requirement to 95 percent for all conventional mortgages it purchases (which went into effect in June 2011).

With only 5 percent skin in the game, can homeowners be protected from the potential risks of negative equity if home values decline? Does just a 5 percent equity stake instill pride of long-term homeownership? Has the paraphernalia of the credit bubble not taught US regulators any lessons? Without serious reform related to sufficient down payments, it could soon be a case of "here we go again."

On the other hand, the delinquency rate of loans made to apartment investors and developers, which are underwritten with low loan-to-value ratios (with more skin in the game) are extremely low. Figure 10-5 shows Fannie Mae-purchased apartment loans and mortgage-backed securities that are ninety days or more past due. Between 2006 and 2010, these apartment loans and MBSs had delinquency rates below *1 percent*.

Figure 10-5: Fannie Mae Apartment Loans
(Serious Delinquency Rate)

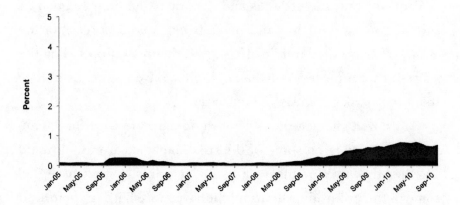

Source: Fannie Mae. Includes loans and securities ninety days or more past due.

Conclusion

In the years leading up to the crisis, lenders could hand off loans (many of them high-risk) to other companies for a fee. Without skin in the game, they could continue to make risky loans galore. As such, properly aligned economic incentives are the best check against careless underwriting. Risk retention will help promote better standards for underwriting and securitizing mortgages which is needed for the long-term health of the US housing market.

In addition, lack of skin in the game promoted systemic risk on both Main Street and Wall Street. Although better than nothing, the 5 percent (or risk retention) rule proposed by Dodd-Frank is just a drop in the bucket. To avert a repetition of the crisis, the agents involved must have a better alignment of interests, so the risk retention rule (which is expected to be implemented in 2013) isn't more symbolic than substantive.

But why only target MBSs and real estate lending? Regulators should go a step further and make banks hold 5 percent of the equity of their initial public offerings. If the institution selling the shares keeps a piece of the game, it gives buyers some assurance that their stock purchase will make sense.

Moreover, clients would be more prepared to trust fund managers if they took on some of the risk. Managers are usually paid whether the investor makes a profit or a loss. If they accepted some of the downside, clients might have more faith in their fund managers. For example, a client invests $200,000. If the fund managers produce a decent return on that money, they collect a percentage of the profit. On the other hand, if the fund fails to return the original $200,000, the managers pay the investor a percentage of the loss. This way the fund managers have put some money where their mouths are and are sharing in the risk. This should moderate the more excessive claims of some investment funds and force managers to be more realistic about what they can achieve, boosting investor confidence. It could also eliminate some of the worst performing funds from the thousands operating in the overcrowded capital markets arena. This needn't apply only to fund managers. All the advisors who take a fee or commission for recommending investment products would win more esteem from their clients if they shared some of the risk. If they really want to win the trust of investors, they need to have skin in the game.

———

Critics of the Dodd-Frank act's 5 percent rule (mostly lenders, mortgage brokers, and real estate agents) claim that the capital available for mortgage lending will shrink, and skin in the game will act as a brake on property lending and economic activity. They also claim that skin in the game is "death by a thousand cuts" and that it will limit financial institutions' abilities to diversify their asset holdings. That is, the institutions will be required to retain mortgages and will not be able to decrease that asset class to diversify their lending risk. But the truth is that those who can no longer do things that they have found extraordinarily profitable vigorously object when told to stop.

In my view, the long-term benefits of having more skin in the game far outweigh the costs. US banks used to be really careful about whom they lent money to because their own money was on the line. Over the years, banks and mortgage lenders started making MBS loans that were sold to thousands of "faceless" investors, and when that happened some lenders became more like sleazy salespeople. Dodgy mortgage brokers and loan officers also got their commissions regardless of whether a loan was good or bad. They basically didn't give a crap, and in most cases they cared little for the credit fundamentals of borrowers. All they cared about was getting their big bonuses.

A lender doesn't care as much about the riskiness of a loan or the eventual likelihood of default if he's going to sell it and not retain any risk. Single-family residential and MBS lenders didn't have skin in the game because they were not lending homebuyers their own money. Although housing lending was once primarily done by banks, the process of securitization came to dominate the residential and commercial property markets. In the mid-2000s, this way of doing business took away the incentive of lenders and others to properly scrutinize borrowers and helped lead to the real estate meltdown that struck across the financial system and caused the worst recession since the Great Depression.

No skin in the game has been a serious problem in the US financial system since the proliferation of LBOs in the 1980s and 1990s, but the Dodd-Frank act—albeit not without its glitches and imperfections—should have a positive influence on the future of the real estate sector. With skin in the game, the increased chance of a loan originator feeling pain if the borrower runs into trouble will make those lenders more careful when providing mortgages. Again and again, history has showed that the more equity borrowers have in their houses the less likely they are to default on their mortgages.

The following chapter presents unresolved problems in the US economy, with a focus on five long-running dilemmas in the real estate sector. If these lingering problems aren't addressed properly, another unforeseen real-estate-driven crisis is likely to beckon.

Chapter 11: Facing the Music

Success is not built on success.
It's built on failure. It's built on frustration.
Sometimes it's built on catastrophe.
—Sumner Redstone, media mogul

In addition to the underlying problem of no skin in the game discussed previously, this chapter discusses additional unresolved problems in post-crisis America. Since a detailed debate of politics, the machinations of elected officials, and macroeconomics is beyond the scope of this book, I only highlight three big picture problems (or so-called "tail-risks") that linger in the US economy and have an indirect effect on real estate. I then focus on the specific troubles that continue to impact the nation's property sector, possible answers to which are provided in chapter 12.

You Are What You Owe

The burgeoning debts of the United States, the biggest in the history of the world, are particularly worrying because they threaten to destroy the financial future of generations of Americans. Failure to address the problem is to irresponsibly kick the fiscal can down the road.

On May 16, 2011, total national debt reached $14.3 trillion (the previously-set debt ceiling) or approximately 99 percent of GDP—not far from the 1946 peak of 121 percent (see figure 11-1). This makes the United States number four in the world rankings of debt-to-GDP ratios (after fiscally troubled Japan, Italy, and Greece, respectively). Furthermore, the alarming debt of $14.3 trillion fails to take into account the $3 trillion owed by state and local governments, not to mention further shortfalls in state and local pension systems. That is why Congress was forced to raise the national debt ceiling to a nauseating $15.2 trillion in August 2011.

Figure 11-1: US Public Debt-to-GDP-Ratio

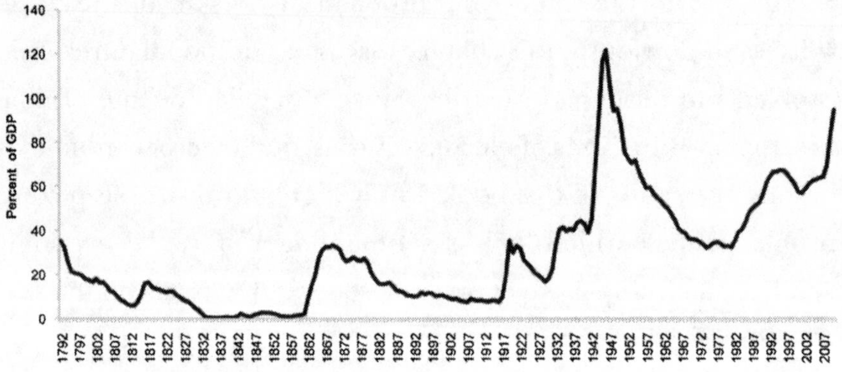

Source: USGovermentSpending.com

Most of us don't easily comprehend the vastness between one million, one billion, and one trillion dollars. For better appreciation, look at the government's total debt as if it was a unit of time: one million seconds is approximately 11.5 days; one billion seconds is nearly 32 years; and one trillion seconds represents more than 30,000 years!

Excessive debt is a national enemy that can severely affect inflation, interest rates, and taxation. It could also form the nexus of systemic financial risk in the years to come. In addition, disproportionate national debt can place pressure on the value of the US dollar, heightening the risk of its devaluation and creating challenges to the dollar's role as the world's reserve currency.[1]

During fiscal year 2011, the US Treasury was on track to pay upwards of $500 billion just in interest payments on existing debt. Excessive debt levels can also impact economic growth rates. Kenneth Rogoff, of Harvard University, and Carmen Reinhart, of the Petersen Institute for International Economics, report that among the twenty industrially advanced countries that they studied, average annual GDP growth was 3 percent to 4 percent when total national debt was relatively moderate or low (under 60 percent of GDP), but it dips to just 1.6 percent when debt is too high (above 90 percent of GDP).[2]

The Government Accountability Office (GAO) warned that the country is on a fiscally "unsustainable" path.[3] Furthermore, the Congressional Budget Office (CBO) has reported several risk factors related to rising debt levels:

- A growing portion of savings would go toward purchases of government debt, rather than investments in productive factories and capital goods such as computers, leading to lower output and incomes than would otherwise occur.
- If higher marginal tax rates were used to pay for the resulting increase in interest costs, savings and investments would be reduced even more than their current levels.
- Rising interest costs would force further reductions in important government programs.
- Restrictions on the ability of policymakers to use fiscal measures to respond to economic challenges.

- An increased risk of a sudden fiscal crisis, during which investors would demand higher interest rates.

Several other government agencies, including the Office of Management and Budget and the Treasury have reported that the United States is facing a series of critical long-term challenges. This is because expenditures related to entitlement programs such as Social Security, Medicare, and Medicaid (which already suffer from unfunded long-term commitments) are growing considerably faster than the overall economy, especially as the US population grows older.

These agencies have also warned that sometime between 2030 and 2040 mandatory spending (Social Security, Medicare, Medicaid, and interest on total national debt) will far exceed tax revenues. If significant reforms are not taken, benefits under entitlement programs will exceed government income by over $40 trillion over the coming decades. According to the GAO, this will cause debt ratios relative to GDP to double by 2040 and double again by 2060, reaching 600 percent by 2080. In other words, all discretionary spending (defense, homeland security, law enforcement, education, etc.) will require borrowing.[4] To that end, austerity measures such as higher tax rates, borrowing even more from other nations via the issuance of Treasury bonds, and further cuts in essential spending would have to be implemented to rein in national debt to sustainable levels.

———

No nation, agency, or organization has the authority to dictate terms to the United States government. Nevertheless, the financial markets have always been able to exert significant influence over nearly every aspect of national affairs. Standard & Poor's, Moody's, and Fitch were a cause of the near collapse of the US economy in 2008 due to their disastrously flawed assessments of mortgage-backed securities. Unfortunately, no alternative has emerged as a viable substitute to the credit rating agencies, simply because unrated debt issues are not marketable.

When Standard & Poor's (S&P) lowered its long-term sovereign credit rating on the United States from AAA to AA+ on August 5, 2011 it was a shot heard around the world. Stock markets plummeted, investors covered their eyes, consumers' confidence and pocketbooks took another beating, and the blame game engulfed politicians and S&P itself. It was a big wake-up call (assuming of course that the agencies have since improved their abilities to assess debt risk).

The United States, the world's most impressive prosperity machine, has never missed a debt service payment in its history and was rated AAA since 1917. Moreover, the country still has the *capacity* to meet its debt obligations. Despite the fact that S&P stripped the US government of its AAA credit rating to a lower level that is on par with Belgium, the controversial agency recently gave that coveted rating to securities backed by subprime home mortgages. The loans receiving the high rating are the same types that were largely responsible for the housing crisis. More specifically, S&P gave 59 percent of the Springleaf Mortgage Loan Trust 2011–1, which is a set of bonds backed by $497 million loaned to homeowners with below-average credit scores and very little property equity, an AAA rating. The mortgages underlying the Springleaf securities that received the AAA rating represent 96.6 percent of the current value of the homes. The credit scores of the borrowers have an average of 651 (the median credit score in the US is 711).

A congressional investigation in early 2011 held S&P partly responsible for the recession because of the firm's inflated grading of bonds from 2005 through 2008. S&P blamed the mistakes that led to the financial crisis on the misunderstanding of cash flows and conflicting methods of securities analysis. Securitization enabled by S&P contributed to more than $2 trillion in losses and write-downs at the world's largest financial institutions, and caused the collapse of Lehman Brothers in 2008, which ultimately froze credit markets and spurred a global recession. In my view, these are inaccuracies that could cause planes to crash if this was aeronautical engineering. So whether or not we believe in the accuracy of S&P's downgrade of America's long-term sovereign credit rating, it's clear as daylight that the United States has colossal problems related to its spending.

The larger impact of S&P's downgrade on US real estate—mainly commercial property—is likely to be on the demand side. Companies and consumers are already hesitant to spend. Downgraded US debt will increase that hesitancy, given the increased uncertainty it creates. Any negative impact on consumer and business confidence and, thus, spending, could translate into reduced economic activity, and as a result, reduced commercial real estate demand (at least in the near-term).

At the corporate level, from 1978 to 2007 the amount of debt held by the financial sector soared from $3 trillion to $36 trillion, more than doubling as a share of GDP. During that period, the very nature of many Wall Street firms changed—from relatively staid private partnerships to publicly traded corporations taking greater and more diverse risks. In 2005, the ten largest US commercial banks held 55 percent of the sector's assets, more than double the level held in 1990.[5] In 2006, financial sector profits constituted 27 percent of all US corporate profits, up from 15 percent in 1980.

In the years leading up to the crisis, too many financial institutions, as well as too many households, borrowed to the hilt, leaving them vulnerable to financial distress or ruin if the value of their investments declined even modestly. For example, in 2007 the five major investment banks—Bear Stearns, Goldman Sachs, Lehman Brothers, Merrill Lynch, and Morgan Stanley—were operating with extraordinarily thin capital. By one measure, their leverage ratios were as high as 40 to 1, meaning for every $40 in assets, there was only $1 in capital to cover losses.[6]

Something Has To Give

The financial crisis left behind alarmingly high levels of consumer debt, and to reduce them US consumers have been increasing their spending but by *less* than any rise in their incomes, leading to anemic growth in consumption. At the same time, and for different reasons, US consumers have been trying to unwind their heavy debt loads.

Consumer de-leveraging, or the paying down of excess debt, is one of the double-edged reasons why the economic recovery since 2009 has been so slow. The ratio of household debt-to-after-tax income fell in 2010 to 1.16, down from its peak of 1.35 in 2007, but has a lot further to go. (Before 2000, the ratio was less than 1).

In addition, the personal savings rate peaked in mid-2009 at 7.2 percent and was forecast to be approximately 5 percent of disposable income in 2011. That may be up from the rock-bottom

1.2 percent in mid-2005, but it is far short of the 8 percent norm during the last thirty years of the twentieth century.

The decline of these metrics has been largely *involuntary* because of restraint by lenders, and due to the Great Recession's millions of job losses. Much of the de-leveraging has been involuntary also because consumers are spooked from using debt due to the weak economy. Put another way, the conundrum of US consumer de-leveraging has been *reactive*, not proactive.

Consumer spending is at an unhealthy 71 percent of the economy, which is well above the 63 percent average of the 1950s. The difference over that lengthy period has been the massive increase in revolving credit and accessible lending (i.e., second-mortgages, home-equity lines of credit, credit card debt, etc.).

Chapter 1 discussed how America is a pure consumption-based economy and that the US consumer is excessively debt-ridden due to years of credit-fuelled buying sprees. When Americans go wild with their credit cards, it boosts economic output. But they cannot keep shopping forever; at some point they have to cut back and pay the bill, especially as wages are stagnant.

It will probably be a while before American consumers resume their spending ways, assuming that a new frugality doesn't suddenly overcome the nation. In a similar way, the public sector is wielding its metaphorical credit card with little thought for the future. That should be good for the economy—for corporate profits and for equities—right up to the moment of reckoning: switching from spending to paying off the bill.

Despite spending less time at the mall, throttling back consumption, and increasing their personal savings rate, US consumers still find themselves with too much debt and too little savings. Even worse, they lack the income or the equity to fund their previous "I want it all *now*" lifestyles. Something has to give.

The need for high levels of spending by consumers to boost the economy is controversial because their debt levels remain high by historical benchmarks. For example, current total household debt is about 85 percent of GDP and it will take years of US household de-leveraging to return to the 50 percent level seen in 1986.

Devil's advocates claim that US consumers don't need to stop saving, they just need to stop increasing the *rate* at which they save for the economy to grow. That point of view is faulty because excessive consumer debt and irresponsible spending are two obvious reasons why many Americans are in financial distress today. The uncertainty of consumer de-leveraging—which is closely connected to personal spending, savings, and the housing market—is a big risk confronting the US economy. It is a major risk because consumers are conditioned to spend more than save, something that has been ingrained in American culture for decades. Therefore, consumer de-leveraging will be a gradual and grisly process that will most likely last for years. Instead of relying on American consumers to de-leverage, the government needs to focus on enforcing new reforms and reworking the financial system from one of rampant speculation to one that helps create jobs and genuine prosperity for the country.

Getting Squeezed

The American workforce can be sliced in many ways. People who get paid a decent wage for skilled but routine work in manufacturing or services are getting squeezed by a double envelopment of technology and globalization.

An MIT study reveals the so-called "polarization of job opportunities" in America.[7] The study indicates that job growth is divided into three categories. On one side are managerial, professional, and technical occupations, held by highly educated workers who are adapting well to the global economy. On the other end are service occupations, those that involve "helping, caring for, or assisting others," such as security guards, cooks, and waiters. Most of these workers have no college education and get hourly wages that are on the low-end of the scale. But jobs in this segment have also been growing.[8]

In between are the skilled manual workers and those in white-collar operations such as sales and office management. These jobs represent the heart of the American middle-class. Those in such jobs made a decent living, normally above the US median family income of approximately $49,000, and they fared quite well in the twenty years before 2000. But since then, employment growth in those jobs has lagged the economy in general.

Moreover, since the Great Recession of 2007–09 it has been these middle-class people who have been clobbered. The MIT study reveals that the main reason for this trend is technology, followed by global competition, which have played the largest role in devaluing the routine tasks that once characterized middle-class work.

But the slow economic strangulation of millions of middle-class Americans started long before the Great Recession, which merely exacerbated the "personal recession" that ordinary Americans had been suffering for years. Dubbed "median wage stagnation" by economists, the annual incomes of the bottom 90 per cent of US families have been essentially flat since 1979—having risen by only 10 per cent in real terms (adjusted for inflation) in nearly three decades. Over the same period the incomes of the top 1 per cent have tripled.[9] The Great Recession has deepened the divide between America's squeezed consumers and its sprightly ones.

This trend has only been getting worse. Many economists see wage stagnation as a structural problem—meaning it is immune to the business cycle. In the last expansion, which started in January 2002 and ended in December 2007, the median US household income (adjusted for inflation) dropped by $2,000—the first ever instance in which most Americans were worse off at the end of a cycle than at the start. Worse is that the long era of stagnating incomes (see figure 11-2) has been accompanied by something very un-American: declining income mobility. This means that nowadays you have a smaller chance of swapping your lower income bracket for a higher one than in almost any other developed economy.

Figure 11-2: US Real Hourly Earnings

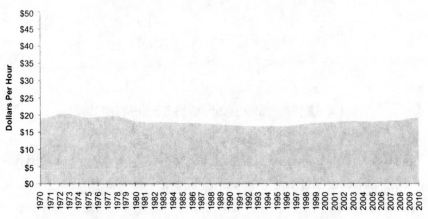

Source: US Department of Labor, Bureau of Labor Statistics

Middle-class in America is also being hollowed out as income inequality becomes more entrenched (see figure 11-3). The increased costs of private health insurance and pension payouts by state and local governments are limiting competitiveness, which could mean for some that the United States isn't the land of opportunity it once was (at least from late 2007 to 2011).

Figure 11-3: Income Inequality: Percentage Growth in Real After-Tax Income

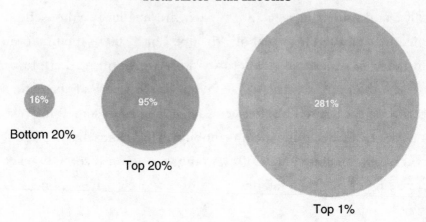

Source: Congressional Budget Office (percentage growth from 1979 to 2007)

The Unresolved Problems in US Real Estate

There are, without doubt, additional unresolved problems and lingering perils facing the US economy, such as marginal economic growth with high inflation; stubbornly high unemployment; the possibility of a massive sell off of Treasury bills by the Chinese government; rising energy costs; and the impact of Eurozone sovereign debt defaults; among others. However, and as noted at the beginning of the chapter, their analysis is beyond the scope of this book.

In addition to the problems stemming from excessive debt and no skin in the game that I discussed previously, the next section focuses on five unresolved problems in American real estate. Although interrelated, these problems are not ranked in order of importance; rather, they are broadly clustered by sector (i.e., those related to residential real estate and those related to commercial property):

1. Misconceptions about housing.
2. Negative home equity.
3. Delinquencies, defaults, and foreclosures.
4. Commercial debt maturities.
5. Private-label mortgage-backed securities.

Problem #1: Misconceptions about Housing

No investment alternative was ballyhooed as a way to get rich quick than housing. With inflation a fact of life for more than half a century, this inflation-sensitive investment, with its high potential for leverage and its tax benefits, provided millions of average Americans with nest eggs in the form of home equity. But today, for-sale and foreclosure signs proliferate across the country, reflecting demand that is fundamentally weak, as fewer and fewer buyers accept housing to be a safe investment. Household formations have slowed by some 1.5 million a year and an overhang of unsold properties continues to dampen any early stage recovery in housing markets.

The urge to own a home is part of the problem with the US economy today. It's what helped get many Americans into excessive

debt. During the mid-2000s, Americans became addicted to speculation of higher prices, which created—together with easy-to-
get mortgages—artificially high levels of homeownership. In a
country where there is huge cultural pressure for homeownership
after decades of price appreciation, a fundamental lesson of the
financial crisis is: not everybody, especially those with low credit
scores, should own a home, which means that several of the most
cherished beliefs about the value of a home don't necessarily hold
true. Accordingly, the following section debunks five myths about
homeownership in the United States.

Myth #1: Housing Is Always a Good Long-Term Investment

Before the housing bust, Americans thought their homes were
their best and most important investments, a view that was heavily
promoted by Washington policymakers who made homeownership a top priority. Karen Pence, who runs the Federal Reserve's
household and real estate finance research group, argues that
homes can actually be a bad investment. Putting aside the fact that
home prices have fallen dramatically, she notes that several factors
make a home an over-rated investment:[10]

- It is an indivisible asset. If you own stocks and bonds and
  suddenly need a little cash, you can sell some of your
  stocks or bonds but not all. With a home, on the other
  hand, you can't just slice off your kitchen and sell it on
  the market.

- It is undiversified. You can buy stocks or bonds in industries or countries all over the world. A home is a big bet on one single neighborhood.

- Transaction costs are very high when you buy or sell a home because of real estate agent commissions, mortgage fees, and moving costs.

- It is asymmetrically liquid, meaning it's easy to get money out when home prices are going up. But it's hard to take money out when prices are going down because refinancing becomes very difficult. Put another way, the leverage that you have in your house with a large mortgage means your investment does well in good times but could be a disaster in tough times.

- It is highly correlated to the employment market, meaning that home prices in a neighborhood tend to rise when the job market is improving in the area and fall when it's worsening. This infers that your main financial asset provides the smallest cushion for you when you might need it most.

———

Historically, the value of owner-occupied homes has risen at a fairly low rate, one that pales in comparison to the long-term performance of stocks and bonds. Between 1975 and 2008, the price for houses of comparable size and quality appreciated an average of approximately 1 percent per year (adjusted for inflation).[11] Americans would have earned over 2 percent per year had they invested in Treasury bills over the same period. They would have earned even more on other investments. For example, Moody's corporate bond index increased an average of 6 percent per year between 1975 and 2008 (also adjusted for inflation), while the S&P 500 stock index grew an average of 8 percent per year. Most of the return from owning a home shouldn't come in financial gains but in the benefits enjoyed by living there.

Moreover, homeownership in a downturn has a big disadvantage: Most people buy stocks all-cash, but homes are typically acquired "on margin" (i.e., they put down a small stake, if anything). If stock prices fall by, say, 20 percent, you lose 20 percent; if house prices fall by 20 percent, you may lose your entire savings. This undermines the claims that homeownership is *always* a good long-term investment.

Myth #2: It's Prudent to Buy a House with a Very Low Down Payment

As discussed in chapter 10, the FHA currently insures mortgages backed by down payments as low as 3.5 percent (the minimum requirement, which is ridiculously low in my view). Therefore, some Americans might think that buying a house with a low down payment is safe. But in the case of a 3.5 percent down payment, a borrower ends up carrying $96,500 of mortgage debt for every $3,500 of home equity (assuming the house is worth $100,000). Moreover, the less equity you have in your home, the greater the chance that a fall in prices will leave you owing more than the house is worth. In this example, housing prices only need to fall by 4 percent (or by $4,000) to leave a buyer underwater, not to mention the impact of upfront title fees and commissions.

Home mortgages with down payments of less than 10 percent are viable loans *only* when home prices are going up. When prices are falling, negative equity leads to mortgage defaults since the homeowner is unable to sell the home at a price to pay the closing costs and the mortgage. When buyers default, they lose not just their down payments but also closing costs and the value of any improvements they've made to their homes. Even if buyers don't default, they may not be able to move for employment because they don't have enough money to pay off their old home loans.

Households with negative home equity (being "underwater" or "upside down") are much less likely to move as similar households with positive home equity. As a result, the American borrowing binge during the recent boom has left many people locked into their current homes until they are either foreclosed on or prices increase to levels that are high enough to pay off their mortgages, which in many markets in the United States could take years. Many families are going to be stuck in declining parts of the country, unable to take advantage of better labor market conditions elsewhere.

Myth #3: Owning a Home Is Cheaper than Renting

Most real estate agents will make that claim, but the argument doesn't survive scrutiny. It's true that if you own, you don't have to write a check to a landlord. However, as an owner you have to cover all the costs of maintaining the house. It's the same house with the same operating costs, whether you pay them directly or whether you pay rent to cover them. By covering these costs as the owner-occupier, what you spend (including your mortgage payment) comes very close to what you would have spent if you rented your house.

According to Capital Economics, for the first time since at least 1981, the median monthly rent in the US is now higher than the median mortgage payment, and the winners are buy-to-rent investors. In addition, the average rental yield on a US house has moved toward 5.5 percent, the highest in a generation.

Many Americans own a home because they believe it's a way to commit to saving by building equity over time, but they shouldn't expect to make large profits. Housing is an expensive and durable product and durable goods are costly to maintain. The main reason to own is because you really like your home, not because you think it makes you money. It usually doesn't.[12]

Myth #4: With Housing Prices So Low, You Can Buy a House for the Same (or Less) than You Can Rent

This is a trap that many Americans fall into. It's easy to look at lower house prices and think that it would be cheaper to buy a house than to pay the rent on an apartment.[13] Mortgage lending websites like to use this to lure customers by putting monthly payment calculators on their websites that tell you that you can have a $140,000 home for less than $1,000 per month. What they're basically trying to say is that you can have a house that you'll own for approximately the same price as a two-bedroom rental apartment in many parts of the country. This might seem like a no-brainer, but those calculators only show a fraction of the actual costs of owning a home.

First, the payments are usually calculated with a 20 percent or higher down payment, which many first-time homebuyers cannot afford to make. Second, many don't account for property tax rates (which can fluctuate) and extra money for private mortgage insurance (PMI) and homeowner's insurance, all of which can increase your monthly payment by another 30 percent or so. Third, the monthly payment doesn't account for maintenance and any ongoing repairs that may be needed on your house. If these repairs and maintenance costs are financed on a Home Depot or Lowe's account, this will increase your monthly costs even more. Once all the other required payments are factored in, including repairs and maintenance costs, that $1,000 mortgage payment can quickly go up to nearly twice the amount.

This means that you shouldn't take the word of dodgy online calculators to decide how expensive a house to own is. It's better to make your own budget and figure out how much you can afford for housing each month. Subtract around $300 per month for maintenance and emergency repairs. Then take that amount and talk to some honest agents and mortgage companies to see if you can get a payment below that amount, including taxes and PMI. Additionally, call your insurance company to see how much it would cost for homeowner's insurance, and adjust your housing budget accordingly. If the total of all these different expenses add up to more than the allocated housing budget, then you cannot afford to buy the house.

With a rent payment, at least the monthly amount is fixed annually and you don't have to worry about additional maintenance or unexpected repairs. Lastly, renter's insurance is also generally inexpensive (under $50 a month) when compared to homeowner's insurance.

Myth #5: A Home Will Increase in Value and You Can Always Sell It for a Profit

The biggest issue with this myth is that it all depends on *when* you sell your house.[14] It's true that if you buy a home now and wait for the housing prices to go up again, you can probably make a profit; however, you'll probably have to wait several years or maybe even a decade before the property value goes up enough, given the current woes of the US housing market.

When you consider that the first five years of mortgage payments are paid toward interest—and not toward the loan principal, that means if prices don't increase for five years you have to make payments for that duration *before* you can sell your house to come out even. So if there is any chance that you might need to move within five years, you could end up losing money rather than making more of it. This can cause problems when you're trying to finance a new home because most people count on the money from the sale of their previous home to put toward the down payment of their new home.

———

These are just a few of the reasons why owning a home is not for everyone and every situation. It's easy to listen to the constant happy-talk that owning a home is the very embodiment of the American Dream, and it's the best thing for everyone. The truth is that nothing is the right choice for everyone.

A Fannie Mae national housing survey indicated that most Americans still aspire to own a home, as well as maintain homeownership, despite ongoing turmoil in the housing market. However, demographic trends such as fewer married couples and shrinking household formation, combined with financial caution among consumers, are contributing to an increased willingness to rent. The data means that more Americans are viewing rental housing as an attractive and sustainable option. According to Fannie's survey, 33 percent of Americans would be more likely to rent their next home than buy, up from 30 percent in 2009. Among renters, 59 percent indicated they would continue to rent in their next move.

Despite most Americans' desire to own their homes, the survey revealed that the recent grisly economic events have greatly influenced families' decision to rent. This trend has caused consumers to approach homeownership with more caution and thoughtfulness. The worst economic downturn since the Great Depression has caused a 4.1 percent decline in the homeownership rate (at 66.4 percent in 2011) and possibly a change in the perception of homeownership as the main pillar of the American Dream (see figure 11-4).

Figure 11-4: US Homeownership Rate

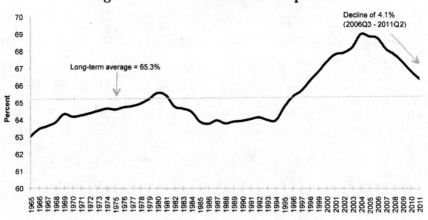

Source: US Census Bureau

Lastly, on the housing policy side, there's a downside to hefty sub-sidies funneled to homeowners, namely that the United States is potentially investing too little in other vital areas such as educa-tion, infrastructure, and technology. At the height of the housing bubble in 2005, mortgages accounted for more than half of all US debt issued that year—about double the historical norm—accord-ing to Haver Analytics.

"We've over-emphasized our investment in housing and neglected to invest in education and infrastructure," said Bill Gross, the founder of Pimco, the world's largest bond fund. "We need to refocus on the production of 'things' rather than the pro-duction of financial products and houses."[15]

Problem #2: Negative Home Equity

Earlier I identified three broad factors underlying the mortgage crisis that led to the Great Recession: (1) The widespread slow-down in house price growth followed by actual declines in prices in most areas of the country; (2) weak economic conditions in selected market areas; and (3) substantial growth in the volume of risky loans originated—made even riskier by loose underwrit-ing and lender quality control in the years leading up to the meltdown.[16]

The more fundamental cause of the mortgage crisis was the surge beginning in 2003 in the origination of subprime loans that were at high risk of foreclosure due to a combination of unafford-able initial-payment levels relative to borrower incomes, coupled with loan terms that would make these loans even more unafford-able over time.[17] The riskiness of these mortgages was masked by rapid house price appreciation through 2004–06 that allowed many—but certainly not all—borrowers to avoid foreclosure by either refinancing into a new mortgage or selling their home for more than they had originally financed. In fact, the surge in risky lending itself fed the rapid house price growth that occurred since 2004. Once risky mortgage credit originations was curbed in late 2006, house price growth reversed to a pattern of rapid deflation in prices.[18] With very little equity in their homes to protect them from a drop in prices, lots of high-risk borrowers quickly became submerged when the bubble burst.

According to CoreLogic, an estimated 10.9 million homes (or nearly 23 percent) were worth less than their mortgages in 2011. An additional 2.4 million borrowers had less than 5 percent equity, meaning they'll be underwater with even slight price declines. Moreover, in 2011 average US house prices were projected to fall approximately 33 percent from their peak in July 2006, accompanied by a level of delinquencies, defaults, and foreclosures without precedent in the post-World War II era.

———

Negative equity is one of the best predictors of default, which is why loan-to-value ratios must be taken seriously. Negative equity is also what burdens banks with losses when homes end up in foreclosure. House price declines, which led to negative home equity, were further exacerbated by an oversupply of new inventory, particularly in markets where rapid price growth had spurred significant housing demand by investors and borrowers who were aided by the super-easy availability of mortgage financing.[19] As house prices softened, demand by both investors and owner-occupiers

dropped sharply, leaving an excess supply of new housing (especially in the second-home market) that further added to the downward pressure on prices. Foreclosures also added to this downward
pressure in the form of a negative feedback-loop.[20]

As such, declining house prices are viewed by some as a result
of the surge in risky lending rather than a direct cause of the mortgage crisis.[21] As the crisis matured, a downward spiral took hold
as declining house prices exerted their own influence to increase
foreclosures, which, in turn, depressed prices further.

Housing market analysts often explain mortgage defaults as
a consequence of life events such as divorce, illness, or job loss.
No doubt, such events figure most importantly in a borrower's
ability to repay a mortgage. However, except for unemployment,
life events tend to occur with unfortunate regularity. By contrast,
mortgage default rates vary substantially over time. It is clear then
that life events lead to defaults when they occur in combination
with some other factor. It seems most likely that this other factor
is deflation in house prices.[22]

Defaults and foreclosures are costly for borrowers who would
rather avoid these expenses by selling their houses and prepaying
their mortgages instead of defaulting. However, they can only sell
when home prices are increasing or are at least stable. The default
rate increases in periods when house prices have fallen, making
mortgage prepayment through resale or refinancing prohibitive
for over-leveraged homeowners. Additionally, the practice of strategic defaults is more widespread in the many American states where
lending is non-recourse, meaning that lenders cannot come after a
defaulting borrower for any debt left over when the property is sold.

Speculative purchases also made things worse as people are
more likely to give back the keys to homes they are not living
in. The 2011 report of the Financial Crisis Inquiry Commission

pointed out that by the first half of 2005, the peak year for the number of housing sales, more than one in every ten house sales in America was for an investment or a second-home.[23]

Given the importance of falling home prices as a factor in defaults, it is natural to ask how far they must drop before it serves the borrower's interest to strategically default; that is, to walk away from a mortgage even in the absence of a life event. A common answer is that home prices must fall to a point where the value of the house is less than the remaining loan balance. But strategic defaults can wreck consumer credit scores for many years, not to mention the social problems that can arise from forced reloca-tion. On the other hand, it's worth mentioning that proponents of strategic defaults claim that the relief such actions provide to distressed homeowners—who know that they're no longer in a bottomless hole of debt—can have some psychological benefits (i.e., self-esteem and confidence).

———

In 2000, underwater borrowers were a rarity. The actual default rate in the United States was close to 2 percent.[24] The underwater mortgage landscape today, of course, looks completely different. Over the period of 2000-06, underwriting standards declined dra-matically and some greedy lenders became more willing to extend mortgages to borrowers with poor credit histories and those who made small down payments, if any at all.

In August 2006, house prices began their steep decline. The combination of small initial equity stakes and oversupply, followed by falling home prices that started at the time, produced a sharp jump in the proportion of underwater mortgages. For example, in Florida, Nevada, Arizona, and California the average number of mortgages with principal balances that are greater than the estimated home values is more than 50 percent.[25]

Given the importance that has long been assigned to home price declines in explaining foreclosure trends, it is perhaps not surprising that most reviews of the mortgage crisis begin by pointing to the slowdown in house price growth that began in August 2006 as one of the indirect factors precipitating the sharp rise in delinquencies, defaults, and foreclosures.[26]

––––––

In 2009, the FDIC issued new guidelines for bank regulators to streamline and standardize the way banks are examined. One notable feature is that as long as a bank has evaluated the borrower and the asset behind a loan—if the bank is convinced that the borrower can repay the loan even if it goes into a workout with the borrower—the bank doesn't have to reserve for the mortgage. In other words, it doesn't have to take a hit against its capital. So if the collateral all of a sudden drops to, say, 60 percent of the original loan balance, the bank doesn't have to take any write-down. That allows banks to sit on weak assets instead of liquidating them or try to raise more capital, thus skewing their balance sheets.

That's quite significant because it infers that the FDIC and the Treasury have decided rather than see a thousand banks fail and then create another 1980s-style Resolution Trust Corporation to sort through all the toxic assets, they'll let the banking system "warehouse" the bad assets. It appears that their plan is to leave the assets in place, and then—when the market eventually changes—let the banks deal with them.

––––––

Mortgage principal write-downs, reducing the principal owed on underwater homes, is a highly controversial issue for US banks, further complicating the unresolved problem of negative home equity. Financial institutions have grudgingly modified mortgages for distressed homeowners by lowering interest rates, spreading principal repayments over more months, even forgiving some overdue interest. But many banks have been reluctant to lower the mortgage principal owed. The reasons for their resistance are several, although the advantages to homeowners are numerous. Table 11-1 provides a summary of the pros and cons of mortgage principal write-downs.

Table 11-1: The Pros and Cons of Mortgage Principal Write-Downs

Pros	Cons
• Increase the willingness of homeowners to work hard and sacrifice to keep their mortgage payments current. • Lower mortgage payments can save underwater borrowers from drowning in debt. • Borrowers who have new loan balances in line with their decreased home values have a cushion if they lose a job or face other financial setbacks.	• A large program of principal write-downs could ratify the view that house prices are not going to recover any time soon. • Powerful financial institutions worry that if they reduce principal at no cost to the borrower, the losses they'd have to take would erode their capital cushions. • In many cases, mandatory reductions don't make financial sense because contracts with some investors who own bonds backed by mortgages don't permit write-downs.

(Table continued on next page...)

Pros	Cons
• A targeted program to lower principal for struggling homeowners can help shrink the overhang of foreclosures.	• Lower the fees collected by mortgage servicers and cut into their profits.
• Prevent value-destroying foreclosures and discourage homeowners from strategic defaults.	• Create an immediate tax liability (e.g., a homeowner making $80,000 looking for a $40,000 write-down immediately increases his taxes).
• Allow homeowners to sell rather than go through foreclosure if they have an "income shock," or need to move.	• Create the potential problem of moral hazard. That is, letting buyers who bought more house than they could afford get off the hook for their bad decisions.
• Force banks to value assets accurately on their balance sheets, making banks underwrite their loans more carefully. Nothing is more dangerous for the financial system than overly optimistic balance sheets.	• By offering to reduce the amount a borrower owes, it would encourage other borrowers who owe more than their home is worth (but could afford to continue making payments) to default on their loans, as they too would try to freeload and get their principal reduced.
• Limit the problem of future adjustable rate mortgage (ARM) resets, once interest rates rise in the future.	• Mortgages with second-liens with no real economic value pose serious problems (as discussed later).
• Give the housing market a fresh start by clearing up financial logjams.	

Second-liens (also known as second-mortgages or junior-liens) are one of the major knots standing in the way of a US housing recovery because they could further destabilize the mortgage and credit markets. Second-lien loans include home-equity lines of credit as well as "piggyback" mortgages—the high-interest loans that were typically used to finance 15 to 20 percent of a home's cost. What makes second-lien loans especially troubling is that the Treasury estimates that 50 percent of at-risk mortgages involve these kinds of instruments.

Second-lien portfolios are among the largest and most risky liabilities on bank balance sheets today. The four largest banks in the US hold approximately $420 billion of these loans on their books—more than 40 percent of the approximately $1 trillion in outstanding second-lien loans.

Housing prices have dropped 33 percent since 2006, and many of the second-lien portfolios will be worthless if the foreclosure fiasco continues. That is because, according to the established legal concept of "lien priority"—in which the first-lien holder must be fully compensated in a foreclosure *before* subordinate holders, if the property is underwater by more than the amount of the second-lien, the institution holding the second-lien doesn't get any money.

As such, mortgage servicers like Bank of America Merrill Lynch have a disincentive to write-down or modify a second-lien loan they own, especially when the first-lien on the same property is packaged into a mortgage-backed security owned by other parties, such as pension funds or private investors. This situation allows banks to defer losses—the practice known as "extend and pretend"—even though it leaves the borrower with unsustainable debt loads.

Underwater borrowers with second-lien loans are between a rock and a hard place: they cannot take what would be the most logical route for someone drowning in debt—selling their home at its current market value—because the holder of the second-lien loan in many cases will object to, and prevent, a sale price that will not pay off both the first- and second-lien mortgages. Economist Joseph Stiglitz describes the problem in his book *Freefall*:

> If there had been a *single* mortgage for 95 percent of the value of the house, and if house prices fell by 20 percent, it might make sense to write-down the mortgage to reflect this—to give the borrower a fresh start. But with two separate mortgages, doing so would typically wipe out the holder of the second-mortgage. For him, it might be preferable to refuse to restructure the loan; there might be an admittedly small chance that the market would recover and that he would at least get back some of what he lent.

Second-liens are also a major threat to bank solvency. According to the Congressional Oversight Panel, Bank of America Merrill Lynch in 2011 had more than $137 billion worth of second-lien loans on its books. This represented 83 percent of its Tier 1 capital, the principal measure used by regulators to determine bank solvency. The situation at Wells Fargo was even worse. Its second-lien portfolio was 116 percent of its Tier 1 capital.

In 2009, during the Treasury's first round of stress tests, second-lien portfolios were valued at 86 cents on the dollar under an "adverse scenario." In 2011, banks were carrying their second-lien portfolios at 85 cents to 93 cents on the dollar, according to the research company Graham Fisher. Current accounting standards allow banks to greatly overinflate the value of second-lien mortgages and keep large portfolios of them on their balance sheets at close to pre-bubble values. Depending on their date of issue and other variables, second-lien loans are probably only worth 40 cents to 60 cents on the dollar, according to Graham Fisher.

Many underwater borrowers with second-liens need a fresh start, or they will end up in foreclosure. So far, four million homeowners have lost their homes since the beginning of 2007, and another 4.1 million are at immediate risk of foreclosure. The Congressional Oversight Panel predicts that by the time the housing crisis has fully abated, some thirteen million additional foreclosures will have occurred.

Problem #3: Delinquencies, Defaults, and Foreclosures

As discussed, declining housing prices and the prevalence of negative home equity were clearly an important precipitating factor in the mortgage crisis. The sharp rise in mortgage delinquencies and foreclosures was also the result of rapid growth in loans with a high risk of default—due both to the terms of these loans and to loose underwriting controls and standards.[27]

With home prices declining for a fifth consecutive year in 2011, measures to solve the problem have proven largely ineffective. As such, the effects of housing declines were obviously still having a serious impact on the US economy. The American housing market is still putting the brakes on any sustained US recovery, and politically and socially the foreclosure crisis continues to create huge problems. The after-effects of the housing bubble, which was enlarged by the easy credit made available due to strong global investor demand for securitized mortgages, are still being felt across the United States.

Already, some 4.1 million homes were in some stage of foreclosure, meaning that the borrower was at least ninety days behind on payments—a record number of bad loans, while as many as 1.8 million additional borrowers were expected to be taken in foreclosure in 2011. To complicate matters even more, there were a growing number of American borrowers who had loan modifications re-default on their home loans even after their payments were substantially reduced through federally sponsored foreclosure relief programs.

The mortgage crisis was actually unusual in that general economic weakness didn't play a significant role in producing delinquencies and foreclosures in most market areas—at least not initially. Instead, it was the slowdown in house price growth that removed the primary safety valve for the high volume of unaffordable mortgages that had been made, which was for borrowers to take advantage of a robust increase in home prices to avoid foreclosure by refinancing into a new loan or selling the property for a profit.

The seeds of the financial crisis were sown long before 2008, but detecting them was complicated by unprecedented house price appreciation between 2004 and 2006—appreciation that masked the true riskiness of subprime mortgages.[28] Or, as Mark Zandi, of Moody's Economy.com, more prosaically put it: "Skyrocketing house prices fed many dreams and papered over many ills."[29]

_____

When you agree to your mortgage terms and sign your contract, one of the key points will be the date on which your payments are to be made. For most people, their mortgage payment is due on the first of the month. If you should fail to make your payment on time for any reason, your mortgage loan will technically be in *delinquency*. Depending on how long you go without making a payment, you're risking late fees, a higher interest rate, and going into default.

Generally, mortgage *default* occurs when a borrower has missed three payments and a fourth one is due. A default leads lenders to initiate the foreclosure process, although historically some 60 percent of defaults have been resolved without a foreclosure actually occurring. Depending on your lender's policies, it could be anywhere from sixty to 150 days before your mortgage takes the dive from delinquency to default. You'll typically receive a notice of default and information about the next steps your lender might take. At that point, your lender has the right to foreclose your home if you still don't make any payments on your mortgage. Like delinquency, mortgage loans in default will show up on your credit report with a negative effect on your FICO score.

Furthermore, *foreclosure* is a process that allows a lender to recover the amount owed on a defaulted loan by selling or taking ownership (repossession) of the property pledged as collateral that is securing the loan. The foreclosure process begins when a borrower defaults on mortgage payments and the lender files a public default notice based on either judicial- or non-judicial-state laws. The foreclosure process can end in one of four ways:

1. The borrower reinstates the loan by paying off the default amount during a grace period determined by state law. This grace period is also known as "pre-foreclosure."
2. The borrower sells the property to a third party during the pre-foreclosure period. The sale allows the borrower to pay off the loan and avoid having a foreclosure on his or her credit history.
3. A third party buys the property at a public auction at the end of the pre-foreclosure period.
4. The lender takes ownership of the property, usually with the intent to re-sell it on the open market, but at a discount. The lender can take ownership either through an agreement with the borrower during pre-foreclosure via a short-sale or by buying back the property at a public auction. Homes repossessed by the lender are also known as bank real estate-owned (REO) properties.

Depending on the specific terms of a loan, mortgage lenders can lose when foreclosures occur because by the time foreclosed houses are sold, approximately 27 percent of the value of the home is lost (as will be discussed later). However, lenders bear only *part* of the costs of foreclosure. Homeowners who experience foreclosure also lose because they are forced to move, which destroys their neighborhood ties, leaves some of them homeless, and increases their children's chance of dropping out of school before graduating.[30]

In addition, research by Janet Currie of Princeton and Erdal Tekin of Georgia State University shows a direct correlation between foreclosure rates and the health of residents in New Jersey, Florida, Arizona, and California. Both economists concluded that an increase of one hundred foreclosures corresponded to a 7.2 percent rise in emergency room visits and hospitalizations for hypertension, and an 8.1 percent increase for diabetes, among people aged twenty to forty-nine. Each rise of one hundred foreclosures was also associated with 12 percent more visits related to anxiety in the same age category. The same rise in foreclosures was associated with 39 percent more visits for suicide attempts among the sample group.

Renters are also harmed when landlords default and rental housing units (apartments) are foreclosed on, because leases are abruptly terminated and renters are forced to bear the costs of unexpected moves. In addition, foreclosures harm communities because vacant homes deteriorate, causing neighborhoods to become blighted. Foreclosures impact local governments as well, since property taxes are their main source of revenue. When property values fall, tax revenues fall, and local governments are forced to cut expenditures on schools, police, and other public services. Lastly, defaults lead to more defaults and foreclosures lead to more foreclosures in a negative feedback-loop.

The fact that mortgage lenders can incur losses on their loans when they foreclose suggests that in some cases they might be better off if they voluntarily reduce homeowners' mortgage payments and allow homeowners to remain in their homes rather than foreclosing. However, and as discussed earlier, most residential lenders have resisted reducing mortgage payments, choosing foreclosure when default occurs.[31] In other cases, if the lender goes down the foreclosure process it's because the homeowner can no longer pay or make up payments as a condition for a loan modification.

Two explanations shed light on lenders' unwillingness to change the terms of mortgages. One is that when mortgages are securitized, a mortgage servicer acts for the investors and most mortgage servicing agreements give servicers strong economic incentives to foreclose rather than to modify mortgage terms. The other explanation is that residential lenders, as discussed previously, might be better off if they foreclose. This is because many mortgages that default are reinstated (or "self-cure") and many of those whose mortgages are modified with their payments reduced end up re-defaulting anyway, so foreclosure is only delayed rather than prevented. But the narrative is that even if lenders are better off foreclosing, it would be more socio-economically efficient to modify mortgages if possible so as to avoid the high external costs of foreclosures.[32]

As can be deduced, the hard job of fixing the US mortgage market is very complex and remains unresolved. Such a huge unresolved problem is dragging down households' optimism and impeding the clearing of the housing market. Furthermore, with millions of Americans falling into hardship, more foreclosures will certainly hurt the US economy at this critical point in the recovery, undermining already-fragile consumer confidence.

The current recovery has been slow in part because the housing sector remains weak. The housing sector remains weak because the inventory of unsold houses remains high, and the inventory of unsold houses remains high because the foreclosure problem has yet to be solved. While US government programs have been aimed at reducing foreclosure filings and encouraging cancellations once filed, they have not focused on mortgage delinquencies per se. If there were no delinquencies, there would be no foreclosures. The problem is that the number of loans starting

foreclosure has been very high in the subprime segment (see figure 11-5). Another problem is that it's basically impossible to manage the amount of delinquencies.

Figure 11-5: Number of Loans Starting Foreclosure by Type

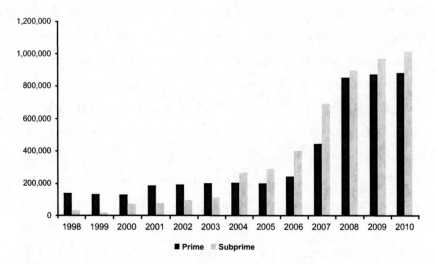

Source: Mortgage Bankers Association, Bank of America Merrill Lynch

No part of the financial crisis has received so much attention,
with so little to show for it, as the tidal wave of home delinquencies
and foreclosures that continues to impact the American economy.
Equally distressing is negative home equity. As indicated earlier, in
2011 some 4.1 million homes were more than ninety days behind
on payments or near foreclosure. Few of these delinquent loans
are being cured. In 2005, homeowners reinstated (or self-cured)
66 per cent of the loans delinquent for ninety days or longer; by
2009, that number had shrunk to just 5 percent. In addition, four
million homes have been repossessed by the banks since January
2007. The result is a heavy weigh-down on homeowners' confidence and the US economy. Therefore, it is believed that it might

take at least five more years to a decade before housing markets can return to normal conditions.[33]

———

The foreclosure problem, of course, is a result of the frenzied home price boom and bust in the past decade. Mortgage originators made foolish loans, and borrowers willfully signed up for them—only to default later—as home prices and the economy slumped. Mortgage servicers rushed to reclaim properties, launching a record number of dubious foreclosure proceedings that culminated into the notorious "robo-signing" fiasco, with numerous allegations that mortgage servicer employees rubber-stamped paperwork, therefore subverting the foreclosure process.[34]

A foreclosure doesn't only damage credit reports, but it also restricts getting home loans in the near future. If a foreclosed-upon homeowner wants to purchase a new house in the immediate years to come, it would be almost impossible. The buyer would need to wait for at least seven years before he or she can get a good loan that would provide the chance to acquire a new house (the FHA restricts foreclosed-upon homeowners from getting a loan from it for seven years). It takes that long for a foreclosure to clear a credit report. This is a major issue for previous homeowners who have cleared up their credit and gotten a job, because they are locked out of buying another home, further depressing the demand for housing.

Homes in foreclosure also depress the price of homes around them. Houses stuck in limbo fall into disrepair. According to a study by researchers at Harvard and MIT, a foreclosure reduces the value of a home by nearly 27 percent, and accounts for a much steeper price drop than other forced sales.[35] That impact will only get worse the longer foreclosures drag on.

Both the George W. Bush and Barack Obama administrations initiated programs to reduce the number of foreclosures by encouraging lenders to lower homeowners' mortgage payments. The Bush administration programs were completely unsuccessful, while the Obama initiatives have received mixed reviews at best.

A problem with both the Bush and the Obama administration programs is that while homeowners apply to have their mortgage payments reduced, lenders have the right to veto any changes. Lenders obviously have an interest in approving only a small number of mortgage reductions in order to discourage applications by homeowners who actually can afford to pay. Because lenders have the right to veto, and since they tend to ignore the external costs, these programs have prevented too few foreclosures.

More specifically, the government interventions seen in recent years, while clearly well intentioned, have done little more than add delays to the notorious foreclosure process, allowing investors to avoid losses by pushing the problem off to another day. Programs such as the Home Affordable Foreclosure Alternatives initiative, which offers short-sale and deed-in-lieu of foreclosure options; as well as revisions to the Home Affordable Modification Program (HAMP), which addresses principal reduction, have been inadequate. For example, if current trends hold HAMP will prevent some 760,000 foreclosures—far fewer than the four million foreclosures that the Treasury initially projected. As a result, the HAMP program could be killed in the House of Representatives before its scheduled closing in December 2012.

An offshoot of foreclosures is shadow inventory—homes whose owners are seriously behind with their mortgage payments or in foreclosure and which will eventually come onto the market. Even though American house prices in 2011 were back at fair value (i.e., the ratio of house prices-to-rents is back to its long-run average), this pipeline of distressed properties is putting prices under continued pressure.[36] How quickly the glut of unsold houses might diminish is hard to know. It depends, above all, on the unemployment rate. But it also depends on the speed and outcome of the burdensome foreclosure process and on the efficacy of US government interventions. According to CoreLogic, shadow inventory—while declining—still remains high (see figure 11-6).[37]

Figure 11-6: Months' Supply of Shadow Inventory

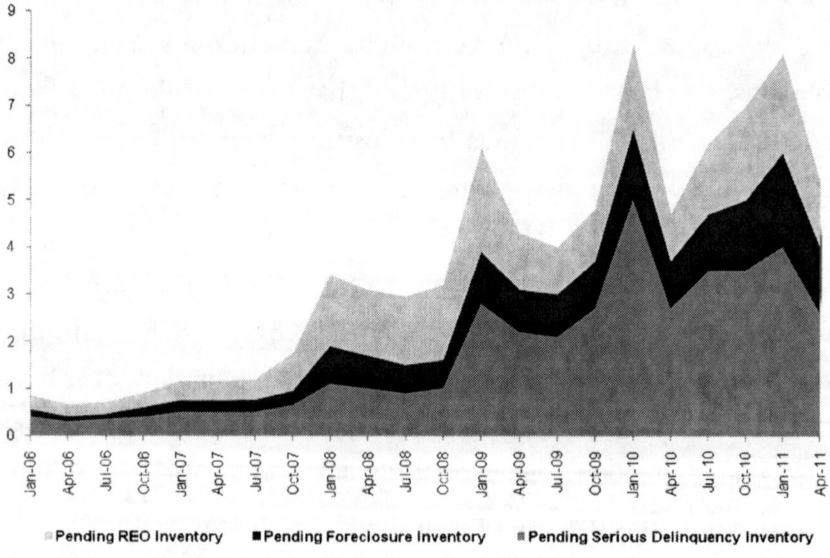

Pending REO Inventory   Pending Foreclosure Inventory   Pending Serious Delinquency Inventory

Source: CoreLogic

Moreover, the weak demand for housing is significantly increasing the risk of further price declines in the US market. This is being aggravated by high levels of shadow inventory that are likely to persist due to the lengthy time it takes mortgage servicers to execute a liquidation sale.

Shadow inventory helps explain why America has suffered such a sharp fall in prices relative to rents after the bust (see figure 11-7). House prices are generally "sticky" on the way down, in part because people are averse to selling at a loss. But America's bust has brought waves of distressed sales, forcing prices down rapidly.

Figure 11-7: Ratio of US House Prices-to-Rents

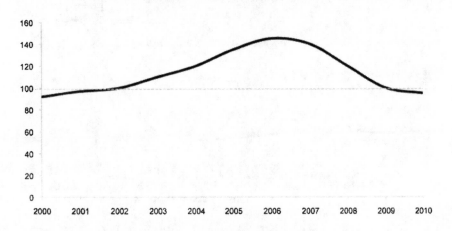

Source: ESRI, Nationwide, Standard & Poor's, Thomson Reuters

In addition to the residential real estate sector, and as discussed in chapter 7, commercial property in the US has been having several problems. During the past three years, this sector generally has not grabbed as much attention, since events in it haven't been as dramatic as in the residential market.

Since 2006, the average default rate on US commercial real estate loans rose from 1.1 percent to close to 4.5 percent in 2010. In addition, according to research firm Trepp LLC, average default rates on commercial mortgage-backed securities (CMBSs) have increased from 0.5 percent in 2006 to approximately 9 percent in 2010, and were projected to increase further in 2011 (see figure 11-8). Balance sheet-originated commercial real estate (CRE) loan defaults, on the other hand, are experiencing a decline.

Figure 11-8: Default Rates of US CMBS and Commercial Real Estate Loans

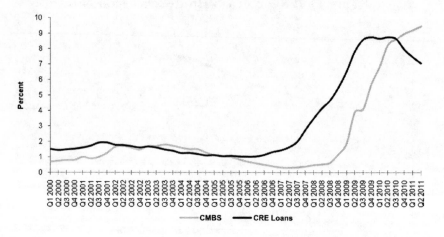

Source: Federal Reserve Board, CRE Finance Council, Trepp LLC

When commercial properties fail, it is the result of a downward spiral of economic contraction; vacant retail outlets and office buildings; as well as the failure of banks serving those communities. These are the same small banks that provide loans to the small businesses that create jobs and boost productivity. If hundreds more of community banks go under, the effect could be like dumping sand in the gears of the US economic recovery.

Because commercial real estate loans typically have five- to ten-year terms, those loans are constantly being refinanced. The problem is that loans made at the height of the commercial property boom—2005 to 2007—were based on inflated prices during a time of easy money. In 2011, those loans were coming to the end of their terms. There was a big commercial real estate price bubble that burst with prices deflating by as much as 44 percent, meaning that there could be ongoing losses to be borne by investors and banks.

Problem #4: Commercial Debt Maturities

Before discussing the unresolved problem of commercial debt maturities in the United States, it's important to first compare residential and commercial real estate debt. There are important differences between residential and commercial property debt that make it difficult to compare causation factors.[38]

The most common residential default is failure to make monthly loan payments because the borrower has suffered an economic setback, such as unemployment, or because the loan was structured so that payments dramatically increased at some point during the term. In some cases, particularly if a property has suffered increased vacancy, commercial borrowers also default due to a failure to make monthly payments. But the increasingly common commercial defaults are related to "maturity," in which the borrower is unable to borrow a large enough sum to pay off an expiring loan. The difference between the balloon payment owed on the maturing loan and the amount that can be borrowed today is the "equity gap." The equity gap is caused by two factors: falling valuations of commercial real estate and a lack of liquidity.[39]

All lenders use written and informal guidelines to analyze potential loans to residential and commercial borrowers. These underwriting standards are a product of market conditions, guidance from federal banking supervisors, and internal decisions about risk tolerance. Underwriting criteria include pricing decisions (fees and interest rates), loan-to-value ratios, and the creditworthiness of the borrower as well as loan covenants. The extent to which a lender conducts due diligence on the property and borrower is also determined by underwriting standards.[40]

A residential real estate loan is underwritten by evaluating both the market value of the property and the creditworthiness of the borrower. The value of residential real estate is primarily determined by analyzing the sales prices of comparable properties, and, thus, values can fluctuate widely over time. Regardless of the value of a home, the borrower's financial stability and ability to repay the loan are critical components of residential underwriting.

Slipshod underwriting standards clearly contributed to problems in residential real estate because many homes were overvalued during the mid-2000s, and many borrowers qualified for loans that they were unlikely to repay even in the most optimistic circumstances.[41] On the other hand, in commercial lending the collateral and the borrower are both evaluated, but the emphasis is on the ability of income-producing real estate to continue to generate cash flow in an amount sufficient to cover operating expenses and debt service.

Most commercial real estate is owned in a single-asset limited liability company (LLC) or a limited partnership (LP), which segregates exposure to contract and tort liability. These ownership structures are significant in the debt context because most permanent commercial real estate loans are non-recourse or limited-recourse to the parent company. Therefore, the creditworthiness of that parent company is not a significant factor in underwriting because it's unlikely that they'll be called upon to satisfy a deficiency. The experience and ability of the owner to operate the collateral to obtain maximum return, however, is highly relevant.[42]

———

In 2007, the US commercial property market entered a state of euphoria. Champagne corks popped as investors splashed hundreds of millions of dollars on trophy assets, more often than not funded with cheap debt. However, according to the MIT Center for Real Estate, commercial property dropped in value by approximately 44 percent from the height of the market in 2007 to 2009. That decline was the result of two main factors: (1) Downward pressure on rent and increasing vacancy rates; and (2) increasing capitalization rates (cap rates). The value of commercial real estate is generally estimated by dividing the net operating income of a property by a cap rate. Cap rates have increased in most tertiary markets since 2007, which has in turn reduced appraisal values of commercial real estate. As a result, many borrowers who have no problem making monthly mortgage payments find themselves in technical default because of low appraisals that don't satisfy required loan-to-value ratios.[43]

The more significant problem is that commercial real estate borrowers of performing assets are finding themselves in maturity defaults, unable to refinance expiring debt. Unlike residential loans, which normally fully amortize over a thirty-year term, permanent commercial loans normally partially amortize over a ten-year term. As a result, every five years the borrower must refinance a balloon payment.

As indicated in chapter 7, approximately $1.15 trillion in commercial debt will mature before 2015. Combining the increase in cap rates in tertiary markets with the stringent capital markets, borrowers and lenders are faced with a significant equity gap that some analysts have estimated could exceed $800 billion.[44]

Determining how that equity gap will be satisfied and by whom could be a major challenge over the next few years. If borrowers cannot raise the funds, then lending institutions, particularly local and regional banks and thrifts, could be confronted with losses. Therefore, government action might be needed to prevent commercial real estate debt from impacting America's fragile economic recovery.[45]

Commercial property tends to lag behind what happens in the broader economy. Companies are still looking for ways to cut costs, many are continuing to reduce workers and reduce their space needs. As a result, commercial rental rates in some segments continued to decline in 2011.

While the housing sector continued to show weaknesses, the commercial property sector—according to pessimists—was a potential debt time bomb because of the approximately $1.15 trillion worth of commercial real estate loans coming due. Moreover, commercial real estate exposure currently represents more than 25 percent of total US bank assets. Importantly, this exposure increases markedly for smaller banks. For the four largest banks (on the basis of total assets), this exposure is 12.3 percent; for the five to thirty largest banks, the exposure is 24.5 percent; while for the thirty-one to one hundred largest banks, the exposure grows to a heart-burning 38.9 percent.

The approaching wave of commercial real estate debt maturities over the next few years is creating uncertainty in the US property markets in 2012. If commercial loan defaults continue to increase, they could result in more distressed properties and foreclosures, as mounting problems with these loans could impact the broader economic recovery.

As noted earlier, US commercial property experienced an average 44 percent decline in prices from its peak in October 2007 to its lowest point in October 2009. This drop is considerably worse than the 27 percent commercial real estate decline associated with the S&L crisis of the late 1980s. The S&L crisis precipitated the government-run Resolution Trust Corporation and the resulting seizures and auctions of hundreds of S&Ls around the country. The same conditions that caused the residential housing bubble—the Fed's easy credit, lax lending standards, and the generous underwriting of mortgage-backed securities—had all caused the over-valuation of commercial property. These conditions also resulted in unsustainable real estate debt growth and the missed assessment of US real estate debt risk (as discussed in chapter 8).

In addition, research by Moody's and Real Capital Analytics indicates that about half of the commercial real estate acquired or refinanced in the last five years are now upside down on their loans, with asset prices falling below the mortgage amount. With huge amounts of US commercial property debt coming due, Deutsche Bank and CoreLogic also estimate that 65 percent or more of CMBS loans could fail to qualify for refinancing, especially the loans taken out in 2005–08, the most toxic vintage.[46] The problem is that high vacancy rates may continue in tertiary markets as long as investor risk tolerance remains low.

As discussed in chapter 7, US banks have been applying the so-called extend-and-pretend approach, or the "ever-greening" of over-leveraged commercial loans, basically extending the maturities and practicing forbearance to avoid recognizing losses, meaning that they're kicking the can down the road. Banks have been extending these loans and snow-plowing them to the present, but extend-and-pretend won't last forever.

Banks and borrowers have been able to conduct such ever-greening because interest rates have been extremely low. But when rates rise, this ever-greening will be harder to maintain. What makes this doubly harmful is that the rise in rates (expected in late 2014) will hit just as the sector is in the midst of a wave of refinancing. Therefore, it seems hard to believe that the $1.15 trillion in refinancing will occur smoothly, meaning that commercial defaults could rise further. If that is the case, the problem of debt maturities will hurt many small- and medium-sized US banks. Moody's, for example, estimates that US banks have barely recognized half of their commercial real estate losses, far less than for residential mortgages.

Another looming problem is the gap between the amount of commercial property debt maturities due and the amount of commercial mortgage-backed security deals in the pipeline. That is, the yawning gap between the approximately $32 billion of commercial mortgage-backed security deals that were expected in 2011 and the estimated $295 billion worth of commercial debt maturing in the same year. This gaping $263 billion hole could grow larger if a proportion of CMBS deals are allocated to new loans. The same problem could occur between 2012 and 2015, unless CMBS issuance really takes off or commercial property values increase significantly. US commercial real estate investors who bought into lower-grade properties backed by massive amounts of debt before the financial crisis are the most exposed. Vacancy rates in Class-B and Class-C properties are still double their pre-crisis levels in tertiary markets, and interest rates won't remain low forever.

As we are well aware, thousands of loans made on US commercial properties are coming due, but many of those property owners might be unable to pay the loans off or roll them over. This is because the market values of those properties have fallen significantly since the loans were made. In addition, most banks are no longer willing to make senior mortgages at loan-to-value (LTV) ratios of more than 65 percent—lower than the 70 to 90 percent ratios they used from 2000 to 2007. This means that owners could be asked to come up with a lot more equity capital to cover their loans.

The only way for the US to avoid widespread commercial property foreclosures and losses in asset values would be for other investors to put up capital to cover the equity gaps. Table 11-2 provides an example of the equity gap problem. As shown, if the market value of a property has fallen significantly, the LTV ratio will rise (since the LTV ratio is the loan balance divided by the value). Assuming the borrower has a lender who is willing to refinance the loan, the borrower will need to come up with additional equity in order to stay under the lender's LTV ratio limit. In order to refinance, the borrower in this example needs to come up with $1,875,000 to refinance because of the property's declining value (even though there is $500,000 in equity remaining in the property). Increased underwriting standards would exacerbate the equity shortfall in this example, requiring an additional $750,000 ($2,625,000 - $1,875,000) to refinance based upon a more conservative 65 percent LTV limit.

Table 11-2: Example of Equity Gap

2007 (Property Financed with 5-year Loan)	
Property Value	$10,000,000
Outstanding Principal Balance	$7,500,000
Equity	$2,500,000
LTV	75.0%
2012 (Loan Matures—Borrower Must Refinance)	
Reduced Property Value	$7,500,000
Outstanding Principal Balance	$7,000,000
Equity	$500,000
LTV	93.3%
Available Loan with 75.0% LTV	$5,625,000
Equity Gap at 75.0% LTV*	**$1,875,000**
Available Loan with 65.0% LTV	$4,875,000
Equity Gap at 65.0% LTV**	**$2,625,000**

*Reduced property value less available loan ($7,500,000 - $5,625,000).

**Reduced property value less available loan ($7,500,000 - $4,875,000).

The equity gap amounts exclude the $500,000 in existing equity.

Underwater commercial property borrowers could be put in an even worse situation. Borrowers in such a situation may even own a property that is fully leased and generating more than enough rental income to cover debt service. Simply due to the decline in property values, thousands of otherwise healthy properties could face default and foreclosure because of this problem.

The banking system itself is unable to refinance such loans by supplying the capital required to close the equity gap between the original loans and the equity needed to pay off or roll them over. De-leveraging (i.e., lower LTVs) in general could make that difficult. Furthermore, commercial real estate bankers most likely won't repeat the favorable lending terms they offered from 2003 through 2007.

Many distressed commercial loans that result in foreclosures could be worked out if certain basic steps are taken by both lenders and borrowers to cooperatively negotiate a consenting resolution. Additionally, borrowers need to accept that times have changed and they could be required to bring in new equity from market players if they want to keep their assets.

However, there remains the bigger systemic question of how the commercial real estate debt problem will impact the overall economy. Although there is no magic wand here—no quick fix—the problem of commercial debt maturities must be addressed. Regulatory measures that give banks a way out of their losses without signing their own death warrants and expediting more commercial loan workouts may be part of the solution.

Problem #5: Private-Label Mortgage-Backed Securities

Some private institutions, such as mortgage brokers, mortgage bankers, credit unions, commercial and investment banks, and homebuilders also securitize loans, known as "private-label" (or non-agency) securities, which are traded in the primary mortgage market. After being originated in the primary market, most mortgages are then sold into the secondary market. Most mortgages usually end up as part of a package of loans that comprise an MBS.

The first private-label MBS was sold in 1977, several years after US government-guaranteed RMBSs emerged. At the time, there were many questions about whether investors would ever buy RMBSs without a government guarantee, or whether investors not used to buying mortgage debt would actually venture into these new securities. Similar questions are being asked again because of the complete loss of confidence in the ratings of RMBSs. According to Amherst Securities Group, roughly 30 percent of private-label securities have missed at least two payments, signaling further concerns over US mortgage defaults.

In many respects, 2010–11 were the best of times in the secondary market and the worst in the primary market. The private residential mortgage-backed securities market has been shrinking. In 2011, it was down by nearly $725 billion since its peak in 2005 (see figure 11-9), which has buoyed demand for government guaranteed debt.

Figure 11-9: US Non-Agency RMBSs

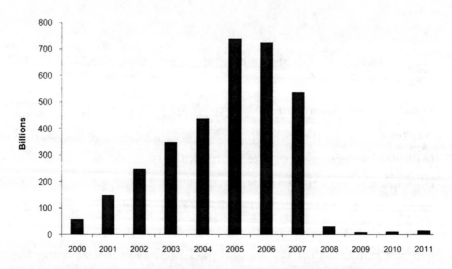

Source: Securities Industry and Financial Markets Association (SIFMA)

However, the lack of new deals doesn't mean that there are no new home loans being made in the United States. Instead of being privately financed, new mortgages are almost entirely funded by the US government, through its backing of Fannie, Freddie, and the FHA. These enterprises have bought the vast majority of new mortgages from banks and repackaged them into government-guaranteed RMBSs in the secondary market.

Although recent public opinion has focused on what went wrong with securitization, once again it's important to recognize its benefits when applied with prudence and restraint. Securitization has played an expanding role in the US economy, growing over the past twenty-five years to an important source of credit. Given the pivotal role of securitization as an alternative and flexible funding channel, failure to restart private-label securitization would come at the cost of prolonging funding pressures on banks and a diminution of credit. For example, the International Monetary Fund (IMF) reiterates this in its *Global Financial Stability Report*, noting that restarting private-label securitization markets in the US is critical to limiting the fallout from the financial crisis.[47]

Those Damn Foreigners!

I would like to end this chapter with a comparative overview of mortgage finance in other countries. As of 2007, US mortgage finance went from being the envy of the world to a case study of spectacular failure. Therefore, it should be beneficial to take a look at other countries that weren't heavily impacted by the global credit crunch, namely Canada and Germany.

O Canada!

Canada's housing market is vastly outperforming that of the US because it didn't experience an American-style housing collapse. The weak lending practices and high-risk mortgage products that caused the financial meltdown in the United States were largely absent in Canada. At 68 percent, Canada's current homeownership rate is generally comparable to that of the United States. However, the US' northern neighbor doesn't have the equivalent of Fannie Mae or Freddie Mac, which buy mortgage loans in the secondary market. Canada also doesn't protect defaulting homeowners from being sued by banks for deficiencies, and the vast majority of its banks hold onto—rather than securitize—mortgage loans. In addition, Canada's tax code doesn't encourage its residents to take on excessive mortgage debt by making mortgage interest tax deductible, as in the United States.

Canadian private banks typically require 20 percent down payments. While mortgage borrowing with a loan-to-value above 75 percent requires the purchase of insurance (similar to the FHA) from the Canada Mortgage and Housing Corporation (CMHC)—the dominant credit insurer of mortgages in the country—unsecured loans represent a small percentage of the overall loan market. Canada's mortgage delinquencies have also remained significantly lower than in America, with the percentage of loans delinquent thirty days or more at just 0.5 percent.

Canadian mortgage lenders have full recourse to the mortgage borrower's other assets and income, in addition to having the house as collateral. This means there is little incentive for borrowers to simply walk away from their mortgage like some Americans do with strategic defaults. Mortgage lending in Canada is clearly more conservative than the United States and is much more creditor-friendly. This relative creditor conservatism has meant that Canada and its banks came through the global financial crisis in much better shape than their US counterparts.

Rollover mortgages are the dominant residential lending product in Canada. As will be discussed in chapter 12, these loans have a fixed rate for up to five years, with a twenty-five-year amortization period. At the end of the fixed rate period, the rate adjusts to the new market rate, while there is a prepayment penalty during the fixed period.

Germany—Simply Inspiring

Germany has been posting inspiring economic growth numbers, easily outdistancing those of the United States. Its top-notch exports are booming, especially in China, where its brands are in high demand. Germany's unemployment rate, at 6.6 percent, is nearly two full percentage points below that of the United States and about in line with Canada's.

The combination of engineering excellence, impeccable quality, and technical innovation of German manufacturers enables them to command a premium price around the world. Although some German lenders haven't been successful with their US real estate ventures, it's clear that Germans know how to do things right domestically, especially with their housing finance system.

Mortgage banks are major residential lenders in Germany. They are regulated by a single financial regulatory agency, the BaFin. In Germany, bank-issued *pfandbriefe*, which are often referred to as "covered bonds," constitute the largest and most liquid market for private sector debt securities. Pfandbriefe, besides being secured by a mortgage portfolio, are also senior liabilities of the bank. In contrast, US residential mortgage-backed securities are much riskier, with an investor's claim limited to a mortgage pool held by a special purpose entity with no skin in the game.

As will be discussed in the next chapter, covered bonds are dual recourse instruments, meaning that investors have a priority claim on the performing mortgage assets in the event of an issuer default, as well as a general claim on the assets of the issuing institution. Therefore, the lender bears the credit risk of the mortgage. Underwriting requirements are also very strict in the covered bond model. As a result, mortgage delinquency rates in Germany have been very low, to the tune of 1.6 percent.

———

Like Canada, rollover mortgages are the dominant lending product in Germany. The country has a current homeownership rate of only 43 percent (which has remained quite constant over the last five years), mainly because of laws that are very favorable to tenants, including limits on rent increases and generous depreciation allowances for rental properties. The annual allowance for depreciation of newly constructed rental housing is 7 percent for the first four years after completion; 5 percent for the next six; 2 percent for the following six; and 1.25 percent for the last twenty-four years.[48] The requirement for a large down payment, often 20 to 30 percent of the home's price, is also a major factor for Germany's low homeownership rate.

Table 11-3 summarizes key mortgage-related statistics for Canada, Germany, and the United States. As presented, the 2008 mortgage debt-to-GDP ratio (at the height of the global credit crunch) was 62 percent in Canada, 43 percent in Germany, and a monstrous 93 percent in the United States. Another alarming statistic is the US mortgage delinquency rate in 2009 (at the end of the Great Recession), which stood at 12.1 percent, compared to 1.6 percent in Germany, and 0.5 percent in Canada. This explains why there was little, if any, good news about housing in the United States in 2011. So believe it or not, we Americans can learn a thing or two from other countries.

Table 11-3: Key Mortgage-Related Statistics

Country	Home-ownership Rate ('06)	Average LTV of New Loans ('06)	Mortgage Debt-to-GDP Ratio ('08)	Decline of Home Prices ('08)	Mortgage Delinquency Rate ('09)
Canada	66.0%	75.0%	62.0%	-3.1%	0.5%
Germany	42.0%	75.0%	43.0%	-1.8%	1.6%
US	69.0%	80.0%	93.0%	-18.1%	12.1%

Source: International Monetary Fund (IMF), World Bank, central banks

Conclusion

Unrealistic assumptions, layers of over-leveraged investors, sky-high prices, an oversupply of money, and cronyism—all stemming from the financial crisis—are making it hard to clean up the mess in American real estate. For those reasons, the economy won't be easily lifted out of its weakness as has typically happened after previous recessions. And for those reasons, the US property sector still has to face the music and deal with its unresolved problems.

Bankers, in their rush to make more and more loans, accepted borrowers' wild optimism and overlooked lots of shortcomings on loan applications. They did so in part because they could easily sell their debt to investors in the form of mortgage-backed securities. As the market overheated, the MBS segment had significantly deteriorating loan underwriting standards and the credit ratings incorrectly assessed the risk of new mortgage-backed security issuance.

For the banks and investors whose money drives the economy, this poses unresolved problems. Their losses could cast a cloud over real estate lending for years to come. In the short-term, toxic securities are creating a problem that is weighing heavily on the market—a web of tangled investors fighting over the leftovers of the properties they own. In the past, the damage was limited to a handful of lenders who invested directly in any given property. Today, the arena is filled with dozens of groups of investors, each with its own hidden agenda.

Although not insurmountable, real estate in the United States still has troubles to deal with, and those ignoring the unresolved problems do so at their peril. Whatever is done or not done will have important implications for the evolution of the US economy.

The next chapter discusses possible solutions to these long-running dilemmas which, if applied properly, should bolster the economic recovery and shorten the pains of post-crisis real estate investments. The time has come for an American renewal.

Chapter 12: An American Renewal

Those who cannot remember the past are
condemned to repeat its errors.
—George Santayana, philosopher

As presented in the previous chapter, real estate in America has serious unresolved problems that lie underneath its flawed financial system, potentially impacting the US economy for years to come. If I were a naysayer, the concluding chapter to this book would have been titled: "After the Good Life Goes Sour." But I'm an optimist who believes that a new American model will shine again. It will shine again—albeit in a different way—if the financial system learns from its major blunders and its unresolved problems are properly fixed.

"You only find out who is swimming naked when the tide goes out," Warren Buffett once mused. The previous American model has been exposed as a costly disaster that cannot be repeated, with many of the players in US real estate swimming buck-naked when the financial crisis hit, exposing the glaring errors they made.

Live and Learn

For a nation as large and complex as America, it will take many years to fundamentally change its old ways. However, some change is already underway. The first thing that has changed is that Americans have finally learned that housing prices don't go up forever, and that the recent boom will probably never happen again in their lifetime.

Lenders have seen that underwriting guidelines for property loans in the securitization markets were deeply erroneous. They realized that most properties had been financed too aggressively, although very few predicted a wholesale price collapse in real estate. Banks have grasped that they must be more prudent with loan underwriting, especially after the failure of so many of them since 2008.

———

Memories of US real estate cycles are short and some of the lessons are never taken on board at all. So the question is whether we're smart enough this time around to use what happened and actually learn from our mistakes.

Before I discuss the possible solutions to the unresolved problems in US real estate, it would be beneficial to first provide a summary of ten broad lessons from the financial meltdown. If the following lessons have indeed been learned, then America is on its way to happier days. If not, then the United States risks becoming a grand celebration of incompetence and mediocrity—diminishing the "American experience."

1. **Underwrite Your Own Risk**. It's back to basics as the real estate lending business relearns some old credit lessons. During the easy money environment from 2003 to 2007, many banks abandoned the fundamental responsibility of underwriting their own risk and ignored the basic

principles of sound lending. The crux of the problem was an explosion of the originate-to-sell loan model.[1]

To avoid repeating the abandonment of underwriting risk, lenders should originate-to-*hold*. Many banks found that they had the blame thrust on them when the credit markets froze, and they were unable to sell mortgages they had no intention of holding in the first place. This isn't to say that the originate-to-sell model won't eventually return in a modified form, but if we want to avoid a similar catastrophe in the future it is incumbent on lenders to at least make sure that the front-end underwriting is sound.[2]

Second, lenders shouldn't rely solely on third parties to grade risk. Many commercial mortgage-backed security buyers were completely reliant on the "spaced-out" rating agencies to assess risk. Credit risk ratings should only be a component of a bank's risk rating system; therefore, independent due diligence must always be completed.

Third, if lenders don't understand the risk involved in a transaction, they ought to just say no. Many banks that refused to follow the herd and steered clear of seemingly attractive capital market products did so because they didn't adequately understand the risk in the transactions. A wise banker once said, "If you can't explain the risk in a transaction to your mother in five minutes or less, then you probably should decline the request."[3]

Fourth, changes to risk management and underwriting practices are needed. That is, more emphasis on affordability, more rigorous stress-testing, and better pricing for borrowers who have more equity to put in a deal.

2. **Make Loans That Can Actually Be Repaid**. Capacity (or cash flow) is one of the "Five Cs" of credit (character, capacity, capital, collateral, and conditions), but it was largely ignored during the housing boom.

   There is plenty of blame to go around for the market malaise that has plagued real estate lending. The government made it too easy to borrow money with low rates, an abundant money supply, and the quasi-public entities Freddie Mac and Fannie Mae that purchased subprime loans on the cheap. Mortgage borrowers sometimes misrepresented information to obtain credit, and Wall Street geeks created a fee-frenzy with complex debt structures to shift risk around. But every loan starts with a borrower, and it's incumbent on every lender to confirm that the borrower can actually repay that loan.[4]

3. **Demand Equity**. If there is one collective lesson from the past, it is that excessive leverage is lethal. Increasing the amount of equity that banks have to hold is one way of keeping down the amount of debt that easily finds its way into real estate. The best way to limit the damage from a property bust is to exercise more direct control over the amount of debt available to property owners and developers, whether through discretionary interventions or standing rules.

   One of the prevailing characteristics of the easy-credit environment was a seemingly unlimited tolerance for excess leverage. It started with some of the lenders in the unregulated investment banking arena that operated with leverage ratios of 30:1 and higher.[5] In the lending arena, the chronic lack of required equity was evident in a number of different segments, particularly in real estate-related credit. As the housing bubble continued to expand, development loans were extended with as little as 10 percent in "equity," often allowing the borrower to trickle it in as the work was completed.[6] Home construction loans were done at 80 percent to 85 percent of appraised value, which often allowed builders to put money in their pockets out of the proceeds. Once the house was complete, an eager buyer quickly purchased it with the equally eager first-lien mortgage lender who routinely provided 100 percent financing.[7] The homeowner could then find any number of lenders to whack on a home-equity line of up to 125 percent of the house value. As a result, defaults quickly reached record levels when the housing bubble burst, due to the negative equity position in which many homeowners found themselves.[8]

With similar leverage tolerance levels in the commercial mortgage-backed securities market, we have seen similar problems. The lack of skin in the game leaves no cushion for the lender or borrower to work through an economic downturn. To that end, at least 15 percent in equity should be considered as a core component of most lending decisions.

4. **Stick to Your Core Competencies**. Generally, the mega-banks are very good at serving the needs of the large corporate sector. Many regional banks thrive in middle-market and small business lending, while community banks focus on local businesses and individuals. Some banks are particularly adept at mortgage lending, while others have mastered certain types of specialized lending such as asset-based financing, leasing, and credit cards.

During the lending mania, many banks got greedy and moved away from their core competencies. Nearly all of the large banks incurred significant subprime exposure either by originating it themselves or by buying it in the form of mortgage-backed securities. Of course, insurance companies, financing firms, and hedge funds also joined the subprime rhapsody. Many players had limited mortgage expertise, while some regional banks moved away from their bread-and-butter lending in markets with which they were most familiar.[9]

5. **Know Your Counterparties**. One of the many shifts of the credit boom was the use of credit-default swaps (CDSs), or debt repayment insurance, to offload risk. Before 2000, if a bank wanted to reduce risk exposures to a "single-name," there were two basic options: (1) Find participants to buy specific positions in a specific transaction, or (2) purchase CDS insurance. (The simplest—and most common—type of credit-default swap was one where there was just one borrower. This is called a "single-name" CDS). In either case, the counterparty risk was generally known to the bank and could be underwritten and monitored easily.[10] If the primary borrower defaulted, the bank could go directly to the insurance company with a CDS claim.

Then the market aggressively introduced "naked trading" of CDSs with neither party actually having to hold the bonds being insured, which allowed banks (and many others) to trade single-name risk on public companies just as they might trade a stock or swap interest rate risk. Because CDSs were traded over-the-counter with no central exchange, no one knew for sure how much exposure there actually was in the system, though most estimates place the global notional, or face, value—calculated at several times the actual level of debt in the market—at more than \$60 trillion.[11] That's because with no transparent market for CDSs, risk positions were hedged and rehedged. So if a bank purchased CDSs there was no control over the ultimate counterparty guaranteeing the risk. It was like buying a life insurance policy on someone you barely know, with the party doing the insuring not necessarily having the money to settle the claim if the third party dies.

6. **Invest Long-Term**. Investment banks such as Bear Stearns and Lehman Brothers financed much of twentieth-century America. That disappeared years later when they fell into the hands of short-termists intent on instant profits. They were merchants of fast transactions rather than long-built relationships. The same applies to real estate, which shouldn't be considered as a short-term play but as a long-term hold.

7. **Don't Trust the Financial Models**. Dick Fuld, the fallen CEO of Lehman, bet on the algorithms that said financial instruments backed by subprime mortgages could not fail. Predictions and complex financial modeling often give the seductive allure of accuracy. Analysts put the standard inputs into their "black box" models and spat out predictions twelve months hence. Some probably didn't even put a confidence interval around those predictions, let alone acknowledge that alternative, high-risk scenarios existed. The financial crisis revealed that such methods ultimately lead to complacency and a false sense of infallibility.

It's better to acknowledge uncertainty, and it makes more sense to look at likely scenarios and the rough probabilities that unforeseen cyclical problems will occur. House prices, as we have learned at great cost, don't go up forever. In addition, mortgage markets can over-discount the risk of a market collapse, leading to the reduced pricing of debt risk.

8. **Don't Sell Garbage**. Oftentimes, capitalism makes money by betting on failure rather than success (think credit-default swaps). The investment banks of old were enterprises that dealt in goods of *real* value. The ones that went bust did so when they were caught peddling junk like screwed-up derivatives that bet on the default of lower-middle-class Americans.

9. **Incentives Matter**. Some loan officers, mortgage brokers, real estate agents, and appraisers were only focused on volume maximization in order to earn more in fees—they did *anything* to get loans approved. The same maximization of fee income at any cost applied to the pre-crisis investment bankers, private equity principals, and hedge fund managers.

10. **Don't Get Caught Up in the Hysteria**. Have the discipline to stop or watch from the sidelines. Watch and listen to market fundamentals, then act. When equity becomes much cheaper than debt, have the courage to tell your investors it's time to take a break. Don't invest because you have to; invest because you want to.[12] Therefore, it's best to rely on objective analysis, disciplined logic, and original thought. It's also better to keep an emotional distance from the market and not get too caught up in the media-induced hype and sensationalism that spark contagion.

Possible Answers and Solutions to the Unresolved Problems in US Real Estate

The US real estate sector still has numerous yet not insurmountable challenges. To try to provide answers and solutions to the unresolved problems of the property sector is a tricky task, especially when a multitude of financial regulations are still being formulated and the lingering effects of the Great Recession are still playing out.

At the macro-level, growth in gross domestic product (GDP) and the consumer price index (CPI), together with the control of unsustainable debt risk and more skin in the game, will stabilize the American real estate markets. However, there is plenty of additional fixing that needs to be done at the grassroots level, coupled with tectonic shifts in the way that homebuyers, investors, lenders, and regulators view debt and real estate.

This next section provides the possible answers and solutions to the five unresolved problems in US real estate that were discussed in the previous chapter. Although not without their costs, risks, legal intricacies, and trade-offs, the following summarizes what needs to be done, starting with the most pressing items and ending with the most complex.

Possible Answers to Problem #1: Misconceptions about Housing

Since the end of World War II, homeownership has been the very personification of the American Dream. A variety of government policies and programs significantly increased homeownership, but for millions of Americans, owning a home has not turned out as they expected.

Before the Great Depression, only a minority of Americans owned a home. But in the 1930s and 1940s, aggressive government policies brought about longer-term mortgages that lowered payments and enabled more people to buy a house. Fannie Mae was created to purchase those mortgages and grease the system. The tax deduction on mortgage-interest payments, around since 1913 when the federal income-tax system was created, privileged home buying over other types of spending.

Between 1940 and 1960, the homeownership rate rose from 44 percent to 62 percent, and from the 1970s to the 2000s, Americans over-leveraged their homes to the detriment of the US economy. In addition, incentives for homeownership distorted demand, encouraging people to buy bigger homes than they otherwise would. Artificial demand for bigger houses also skewed residential patterns, leading to excessive suburban sprawl.

Fannie Mae, Freddie Mac, and Wall Street built a massive home mortgage production machine to automate loan approvals and assemble and trade MBS pools—all of which exposed households to catastrophic risks.[13] In other words, for homeownership to live up to its promise, consumers and communities have to be insulated from destructive gyrations in property values and interest rates that can cause major instability.

———

Owning a home has been perceived as being the ultimate goal for most Americans, but it's not meant for everyone because of the economic realities of modern life. A house is a major investment that should not be underestimated. At the same time, it should not be pushed onto people who can't afford it. As such, the alternative of renting should be promoted by policymakers as being a viable socio-economic solution to not owning a home, and the United States should create incentives for people to put property out to rent. Tax laws that allow landlords to write off the first few thousand dollars they receive in rent, or a portion of their rental property's mortgage interest, would create incentives for renting.[14] In addition, and as is done in Germany, landlords should have access to a generous depreciation allowance that can be used to offset income from other sources.

An often-scorned mode of living, renting should be viewed more positively, especially after the disastrous impacts of the financial crisis, rendering the American Dream a hazy myth for many of those affected. Moreover, renters in America should have the option to do more than choose between two demanding masters: landlord or bank.

A form of ownership that could encourage more renters is the "land-trust model," which combines most of the benefits of homeownership with some of the best features of renting. There is no down payment, and closing costs are modest. If the home needs repairs, low-cost financial assistance is available. Even a market downturn wouldn't necessarily spell disaster.[15]

Land trusts are a type of "shared equity" financial structure named for the premise that a homeowner is not alone with the risks of property ownership. By one count, approximately 800,000 homeowners in the US have some kind of economic co-sponsor, whether they live in a home whose deed dictates that it remain affordable over time, a housing co-op, or a mobile-home park.[16] The shared equity model has been promoted by the well-endowed Ford Foundation, although the biggest challenge so far has been securing stable sources of the subsidies that actually put the "equity" into shared equity.

In a survey released by Fannie Mae, just 65 percent of respondents said that they preferred owning to renting, down from 89 percent fifteen years ago. The survey also indicated that the most common reason respondents gave for wanting to buy a home as opposed to renting was the quality of local schools, followed closely by safety. Both outranked purely economic reasons as a driving motive. In other words, it isn't ownership that the respondents seek but access to better services.

Owners stay in one place longer than renters, and they literally have an investment in their community. Therefore, offering renters an investment share in their local housing market is necessary.[17] Such an idea is already at work in Cincinnati, where the Cornerstone Community Loan Fund offers "renter equity," in which residents of its apartments receive credits each month, provided that they satisfy the terms of their leases. Tenants finish accumulating credits after five years and end up with the cash equivalent of close to $3,500.[18] The objective is to embed in residents the same pride as in the pride of ownership, in addition to creating a financial incentive for renters.

———

Most Americans view homeownership as a market-based commodity. But homes are not primarily investments—they are shelter, and the benefits of stable ownership to individual families and communities should be much more important than just a chance

to speculate on making a big payoff from owning a home.[19]
Therefore, and in the wake of the financial crisis, the unjustified
stigma associated with renting should be diminished via a viable
government-funded public relations campaign.

The goals of housing should be that people are well housed,
not necessarily that they are homeowners. That is, the United
States needs sustainable homeownership, not just homeownership for ownership's sake. While house prices soared in the past
decade, over the longer-term they have generally increased by
about 1 percent a year above the national rate of inflation. In that
respect, stocks have generated a far higher return. A $100 invest-
ment in housing in 1933 is now worth $178, adjusted for inflation.
A similar investment in stocks would be worth $932 in today's dol-
lars, according to Robert Shiller of Yale.[20]

Buying a home also includes legal fees and other costs. For
such costs to be recovered, owners usually must stay in their homes
for at least five years, and that's in a normal market, not one where
prices have declined significantly. These are economic realities
that potential homebuyers must be made aware of, reminding
them that homeownership is not an American nirvana.

————

As many of us know, if you own a home in the United States today
you get a tax deduction on your mortgage interest. The mortgage-interest deduction basically works like this: say a homebuyer
makes $60,000 a year and paid $6,000 last year in interest on his
mortgage. If he claimed his mortgage-interest deduction, the IRS
would tax only $54,000 of his income (or less if he claimed other

deductions). The IRS also lets people claim deductions on interest they pay on a second-home or a home-equity loan. The home mortgages must be $1 million or less, and the home-equity loans must be $100,000 or less.

I would like to take the opportunity to discuss the controversial issue of whether the mortgage-interest deduction should be phased-out, but the following questions first need to be considered: Who gains, who loses, and by which mechanisms? Is the change desirable?

There has been a growing push to get rid of this major government subsidy. The disparate arguments, which touch on the questions above, are as follows:[21]

- The policy should be changed because it doesn't really encourage homeownership as it's supposed to.
- The government shouldn't be encouraging or subsidizing homeownership, especially following the disastrous effects of the recent mortgage meltdown.
- The government can't keep giving out such a big tax break when it faces huge debts and resulting deficits.
- The policy isn't giving enough of a tax break to lower-income families.
- The deduction has encouraged investment in housing over other sectors of the economy.

Despite the objections, it will be difficult to revamp a tax deduction that's been in place for nearly a century. The housing sector's powerful lobby—realtors, homebuilders, bankers, and everybody who has a vested interest in preserving the deduction—is sure to fight any proposal that would discourage home buying, particularly given the weakness of the US housing market. In addition, both Congress and the White House would have to approve any changes to the tax code, and they will certainly be reluctant to debate such a controversial issue before the 2012 presidential election.[22]

At any rate, consumer groups say the government should replace the deduction with a tax credit of up to $5,000 a year for moderate- and low-income families buying mid- or low-priced homes. (A $5,000 credit, unlike a deduction, would wipe out the first $5,000 of tax owed to the IRS). The Greenlining Institute says this plan would add to the government's tax coffers while giving tax breaks to the people who most need them.

The Obama administration's 2012 budget leaves the deduction in place, but it puts limits on the deductions claimed by families making more than $250,000 a year. The president's deficit commission also advocates changing the tax deduction to a tax credit, which would cap eligible mortgages at $500,000 instead of $1 million, and eliminate any tax benefits for second-homes and home-equity loans. Further, the Office of Management and Budget (OMB) estimates that the mortgage-interest deduction cost the government $79 billion in forgone taxes in 2010. That could rise to as much as $144 billion in 2016, according to the OMB, strengthening the case that the government should get rid of the deduction to help plug its massive budget gap. The advantages and disadvantages of the contentious mortgage-interest deduction are summarized in table 12-1.

Table 12-1: The Pros and Cons of the
Mortgage-Interest Deduction

Pros	Cons
• It is helpful for people who bought their homes recently. That's because when you first buy a home, a large portion of each monthly payment goes toward paying down the interest. Over time, the portion of your monthly payment that goes toward interest will shrink, and the portion that goes toward principal will increase, at least in most home loans. • A National Association of Realtors (NAR) survey of almost 3,000 homeowners and renters indicated that nearly 75 percent of the homeowners and 66 percent of the renters said the mortgage-interest deduction was "extremely" or "very" important.	• Changes to the mortgage-interest deduction now or in the future could erode home prices. • The government shouldn't subsidize homeownership. The government pushed homeownership hard in the 1990s and early 2000s, and many of the borrowers couldn't afford their homes. Most experts agree that this was one of the causes of the financial meltdown. • The tax deduction encourages more mortgage debt. • It doesn't fulfill its stated purpose to increase home buying. Australia and England don't give tax deductions on mortgage interest, and they have higher homeownership rates than the US.

(Table continued on next page...)

Pros	Cons
• Encourages people to buy homes with the idea that homeowners take better care of their property, contribute more to their neighborhoods, and can build wealth. • Middle- and lower-income homeowners tend to get a better deal by claiming the standard deduction instead of itemizing to claim the mortgage-interest deduction.*	• Tends to disproportionately benefit families making $100,000 or more a year, largely because they have the biggest houses and the biggest house payments. • It's doubtful that the mortgage-interest deduction is *the* deciding factor when a family chooses to buy a home, though it may encourage some families to buy bigger homes.

*The standard deduction for most single adults was $5,700 in 2011 (or $11,400 for married couples). So, all else being equal, the homeowner who pays $5,000 a year in mortgage interest would be better off claiming the standard deduction instead of the mortgage-interest deduction.

The issue of the mortgage-interest deduction is obviously highly controversial, with several pros and cons depending on which standpoint is considered. Perhaps what needs to be considered by regulators is a midway point. That is, the government should consider capping or gradually cutting the tax deduction, which is the only such subsidy of its kind in the West.

The US government's support of the housing market has been pervasive but has not yielded many of the expected benefits to prospective or existing homeowners. The US provides a plethora of tax breaks and subsidies at the federal level, as well as state and local property tax deductions and exclusions from capital gains taxation. To that end, it's clear that an overhaul is needed, including a gradual phasing-out of the expensive and regressive mortgage-interest deduction in America.

Possible Answers to Problem #2: Negative Home Equity

US home prices are in a double dip that has erased all of their bounce since the recession and threatens to derail a stuttering economic recovery. According to Capital Economics, house prices in 2011 were 33 percent below their peak in 2006—a sharper fall than the 31 percent drop during the Great Depression. Roubini Global Economics forecast a year-on-year fall in house prices of 8 percent for 2011.

As home prices continue to fall, the problem of negative equity has grown and keeps getting worse. US mortgages are suffering from two serious unresolved problems that continue to delay a recovery in the housing market, threatening the broader economy. First, estimates by CoreLogic put as many as 23 percent of US homes in 2011 as being underwater. It is also estimated that about 1.8 million homes are more than ninety days delinquent—shadow inventory that's set to add to the 2.3 million homes already in foreclosure, and the unsold supply of approximately 3.9 million previously owned homes already on the market. In many cases this is a result of poorly informed households buying homes at the peak of a housing bubble with reckless lenders allowing them to be significantly over-leveraged. Second, the current anemic job growth continues to cause additional mortgage delinquencies (and subsequent defaults and foreclosures).

Loan-to-value (LTV) is one of the risk factors that lenders assess when qualifying borrowers for a mortgage. The likelihood of a lender absorbing a loss in the foreclosure process increases as the amount of equity decreases. Therefore, as the LTV ratio of a loan increases, the qualification guidelines for mortgage programs must be stricter.

There's no doubt that the need for mortgage financing is essential to facilitate property ownership. However, due to the liquidity risk associated with long-term financing through mortgages, and given the disastrous effects of over-leveraged real estate, US regulators should consider limiting banks to offer loans secured by real estate at a ceiling of 10 percent of their total assets (compared to a whopping 38 percent in 2007).[23] This would protect bank balance sheets from being over-exposed to property risk.

It's important to highlight that the excessive real estate exposure and lack of diversification of small and regional banks has been a major factor in bank closings, and is likely to continue pressuring these institutions going forward. Moreover, regulators should also consider putting a cap on allowable LTVs. That is, most borrowers shouldn't be allowed to get loans that are higher than 85 percent of a home's value.

The proposed 5 percent rule discussed in chapter 10, known as "risk retention," would require that mortgage lenders invest in the loans they make, so if the loans go bad, the lender would suffer. Lenders would have to accept 5 percent of the losses. But banks would not have to retain any risk for mortgages made to borrowers who put down at least 15 percent, making the loans relatively safer. As a result, the cost to the banks would be less, and they would be able to offer lower interest rates for these loans.

Some critics have noted that these conditions would keep eligible borrowers from getting good terms on their loans. In other words, if lenders require higher down payments to get a loan, broad swaths of working- and middle-class people would not be able to get a mortgage. I fully respect the opinion of the critics; however, the subprime crisis and the resulting financial meltdown should have taught us that homeownership isn't for everyone. I'm also aware that imposing rigid limits on how much people can borrow either disenfranchises some (first-time buyers and the self-employed tend to suffer the most), or risks encouraging them to find a way around the rules by maxing-out their borrowing with more expensive, unsecured financing. Some lenders also express concern that if underwriting becomes too stringent, borrowers are relieved of taking responsibility for their own actions. These are legitimate worries, and they resemble disturbing reverberations of arguments that were put forward by some analysts and academics at the height of the recent housing boom.

However, putting a ceiling on the amount of loans that banks can lend in the high-risk residential real estate sector and placing a cap on allowable LTVs would prevent the risks of excessive housing leverage from impacting the US financial system once and for all. Moreover, holding a higher equity stake in one's home has benefits that extend beyond the owner. First, it helps make the housing market more stable. One of the reasons that there are still high rates of home foreclosures today is the high incidence of households that have no equity. Homeowners with more equity are less likely to abandon their homes when faced with financial hardship.[24]

Secondly, higher equity stakes allow for greater labor mobility and, therefore, a more efficient allocation of human resources. Homeowners with higher equity are better able to absorb transaction and moving costs when relocating in pursuit of better employment, especially in times when unemployment is high and home prices are falling.

The recent sharp drop in homeowner equity is of major concern for the US economy. Since the Great Recession began, owners' average equity as a percentage of household real estate has fallen below 40 percent for the first time since 1945.

———

According to MIT economist William Wheaton, to fix the negative home equity problem existing mortgages could be restructured into two parts: (1) A standard new mortgage against the current (reduced) value of the home, and (2) a claim against some fraction of any capital gains (above the reduced value) when the home is sold.[25] When a household sells their home, they would have to pay off both claims and take away their share of any gains accrued. Most likely, the lender's claim on future gains would be capped, for example, at a value equal to the difference between the original mortgage balance and the amount created in part 2 above.[26]

To illustrate, consider the tight spot of an owner whose original house and loan were established at $100,000, but whose house is currently valued at only $60,000. The loan is therefore 40 percent underwater ($60,000 - $100,000 = -$40,000).[27] When restructured, the loan would be divided into a $60,000 traditional mortgage and a claim of, say, 50 percent of the future appreciation (but capped at $40,000). The borrower's payments would fall by 40 percent, but later when he moves and the property sells for, say, $90,000, he would surrender $15,000 of the sales proceeds ($90,000 - $60,000 = $30,000 x 50% = $15,000) to the lender. The lender might even recover all its money if, later on, the property sells for $140,000. The owner's gain in this case would be reduced from $80,000 to $40,000, but at least he's getting something out of his underwater mortgage.[28] Since the claim is in "current" dollars, inflation alone supports the prospect for eventual loan recovery.

For borrowers, this financing structure would eliminate the growing potential of strategic defaults, where owners just walk away from their underwater loans, suffering potential bankruptcy and the loss of credit for at least the next seven years. The new loan's payments in the example above would be less, yet would be more in line with what current buyers of similar homes would be experiencing. Owners would also maintain a stake in the value of their property, which would align home-maintenance incentives.[29]

There is a possible concern here that borrowers might sell their homes right away to try to release their second-claim obligation. Doing so would leave them with no equity, and hence (in today's market) the inability to buy another house. But the combination of reduced payments *and* some future stake should enable most to relocate whenever such need or opportunity arises.[30]

From the lender's perspective, we are seeing substantial resistance to restructuring mortgages (principal write-downs) since restructured loans sometimes re-default. Most lenders believe that loans left alone could eventually get reinstated (i.e., the loans work themselves out based on the basic forces of supply and demand).[31] But this type of restructuring proposed by William Wheaton of MIT actually makes "self-curing" more likely and re-default *less* likely.

In addition, with a contingent claim (a claim that can be made only if one or more specified outcomes occur), lenders are also able to add an additional (fully liquid) asset on their books relative to a conventional modification. The value of this contingent claim would, of course, vary by market. Those areas that experienced more modest price bubbles and subsequent price declines (i.e., Texas) are likely to experience full price recovery. On the other hand, markets that went overboard (i.e., Florida, Nevada, Arizona, and California) would take much longer, hence a lower value for a contingent claim in those markets.

Moreover, such a restructuring would help owners who aren't able to make payments, even though their mortgage might be giving them some positive equity. Existing borrowers would certainly accept a lower share of the upside in exchange for reduced payments and a lower mortgage balance. To induce lenders into such an arrangement, the costs of foreclosure (plus the value of the contingent claim) would have to equal or exceed the write-down in balance with what each particular owner could afford. Such restructuring would not work for everyone, but it should help some homeowners with negative equity.[32]

There's actually a precedent for a similar form of mortgage restructuring. In the early 1980s, the Department of Housing and Urban Development suggested "shared appreciation mortgages" as a way of lowering payments for first-time buyers. A shared appreciation mortgage is one where a lender agrees as part of a loan to accept some or all payment in the form of a share of the increase in value (appreciation) of a property over time.

In the current environment there is sufficient opportunity for the US government to lead in such mortgage restructuring. Troubled loans on the books of Fannie Mae and Freddie Mac could be repackaged as such and possibly a secondary market could be created for the contingent claims. The private sector could soon follow, narrowing the gap between house prices and homeowners' negative equity (see figure 12-1).

Figure 12-1: US Homeowners' Equity

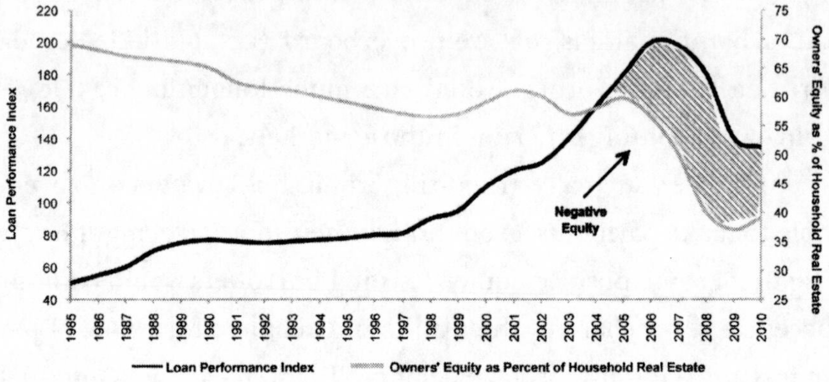

Source: Federal Reserve Board

Another possible solution to the unresolved problem of negative equity is that lenders "re-equify" borrowers by decreasing the loan balances to an amount that is less than the value of their homes.[33] That would go beyond the short-term solution of extending the term of the loan and giving the borrower more time to repay. It would force banks to admit that the collateral backing their loans is diminished, bringing their opaque balance sheets much closer to reality.

The goal from a public policy standpoint should be to have an orderly decline in values back to historical norms without further depleting jobs and savings. But the larger dilemma is that underwater homeowners don't have any more skin in the game left and banks have no incentive to take the write-downs.

Effective principal reductions could also be achieved if the lender, or another owner of the mortgage, sells it at a big discount to an investor. That investor then reduces the loan balance and refinances the borrower into a mortgage insured by the FHA. Now the US government would be holding the bag on a loan that might be sustainable.[34]

Furthermore, there is an option that could be both fair and effective. It requires a marketplace in which third party investors can co-invest in the home with the current homeowner and purchase, as a result, an equity stake in the home itself. That is, the bank receives external capital as an incentive to make an additional write-down. The investor gets a stake in a property he believes will yield a positive return. The homeowner gets a reduced principal and mortgage at the cost of the lost interest in a share of his home. In other words, it is fair to all parties, including the neighbors.

———

Principal reduction is not an across-the-board solution. Not every homeowner with a loan balance that exceeds the value of his home falls behind on his payments, and not every time the cost of the write-down is less than the expected cost of foreclosure should a write-down be done by a lender. For those reasons, principal reduction needs to be used in a very careful and focused way, and it is best to assist borrowers in areas with severe price declines where there is little prospect for the full recovery of home values.[35]

Therefore, principal reductions need to be done on a case-by-case basis and regulators need to be careful not to design a program that induces more people to walk away from their homes (strategic defaults), or one that people view as being selective or unfair. That is, regulators shouldn't reward and incentivize irresponsible behavior on the part of homeowners.

But how would principal reductions induce more people to walk away? For example, your neighbor—who hasn't made any payments on his loan for months—gets a big reduction in his loan balance. Meanwhile, you've been working two jobs to pay your mortgage each month. In this case, your reward from the bank would be zero. Therefore, you might decide to stop paying too in the hope of getting the same deal your neighbor got from the bank (i.e., freeloading).

There's no doubt that the negative equity chaos is impacting America's economic recovery. Millions of homes have already plummeted in value, and if the banks take them back through foreclosure they will be selling them at or below market value. Today's market value is likely to be below the current loan balance for the home, and selling another home at a distressed price adds downward pressure on the surrounding area. As such, this cycle needs to be broken or the US housing might not fully recover.

In addition to the argument mentioned earlier about regulators being selective or unfair, the obstacle of second-liens on underwater homes is another debate against principal reductions. A second-lien is a second-mortgage on a house. The second-lien is junior to the first-mortgage, meaning that if the borrower defaults and the first lender decides to foreclose, the proceeds from the sale go to pay off the first-mortgage; the second-lien only gets paid back if the sale proceeds exceed the amount due on the first-mortgage. That is, if there is any "juice" left in the deal.

Large numbers of second-liens today have little or no real economic value. The first-liens are well underwater and the prospect for any real return on the seconds is negligible. Yet because accounting rules allow holders of these seconds to carry the loans at artificially high values, many banks and mortgage servicers refuse to acknowledge the losses, meaning that willing first-lien holders can't reduce their principal.

First-lien holders are sometimes willing to reduce the principal on underwater mortgages, because it allows them to minimize their losses compared to allowing the property to drift into foreclosure. However, such loan modifications are often blocked by second-lien holders who can no longer claim any equity in the home but still hold out for a share of the compensation. As such, banks and financial regulators need to take the necessary steps to write-down these second-mortgages and allow principal reductions of the underlying first-liens to take place on a practical, case-by-case basis.

A proposal from Congressman Brad Miller of North Carolina supports using eminent domain to buy second-lien mortgages from banks at market value. Although this could put some banks out of business, Miller notes that the Dodd-Frank act has a mechanism to wind down large financial institutions in an orderly way, so as to not cause too much damage to the economy. At least with the government in the driver's seat, millions of homeowners would have a much better chance of staying in their homes. One of the main arguments for not forcing banks to take write-downs on second-lien mortgages is the assumption that housing prices are going to return to pre-2006 levels, but that isn't going to happen unless the country has another real estate bubble. Lastly, one of the problems with mortgage principal write-downs (and as discussed earlier) is moral hazard. That is, by offering to reduce the amount a borrower owes, it would encourage other borrowers who owe more than their home is worth (but could afford to continue making payments) to default on their loans, as they too would try to freeload and get their principal amounts reduced. The following three steps provide a possible approach to solving that problem:

- Provide an option for concerned households to write off a portion of their debt, but at the same time their credit rating would be reduced by certain grades.
- Give the banks an option to clean up their balance sheets by swapping the underwater assets for cash from an independent fund on a case-by-case basis.
- If the banks choose the above option, they need to hand a portion of the equity share to the independent fund. The fund could be set up through private capital raised in the financial markets.

Possible Answers to Problem #3: Delinquencies, Defaults, and Foreclosures

The solutions to the unresolved problem of delinquencies—which as we know often lead to defaults and foreclosures in the housing sector—not only require larger down payments and much stricter underwriting standards; they require both long- and short-term policies. Solving these complex, interconnected problems could take years as there has to be an orderly phase-out of government guarantees and a transition to a de-leveraged, market-based system.

Long-term, the idea proposed by Columbia University's Charles Calomiris—to increase minimum down payments by

1 percent per year over fifteen years, bringing them to approximately 15 percent—should be considered.[36] In addition, Peter Wallison of the American Enterprise Institute has suggested that the private sector be encouraged to grow by reducing the government-sponsored enterprises' maximum mortgage amount by a to-be-determined percentage every year until they are no longer important factors in the mortgage market, and then the GSEs can be privatized or gradually closed down.[37]

To fix the ubiquitous problems of foreclosures, short-term policies that promote de-leveraging need to be implemented. For example, some of the excess supply of foreclosed properties could be sold to buyers who agree to put close to 15 percent down and use the properties as rentals. In support of this, Josh Rosner of the research firm Graham Fisher has suggested that homeowners who voluntarily pay-down a portion of the principal on their underwater mortgage receive a tax credit that also applies toward their mortgage principal.[38] In return, they would forgo future tax deductions of their interest payments (assuming that the tax deductibility of mortgage interest isn't abolished anytime soon).

———

Lender custom-loan modifications for first-liens are usually evaluated by developing an estimated target affordable payment of 28 percent to 36 percent of the borrower's gross (pre-tax) income. Lenders use the lowest percentage for borrowers with the lowest incomes. Once the target payment is calculated for the borrower, lenders test each modification option to see if it will get the borrower to an affordable payment. Concurrently, lenders analyze each option to determine whether the value of the modification exceeds the value expected through foreclosure. Lenders then recommend the modification option that produces both an affordable payment and a positive value result. At the lender level, foreclosure prevention options include the following:

- Payment plans (where a borrower agrees to pay back arrearages over time).
- Deferments (where a borrower agrees to make late payments in the future).
- Borrower stipulations (where a borrower agrees to make a set of payments, often as a prelude to a modification).
- Short-sales/settlements (a form of principal forgiveness where the lender agrees to accept less than the amount of the mortgage in exchange for the underlying property or the proceeds of the sale of the property). Although borrowers do not keep their homes in short-sales and settlements, these may be appropriate solutions when the borrower has no interest in remaining in the home, or simply cannot afford the home over the long-term, even if payments are reduced by a modification.

In addition, and on a more local level, there are four potential roles for lenders in their community to fix the ubiquitous problem of home foreclosures:[39]

- Maintain vacant foreclosed properties that they hold (real estate-owned, or REO, properties) until a buyer can be found (it can take up to twelve months for such properties to be sold).
- Donate REO properties to community groups.
- Pay for demolition when REO properties are beyond repair (i.e., in Detroit).

- Provide access to borrower data that can help local groups with prevention, intervention, stabilization, and revitalization efforts.

To offset the costs associated with these local-level suggestions, regulators would need to provide financial support, such as tax breaks for the banks involved and monetary relief for any associated mortgage write-downs.

———

The all-American fixed rate mortgage (FRM), in which the interest rate on the note remains the same throughout the term of the loan—as opposed to a variable loan, in which the interest rate may adjust or "float"—was first developed by the FHA in the 1930s. Although the FRM has endured for more than seventy-five years, it has caused some serious problems to homeowners due to its lack of flexibility. Perhaps it's time for the US housing market to consider other forms of financing that reduce the risks of foreclosure.

An alternative financing structure that should be considered for purchasing residential real estate in the United States is the rollover mortgage, which is used extensively in Canada and Germany (as discussed in chapter 11). A rollover mortgage is not an adjustable-rate mortgage (ARM), which changes every set time period to the market rate based on an index such as Treasury securities or the London Interbank Offered Rate. But unlike a rollover mortgage, an ARM has a cap on how high or low the rate can go.

A rollover mortgage (RM) is one in which the amortization of principal is based on a longer-term, but the interest rate is established for a much shorter-term. The loan may be extended, or rolled over, at the end of the shorter-term at the current market interest rate. For example, a borrower obtains a rollover loan where the amortization term is for twenty-five to thirty years and the interest rate is 5 percent for five years. After five years, the borrower must renew the loan at the going interest rate, or refinance with a new loan. In other words, the rate is reset or refinanced to a second fixed rate.

More specifically, rates for the five-year term are dictated by market forces and are not linked to any external reference rate (an index). At the end of the five-year term, the principal becomes due and payable. The borrower has the option of paying off the unamortized principal or refinancing it with a new five-year loan at the going interest rate with payments geared to fully amortize the principal over the remainder of the original amortization period. Therefore, if interest rates decrease over the five-year period, the borrower's monthly payment will be less. Lenders can also reduce the rollover period on residential mortgages to one year to give borrowers more flexibility in managing interest rate risk by shopping around for the best loan terms.

In addition, the refinancing of RMs doesn't involve any new closing costs and certain changes can be made without incurring closing costs. For example, the borrower can repay part of the loan or reduce the amortization period but would face prepayment penalties during the fixed rate period.

RMs also allow for a high degree of asset and liability matching for lenders with no rate ceilings. In the case of large-scale residential and commercial developments, however, FRMs matching the amortization period would probably be favored because bor-rowers prefer the fixed contracts due to fears that rent increases would not match interest and price level increases.

An RM typically has lower rates than an FRM during its first few years. The lower rate is to compensate for the potential risk in the later years. As such, it allows the borrower to capitalize on current low interest rates and it gives the lender the opportunity to capitalize on any higher interest rates in the future.

A second alternative product is the "declining jackhammer interest mortgage," which automatically rewards a history of on-time payments by reducing the loan's rate.[40] For example, a lender offering a start rate of 7 percent on a mortgage with 15 per-cent down could steadily drop that rate to 5 percent over the first fifteen years of the mortgage. The process of dropping interest rates could go faster if the appraised property value moves up rap-idly. Borrowers then would have less incentive to refinance with another lender as they build equity. Better management of both default and prepayment risks would also make it easier for lenders to approve credit-worthy borrowers, thus decreasing the number of foreclosures.[41]

A third alternative is the "ratchet mortgage," which could mit-igate lending risks.[42] Falling interest rates trigger an automatic, no-cost rate drop on the ratchet mortgage, yet higher rates in the future wouldn't cause the borrower's payments to increase. Ratchet mortgages would be linked to a bond or mortgage-backed security whose rate moves in sync with the ratchet loan. Start rates would be equal to an FRM available to the borrower. In addition, lenders would maintain their interest rate spread and reduce pre-payment risk, while passing the risk of rate increases on to final investors.

Eliminating refinancing costs via ratchet mortgages should reduce foreclosures, because at-risk borrowers could find their monthly payments dropping without having to pay anything extra and without having their credit checked again (which reduces their FICO score). Originators, however, would be taken out of the refinancing process. But that could be resolved by increasing the initial commissions paid. Since the automatic refinancing provision would tend to increase the life span of ratchet mortgages, those additional origination expenses could be recouped by the lender's spread over funding costs.

———

Lastly, the US government could amend the bankruptcy law to allow people to include their prime residences in personal bankruptcy, thereby giving homeowners more leverage to get mortgage lenders to mitigate the terms of their loans. Bankruptcy judges have the right to reduce and even eliminate creditor claims in virtually all forms of bankruptcy—except when the debt is secured by a prime residence. For instance, if someone is bankrupt and owns a vacation house, a yacht, or a private jet, the judge has full authority to reduce the size of the debt and change the terms, but not for a prime residence. An amended bankruptcy law would be a way out of foreclosure hell for homeowners, offering them a fresh start.

Possible Answers to Problem #4: Commercial Debt Maturities

As previously discussed, the US real estate market faces a towering $1.15 trillion in commercial debt maturities. In an attempt to solve this potential problem, lenders need to shift more toward restructuring commercial loans (i.e., lowering the interest rates, case-by-case principal write-downs, or allowing for additional collateral), instead of simply extending maturities and kicking the can down the road. Restructuring commercial loans would assist borrowers because the "pay me later, pay me more" approach would only cause more damage to the sector.

While it has served as a Band-Aid practice right after the Great Recession, the practice of extend-and-pretend (loans continuing without significant changes to defer losses) is expected to unwind. In the meantime, distressed real estate with maturing loans could be foreclosed on and put on the market, putting further downward pressure on commercial property prices. As a result of the threatening debt maturities and the uncertainty surrounding loan modifications, commercial real estate investors have been lowering their return expectations as they enter "an era of less."[43]

In the next couple of years it will be very important for lenders to pay close attention to borrowers. There are many new loan requests reporting that they have to pay off their loan in thirty to sixty days. Some of these borrowers have solid credit, good pay histories, and financials, yet their banks are requiring them to pay off their loans. This is causing many borrowers to raise additional capital by selling other real estate holdings, causing financial duress to such in-good-standing borrowers.[44]

Some banks such as JPMorgan Chase and Wells Fargo are accepting short-sales on these loans just to get them off their books. The problem today, however, is that the banks aren't listening enough to the borrower. Instead of working out an "amicable" solution, some banks are throwing these good-credit customers out the door. Of course, not all loans are workable, so the lender has to really listen to the borrower to see if there is a possible solution, including case-by-case loan modifications.[45]

———

Commercial property owners are expected to have several challenges, even if they aren't in a position where they have to refinance. With vacancy rates still high and rental rates decreasing in some commercial real estate segments, it is important to maintain occupancy levels. Pride of ownership and gamesmanship are big factors, as well as property maintenance. If a landlord wants to keep his tenants, he needs to be sure they are content with their surroundings, because a competitor's building down the street is most likely offering rent concessions to lure them to the building. Although power is shifting from the tenant to the landlord, some owners are still throwing in large contributions to tenant improvements.[46] Under these current conditions, owners who will soon be facing a refinancing event need to be proactive to extend leases and must bring equity to the negotiation table as well. There is no time to wait because if they are not ahead of the game, owners will be shocked when they find out that the bank isn't able to give the amount of loan they were hoping for to refinance.[47]

Furthermore, buyers need to be sure they are paying attention to the market and not just buying what they think will be a "good deal." For example, there are many hidden risks in buying a bank REO property. That is, if a buyer doesn't thoroughly research the local market, he could end up with a cash-guzzling property. Due diligence has never been more important (i.e., Why did the previous owner fail? Is there something wrong with the property? If an investor is buying a distressed asset, the lender typically doesn't know the history—but does the investor know?)[48] It's important to keep in mind that banks selling REO property cannot provide any representations or warranties to a buyer, which increases the risk that a "surprise cost" cannot in any way be remedied by the selling bank after closing.

Commercial real estate agents (brokers) have been having a tough time trying to sell and lease properties in tertiary markets. The property owners are pushing them to sell at high enough prices to pay off the debt, with buyers, on the other hand, wanting to acquire properties at much less than the offering price. The agents need to look for ways to save through property tax appeals and lease restructuring, so they need to plan ahead and create a recovery plan for owners. If owners haven't created a plan before they have losses, they might not have the time to pull themselves out of the debt hole and find ways to fill their properties' equity gaps. To that end, owners need to plan ahead and be ready for potential losses and how to recover from them.[49]

The US banking system itself will be unable to refinance the approximately $1.15 trillion in commercial loans coming due by supplying the capital needed to close the gap between its original loans and the equity needed to pay off or extend those loans. There is, of course, the possibility that banks continue their favorable lending terms, particularly in terms of lower interest rates. That is, if faced with massive defaults, the banks could continue to kick the can down the road. It's already happening in the sense that the Fed has been keeping rates low so that owners can refinance at low rates when their teaser rates expire. By keeping rates low, the Fed is artificially keeping property values higher than they otherwise would be, and it's making it easier for some investors to qualify for larger loans. (A basic rule of thumb is that each one hundred basis points, or 1 percent, in interest rate is worth 10 percent in property value. It appears that rates have been held down artificially by at least one hundred to 200 basis points).

———

Banks are driven by their need to balance increasing liquidity by exiting their real estate loans with a desire not to take any losses beyond those already provided for. To avoid this, they have rolled over many loans to allow for market recovery, or more complex exit strategies. Another mechanism is to sell a property facing a large write-off, with the loan still attached and then share profits (depending on its subsequent performance). If a bank has an over-leveraged asset, it can inject equity and restructure the loan, so it will have good collateral and a good loan that will come back on its balance sheet. At the end of the day, it's all about the equity in the underlying collateral.

So far, most lenders have been under political pressure to either not foreclose or delay foreclosing. Many observers, including economist Nouriel Roubini of New York University, have called for principal forgiveness by lenders. Lenders have resisted wholesale principal forgiveness; however, if push comes to shove, they could eventually be forced into some kind of "give-and-take" situation. While there may be opportunities for new equity in the capital markets, one can't assume that equity is going to fill *all* the funding shortfalls. Lenders could extend and/or refinance at different LTVs; they could even take bigger write-offs than we might think. Time will tell.

At any rate, where would the needed equity come from? Table 12-2 summarizes four potential sources that could help work out the unresolved problem of commercial debt maturities.

Table 12-2: Potential Sources of Capital to Fill the Equity Gap[50]

Source of Capital	Comments
Opportunity and private equity funds	Most such firms have no interest in holding the properties concerned for long periods; rather, they want to sell them at a profit within one to a few years. These firms could buy the potentially delinquent properties from their current owners at distressed prices in the hope of improving cash flows and then selling them at a profit. Or they could simply resell the properties at slightly higher prices than they paid for them without improving cash flows. However, this group has to raise money for its activities by getting other investors to put up cash. In the past, these funds have raised large amounts of money by promising investors high leveraged yields, in the 17 percent to 30 percent range, very unlikely in today's economic climate. Some funds that concentrate mainly on core properties may be able to attract funds with promises of lower yields than those they promised in the past. But it is unlikely that more aggressive opportunity and private equity funds—which traditionally promised high yields—will be able to attract enough capital from their own investors. This potential source would not be enough to provide a large amount of the missing equity necessary to cope with all the commercial debts soon coming due, especially with such properties throwing off lower yields than in the past. Opportunity and/or private equity funds will not be able to produce the high yields such groups have traditionally promised their investors. Hence, except for some core investment funds, they will find it harder to raise capital than in the boom years of the mid-2000s.

(Table continued on next two pages...)

Source of Capital	Comments
Publicly held real estate investment trusts (REITs)	Most REITs are only leveraged with debt by 50 percent, so they are not very susceptible to bankruptcy—a key reason they are usually able to raise more capital. REITs can raise large amounts of capital in public markets, and can use it to de-leverage their balance sheets. But REITs could use their capital to buy many of the properties with debts coming due in the next few years (assuming that REIT stock prices will rebound once again). Investors who have been putting capital in REITs would, therefore, make it possible for lenders with their loans coming due to recoup some of their possible loan losses by selling the properties concerned to REITs, or persuading their borrowers to do so. Given the ability of REITs to raise funds in capital markets, this seems the most likely way to put large amounts of equity into paying off the debts that the present debtors cannot pay. In many cases, this would require banks and other lenders to take back the properties concerned and then sell them to REITs, possibly at prices below their original values. REITs seem most capable of raising a lot of additional equity and other capital through public securities markets or unsecured loans. Then, investors with money to put out can buy the shares or bonds of REITs that purchase such delinquent properties.
Commercial banks and other lenders	These lenders extend their loans coming due far enough into the future so that more active bank lending may be available by the time the loans become due again. Lenders could simply extend their loans outward for several years in the hope that economic conditions will improve in the meantime. Then, either banks would resume lending funds to the borrowers involved, or a steadily recovering economy would enable the borrowers to make enough more money to pay off (or roll over) their loans without added equity. That is what many banks and other lenders have been doing (and hoping for) up until now. For two reasons, those lenders have not wanted to take over the properties concerned. If they did so, they might be forced to show large losses on their books, plus they would have to manage the properties themselves, something they are not likely to do well. However, such loan extensions do not

	solve the problem of obtaining enough equity to cover *all* commercial mortgages coming due; they just defer the problem to the future. Yet many banks and other lenders may continue granting extensions in order to avoid both absorbing write-downs on their now-overdue loans and managing the properties concerned. Such extensions are especially likely if the lenders are, in effect, capturing almost all the cash flows from such properties *without* having either to own them or manage them. Extending loans well into the future merely defers the equity gap problem in the hope that borrowers will by then be able to raise more capital. This category also involves lenders who "swallow the equity gap." That is, they take back the properties concerned and absorb the equity losses themselves. In this approach, banks and other lenders foreclose immediately when their loans come due, and take ownership of the properties concerned. This compels them to write-down the original values of the loans on their books, which may often be larger than the then-current market values of the properties they thus assume. The foreclosing parties then must either manage their new properties or try to sell them at a loss compared to the original book values of the property loans. Having banks and other lenders foreclose immediately and take ownership of delinquent properties fails to solve the equity gap. Instead, it forces lenders to absorb losses when the borrowers cannot pay the loan payments due.
Mortgage servicing firms assigned to cope with over-due commercial loans	These entail special servicing firms that are trying to cope with delinquent mortgage borrowers to work out some form of settlement that satisfies both lenders and borrowers. But this seems unlikely in many cases of major commercial delinquencies for three reasons. First, special servicers have no ready access to sources of capital. Second, there is a huge gap between what the borrowers owe and their ability to pay. Third, the complexity of creating such deals requires lengthy negotiations among borrowers, servicers, and lenders. Up to now, this time-consuming method has succeeded in remedying very few delinquent commercial loans. Relying on under-staffed special servicing firms to structure successful deals probably cannot achieve enough volume to cope with the equity gap problem.

The four options discussed in table 12-2 are unlikely to plug the funding gap entirely; therefore, mezzanine capital could step in as a last resort to fill the hole. Mezzanine capital refers to subordinated debt (or preferred equity securities) that often represent the most junior portion of a company's capital structure that is senior to the company's common equity. Mezzanine capital, which is often provided by private equity funds, allows companies to borrow additional capital beyond the levels that traditional lenders are willing to provide through bank loans. In compensation for the increased risk, mezzanine capital holders require a higher return for their investment than secured or other more senior lenders.

Mezzanine lending is riskier than mortgage lending, but is less risky than straight equity contributions. This is because a mezzanine loan is not secured by the property, but is instead secured by the owner's stake in the real estate firm. Upon default, the lender may take over the owner's equity position in the firm; therefore it can be referred to as "disguised equity."

More specifically, preferred equity securities (also called "preferred shares" or "preferreds") are a special security that have characteristics of both an equity and debt instrument, and are generally considered as a hybrid instrument. Preferred shares are senior or higher-ranking to common stocks but are subordinate to bonds. Similar to bonds, preferred shares are rated by the major credit rating agencies. The rating for preferred shares is generally lower since preferred dividends do not carry the same guarantees as interest payments from bonds, and they are junior to all creditors.

In sum, the solution to the significant refinancing gap will be multi-faceted. The capital markets—in the form of a refined

CMBS model, together with debt of a longer duration in order to attract additional sources of funding such as pension funds—will also form an essential part of the solution.

Possible Answers to Problem #5: Private-Label Mortgage-Backed Securities

The mortgage-backed security (MBS) market is a particular cause for concern, not only because there are major uncertainties about the size of the total market and its maturity structures, but also because the investor structure that is comprised of separate agendas makes a restructuring of MBS debt via maturity extensions much more difficult.[51]

Real estate is always volatile and financial crises are always destructive. Therefore, the main aim for policymakers must be to sever the connection between the two. This often lethal connection can be severed by introducing financial products to the US markets with skin in the game such as covered bonds.

The widespread introduction of a deep and highly liquid covered bond market in the United States will help vent part of the pressure from the unsatisfied volume of private-label MBS refinancings. Covered bonds are securities issued by a bank and backed by a group of performing and eligible mortgage loans (commercial and residential) known as a "cover pool."

Prussia under Frederick the Great introduced covered bonds, known as pfandbriefe, in 1769 to finance public works projects. Since then, twenty-four other countries in Europe have adopted the covered bond structure, each with its own unique laws.[52] Although considered an old-fashioned debt instrument, what is impressive about pfandbriefe is the fact that not one issue has ever defaulted in the nearly 240 years of their existence.

In 2011, $32 billion in covered bonds were sold to American institutional investors by European, Norwegian, or Canadian banks—but not by US banks. So far, the covered bond market has been met with little acceptance in the United States primarily because Fannie Mae and Freddie Mac, which dominate the US mortgage market, offer a government-guaranteed enhancement to securitized financing, which has far reaching influences throughout the US financial system. But this should change as the two obsolete mortgage bundlers are eventually phased-out.

There are two different types of covered bonds: those backed by high quality mortgage loans and those backed by public sector loans. If the issuing bank becomes insolvent, the assets in the cover pool are separated from the issuer's other assets solely for the benefit of the covered bondholders. Asset eligibility for the cover pool (and the process in the event of an issuer's insolvency) is determined by bankruptcy laws specific to each country.

Based on the high quality of the loans in the cover pool and the strength of the issuing banks, most covered bonds justifiably receive high credit ratings of AA or AAA. In general, their maturities range from two to ten years, although there is a recent trend in Europe toward long-term securities greater than ten years.

Covered bonds are similar in many ways to mortgage- and asset-backed securities, but with one major difference: the loans backing a covered bond remain on the balance sheet of the issuer (typically a bank). The bonds are, therefore, obligations of the issuing bank and the issuer retains control over the assets (skin in the game).

Under the direct-issuance structure of covered bonds, the issuing institution must designate the cover pool of mortgages as collateral for the bonds, which remain on the balance sheet of the depository institution. Issuers of covered bonds must provide a first priority claim on the assets in the cover pool to bondholders, and the assets in the cover pool must not be encumbered by any other lien. The issuer must also clearly identify the cover pool's assets, liabilities, and security pledge on its books.[53]

This structure can change the make-up of the loan pool to maintain its credit quality—which benefits investors—and can also change the terms of the loans. By contrast, mortgage- and asset-backed securities are typically off-balance-sheet transactions (no skin in the game) in which lenders sell loans to murky special purpose vehicles (SPVs) that issue bonds, thus removing the loans—and the risk associated with those loans—from the lenders' balance sheets. In addition, interest is paid from an identifiable and projected cash flow, not just out of vague financing operations. Since non-performing or prepaid loans must be replaced, the pool is always performing.

Unlike the "securitization method"—which is designed to transfer risks with significant contractual, regulatory, and governmental restrictions on the ability of the securitization vehicle (a trust or conduit) to replace or effectively modify mortgage loans—covered bonds are designed to allow the replacement of non-performing loans to keep the overall portfolio performing.[54]

Although both mortgage-backed securities and covered bonds are a potential source of long-term funding for mortgage loans, there are several other noteworthy differences between covered bonds and MBSs that make them attractive to different types of investors:[55]

- The cash flows from the mortgages and credit enhancements in mortgage-backed securities are generally the only source of principal and interest payments to the MBS investors. In a covered bond, principal and interest are paid by the issuer's cash flow, while the mortgages in the cover pool serve as collateral for investors.

- The collateral underlying covered bonds is dynamic, and non-performing (or prepaying) assets within the cover pool must be substituted with performing mortgages. Mortgages underlying MBSs are static and remain in each MBS until maturity.

- In the case of an issuer default, covered bonds are structured to avoid prepayment prior to the date of maturity. This is accomplished through swap agreements and deposit agreements (guaranteed investment contracts). MBS investors, in contrast, are exposed to prepayment risk in the case of a mortgage default or prepayment.

- In the event that the covered bonds accelerate and repay investors at an amount less than the principal and accrued interest, investors retain an unsecured claim on the issuer. MBS investors, on the other hand, generally do not retain any claim on the issuer in the event of repayment.

———

In order to facilitate a covered bond market in the United States, Republican Congressman Scott Garrett introduced the Covered Bond Act in the House of Representatives in 2011. The act, co-sponsored by Democrats Carolyn Maloney and Paul Kanjorski and Republican Spencer Bachus, expands upon legislation that Garrett previously introduced in 2008, the Equal Treatment of Covered Bonds Act, which was never passed into law.[56] However, in June 2011 the House Financial Services Committee voted in favor of a bipartisan bill to establish a covered bond market in the United States. Analysts believe the Covered Bond Act of 2011 has a good chance of reaching President Obama's desk in 2012. The National Association of Realtors, Mortgage Bankers Association, and Securities Industry and Financial Markets Association all support the bill. Progress of the Covered Bond Act will not necessarily be plain sailing. A key part of any legislation would involve altering US bankruptcy laws to protect the pool of assets backing covered bonds in the event of the sponsoring bank's collapse. As such, covered bonds are a long-term, yet essential, solution for the hard-hit US real estate sector.

Conclusion

If the US property market has learned its lessons from the financial crisis and applies some of the possible solutions to the unresolved problems presented in this chapter, I am confident that better days are ahead for America. But there are also some new realities with which Americans have to come to terms.

Conventional thinking dictates that the larger economy must first stabilize before the country experiences a decline in joblessness and a resulting increase in consumer spending; however, as we know this time around it's much different. A rising tide won't be lifting all boats because some of the ongoing problems in the US economy, namely unemployment and weak housing markets, appear so far to be structural. Americans need to come to terms with the possibility that unemployment levels could remain on the high side for at least five years to come—if not longer—due to the forces of technology and globalization. In addition, the unresolved problems in US real estate need a sustained increase in values. An increase in property values will only come when there is a remarkable new "story" about the US economy that fundamentally changes investor and consumer sentiment. A sustainable recovery also requires a sustainable return of confidence.

The reality is that such a story is going to take a while to unfold, meaning that households will be dealing with such deep problems as foreclosures and negative equity for some years to come. The same applies to the commercial real estate sector with its debt maturities and bruised securitization market. But all these issues don't mean that something isn't already stirring in the US economy.

Although it's not "morning in America" yet, there are hints in 2012 of dawn on the horizon. In the cycle of market emotions, I believe that the country is at the "hope" stage (see figure 12-2), and a new story is slowly starting to unfold, although so far not a very remarkable one.

Figure 12-2: The Cycle of Market Emotions

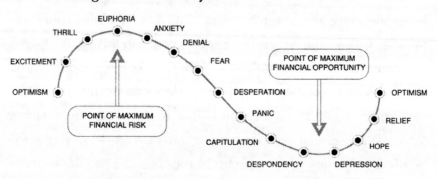

Source: Westcore Funds

The story so far is that after a desultory three years from the official ending of the Great Recession, the United States might be drifting along in a Japanese-style funk. Be that as it may, the ticker tape of economic statistics has started to reveal modest encouragement. For example, personal consumption was predicted to increase by 2.2 percent in 2011 (compared with 1.7 percent in 2010); unemployment was forecast to average 8.5 percent (compared with 2010's 9.7); while GDP was predicted to chug along at close to 1.7 percent.

Furthermore, after the major shakeup on Wall Street, some of the best minds will probably be redeployed from high-finance to science and technology. This will be a positive and much needed trend, since the United States has fallen behind the rising economic powers of China, Brazil, India, and South Korea in several sectors.

———

Battered by the economic collapse that was triggered by the financial and real estate sectors, American business and political leaders must rebuild growth and employment that's based less on excessive debt, consumption, construction, and imports, and more on manufacturing and exports. For a sustained US recovery and a brighter future, America needs to get the macro-medicine of its real estate sector right, have much firmer foundations than the mortgage-fuelled consumer spree of the mid-2000s, together with growth in GDP and more skin in the game.

The particular road on which Americans were embarked at the debut of the twenty-first century was a feature of their own unique situation. A half century of economic progress and a twenty-five-year bull market had led them to believe things that were not true or sustainable and to expect things that they were not likely to get. Never in the history of humanity had any people been able to get rich by spending money; nor had investment markets ever made the average buy-and-hold investor rich; nor had paper money (unbacked by gold) ever retained its value for very long. It is therefore hoped that the financial crisis of 2008 was the end of that surreal road and the beginning of an American renewal.[57]

An American renewal requires a financial system that ensures that a debt-driven boom in real estate never happens again. Otherwise, only repeated consumer-credit bubbles will—temporarily—sustain the US economy, until they burst once again.

Epilogue

Change always comes bearing gifts.
—Price Pritchett, business advisor

The objective of this book is to convey the unresolved problems in the post-crisis US financial system and real estate sector in particular, alerting readers to the looming risks which, if dealt with effectively, can enable the US property space to be better prepared for inevitable crises in the future.

The financial world is a messy and risky place, full of sharp bumps and fogbound hollows. One of the risks impacting the US financial system is that many Americans are addicted to excessive consumption and debt. The prudent use of debt does, of course, propel growth, but the bigger problem is that most Americans haven't always had a good handle on the risks that heavy borrowing poses both for them and for the US economy.

The US economic model that drove the long boom from the 1980s to 2008 is in need of a major changeover. Considering the scale of the recent bust, and the system malfunctions that have been exposed, one could argue that the 2008 financial crisis has bequeathed a once-in-a-generation crisis of capitalism.[1] It is a crisis of capitalism because our economic model and policy settings cannot produce sustainable growth, adequate income formation, or employment creation. We have lost (at least for now) the housing, financial services, and credit-creation growth drivers and been left with excessive levels of personal and government debt to unwind, a dysfunctional financial system, and weak labor markets. The capacity to produce and sell goods and services has outstripped that of US consumers to borrow and spend. Without prudent credit and jobs, other fault lines have been exposed, including the fragile real estate sector, the long stagnation of wages, and extremes of income inequality.[2]

———

In deciding how much to bid for a home, leveraged homebuyers focused on monthly payments, and lower mortgage rates allowed them to chase prices higher in the context of housing markets that were tight. Once home price appreciation took off, backward-looking price expectations led both homebuyers and mortgage investors to count on rapidly rising values, which further fuelled the speculative mania.

The seeds of destruction were sown from the beginning: the supremely risky nature of the loans tolerated in the United States, the sheer volume of them, the large share of them made to speculators, and the way they were bundled into securities and written into high-risk CDOs and CDSs—all caused greater damage to the global financial markets than did mortgage loans originated in any other country.

The global order of high-tech derivative marketing and Nobel Prize-winning mathematical models turned out to be a prescription for financial destruction.[3] When all is forgotten and we've moved on to our next financial crisis, there will be certain fingers frozen in time pointing at the subprime loans as the direct cause of the calamity. But the reality is that the subprime loan tragedy was merely a catalyst that exposed the mega-tiered securitizations of securitizations, the massive leverage chain of derivatives attached to nothing concrete, and the ineffective regulatory restraints. All of which led us down the rabbit hole of the Great Recession.[4]

———

As much of the industrialized world tries to emerge from a financial crisis and recession that had its roots in the US housing market, the role of real estate in economic activity is finally getting a closer look after many years of neglect. Of course, real estate is not the only asset class to experience bubbles and crashes; stock markets do it all the time. But when property markets experience extreme volatility, the knock-on effects are more damaging to the wider economy than for any other asset class. The bursting of the dot-com bubble in 2000–02, for instance, did not produce anything like the Great Recession.

From the charlatans who pushed unaffordable mortgages and the investment bankers who packaged crappy loans into securities and sold them off as AAA-rated investments to commercial bankers who often prefer to foreclose rather than work with borrowers to keep them in their homes, the Great Recession has wrought well-documented havoc. In addition, pundits keep telling us that America is headed into an assisted-living facility for retired global powers. However, there might be a silver lining amid the financial destruction that has been wrought. The crisis and the changes that it brought aren't entirely bad for the United States, although it is tough for virtually anyone, especially those unemployed or those who lost their homes to foreclosure, to see that now. The

Great Recession should make Americans examine changes and alternatives to their lifestyles that they may never have considered before. This means they ought to be simplifying their lives and shifting from material wealth toward a growing awareness of the impact of excessive debt and consumption. It's also hoped that the Echo Boomer generation, also called the Millennials, will be more naturally attuned to giving priority to quality of life over quantity of possessions—shedding the shallow burden of consumption to remember what's really important.

———

The unresolved problems of the United States will not go away by sprinkling about some fiscal fairy dust or by just grumbling. America is in trouble and Americans must be more receptive to change now than ever before. It's evident that consumer-splurge-dependent patterns of growth established in the second half of the twentieth century are not sustainable in the post-crisis era.[5] Living beyond their means should have shocked Americans into being more financially responsible.

Galileo Galilei once said: "All truths are easy to understand once they are discovered; the point is to discover them."[6] Therefore, it is hoped that the Great Recession has enabled US real estate investors and consumers to discover four needed changes in their behavior:

- **Avoiding Complacency**. Real estate investors have to ensure that the risk of complacency doesn't come back. This is known as "black swan fatigue"—weariness with the idea that an extremely unlikely event could take place and cause havoc in the financial and property markets.[7]

- **Caution**. While an excessive focus on analysis can temper financing and development activity, a healthy degree of caution requires more fiduciary responsibility and realistic expectations for returns going forward.

- **Doing More with Less**. This isn't just a function of relentless cost cutting. There needs to be a genuine recognition that many common business practices in the past four decades were simply misguided.

- **Obsessing Less about Money**. Americans need to be focusing on what is important and to prioritize what is meaningful, both as human beings and through their organizations—obsessing less about money with a drive toward achieving more than just profits.

The US real estate sector will be viable provided it embraces changes that are essential. That is, more skin in the game, a disciplined approach to investing, stricter underwriting practices, proper disclosures, and fiscal prudence. This is in marked contrast to the past, when an apparent limitless supply of capital drove many investors on a wanton hunt for yield at any cost.

———

US consumer confidence continues to be volatile, foreclosure rates are high, and GDP is moving only by inches, but as economist Carmen Reinhart notes, "Recovery from a recession of purely financial origins is much slower, like the difference between recuperating from open heart surgery versus having a broken bone set."[8] That's why the government's stimulus programs and new financial regulations, while certainly no panacea, have been essential. There's no doubt that without such interventions a recovery would have been still slower and unemployment still higher. Foreclosures must and will eventually burn off, and policies to re-liquefy the mortgage markets—even if they don't sound like much—are much better than doing nothing.

One of the country's biggest problems is its low personal savings rate, which prior to the meltdown was close to zero. The over-leverage of the American consumer and the highly questionable financial instruments were all consequences of the low personal savings rate. An economy cannot live off borrowed money (i.e., US government bonds) forever, especially when it is that of overseas investors. But I am confident that the weakness of the US economy due to the low savings rate, excessive reliance on over-leveraged consumers, and the dependency on foreign debt will eventually change. The passage of time and the recognition of problems are the best healers for all woes.

———

In the current era of US self-doubt, beset by intimations of economic decline, the era of American financial hegemony seems distant, although as recently as the mid-2000s globalization seemed to be remaking the world in the US mold. But America has a dynamic and entrepreneurial culture, flexible labor markets, high productivity performance, the rule of law, favorable demographics, and other great strengths that enable it to make a sustained comeback.

Change is our home field. It is who we are and what we do. Therefore, it's never too late for the country to get a grip on its problems, and pessimism about America rarely pays off in the long-run. Today's headwinds reflect structural adjustments that will, in the longer-term, place the US economy on a stronger footing. The preconditions for strong future growth are reduced uncertainty, improved consumer confidence, stabilized household finances, and healthy credit markets. The American Dream is still alive, even though the new goal is not for *every* American to become a homeowner.

The United States is a resilient place and Americans are hardwearing people. There is nothing like the American spirit. There is nothing like American ingenuity. While the country is undergoing some major challenges, changes, and adjustments, I believe that it is ultimately going to come out better than before if the lessons discussed in this book have been learned and the unresolved problems in American real estate are properly addressed. The country cannot afford to return to its unsustainable pre-crisis procedures, and it must emerge as a powerful exporter with domestic investment rather than compulsive consumption being its real strength.

Excessive debt and a concentration of losses in highly leveraged institutions that cause real estate booms and busts—coupled with disruptions in the credit markets, poor regulatory oversight, and reckless self-interested behavior—cannot be allowed to unleash their venom on American society again. But it would be naïve to assume that financial crises won't happen in the future. They will happen again but in different ways for different reasons with different consequences. America's capital markets continue to be based on speculation, and some of its players continue to find loopholes to beat the system. Rules will always be gamed. It's just how it is.

My aspiration is that as more skin in the game is adopted, the next American financial meltdown is *not* caused by the property sector. Real estate has already caused far too much damage to the US economy and social fabric. Therefore, everything possible needs to be done to avoid another *purely* property-driven crisis. "Never again" should be the watchword.

As we reach the end of this book, I would like to leave the reader with the words of Robert Rubin, the United States Secretary of the Treasury during the Clinton administration, which bring to light the true essence of the American spirit of change, hope, and renewal: "The historic resilience of our political system, our economy, our culture, and our society is a hopeful augur. We have risen to difficult challenges many times in the past and we can do so again. But there is still much to do."[9]

Acknowledgments

This book would not have been possible without the unsparing assistance of Marc Thompson—a savvy real estate banker, scholar, and gentleman. Marc shared his extensive research on real estate debt risk, his vast knowledge about property finance, and guided me to the most accurate sources.

My wife, Gigi, was patient with my long hours, giving me a quiet space to write, bringing me coffee when I needed a break, and reading over the early manuscript to make sure it was enjoyable. I am most grateful for her love and support. My twin daughters, Dahlia and Ameera, were also kind and understanding about my holing-up in the home office to write when they wanted to play.

My sincere gratitude goes to Abdul Suleman, my friend, mentor, and boss at Equinox Hospitality Group, who generously allowed me to take time off to pursue this project.

Great thanks go to Gary Carr for reviewing the initial manuscript, Jenny Lee for creating the data charts, and Rayhab Saeed for producing the illustrations.

Last but not least, I would like to acknowledge the following outstanding individuals for providing their excellent insight: Mike Burrichter, Tom Callahan, Don Clark, Chip Conley, Mike Depatie, Jim Gavin, David Geltner, Henry Gjestrum, Amr Hamdy, Joel Hiser, Peter Ingersoll, Crystal Lee, John Lee, Corey Limbach, Glenn Mueller, Nick Peterson, Michelle Smee, and Tony Wood.

Thank you all for making it happen.

Financial Acronyms Used in the Text

Acronym	Meaning
ABS	Asset-backed security
AIG	American International Group
AMC	Appraisal management company
ARM	Adjustable-rate mortgage
AVM	Automated valuation model
BIS	Bank for International Settlements (Basel, Switzerland)
BOD	Board of directors
BPO	Broker price opinion
CDO	Collateralized debt obligation
CDS	Credit-default swap
CMBS	Commercial mortgage-backed security
CMO	Collateralized mortgage obligation
CPI	Consumer price index
CRE	Commercial real estate
EBRD	European Bank for Reconstruction and Development
EPS	Earnings per share
FASB	Financial Accounting Standards Board
FDIC	Federal Deposit Insurance Corporation
FHA	Federal Housing Administration
FICO	Fair Isaac Corporation (credit scores)

(Table continued on next page…)

Acronym	Meaning
FRM	Fixed-rate mortgage
FTSE	Financial Times Stock Exchange
GDP	Gross domestic product
GSE	Government-sponsored enterprise
HAMP	Home Affordable Modification Program
HUD	Department of Housing and Urban Development
LBO	Leveraged buyout
LTV	Loan-to-value (ratio)
MBS	Mortgage-backed security
MLS	Multiple listing service
MSA	Metropolitan statistical area
NAREIT	National Association of Real Estate Investment Trusts
NCREIF	National Council of Real Estate Investment Fiduciaries
NCSHA	National Council of State Housing Agencies
NOI	Net operating income
NYSE	New York Stock Exchange
OFHEO	Office of Federal Housing Enterprise Oversight
OTC	Over-the-counter (derivatives)
P/E	Price-earnings (multiple or ratio)
PLS	Private-label securitization
PMI	Private mortgage insurance
REIT	Real estate investment trust
REMIC	Real estate mortgage investment conduit (of MBSs)
REO	Real estate-owned (by banks)
RM	Rollover mortgage
RMBS	Residential mortgage-backed security
ROE	Return on equity (ratio)
RTC	Resolution Trust Corporation

(Table continued on next page...)

Acronym	Meaning
R&D	Research and development
S&L	Savings and loan
SEC	Security and Exchange Commission
SIV	Structured investment vehicle
SPV	Special purpose vehicle
TARP	Troubled Asset Relief Program
USPAP	Uniform Standards of Professional Appraisal Practice
YSP	Yield-spread premium

Note: For the plural of several acronyms in the book, an "s" has been added (i.e., "ABSs" for "asset-backed securities").

Description of Different Types of Mortgages

Having described in chapter 2 how loan securitization and derivatives are supposed to work, in the following section I'll briefly dissect the different types of loans and borrowers that were the "raw material" of the mess we are in today.

Nightmare Mortgages

A method developed by the Minneapolis-based Fair Isaac Corporation assigns borrowers a score, known as the **FICO credit score**, ranging between 300 and 850. This is a measure of the borrower's probability of delinquency and default, where a lower score implies a greater risk to the lender. It is broadly accepted that a FICO score less than 620 is considered nonprime, or **subprime**.

A subprime borrower is usually one who has a high debt-to-income ratio, a not-so-good credit history, or other characteristics that are correlated with a high probability of default, compared to borrowers with good credit. Because these financially volatile borrowers are essentially riskier, subprime mortgages are originated at a premium above the mortgage rates offered to individuals with good credit.

Despite having a lower FICO score, subprime borrowers typically got a loan-to-value (LTV) in excess of 80 percent. (A high LTV means that the borrower is making a smaller down payment). Therefore, the lender assumes more risk with these borrowers because it will be harder to recover their invested capital from the collateral (in this case a home) if the borrowers default on their loans. This is a scenario where home price appreciation is flat, or negative.

However, at the height of the lending frenzy, subprime mortgages went to all kinds of borrowers, not only to those with impaired credit. A loan can be labeled subprime not only because of the characteristics of the borrower it was originated for, but also because of the *type* of lender that originated it, features of the mortgage product itself, or how it was securitized.[1]

If a loan was given to a borrower with a low credit score or a history of delinquency or bankruptcy, lenders would most certainly have labeled it subprime. But mortgages could also be labeled subprime if they were originated by a lender specializing in high-cost loans—although not all high-cost loans were subprime.[2] Also, unusual types of mortgages generally not available in the prime market, such as "2/28 hybrids," which are discussed later, would be labeled subprime even if they were given to borrowers with credit scores that were sufficiently high to qualify for prime mortgage loans.

The process of securitizing a loan also affected its subprime designation. Many subprime mortgages were securitized and sold on the secondary market. Securitizers ranked ordered pools of mortgages from the most to the least risky at the time of securitization, basing the ranking on a combination of several risk factors, such as credit score, loan-to-value, and debt-to-income ratios. The most risky pools would become a part of a subprime security. All the loans in that security would be labeled subprime, regardless of the borrowers' credit scores.[3]

———

Alt-A mortgages are typically loans to borrowers with near-prime credit scores, loans requiring little or no income documentation, or that allow high debt-to-income or LTV ratios. But Alt-As were just crappy mortgage loans for which lenders hadn't even bothered to acquire the proper documents to verify the borrower's income.

"A" was the designation attached by the bond markets to the most creditworthy borrowers, and Alt-A, which stood for "Alternative A-paper," meant an alternative to the most suitable to receive credit, which of course would sound a lot more fishy if it were labeled that way. As a rule, any loan that had been turned into an acronym or abbreviation could more clearly be called a "subprime loan," but the bond markets didn't want to be clear.[4] In addition, interest-only and payment-option adjustable rate mortgages (ARMs) were loan products that saw only limited use prior to the go-go 2004–06 period. **Interest-only loans** expose borrowers to payment resets when principal payments kick in after a prespecified period, while **payment-option ARMs** can result in negative amortization, which means that borrowers can choose to make payments so low that their mortgage balance *rises* every month instead of going down.

The **adjustable rate mortgage** is defined by variable periodic payments as determined by a benchmark index (reference base), such as the twelve-month London Interbank Offered Rate, or one-, two-, and five-year Treasury securities. That's why ARMs typically have reset periods of between one and five years. The interest rate at the reset date is equal to the benchmark index plus a spread (or variance). The variance is typically between 1 percent and 2 percent, reflecting market conditions, the features of the ARM, and the increased cost of servicing an ARM compared to a fixed-rate mortgage (FRM), the hallmark of American housing finance. The 1980s saw the first major production of ARMs, and the first state to use this type of loan was trend-setting California.[5] The frequency at which the ARM note rate adjusts is usually either monthly, semiannually, or annually. Both of these products typically have an amortization period of thirty years with monthly payments.

An Alt-A mortgage is considered riskier than an A-loan (or prime), but less risky than subprime, the riskiest category. ARMs had been popular with lenders because they shift interest rate risk from the lender to the borrower. It should be pointed out that, over the long-term, a thirty-year mortgage can actually be more expensive than an ARM. The ARM, however, is subject to fluctuations of a number of indicators in the market and therefore carries great risk for the borrower. In the end, buyers who value a safer home loan and who can resist the lure of more risky but possibly cheaper financing, the thirty-year FRM offers the more prudent long-term bet.

Lastly, the **2/28 hybrid loan**—a lethal lending product before the financial crisis—had a fixed, low interest rate for the first two years (known as a "teaser"), and then became adjustable semiannually for the next twenty-eight years as the note rate reset to the value of an index plus a margin.

————

A loan can be for a home purchase, for **refinancing** an existing mortgage (commonly known as a "refi"), or for refinancing an existing mortgage and instantaneously borrowing cash against the equity in the home (called a "cash-out refi" or simply a "cash-out").[6] This occurred when a homeowner took out a larger mortgage, paid off the previous one, and pocketed the difference. With mortgage rates low and falling, homeowners could increase the size of a loan without increasing the monthly payment.

In the case of the subprime sector, the lure of such windfalls made refis very popular. Because cash-out refis allow the borrower to tap into built-up equity in a property, the borrower was able to benefit directly from the appreciation of home prices. Prudent refinancing can stimulate the economy by allowing homeowners to extract equity and lower their borrowing costs, but such borrowers tend to be more interest-rate sensitive. Today, however, refinancing is difficult because of high unemployment, tighter underwriting standards, and **negative home equity** (being "underwater" or "upside down").

————

A significant impact on the US economy came from **mortgage-equity withdrawals** (or home-equity loans) and the consumer spending that it enabled. For most of the 1990s, the net equity pulled out by homeowners—either through sales or through home equity refis—was quite modest. It accounted for nearly $25 billion dollars per quarter and was approximately 1 percent of US personal disposable income. After slumping in the late 1980s and early 1990s, home prices began to rise modestly. By the late 1990s, gains had returned to the historical mean. That allowed some withdrawal of equity. But even then, it remained a relatively modest amount, averaging about $37 billion per quarter, or 2 percent of disposable income.

The impact of mortgage-equity withdrawals began to accelerate once the Fed dramatically cut interest rates. By mid-2002, the quarterly average of mortgage-equity withdrawals was more than $100 billion, which was greater than 4 percent of disposable income and up nearly 400 percent from 1997. By 2003, those quarterly numbers were $150 billion and 6 percent, respectively. Then in 2005 things began to spin out of control, as quarterly mortgage-equity withdrawals were almost $250 billion dollars, or over 10 percent of disposable income. To put that into context, that was nearly a *900 percent* gain over 1995.

According to CoreLogic, 38 percent of borrowers who took cash out of their residences using home-equity loans were underwater in 2011. By contrast, 18 percent of borrowers who didn't are burdened by underwater loans.

The All-American Johnsons

Indeed some people were dishonest, greedy, and reckless and probably deserved to lose their homes. But at the same time we have a sympathetic view toward the millions of homeowners who are now in trouble, most of whom were simply trying to realize the American Dream of providing a decent home for their families. They fell victim to the illusion that home prices would go up forever, trusted their lenders who sold them lethal mortgage products, and simply didn't understand the financial implications of their mortgages.[7]

———

Probably the easiest way to explain one type of these lethal mortgage products is to create a scenario with an imaginary lower middle-class American family, the Johnsons.

In 2004, Steve Johnson got a job in Las Vegas making $40,000 a year. At the time, he and his family were living in a two-bedroom apartment near the UNLV campus. The residential real estate market started to rise in value. The average home prices in the surrounding market area went from $150,000 to $200,000 in six months, and Steve started to worry that if he didn't buy a house now he would never be able to afford one. He didn't want to be left out, so he decided to jump on the bandwagon.

The Johnson family found their dream home in a suburb of Las Vegas for $200,000 and went to a local mortgage broker named Jack. Jack told Steve that his monthly payment will be $1,079,[8] plus taxes and private mortgage insurance (PMI), which could run up his total payments to nearly $1,200 a month, nearly half of Steve's monthly paycheck (after income tax). In order to close the deal, Jack tells Steve about some other ways that he can lower his monthly payment, such as the payment-option

ARM, probably the worst mortgage product that was ever sold—mainly to unsuspecting or unsophisticated borrowers during the housing boom. As discussed earlier, an option ARM is a mortgage with an initially low adjustable teaser rate for which borrowers can pay *less* than the interest accruing on the loan for, say, five years (which is then added to the unpaid principal balance).

Jack easily convinces Steve that his home value will keep rising enough to refinance the mortgage in two to three years, and shows him the fuzzy payment-option math for the ARM, with his initial minimum payment going down to about $750 a month. Steve thinks this is a no-brainer, so he takes the option ARM with the plan to refinance his house in a few years and to cash-in on possible newly created equity.

The Johnsons move into their new home and enjoy the low monthly minimum payments of around $750. Their home value increased $20,000 in three months, and they're really excited. By speaking to his friends and reading the hype in the local newspapers, Steve gets the herd mentality idea that if he remodels his kitchen the value will increase even more. So Steve takes out a $10,000 loan, using his **home-equity line of credit (HELOC)** to start the kitchen remodeling project. Another two months pass, and their home value increases even more.

In two years (by 2006), the Johnson's home increased in value to nearly $300,000 and the family owed about $230,000, because they picked the option ARM that they didn't pay off any principal for (they were only paying a portion of the interest at the low initial teaser rate). In addition, they went a little overboard with their HELOC to buy a new SUV, take a two-week holiday at a four-star resort in Mexico, and get an expensive home-theater TV system.

Suddenly home values had increased way above most people's income ability to pay their mortgages. As a result, individuals and families weren't able to sell their homes as quickly. Then the dreaded drop in home values came. Leverage levels on homes had increased to unsustainable levels when home-sale velocity began to slow. By August 2006, home values were being dropped to stimulate home sales.

Investors and homeowners saw the drop and started to get anxious, so many wanted to sell their homes with the hope of making a quick profit, or to pay off their mortgage obligations immediately after the burn off of the low teaser rate payment. There were too many homes for sale and not enough people who could qualify for financing to buy. As a result, home prices began to drop further, and borrowers were starting to get walloped.

By mid-2007, the Johnsons panicked. Their home value was now $250,000, so they put it up for sale. Months went by and nobody bought it, so they dropped their price to $230,000, the same amount they owed the bank. Still no one bought it. Then Steve got laid off and was really desperate. He had to sell his house or risk losing everything. After three months, Steve still couldn't sell the house and wasn't able to make his payments, so the bank foreclosed on his home, and Steve and his family were forced to move out and live with relatives in Reno—his credit was wiped out. Now the bank owned a house worth less than the loan it had extended to the Johnson family. The bank finally sold the house at an auction for $140,000, losing $90,000.

The notion of subprime lending being a way to help low-income borrowers who otherwise could not buy a home live the American Dream was largely fiction, but it was a myth powerful enough to give subprime lending free reign for a long time.[9] What happened to the Johnsons happened to millions of lower middle-class Americans who were forced into foreclosure by mortgage "pros" who flooded the nation with high-risk, high-profit home loans. The owners of these mortgages had no choice but to sell the taken-back houses for far less than the actual amount of the underlying value of the debt. Almost overnight, owners of mortgages and related derivative products were losing billions of dollars because of similar bad loans. These owners, some of which were banks, were sometimes wiped out because of the write-offs they had to make on their loans that went toxic.

Notes:

1. Yuliya Demyanyk, "Ten Myths about Subprime Mortgages," Economic Commentary, Federal Reserve Bank of Cleveland, July 2009.

2. Ibid.

3. Ibid.

4. M. Lewis, *The Big Short* (New York: W. W. Norton & Company, 2010), 127.

5. F. Fabozzi and F. Modigliani, *Mortgage and Mortgage-Backed Securities Markets* (Boston: Harvard Business School Press, 1992), 103.

6. F. Sabry and T. Schopflocher, *The Subprime Meltdown: A Primer* (New York: NERA Economic Consulting, 2007), 2.

7. W. Tilson and G. Tongue, *More Mortgage Meltdown: 6 Ways to Profit in These Bad Times* (Hoboken, NJ: John Wiley & Sons, 2009), 45.

8. The monthly payment of $1,079 is based on the following assumptions: $200,000 home value; 90 percent loan-to-value ratio; $180,000 loan; 6 percent interest rate; thirty-year fixed loan amortization, excluding taxes and private mortgage insurance.

9. A. Katz, *Our Lot: How Real Estate Came to Own Us* (New York: Bloomsbury, 2010), 66.

Appendix A

The Evolution of US Mortgage Finance, Securitization, and Real Estate Derivatives

The purpose of this appendix is to highlight the sequence of numerous laws and events pertaining to US mortgage finance, securitization, and real estate derivatives, some of which indirectly led to the financial crisis of 2008.

- Long before the first mortgage-backed security (MBS) was invented in 1970, financial institutions engaged in the practice of "participating" in each other's loans. That is, one bank could purchase a "piece of the action" in another bank's loan to a borrower. Among the major commercial banks, this practice dates back to the late 1800s.

- The rating of bonds began in the US in the early 1900s, with government debt and railroad bonds an early focus. Standard & Poor's, Moody's, and Fitch all trace their origins to that time, when investors paid for their analysis. The ratings sector began its dramatic growth in the 1970s, when a rating made it easier to sell debt to a wider range of investors and regulators started using them to assess capital needs. Sellers of debt began paying for ratings, which run on a scale from AAA to B3. (The agencies' failure to spot the Enron collapse in 2001 was widely criticized. The 2008 crisis was the biggest blow to their credibility yet).

- In 1934, and in response to the Great Depression, Congress established the Federal Housing Administration (FHA) to provide government-guaranteed mortgage insurance. Government-insured mortgages are financial instruments that the government agrees to pay if the homeowner stops making payments. This insurance protects the lender from loss.

- In 1938, the Federal National Mortgage Association (FNMA) was chartered to provide a secondary market for FHA-insured mortgages. FNMA, colloquially known as Fannie Mae, or simply "Fannie," originally performed two functions: special assistance and a secondary mortgage market. The special assistance function amounted to a form of subsidy to provide low interest rate mortgages through certain FHA programs. Fannie purchased at par FHA-insured mortgages with artificially low interest rates and, if required, resold the mortgages at discount prices. The loss incurred by Fannie through the special assistance function was borne by the US Treasury. The secondary mortgage market function was limited to FHA-insured mortgage loans. It was not a subsidy and was required to be completely self-supporting.

- In 1940, Congress passed the Investment Company Act. Along with the Securities Exchange Act of 1934, coupled with extensive rules issued by the Securities and Exchange Commission, the Investment Company Act formed the backbone of United States financial regulation. The act applied to all investment companies except hedge funds. (It was updated by the Dodd-Frank act of 2010).

- In 1948, Fannie purchased its first mortgage loan guaranteed by the Department of Veterans Affairs (VA), which was formed in 1930.

- In 1949, the first secondary market transaction between two savings and loan institutions took place.

- In 1954, the FNMA Charter Act converted Fannie into a privately-owned and financed corporation. However, supervisory authority over Fannie remained with the Housing and Home Finance Agency.

- In 1957, the Federal Home Loan Bank Board issued the first regulations permitting the purchase and sale by thrift institutions of participation interests in mortgage loans.

- In 1968, Congress enacted the Truth in Lending Act (TILA) to standardize credit disclosure to consumers, like disclosing a loan's annual percentage rate (APR) and finance charges. Congress also created the Government National Mortgage Association (GNMA), commonly known as Ginnie Mae, or just "Ginnie." Congress transferred to Ginnie the special assistance function formerly performed by Fannie Mae. At that time, Fannie technically ceased to be a "government agency" but remained subject to the oversight of the Department of Housing and Urban Development (HUD) as a privately owned, publicly chartered entity. For purposes of this appendix and as described in the book, however, Fannie is referred to as a government agency or a government-sponsored enterprise (GSE).

- Also in 1968, Ginnie Mae guaranteed the first publicly traded pass-through securities representing interests in pools of FHA and VA mortgage loans. This essentially meant that Ginnie began securitizing mortgages—buying mortgages from lenders, combining them in pools, and issuing securities backed by those pools to lenders, who could then sell them to investors.

- In 1970, Lewis Ranieri, the trading desk guru of investment brokerage house Salomon Brothers, was the first to recognize that mortgages could be widely traded as securities like stocks and bonds.

He is basically the one who invented mortgage-backed securities (MBSs).

- Also in 1970, Congress passed the Emergency Home Finance Act, which established the Federal Home Loan Mortgage Corporation (FHLMC), nicknamed Freddie Mac, or "Freddie," to provide a secondary mortgage market for non-federally insured home mortgages. Congress also authorized Fannie to provide a secondary market for the same type of mortgage loans. (Freddie went public in 1989).

- In 1971, Freddie introduced its first conventional mortgage pass-through certificate.

- Also in 1971, President Richard Nixon unilaterally ordered the cancellation of the direct convertibility of the United States dollar to gold. This act was known as the "Nixon Shock." Virtual credit came to predominate in the United States since it abandoned the gold standard. Debt became intrinsically linked to power, since credit can be used to "control" consumers and homebuyers.

- From 1971 through 1977, virtually all MBSs were either guaranteed by Ginnie Mae or issued directly by Freddie Mac. During that period the volume of outstanding MBSs issued or guaranteed by the two agencies increased dramatically, although Fannie had not yet become actively involved in issuing MBSs. Fannie continued to purchase mortgage loans to hold in its portfolio and did not commence actively issuing MBSs until later. During that period, private institutions developed an interest in creating and issuing their own MBSs without the involvement of the agencies.

- In 1974, Congress created the Commodity Futures Trading Commission (CFTC) as an independent agency of the government to regulate futures and options markets.

- The Real Estate Settlement Procedures Act (RESPA) was passed by Congress in 1974. It was created because various companies associated with the buying and selling of property, such as lenders, real estate agents, construction companies, and title insurance companies were often engaged in providing undisclosed kickbacks to each other, inflating the costs of real estate transactions, and obscuring price competition by facilitating "bait-and-switch" tactics. However, critics say that kickbacks still occur. For example, lenders often provide captive insurance to the title insurance companies they work with, which critics say are essentially a kickback mechanism.

- Also in 1974, Congress enacted the Employee Retirement Income Security Act (ERISA). This legislation required that pension funds be "funded" by investing pension contributions. ERISA put explicit emphasis on the benefits of diversified investment portfolios, including diversification out of traditional reliance on the stock market, to consideration of alternative assets such as real estate.

- In 1975, the Home Mortgage Disclosure Act required lenders to supply the government with details of their loans and the race of the people who applied for them.

- In 1977, Bank of America National Trust & Savings Association (now Bank of America Merrill Lynch), along with Salomon Brothers, became the first private sector issuers of residential mortgage-backed securities (RMBSs).

- From 1978 to 1984, a limited number of private institutions became issuers of MBSs. The big Wall Street investment banking firms established specialized MBS departments. However, the major impediment to the growth of the market for private (non-agency) MBSs was legal restrictions on the ability of regulated institutional investors to invest in private MBSs.

- In 1981, Hewlett-Packard introduces the HP 12c financial calculator, invented by an Iowa farm-boy-turned-PhD who worked in a small HP laboratory in Corvallis, Oregon. That farm boy was

Hewlett-Packard R&D project manager Dennis Harms. In a world of smart phones and tablet devices, the HP 12c financial calculator is a relic, although still widely used by real estate professionals, especially those who entered the business in the 1980s. The 12c offers the abstruse-sounding reverse Polish notation (RPN). The description "Polish" refers to the nationality of logician Jan Łukasiewicz, who invented Polish notation in the 1920s.

RPN is an initially counter-intuitive way of entering sums that many real estate lenders and financial analysts swear by to calculate cash flows, amortization, time value of money, and mortgage payments. More important is the aura of wisdom and financial prowess that a well-worn 12c confers on its owner. By slapping the old HP 12c down on the table, its owner is saying: "I'm a complex thinker, I can handle detail, and I mean business."

In RPN, the "operators" follow their "operands." In mathematics, an operand is the object of a mathematical operation, a quantity/number on which an operation is performed. For example, to add 3 and 4, one would write "3 4 +" rather than "3 + 4." If there are multiple operations, the operator is given immediately after its second operand. So the expression written "3 – 4 + 5" in conventional notation would be written "3 4 – 5 +" in RPN.

- Also in 1981, Fannie Mae issued its first mortgage pass-through securities.

- In 1982, Congress passed the Garn-St. Germain Depository Institutions Act. Garn-St. Germain lifted many regulations on the savings and loan (S&L) sector, allowing it to expand further into new businesses, such as commercial lending and investing in high-risk corporate bonds, namely junk bonds.

- In 1983, Freddie Mac issued the first collateralized mortgage obligations (CMOs).

- Also in 1983, the first securitization in the commercial real estate capital markets occurred when Fidelity Mutual Life Insurance sold $60 million of 100 percent beneficial ownership participation in a pool of commercial mortgages to three life insurance companies through Salomon Brothers Realty Corporation. Fidelity retained responsibility for loan servicing and agreed to advance principal and interest payments, and to repurchase or substitute new mortgages for any loan in the pool that defaulted. This transaction was rated AAA by the rating agencies, and three other life insurance companies went on to use the same format in 1984.

- By 1984, a credit crunch was over and life insurance companies, banks, and savings and loan firms (S&Ls) were under pressure to lend. The commercial mortgage portfolio debt market was driven to all-time highs, displacing CMBS transactions until the early 1990s. In the fall of 1984, Standard & Poor's presented the first commercial real estate risk rating format with actuarial and property-specific guidelines for CMBSs.

- The first multi-property, single-borrower CMBS transaction was issued in 1984 when a Mel Simon shopping center portfolio was securitized.

- The Secondary Mortgage Market Enhancement Act of 1984 became law. The most important change brought about by the act was the removal of restrictions on investments by regulated financial institutions in many private MBSs. Lewis Ranieri, the inventor of MBSs, helped create and defend the bill before Congress.

- In 1985, Lincoln National Life issued a pass-through CMBS, and Midwest Federal of Minneapolis issued the first thrift commercial-mortgage pool securitization. That year, estimated issuance of pooled commercial mortgage-backed securities spiked to $3.7 billion.

- In 1985, the first mortgage derivative was created by Salomon Brothers.

- The International Swaps and Derivatives Association, a trade organization of participants in the market for over-the-counter derivatives, was established in 1985 with its headquarters in New York.

- In the mid-1980s, Charles Sanford, an innovative financier at Bankers Trust, developed the first full-fledged system for measuring the level of credit and market risk, known as RAROC (risk adjusted return on capital). RAROC was based on an idea known as value at risk, or VaR. VaR is a measure of the risk of loss on a specific portfolio of financial assets. For a given portfolio, probability, and time horizon, VaR is defined as a threshold value such that the probability that the mark-to-market loss on the portfolio over the given time horizon exceeds this value (assuming normal markets and no trading in the portfolio is the given probability level).

- The Tax Reform Act of 1986 became law and established real estate mortgage investment conduits (REMICs) as a new tax classification for collateralized mortgage obligations (CMOs) and MBSs. The REMIC tax classification provided greater flexibility to issuers in structuring MBSs and caused a further expansion of the MBS market. In fact, thanks to the lobbying of Lewis Ranieri at the time, the IRS overhaul made the trading of tranched MBSs tax-exempt— opening the gate to their creation on a mass scale.

- After Congress changed the tax code in 1986, eliminating the deductibility of interest payments on all consumer debt except those charged on home mortgages, the stage was set for housing to become America's most favored asset.

- In 1986, Fannie issued the first tranched MBSs providing for the disproportionate allocation of principal and interest between two classes of certificates representing interests in a single mortgage pool. Fannie Mae (and Freddie Mac) purchases helped finance mortgages by providing a market for lenders to sell the loans they made, instead of holding them.

- A basic collateralized debt obligation (CDO) was first issued in 1987 by bankers at Drexel Burnham Lambert under the direction of junk-bond king Michael Milken.

- The Financial Institutions Reform, Recovery, and Enforcement Act of 1989 (FIRREA) was signed into law. FIRREA abolished the Federal Home Loan Bank Board and transferred some of its regulatory functions to the newly created Office of Thrift Supervision. FIRREA also created the Resolution Trust Corporation (RTC) to handle the S&L crisis. FIRREA's new regulations made it more onerous for savings institutions to hold commercial real estate loans.

- By 1989, excessive portfolio lending, an excess of capital, and poor market discipline created an overbuilt commercial real estate sector. In 1990, another credit crunch cut off traditional commercial real estate capital, resulting in portfolio lenders suffering their worst losses since the Great Depression. Thrifts left the business, and the RTC had to find a way to liquefy a huge number of failed thrift assets before its charter expired in 1995. Commercial mortgages were out of favor, so the RTC found that it could not sell whole-loan assets effectively in direct investor-to-investor transactions, so it turned to the capital markets.

- According to research by Richard Milne of the *Financial Times*, in 1991 just 20 percent of securities were rated AAA. But by 2009 the proportion of AAA debt had swollen to a staggering 55 percent of the total.

- In 1991, James Johnson became the head of Fannie Mae, turning it into an aggressive money-making machine. Johnson spotted an opportunity to use a popular cause—increasing homeownership—as a means of building Fannie's power in Washington. Between 1989 and 2009, Fannie spent around $100 million securing lawmakers' affections. Fannie Mae helped build and operate the conveyor belt that fed toxic mortgages and mortgage securities into the financial system.

- Fannie Mae also initiated the $10 billion "Open Doors to Affordable Housing" program in 1991. Its goal was to finance so much low-income housing that Fannie Mae's government prerequisites couldn't be taken away.

- The first credit-derivatives were invented by Peter Freund and John Crystal of Bankers Trust in 1991.

- Also in 1991, a law known as the Federal Deposit Insurance Corporation Improvement Act (FDICIA) was implemented. Walker Todd, a lawyer working at the Federal Reserve Bank of Cleveland, uncovered an obscure amendment to the law that dramatically expanded the federal safety net, increasing the likelihood of tax-payer bailouts in the future. While previously only commercial banks who were members of the Federal Reserve System could request emergency financial support from the central bank in times of crisis, the amendment to FDICIA increased the availability of Fed assistance to include investment banks and insurance companies. "Moral hazard" is the term used by economists to describe what Walker Todd had uncovered. That is, if access to emergency capital made bank managers *less* likely to exercise caution, it would encourage risk taking among banks because their executives knew they could be bailed out if they got into trouble.

- The Federal Housing Enterprises Financial Safety and Soundness Act became part of the law in 1992. The largest change with this act was the creation of a separate overseer for Fannie Mae and its smaller cohort, Freddie Mac. A new and supposedly independent regulator within the Department of Housing and Urban Development called the Office of Federal Housing Enterprise Oversight (OFHEO) was tasked with overseeing the operations of Fannie Mae and Freddie Mac with an eye for "safety and soundness." However, the act actually encouraged unsafe and unsound activities at both Fannie and Freddie by assigning them a new "affordable housing mission." Under the law, Fannie and Freddie had to use their mortgage purchases to provide housing to those across the US who had previously been unable to afford a home. Traditionally, banks had required that borrowers put 20 percent of the property price down to secure a loan, but the 1992 act encouraged Fannie and Freddie to buy mortgages where borrowers put down a nominal amount of 5 percent (or less) of the total loan amount.

- In 1992, the capital requirements of Fannie Mae were set at levels far below those of other banks—2.5 percent versus the 20 percent demanded by banks.

- Starting in 1993, the downward slide in Fannie Mae's lending standards began. Lower underwriting standards meant Fannie could significantly grow its portfolio and its earnings. It also meant that Fannie was moving further out on the risk curve.

- In 1993, United Companies Financial, a publicly traded mortgage lender based in Baton Rouge, Louisiana, sold the first private-label (non-government agency) residential mortgage-backed securities (RMBSs) comprised of $165 million worth of home loans.

- Also in 1993, a program called "Alternative Qualifying" was introduced by Fannie Mae and Freddie Mac. Alternative Qualifying (AQ) did away with long-standing practices requiring that a borrower's monthly housing payment not exceed 28 percent of his or her pre-tax income, and that his or her total debt did not exceed 36 percent of income. The AQ program was the first in a series of steps aimed at easing lending practices and expanding loan volumes.

- In 1994, President Bill Clinton launched the National Partners in Homeownership, a public-private cooperative with one goal: raising the numbers of homeowners across the country.

- In 1994, Blythe Masters of JPMorgan invented the first credit-default swap (CDS). Masters realized that JPMorgan could sell the risk that a borrower won't be able to pay back his debt. Since banking is based on making loans to customers, the risk of default by those customers is a crucial part of the business. A product like the CDS was supposed to reduce that risk—by selling it to somebody else—and had the potential to create a gigantic new market. But a credit-default swap was really just a financial option: An investor paid a small premium and, if enough subprime borrowers defaulted on their mortgages, he got rich.

- Also in 1994, Option One Mortgage, a company that would become a major player in the mortgage mania of the mid-2000s, was approving loans for borrowers whose debt-to-income levels went as high as 60 percent.

- Fannie Mae announced its "Trillion Dollar Commitment" in 1994, an aggressive program that earmarked $1 trillion to be spent on affordable housing between 1994 and 2000. Later in 2006, Countrywide Financial launched its own trillion-dollar commitment, known as "We House America." Fannie and Countrywide were basically pouring gasoline on the fire because people were buying homes they could not afford.

- In 1995, there was a proliferation of family-run subprime lenders, such as Metropolitan Mortgage of Miami. Between 1994 and 1997, subprime mortgage origination boomed, growing from about $40 billion to $125 billion. In 1995, nearly one in five mortgages qualified as subprime.

- Also in 1995, the Department of Housing and Urban Development (HUD) relaxed its rules involving appraisals, eliminating the requirement that those assessing the value of a property before a borrower took out a mortgage on it were independent from other companies involved in the process. Under a rule designed to streamline regulations, HUD said that lenders could hire their own appraisers, setting up the potential for inflated valuations and anything-goes lending. In the mid-1990s, many loose lending programs were springing up, like Arbor National Mortgage's offering to refinance customers' homes through its "50/50 Homeflex" program. Borrowers could be approved even if their debt payments consumed 50 percent of their monthly incomes.

- Ethan Penner is credited with redefining the business of commercial real estate finance in the mid-1990s by developing new sources of liquidity and revitalizing CMBSs. At the helm of the Capital Company of America (formerly known as Nomura Asset Capital Corporation), Penner helped the firm become one of the largest lenders in the US commercial real estate market. The company later sustained huge financial losses in 1998 when the so-called "Asian Flu" spread throughout the global capital markets.

- Also in the mid-1990s, accounting rules allowed companies that pooled loans into securities to recognize as income today what they expected the security to generate over the life of the pool. This was known as "gain-on-sale" accounting.

- During this period, a large subprime lender, Greentree Financial, experienced escalating defaults largely due to its recently introduced loan programs requiring down payments of only 5 percent. Greentree was following Fannie Mae's lead. (The government-sponsored mortgage giant had begun buying low down-payment loans in 1994).

- In 1996, the Fed imposed a rule allowing banks to include in their calculation of Tier 1 capital any holdings they had in trust preferred securities (TRUPS). These complex instruments had characteristics of both debt and equity. By allowing a debt instrument to be counted toward the least risky calculation of capital, the rule essentially allowed banks to make their financial statements appear sounder than they were. More important, the money that banks received when they sold these securities helped fuel the mortgage lending boom that was on the horizon. By 2005, and with that boom in full swing, TRUPS issuance stood at $85 billion, with more than 800 banks issuing them in the US.

- Also in 1996, the Office of Thrift Supervision (OTS), the federal regulator charged with minding the nation's savings and loan companies, changed its interpretation of rules initially governed by the Alternative Mortgage Transaction Parity Act, a 1982 law that removed restrictions on mortgages with features that differed from the standardized thirty-year fixed-rate loan. While the OTS had barred finance companies like Greentree Financial and Metropolitan Mortgage from selling loans with prepayment penalties, the regulator eliminated that restriction in 1996.

- By 1997, the top ten subprime lenders accounted for almost 40 percent of originations across the US mortgage sector. Some companies, like Household International, Associates First Capital, and Beneficial Corporation, originated mortgages and held them on their balance sheets, as traditional portfolio lenders did. Others, however, like NovaStar Financial, ContiMortgage Corporation, FirstPlus Financial Group, Greentree, and Cityscape Financial, securitized their originations. These companies were the go-go engine that produced the greatest growth in the US subprime sector.

- The first public securitization of Community Reinvestment Act (CRA) loans started in 1997. CRA loans are targeted to low- and moderate-income borrowers and neighborhoods.

- In 1997, Andrew Cuomo, the director of HUD, proclaimed that Fannie and Freddie must buy more subprime mortgages. Pushed to buy subprime loans, the degradation of underwriting standards was well underway.

- Also in 1997, investment bankers at JPMorgan created a financial instrument called a Broad Index Securitized Trust Offering, which later evolved into the "synthetic" collateralized debt obligation.

- During 1998, Fannie Mae's total mortgage financing hit the $1 trillion mark.

- At the end of 1998, Fannie held capital of only 3.6 percent of its assets, compared to 8.2 percent for banks insured by the Federal Deposit Insurance Corporation.

- Also in 1998, the global markets went into a tailspin when the Russian government had devalued its currency in an attempt to address a debt crisis sparked by defaults on its bond obligations. When the quantitatively driven hedge fund Long-Term Capital Management (LTCM) imploded, mortgage originations in the US fell sharply, and entities such as United Companies Financial, ContiMortgage, and FirstPlus all vanished. Anything-goes accounting, sleepwalking credit rating agencies, and a merry band of Wall Streeters willing to package dubious loans for sale to unsuspecting investors all took their toll.

- LTCM did business with nearly everyone important on Wall Street. As LTCM teetered, Wall Street feared that Long-Term's failure could cause a chain reaction in numerous markets, causing catastrophic losses throughout the financial system. After LTCM failed to raise more money on its own, it became clear it was running out of options. In September 1998, Goldman Sachs, AIG, and Berkshire Hathaway offered to buy out the fund's partners for $250 million, to inject $3.7 billion, and to operate LTCM within Goldman's own trading division. But the offer was too low for LTCM's partners because at the start of the year their firm had been worth $4.7 billion. Seeing no options left, the Federal Reserve Bank of New York organized a bailout of $3.6 billion by major creditors and Wall Street investment banks to avoid a wider collapse in the financial markets.

- Arranging the bailout of LTCM was a watershed event, because when other brokerage firms had gotten into trouble, they had received no help from the Fed. Helping a hedge fund escape difficulties that it had brought upon itself was beyond the pale. In other words, LTCM sent the message that the Fed was in bailout mode and the barn door was wide open for freewheeling bank behavior.

- Also in 1998, Alan Greenspan made his infamous comment before the House Banking Committee that the "regulation of derivatives transactions that are privately negotiated by professionals is unnecessary."

- In 1999, Byron Dorgan, a Democrat representing North Dakota in the US Senate, said, "I think we will look back in ten years' time and say we should not have done this [deregulation], but we did because we forgot the lessons of the past, and that that which is true in the 1930s is true in 2010."

- Some $160 billion in subprime loans were underwritten in 1999, up from $40 billion in 1994, and in 2003 that figure would jump to $332 billion. Many of the loans wound up in Fannie's and Freddie's portfolios. By 2008, some $1.6 trillion of toxic mortgages, or almost half of those that were written, were purchased or guaranteed by Fannie and Freddie.

- Also in 1999, Congress repealed the Glass-Steagall Act by passing the Gramm-Leach-Bliley Act (better known as the Financial Services

Modernization Act), which allowed commercial banks, investment banks, and insurance companies to merge and interact.

• In 2000, David Li, a researcher at JPMorgan, published a paper presenting a method he had devised for estimating the degree of correlation based on a well-established statistical technique known as the Gaussian copula model. This was basically a way of estimating the degree of dependencies of different kinds among a group of variables. He applied it to CDOs of corporate debt, and his concept quickly spread until almost every bank, rating agency, and investment group adopted it for their own models. The Gaussian copula enabled bankers to craft more and more CDOs faster and faster. ("Gaussian" refers to the assumption of a normal bell-shaped distribution; "copula" in Latin means "combining").

In many ways, Li's work was a boon for the derivatives sector. As the *Wall Street Journal* pointed out, the launch of Li's Gaussian copula model meant that bankers had a method not only to weigh a "bag of apples" (i.e., companies), but also to predict the likelihood they would all rot. That gave bankers the ability to trade different pieces of CDO risk with much more confidence—so much so, in fact, that a new business developed called "correlation-trading," which made investment bets based on how the correlation inside a CDO or between CDOs might move.

But the model also introduced new risks. The more that banks all relied on Li's Gaussian copula approach, the more they were creating a *new* form of correlation risk. Because everyone was using the same statistical method of devising their CDOs to contain risk, in the event of economic conditions that defied that modeling, huge numbers of CDOs would suffer losses all at once. As Alex Veroude, the manager of a CDO for Gulf International Bank, explained, "The problem is that all the structures now are designed the same way, with the same triggers. That means that if there is a storm, all the boats in the water will capsize."

Worse still, the fundamental philosophy behind the Gaussian statistical technique did not appear to be well-suited to cope with a situation where the boats might all capsize, en masse. Like any model, it was only as good as the data that was fed into the "engine," and that data was usually based on what had happened in the past. If something completely unexpected ever occurred—an event that was not in the data set—the model would not work.

Good statisticians tried to avoid that problem by working with as much data as they could. However, the credit-derivatives world was so new that there was not always that much data available. How could the trajectory of a CDO-squared be judged from past data when that "past" was just two years old? Or a subprime-linked derivative, for that matter, that had never been widely traded? And how could the models effectively forecast what might happen if a true investor panic got under way, creating a selling chain reaction that had never been seen before?

As David Li himself said about the model he had fashioned, "The most dangerous part is when people believe everything coming out of it." But even if some observers of the boom were highly skeptical about just how well the risks had really been measured, few had any motive to stop it.

- The Commodity Futures Modernization Act, mandating that derivatives should be exempted from any federal regulation, was introduced in 2000 and was later passed under the Consolidated Appropriations Act. The act provided "legal certainty" for over-the-counter derivatives that would indirectly cause the meltdown eight years later.

- Between December 2000 and July 2003, the Fed made a crucial decision that indirectly contributed to the mortgage lending craze. It slashed its federal funds rate from 6.5 percent to an unheard-of 1 percent.

- In 2001, the Treasury made a move that pushed investors to increase their already sizable holdings in mortgage-backed securities issued by Fannie and Freddie. It stopped issuing its benchmark long-term bonds, those with thirty-year maturities. With no more thirty-year issuance, investors looking for longer-term bonds turned to debt issued by Fannie and Freddie as a substitute for Treasuries. This heightened demand for Fannie and Freddie securities allowed investors to pump up the debt on their balance sheets and vastly increase their mortgage purchases.

- Also in 2001, the Basel Committee on Banking Supervision recommended changes that opened wide the floodgates for the mortgage securities mania. One change significantly reduced the amount of capital a bank was required to set aside on privately issued mortgage-backed securities (MBSs). A second increased the importance of the credit rating agencies (Standard & Poor's, Moody's, and Fitch). But the problem was that the rating agencies made the disastrous decision to accept as gospel the information provided to them by the banks that were putting together the MBS deals themselves (read: major conflicts of interest and corruption).

- In 2003, Maxine Waters, a Democrat from California, pushed the housing finance sector to eliminate down payments altogether. Waters' "American Dream Down Payment Initiative" would free a borrower from having to put any money down when buying a house. Waters clearly ignored that history showed that borrowers who had no investment in their homes defaulted far more frequently than those who had built up equity in them.

- The subprime mortgage CDS was invented by Mike Edman at Morgan Stanley in 2003.

- The Securities Industry and Financial Markets Association (SIFMA) was founded in New York in 2005.

- By the mid-2000s, Orange County, California was home to four of the nation's six biggest subprime lenders. Together, these four lenders—Ameriquest, Fremont Investment & Loan, New Century, and Option One Mortgage—accounted for nearly a third of the US subprime market.

- Major accounting fraud at Fannie Mae involving the intentional manipulation and inflation of management bonuses was uncovered by OFHEO in 2005.

- Also in 2005, Charles Himmelberg, a senior economist in research and statistics at the New York Fed published a paper entitled "Assessing High House Prices: Bubbles, Fundamentals, and Misperceptions." Along with two co-authors, Himmelberg concluded that there was *no* bubble in real estate.

- In 2006, CDS Indexco and Markit launched the ABX.HE (asset-backed securities home equity), a subprime credit-derivative index. An ABX is a credit-derivative swap contract that pools lists of exposures to private-issued residential mortgage-backed securities. From 2007 to 2009, the ABX.HE index fell 70 percent.

- In 2007, as the financial maelstrom was ramping up, Citigroup and other banks were found to have hidden obligations in a manner similar to the way Enron did. They had created special-purpose vehicles (SPVs) to sell short-term commercial paper to investors; the banks used the proceeds from this issuance to invest in mortgages and other longer-term paper. When investors stopped buying this commercial paper, the banks had to bring the entities' massive losses back onto their own balance sheets. This accelerated the mortgage crisis.

- As a result of the financial meltdown of 2008 that was precipitated by the subprime mortgage fiasco, the market for bonds backed by securitized loans was essentially at a standstill between late 2007 and mid-2010, unless the bonds were guaranteed by a federally backed agency.

- In 2012 and beyond, the securitization and derivatives sectors are bound to change given the rulings of the Dodd-Frank act, signed into law in July 2010, and due to the enduring squall of mortgage-related litigation.

Source: G. Morgenson and J. Rosner, *Reckless Endangerment: How Outsized Ambition, Greed, and Corruption Led to Economic Armageddon* (New York: Times Books, 2011), G. Tett, *Fool's Gold: The Inside Story of JPMorgan and How Wall St. Greed Corrupted Its Bold Dream and Created a Financial Catastrophe* (New York: Free Press, 2009), Nomura Securities International, CRE Finance Council, research by the author

Appendix B

Summary of US Government Intervention During and After the Financial Crisis

At the writing of this book, the US government's total commitment to solving the financial crisis had reached $12.6 trillion. The $12.6 trillion would be enough to send a $40,000 check to every man, woman, and child alive in the country today.

Government initiatives designed to address the financial crisis and its aftermath are summarized below.

- Bear Stearns was acquired by JPMorgan Chase in March 2008 for $1.2 billion. The sale was conditional on the Fed lending Bear Stearns $29 billion on a non-recourse basis.
- Independent National Mortgage Corporation (IndyMac), America's leading Alt-A originator in 2006 (with approximately $32 billion in deposits) was placed into conservatorship by the FDIC in July 2008, citing liquidity concerns. A bridge bank, IndyMac Federal Bank, was established under the control of the FDIC.
- The Housing and Economic Recovery Act designed primarily to address the mortgage crisis, was passed by Congress in July 2008.

Some provisions of the law were later modified by the American Recovery and Reinvestment Act of 2009 (discussed below).

- The government-sponsored enterprises (GSEs) Fannie Mae and Freddie Mac were both placed in conservatorship in September 2008 under the regulation of the Federal Housing Finance Agency. The two GSEs were holding mortgage-backed securities (MBSs), mortgages, and other debt with a notional value of more than $5 trillion. The total cost of the bailout to US taxpayers was $164 billion.

- Lehman Brothers declared bankruptcy in September 2008 after Secretary of the Treasury Henry Paulson, citing moral hazard, refused to bailout the investment bank.

- AIG received an $85 billion emergency loan in September 2008 from the Fed, which AIG repaid by gradually selling off its assets. In exchange, the US government acquired an approximately 80 percent equity stake in AIG. The AIG debacle cost US taxpayers a total of $182 billion due to its critical position insuring the toxic assets of many global financial institutions through credit-default swaps. The Fed's rescue of AIG is one of the most controversial chapters of the government's response to the financial crisis.

- Washington Mutual (WaMu) was seized in September 2008 by the Office of Thrift Supervision. Most of WaMu's untroubled assets were sold to JPMorgan Chase.

- In October 2008, the government passed the Emergency Economic Stabilization Act, which established the Troubled Asset Relief Program (TARP). This law included $700 billion that was used to lend funds to big banks (that apparently didn't really need the money) in exchange for dividend-paying preferred stock. TARP officially ended in October 2010. "It wasn't fair, but it was necessary." That comment about TARP from Treasury Secretary Timothy Geithner in April 2010 seemed about the best that anyone would ever say of it.

- In November 2008, the government announced that it was purchasing $27 billion of preferred stock in Citigroup, as well as warrants on 4.5 percent of its common stock. The preferred stock carried an 8 percent dividend yield.

- In November 2008, the Fed also announced a $600 billion program to purchase the MBSs of Fannie and Freddie to help lower mortgage rates.

- The target for the federal funds rate was lowered from 5.25 percent to 2 percent, and the discount rate from 5.75 percent to 2.25 percent. This took place in six steps occurring between September 2007 and April 2008. In December 2008, the Fed lowered the federal funds target rate further to a range of 0 percent to 0.25 percent (or 25 basis points). At the writing of this book, the federal funds rate was still at 0.25 percent.

- Along with other central banks, the Fed undertook "open market operations" to ensure that its member banks remained solvent. These are effectively short-term loans to member banks collateralized by government securities. Central banks lower the interest rates (called the "discount rate" in the United States) that they charge member banks for short-term loans.

- In December 2008, the Fed created a variety of facilities to enable it to lend directly to banks and non-bank institutions against specific types of collateral of varying credit quality. These included the Term Auction Facility and the Term Asset-Backed Securities Loan Facility programs.

- The first round of quantitative easing, nicknamed QE1, covering the period from January 2009 to March 2010, involved the purchase of approximately $1.4 trillion of mortgage-backed securities and Treasuries.

- In February 2009, President Obama signed the American Recovery and Reinvestment Act, a $787 billion stimulus package with a broad spectrum of spending and tax cuts, and with $73 billion specifically allocated to programs intended to help struggling homeowners to avoid foreclosure. The program was supplemented by $200 billion in additional funding for Fannie and Freddie to purchase (and more easily refinance) mortgages. This additional funding is known as the Homeowner Affordability and Stability Plan (HASP), which is funded mostly by the Housing and Economic Recovery Act of 2008. HASP uses cost-sharing and incentives to encourage lenders to reduce homeowners' monthly payments to 31 percent of their pre-tax monthly income. Under the program, a lender is responsible for reducing monthly payments to no more than 38 percent of a borrower's income, with the government sharing the cost to further cut the rate to 31 percent. HASP involves forgiving a portion of the borrower's mortgage balance, where companies that service mortgages get incentives to modify loans and help the homeowner stay current on loan repayments.

- In March 2009, the government provided eligible homeowners the opportunity to modify their mortgages to make them more affordable, mainly through refinancing the existing balance in a program called the Home Affordable Modification Program (HAMP), which was also designed to pay "sweeteners" to lenders to encourage them to soften repayment terms and help avoid foreclosures, with a lofty goal of four million households by 2012. It is estimated that only 760,000 homeowners will have benefited from this controversial program. Part of the reason why participation in this program has been so poor is because of the conflict of interest for servicers, the companies that collect payments and seize homes when borrowers default. It's more in servicers' economic interest to foreclose rather than put borrowers into a HAMP modification. In the case of principal forgiveness, one of the problems is that servicers are paid based on a percentage of the *active* principal. Principal reduction eats right into their bottom-line. Therefore, US Treasury officials should focus on increasing incentive payments to servicers to compensate for losses.

- Also in March 2009, the Federal Open Market Committee (FOMC) increased the size of the Fed's balance sheet by purchasing an additional $750 billion of Fannie and Freddie MBSs, bringing its total purchases of these securities to up to $1.35 trillion in 2009. Additionally, to help improve conditions in private-credit markets, the FOMC purchased $300 billion of longer-term Treasury securities during 2009. The expansion of the Fed's balance sheet means that it was electronically creating money, necessary because the US economy was very weak and inflation was too low.

- Another method of recapitalizing banks is for government and private investors to provide cash in exchange for mortgage-related assets (including toxic assets), improving the quality of bank capital while reducing uncertainty regarding the financial position of banks. US Treasury Secretary Timothy Geithner announced a plan in March 2009 to acquire toxic assets from banks known as the Public-Private Partnership Investment Program, which involves government loans, guaranteeing to encourage private investors to provide funds to purchase toxic assets.

- The $8,000 tax credit for first-time homebuyers and the $6,500 tax credit for repeat homebuyers expired in April 2010. The tax credit applied only to homes priced at $800,000 or less.

- In April 2010, the federal government also provided opportunities for homeowners to avoid foreclosure through a short-sale or deed-in-lieu of foreclosure. This measure is called the Home Affordable

Foreclosure Alternatives (HAFA) program. Short-sales tend to be complex, especially when the seller has also taken out a second-mortgage (a second-lien), or the mortgage has been packaged into a security sold to investors. In 2011, short-sales accounted for only 10 percent of house sales, much less than expected.

- In November 2010, the FOMC announced plans for a second round of quantitative easing (or QE2), which called for the repurchase of an additional $600 billion of long-term Treasuries which ended in June 2011.

- In December 2010, President Obama signed into law an $858 billion bill extending George W. Bush-era tax cuts for two years for all income groups, instead of letting them expire for family earnings that exceed $250,000 a year, the cutoff the administration uses for the US middle-class.

- In July 2011, the United States Consumer Financial Protection Bureau (CFPB) was established. The central mission of the CFPB is to make markets for consumer financial products work for Americans—whether they are applying for a mortgage, choosing among credit cards, or using any number of other financial products.

- Also in July 2011, the Office of the Comptroller of Currency (OCC) absorbed all the functions of the Office of Thrift Supervision. The merger was a provision of the Dodd-Frank act. This means that the ongoing examination, supervision, and regulation of federal savings associations is a responsibility of the OCC.

- In August 2011, Congress voted to extend the US debt ceiling and undertake deficit reduction measures. The national debt ceiling of $14.3 trillion was increased to $15.2 trillion (and counting).

- In October 2011, the Fed started "Operation Twist," which involved buying $400 billion of long-dated Treasuries, financed by selling an equal amount of debt with three years or less to run. The objective was to help lower Treasury yields and mortgage rates with the hope of generating a surge in debt refinancing that would free up money for homeowners to spend on other things.

- Also in October 2011, the Obama administration modified its Home Affordable Refinance Program (HARP). HARP was originally designed to assist homeowners in refinancing their mortgages, even if they owe more than the home's current value. The program failed to meet regulators' expectations when it was launched in March 2009, partly because borrowers who were deeply underwater on their mortgages could not refinance, as HARP limited refinance loans to no more than 125 percent of the value of the home. The new HARP will not have a cap.

- In December 2011, the Securities and Exchange Commission filed fraud charges against former Fannie Mae CEO Daniel Mudd, Richard Syron—ex-chief executive at Freddie Mac—and four other former executives. The SEC alleged that while Freddie Mac said its subprime exposure was $2 billion—$6 billion it was, in fact, $141 billion—$244 billion.

- In February 2012, a $25 billion deal was announced that includes $4.2 billion in cash for forty-nine states to pay for foreclosure-prevention initiatives. Loan servicers are expected to pay $1.5 billion to homeowners harmed by botched foreclosures caused by the "robo-signing" fiasco. The money will test the effectiveness of principal forgiveness in preventing defaults, and may spur a larger-scale program, if it's successful. Critics claim that the deal is too small relative to negative home equity, estimated at $700 billion.

Source: Research by the author

Appendix C

The Basic Mechanics of Bonds

Bond at Original Issue

Sellers	Buyers	Buyer Monetary Return at Maturity	Buyer % Yield at Maturity
Bond is selling at par value $1,000	Buy at par value	Original buyer gets:	Annual interest $60
Term 10 years	Receive 10 annual payments of $60 each	Par value $1,000	Price $1,000
Interest rates 6.0%	Receive par value at maturity	+ Interest x 10 years $600	Bond yield 6.0%
		Price _____	
		- Original cost $1,000	
		Return $600	

Bond 2 Years Later (Assuming Interest Rates Go UP)

Sellers	Buyers	Buyer Monetary Return at Maturity	Buyer % Yield at Maturity *
Original buyer sells 2 years after issue when interest rates go UP	Buying at a DISCOUNT in the secondary market	New buyer gets:	Annual interest $60
The original bond sells at a DISCOUNT	Pay $200 LESS than par value	Par value $1,000	Price $800
Interest rates 8.0%	Receive 8 annual payments of $60 each	+ Interest x 8 years $480	Bond yield 7.5%
Market price of original bond issued $800 estimate	Receive par value at maturity	Price $800	
+ Interest x 2 years $120		- Original Cost $800	
Price $920		Return $680	
- Original cost $1,000			
Loss (Discount) -$80			

Bond 3 Years Later (Assuming Interest Rates Go DOWN)

Sellers	Buyers	Buyer Monetary Return at Maturity	Buyer % Yield at Maturity
Original buyer sells 3 years after issue when interest rates go DOWN	Buying at a PREMIUM in the secondary market	New buyer gets:	Annual interest $60
The original bond sells at a PREMIUM	Pay $200 MORE than par value	Par value $1,000	Price $1,200
Interest rates 3.0%	Receive 7 annual payments of $60 each	+ Interest x 7 years $420	Bond yield 5.0%
Market price of original bond issued $1,200 estimate	Receive par value at maturity	Price $1,200	
+ Interest x 3 years $180		- Original cost $1,200	
Price $1,380		Return $220	
- Original cost $1,000			
Gain (Premium) $380			

* The bond buyer is getting a good deal under this scenario.

Bond Basics:

1) Because the original interest rate stays the same and the bond price will vary accordingly after the original issue, the yield changes. For example, if new bonds selling for $1,000 are offering only 3.0%, you will be able to sell your 6.0% original bonds for more than you paid (i.e., for a premium), since buyers will agree to pay more to attain a higher interest rate.
2) If interest rates go up, as a bond buyer you get a higher yield compared to the original bond issue (but the market price of the bond will be lower than the par value).
3) If interest rates go *down*, as a bond buyer you get a *lower* yield compared to the original bond issue (but the market price of the bond will be *higher* than the par value).
4) Investors try to get out of low interest-rate bonds.
5) Investors try to make profits on high interest-rate bonds.

Source: Research by the author

Notes

Unless otherwise indicated in the references below, all US economic data in the book are from official government sources.

Introduction

1.   To clarify the terminology, the "subprime mortgage crisis" (or the "mortgage crisis") was one of the first indicators of the broader "financial crisis of 2008," which, in turn, was at the epicenter of the "Great Recession of 2007–09."

   In addition, a "mortgage loan" is a loan secured by real estate through the use of a mortgage "note." A note is a document or a clause in a document in which the borrower accepts responsibility for the repayment of a debt under certain terms and conditions. In other words, a note evidences the existence of the loan and the encumbrance of the real estate through the granting of a mortgage which secures the loan. However, in everyday usage the words "mortgage" or "loan" alone are most often used to mean *mortgage loan*. As such, I have used the terms "mortgage" and "loan" interchangeably throughout the text.

2.   "Moral hazard" describes what happens when risk takers are shielded from the consequences of failure; they might take ever-greater risks. In addition, economist Paul Krugman describes moral hazard as: "Any situation in which one person makes the decision about how much risk to take, while

someone else bears the cost if things go badly." The term dates back to the seventeenth century and was widely used by British insurance companies by the late nineteenth century. Early usage of the term carried negative connotations, implying fraud or immoral behavior, usually on the part of the insured party.

Chapter 1: Red, White, and Blue

1. W. Safire, *The New York Times Guide to Essential Knowledge* (New York: St. Martin's Press, 2007), 599.

2. A. Rand, "Introducing Objectivism," *The Objectivist Newsletter* 1 (8): 35.

3. Devin Leonard, "The New Abnormal," *Bloomberg BusinessWeek*, August 2, 2010, 50–55.

4. C. Anderson, *Bubbles, Panics & Crashes: A Century of Financial Crises, 1830s–1930s,* (Cambridge, MA: Harvard Business School Press, 2009), 18.

5. C. Kindleberger, *Manias, Panics & Crashes: A History of Financial Crises* (New York: John Wiley & Sons, 2005), 24–37.

6. A. Downs, *Real Estate and the Financial Crisis: How Turmoil in the Capital Markets is Restructuring Real Estate Finance* (Washington, DC: Urban Land Institute, 2009), 34–35.

7. Anderson, *Bubbles,* Ibid.

8. Based on the analysis by the author presented in the table on pages 439–440.

9. The years during which America's major mail-order catalogues were founded are as follows: Hammacher Schlemmer, 1848; Montgomery Ward, 1872; Sears, 1893; L. L. Bean, 1912; Eddie Bauer, 1920; Lands' End, 1963; and JCPenney, 1963.

US Recessions,* Financial Panics, and Depressions—1775 to 2009		
Year	**Event**	**Gap in Years**
1775	Revolutionary War	-
1793	France and England War	18
1797	Panic of 1797	4
1802	Recession of 1802–04	5
1807	Embargo Depression	10
1815	Depression of 1815–21	13
1819	Primary Post-War Depression	12
1826	Secondary Post-War Depression	7
1837	Panic of 1837	11
1842	Debt Repudiation Depression	5
1857	Panic of 1857	15
1861	Secession Depression	4
1873	Post-Civil War Depression	12
1884	Depression of 1884	11
1893	Panic of 1893	9
1896	Silver Campaign Depression	3
1903	Rich Man's Panic	7
1907	Panic of 1907	4
1910	Panic of 1910	3
1914	World War I Depression	4
1921	Post-War Depression	7
1929	Stock Market Crash/Great Depression	8
1937	Recession of 1937–38	8
1948	Recession of 1948–49	11
1960	Recession of 1960–61	12

(Table continued on next page...)

Year	Event	Gap in Years
1969	Recession of 1969–70	9
1973	Oil Crisis	4
1981	Early 1980s Recession	8
1990	Early 1990s Recession (caused by S&L crisis)	9
2000–02	Dot-Com Crash/9-11	11
2007–09	Financial Crisis/Great Recession	7
Average		**8**

Source: C. Anderson, *Bubbles, Panics & Crashes: A Century of Financial Crises, 1830s–1930s*, (Cambridge, MA: Harvard Business School Press, 2009), the National Bureau of Economic Research. *Recessions lasting for more than one year. The general rule of thumb that technically defines a recession is two quarters of negative GDP growth.

10.   National Bankruptcy Center, *2010 Year-End Bankruptcy Filings Report* (Burlingame, CA: NBKRC, 2011).

11.   A. Novotney, "What's behind American consumerism," *Monitor* 39 (7): 40.

12.   Ibid.

13.   Data obtained from http://www.myfico.com/crediteducation/averages-tats.aspx, (accessed July 10, 2010).

14.   "Amortizing mortgages" or "amortization" refers to the paying off of a mortgage or debt via periodic installment payments over time.

15.   N. Retsinas, "A House Divided: Investment or Shelter?" *Harvard Business School Working Knowledge,* January 23, 2008.

16.   Ibid.

17.   Downs, *Real Estate*, 34.

18.   Ibid., 53.

19.   Ibid.

20.   M. Lewis, *The Big Short* (New York: W. W. Norton & Company, 2010), 210.

Chapter 2: Mumbo Jumbo

1. Since 2008, all investment banks were restructured as commercial bank holding companies to be eligible to participate in the Federal Reserve's "quantitative easing" programs.

2. J. Downes and J. Goodman, *Finance & Investment Handbook* (New York: Barron's Educational Services, 1998), 584.

3. S. Johnson and J. Kwak, *13 Bankers: The Wall Street Takeover and the Next Financial Meltdown* (New York: Vintage Books, 2011), 76.

4. Ibid.

5. Ibid., 84.

6. According to the weekly newsletter *Commercial Mortgage Alert*, the combined issuances by JPMorgan Chase, Deutsche Bank, and Goldman Sachs comprised 68 percent of the total $11.6 billion of CMBSs in 2010.

7. Basel III is the revision of the Basel Accords on financial regulation by the Bank for International Settlements.

8. The ideas on mortgage securitization in this section are based on F. Fabozzi and F. Modigliani's excellent book *Mortgage and Mortgage-Backed Securities Markets* (Boston: Harvard Business School Press, 1992), 2–12.

9. Aline van Duyn, "Foreclosure chaos boosts distressed mortgaged debt," *Financial Times*, October 19, 2010, 25.

10. M. Lewis, *The Big Short* (New York: W. W. Norton & Company, 2010), 7.

11. A "lock-out" provision is a clause in a mortgage that prohibits prepayment during a certain time period. This clause has strong provisions to deter prepayment of all (or a portion of) the mortgage for a predetermined period of time. The reason for a lock-out provision is to protect the yield spread of investors. It helps keep interest rates at a reasonable level. Without this clause, borrowers would have to pay either higher interest rates or higher points.

"Defeasance" of a securitized commercial mortgage is a process in real estate finance by which a borrower substitutes other income-producing collateral for a piece of real property to facilitate the removal ("defeat") of an existing lien (claim of a party, usually a creditor, to hold or control a property of another party to meet a debt or liability) without the paying off (through a transfer of liquid assets) of the existing note.

"Yield maintenance" is a prepayment penalty that, in the event the borrower pays off a loan before maturity, allows the lender to attain the same yield as if the borrower had made all scheduled mortgage payments until maturity. Yield maintenance premiums are designed to make lenders indifferent to an early prepayment by a borrower.

12. S. Meister, *Commercial Real Estate Restructuring Revolution: Strategies, Tranche Warfare, and Prospects for Recovery* (Hoboken, NJ: John Wiley & Sons, 2011), 42.

An "indenture" is a written agreement specifying the terms and conditions for issuing bonds, stating the form of the bond being offered for sale, interest to be paid, the maturity date, call provisions, and protective covenants (if any), the collateral pledged, the repayment schedule, and other terms. It describes the legal obligations of a bond issuer and the powers of the bond trustee who has the responsibility of ensuring that interest payments are made to registered bondholders.

13. Investment-grade ratings by the credit agencies are typically labeled AAA/ Aaa through BBB-/Baa3. Below investment-grade ratings are usually labeled as BB+/Ba1 through B-/B3.

14. Meister, *Commercial Real Estate*, 42.

15. Ibid.

16. Ibid.

17. Ibid.

18. Ibid.

19. Ibid, 43.

20. Johnson and Kwak, *13 Bankers*, 64.

21. M. Sullivan, *The Alarming Tidal Wave of Hotel Mortgage Loan Defaults/Workouts* (San Francisco: HVS Capital Corporation, 2011), 2–3.

22. CMBS loans get modified only after they've been pushed onto special servicing, which often happens because their collateral no longer generates the amount of cash flow needed to service their debt, or because of a pending maturity or risk that a refinancing won't take place. But not all loans in special servicing are modified. Many are simply liquidated in one way or another, or foreclosed. While modifying loans could eventually result in a "positive event" with higher liquidation values, they often generate added fees to CMBS transactions. Special servicers receive workout fees when they modify a loan, which can have a fairly significant impact on any given transaction's liquidity.

   In the "principally secured test," the real estate mortgage investment conduit (REMIC) rules permit changes to the collateral and the credit enhancement relating to a mortgage loan (even a performing loan), so long as the loan remains "principally secured" by real property after the modification. Principally secured means either: (1) That the mortgage has a loan-to-value ratio (taking into account only the real property collateral) of 125 percent or less; or (2) for mortgages with loan-to value ratios above 125 percent, that there is no reduction in the fair market value of the property after the modification. The principally secured test applies to all property releases, including those contemplated by the parties involved when a loan was closed, or for which default is reasonably foreseeable.

   On the other hand, the "imminent default test" has been interpreted as follows: "The Internal Revenue Service will not challenge the tax status of a REMIC due to the REMIC's modification of a commercial loan that is currently performing, but where, in the view of the commercial loan servicer, a significant risk of default exists, even if the default is expected to occur only at some distant future date."

The original loan documents are critical in a CMBS lawsuit because they set out the process for giving control of the loan to one debtholder in the wake of a default. Typically in these situations, there is an appraisal and control of the debt goes to the most-junior debtholder that is "in-the-money," meaning it would get some of its money returned after the sale of the property. For example, after an owner defaults on its debt, the debt is appraised. If the most-junior debtholder's tranche is "out-of-the-money" based on the appraisal, the junior debtholder can oftentimes claim that a clause in the loan documents gives it the right to buy the loan (between the appraisal date and when control of the loan would have reverted to a more senior creditor). This is known as "tranche warfare."

23. Johnson and Kwak, *13 Bankers*, 121–122.

24. Nomura Fixed Income Research, *CDOs in Plain English* (New York: Nomura Securities International, 2004), 1.

25. J. Helwege, S. Maurer, A. Sarkar, and Y. Wang, *Credit-Default Swap Auctions* (New York: Federal Reserve Bank of New York, 2009), 3.

26. Simon Johnson and James Kwak, "Credit-default swaps," *What happened to the global economy and what we can do about it: The Baseline Scenario*, October 4, 2008, http://baselinescenario.com/financial-crisis-for-beginners/#cds.

To further explain a credit-default swap (CDS), the buyer of insurance-like protection against credit exposure pays a fixed fee or premium to the seller of protection for a period of time (a contract). If a certain pre-specified "credit event" occurs, the protection seller pays compensation to the protection buyer. A credit event can be a bankruptcy of a company, called the "reference entity," or a default of a bond issued by the reference entity (borrower). If no credit event occurs during the term of the swap, the protection buyer continues to pay the premium until maturity. Usually there is no exchange of money when two parties enter in the contract, but they make payments during the term of the contract, thus explaining the term credit-default "swap."

In contrast, should a credit event occur at some point before the contract's maturity, the protection seller owes a payment to the buyer of protection; thus, insulating the buyer from a financial loss. CDSs can also be used as a way to gain exposure to credit risk. While the risk profile of a CDS is similar to a corporate bond of the reference entity, there are some important differences. For example, a CDS does not require an initial funding, which allows leveraged positions. Moreover, a CDS transaction can be entered where a cash bond of the reference entity of a particular maturity is not available. Further, by entering a CDS as a protection buyer, one can easily create a "short" position in the reference credit. (A short position is the sale of a borrowed security, commodity, or currency with the expectation that the asset will fall in value). As such, CDSs are *supposed* to be a tool for diversifying or hedging one's portfolio.

The above is based on Nomura Fixed Income Research, *Credit-Default Swaps (CDSs) Primer* (New York: Nomura Securities International, 2004), 1–5.

27.   Ibid.

28.   Ibid.

29.   Ibid.

30.   Ibid.

31.   Ibid.

32.   Ibid.

33.   G. Tett, *Fool's Gold: The Inside Story of JPMorgan and How Wall St. Greed Corrupted Its Bold Dream and Created a Financial Catastrophe* (New York: Free Press, 2009), 46–48.

34.   Johnson and Kwak, *13 Bankers*, 125. "Synthetic" collateralized debt obligations are CDOs backed by a pool of derivatives such as credit-defaults swaps, rather than bonds or mortgage loans.

35.   J. Stiglitz, "Capitalist Fools: Five Key Mistakes That Led Us to the Collapse," in Carter, *The Great Hangover: 21 Tales of the New Recession from the Pages of Vanity Fair* (New York: Harper Perennial, 2010), 145–152.

36.   Peter Foster, "George Soros urges governments to outlaw 'toxic' credit-default swaps," *The Telegraph* (London), June 12, 2009, http://www.telegraph.co.uk/finance/newsbysector/banksandfinance/5514341/George-Soros-urges-governments-to-outlaw-toxic-credit-default-swaps.html, (accessed July 27, 2010).

37.   Aline van Duyn, "Raising the curtain on the private nature of derivatives," *Financial Times*, September 15, 2010, 17.

38.   Louis Story, "A Secretive Banking Elite Rules Trading in Derivatives," *New York Times*, December 11, 2010, A1.

39.   M. Zandi, *Financial Shock: A 360° Look at the Subprime Mortgage Implosion, and How to Avoid the Next Financial Crisis* (Upper Saddle River, NJ: FT Press, 2008), 120–121. For a full description of the complexities of the shadow banking system, see http://www.newyorkfed.org/research/staff_reports/sr458.pdf.

40.   P. Angelides et. al., *The Financial Crisis Inquiry Report* (New York: Public Affairs, 2011), xxv.

41.   Ibid., xxiv.

42.   Ibid.

43.   Lewis, *The Big*, 218.

44.   D. Elliott, *A Primer on Bank Capital* (Washington, DC: The Brookings Institution, 2010), 10, 21.

45.   Lewis, *The Big*, 244.

46.   M. Thompson and I. Broff, "A Missed Assessment of Real Estate Debt Risk: How the Credit Rating Agencies and Commercial Bank Regulators Missed the Assessment of Real Estate Debt Risk, Creating the Largest Real Estate Bubble in US History," *Real Estate Issues* 34 (3): 25–32.

47.   R. Lowenstein, *The End of Wall Street* (New York: The Penguin Press, 2010), 23.

48.   Ibid.

Chapter 3: Drinking the Purple Kool-Aid

1. A. Downs, *Real Estate and the Financial Crisis: How Turmoil in the Capital Markets is Restructuring Real Estate Finance* (Washington, DC: Urban Land Institute, 2009), 41.

2. Ibid., 13–14, 54–56.

3. Ibid., 173.

4. I. Glass, "The American Life," Public Radio International, April 5, 2009.

5. S. Goel, *Crisis Management* (New Delhi: Global India Publications, 2009), 61.

6. Noelle Knox, "43% of first-time home buyers put no money down," *USA Today*, January 18, 2006, A1.

7. D. Kahn and M. Borden, *Complete Idiot's Guide to Success as a Mortgage Broker* (New York: Alpha Books, 2006), 143–152.

8. Downs, *Real Estate*, 38. This estimate includes the residential real estate, finance, and insurance sectors. Fixed residential investment and housing-related spending alone comprised 16.8 percent of gross domestic product in 2005.

9. "FTSE" stands for the Financial Times Stock Exchange. The FTSE NAREIT Equity REIT Index reflects transaction-based returns that include the use of leverage and overhead for expenses associated with managing REITs. The NAREIT Index is comprised of a broad range of income-producing property types, including office, retail, industrial, apartment, hotel, and self-storage facilities. In addition, the NAREIT Index is a total return index (i.e., includes dividends), whereas other major indices such as the S&P 500, Dow Jones Industrial Average, and the NASDAQ index do not include dividends.

10. Downs, *Real Estate*, 12.

11. W. Cohan, *House of Cards: A Tale of Hubris and Wretched Excess on Wall Street* (New York: Doubleday, 2009), 450.

12. A "contract-for-deed," also known as a "land contract" or an "installment sale agreement," is a contract between a seller and buyer of real estate in which the seller provides financing to buy the property for an agreed-upon purchase price, with the buyer repaying the loan in installments.

13. R. Shiller, *The Subprime Solution: How Today's Global Financial Crisis Happened, and What to Do about It* (Princeton, NJ: Princeton University Press, 2008), 130.

14. Rachel Sanderson and Gillian Tett, "Get me into Goldmans," *Financial Times*, August 14, 2010, 15.

15. Zachary Goldfarb, "Fed's image tarnished by newly released documents," *Washington Post*, January 12, 2012, A1.

Chapter 4: Strawberry Pickers and Predators

1. US General Accounting Office, *Consumer Protection: Federal and State Agencies Face Challenges in Combating Predatory Lending* (Washington, DC: GAO, 2004), 18–21.

2. Ibid.

3. M. Hudson, *The Monster: How a Gang of Predatory Lenders and Wall Street Bankers Fleeced America—and Spawned a Global Crisis* (New York: Times Books, 2010), 10.

4. Ibid.

5. Ibid., 37.

6. Ibid., 38.

7. Case number 1:2007cv03325 Illinois Northern District Court Miller, http:// www.enotes.com/topic/Ameriquest_Mortgage, (accessed May 2, 2011).

8. E. Belsky and N. Richardson, *Understanding the Boom and Bust in Nonprime Mortgage Lending* (Cambridge, MA: Joint Center for Housing Studies of Harvard University, 2010), 84–105.

9. W. Lucy and J. Herlitz, *Foreclosures in States and Metropolitan Areas: Patterns, Forecasts, and Pricing Toxic Assets* (Charlottesville, VA: University of Virginia School of Architecture, 2009), 1.

10. Ibid.

11. D. Boclan, P. Smith, G. Green, and P. Leonard, *Dreams Deferred: Impacts and Characteristics of the California Foreclosure Crisis* (Washington, DC: Center for Responsible Lending, 2010), 4.

12. Ibid.

13. Ibid., 5.

14. Ibid., 6.

15. Ibid., 9.

16. Ibid., 10.

17. Ibid.

18. This section is based on a true story; however, the names, dates, and places have been changed to respect the privacy of the individuals involved.

Chapter 5: Wicked Incentives

1. Simon Caulkin, "Cheques and balances: Ballooning chief executive pay has soared free of market gravity. How do we bring it back down to earth?" *Financial Times* (Business Education supplement), December 6, 2010, 16.

2. C. Rossi, *Anatomy of Risk Management Practices in the Mortgage Industry* (Washington, DC: University of Maryland and the Research Institute for Housing America of the Mortgage Bankers Association, 2010), 7–8.

3. Ibid., 14–16.

4. Ibid., 30.

5. In finance, capitalization is a process by which income is converted to one lump sum capital value. The capitalization rate (cap rate) is the initial unleveraged return on an asset to the investor based on the purchase

price and the annual net operating income the property generates. For example, if a hotel produces a net operating income (NOI) of $1,000,000 in the first year of ownership, and the cap rate for that type of hotel is 8 percent, $1,000,000 divided by 0.08 produces a result of $12,500,000 as the estimated market value of the property. The inverse of 8 is 1/8, or 0.125; therefore, 0.125 x 100 = 12.5 (which is the net income multiple) and 12.5 x $1,000,000 = $12,500,000.

———

Beyond being an investment, US Treasuries (bonds) are the core of international debt markets. In a world flooded with debt, Treasuries are the hub and other market interest rates are the spokes, priced and valued against the US benchmark. As presented in Appendix C, when interest rates rise, bond yields increase in tandem, and the values of previously issued bonds decline. The same mechanics apply with cap rates. When cap rates rise, property prices fall, and vice versa. In other words, when the required return is high and the expected NOI is weak, investors will apply a high cap rate to value a property because they know the cash flow of the property is not likely to grow. As such, a cap rate is an indicator that reflects investors' expectations about investment returns and/or NOI growth, typically for the first twelve months of ownership. Said differently, a cap rate is dependent on what investors want to earn on their money when acquiring a commercial property.

A cap rate is also indirectly tied to the prevailing interest rates as investors can choose other choices if real estate doesn't provide a sufficient return. Each building can vary, but there should be a level that is common for most buildings that are in the same market (i.e., property type, condition, and location). Many times the NOI can be misstated, so it's important to check the details to see what has been assumed when the NOI was computed. Otherwise, it's garbage in-garbage out.

The explanation for the strong link between cap rates and inter-est rates is that property competes in the capital markets with alternative investment vehicles (both risky and "risk-free"). However, following the 2011 downgrade of US government debt from AAA to AA+, nothing in the financial markets is 100 percent risk-free. So, for example, when the rates for ten-year Treasuries go down investors will tend to turn to other investment vehicles, such as corporate bonds, stocks, gold, and real estate.

6. Sam Pizzigati, "Executive Pay: Our Myopia Around the Mighty," *Too Much*, July 10, 2010, http://toomuchonline.org/our-myopia-around-the-mighty/, (accessed October 9, 2010).

7. Ibid.

8. Robert Pozen, "Can We Break the Tyranny of Quarterly Results?" *Harvard Business Review*, October 27, 2009, http://blogs.hbr.org/hbr/restoring-american-competitiveness/2009/10/can-we-break-the-tyranny-of-qu.html.

9. Ibid.

10. Ibid.

11. Ibid.

12. Ibid.

13. Ibid.

14. Katherine Sinderson, "Eye on the Issues," *The Advocate for Institutional Investors*, Fall 2010, 14.

15. Amr Hamdy, "Corporate Governance Report: Executive Pay and the Credit Crisis of 2008," (unpublished paper, Graduate School of Business, Fordham University, New York, 2008).

16. Ibid.

17. Ibid.

18. Ibid.

19. Ibid. A claw-back involves money or benefits that are distributed and then taken back as a result of special circumstances.

20. Ibid.

21. Ibid.

22. Ibid.

23. Ibid.

24. Layering is the tendency to accumulate high-risk credit factors: a low FICO score of 620 and below, no income documentation, no asset documentation, and no down payment.

25. Andrew Palmer, "Bricks and slaughter," *The Economist* (a special report on property), March 5, 2011, 15.

26. Robert Shiller is an expert on behavioral economics, real estate, and financial markets. He came to national prominence in 2000 with his bestseller *Irrational Exuberance*, which described speculative bubbles and correctly predicted the dot-com implosion. Following the housing market collapse, which he had also predicted, he wrote *Subprime Solution: How the Global Financial Crisis Happened and What to Do About It*, which is referenced in this book. With Karl Case, and with its origins dating back to 1991, he developed the most widely used housing benchmark, the Standard & Poor's/Case-Shiller Home Price Index.

27. Zachary Karabell, "Big Bad Bankers" *Time*, January 31, 2011, 20.

Chapter 6: Cheese, Sleaze, and Filling in the Boxes

1. Andrew Palmer, "Bricks and slaughter," *The Economist* (a special report on property), March 5, 2011, 4.

2. Ibid.

3. Ibid.

4. Ibid.

5. Douglas Heddings, "Real Estate Agent Accountability for Bad Advice," October 12, 2007, http://www.truegotham.com/real-estate-agent-account-ability-for-bad-advice/, (accessed October 17, 2010).

6. H. Kelly, "The Morphology of the Credit Crisis," *Real Estate Issues* 34 (3): 21.

7. Ibid.

8. Mortgage brokers came under tough scrutiny in the wake of the financial crisis, with lawmakers and regulators sharply critical of underwriting standards and practices that were seen as too loose, helping create the housing price bubble. The SAFE Act specifies that mortgage brokers who are employees of federal agency-regulated institutions must also be listed with the Nationwide Mortgage Licensing System and Registry.

9. A. Katz, *Our Lot: How Real Estate Came to Own Us* (New York: Bloomsbury, 2010), 142.

10. The Uniform Standards of Professional Appraisal Practice (USPAP) is considered the quality control standard applicable for real property, personal property, intangibles, and business valuation appraisal analysis and reports in the United States and its territories.

11. M. Jarsulic, *Anatomy of a Financial Crisis: A Real Estate Bubble, Runaway Credit Markets, and Regulatory Failure* (New York: Palgrave Macmillan, 2010), 97.

12. Ibid., 97–98.

13. M. Hudson, *The Monster: How a Gang of Predatory Lenders and Wall Street Bankers Fleeced America—and Spawned a Global Crisis* (New York: Times Books, 2010), 156.

14. Ibid.

15. T. Kenney, "True Value," *Knowledge Leader*, Fall 2010, 29.

16. Ibid. An automated valuation model (AVM) is the name given to a service that can provide quick property valuations using modeling combined with a database. Most AVMs calculate a property's value at a specific point in time by analyzing the sales prices of comparable properties. Appraisers, Wall Street, and lending institutions use AVMs in their analysis of residen-

tial property. Basically, an AVM is a residential valuation report that can be obtained in a matter of minutes.

17. J. Trice, *Reengineering the Appraisal Process* (Cincinnati: Collateral Risk Network, 2009), 1.

18. CCIM Institute, "Will Dodd-Frank Act Impact Me?" January 18, 2011, http://www.ccim.com/newscenter/will-dodd-frank-act-impact-me, (accessed January 24, 2011).

19. The complete Dodd-Frank Wall Street Reform and Consumer Protection Act (H.R. 4173) can be downloaded at http://www.gpo.gov/fdsys/pkg/BILLS-111hr4173enr/pdf/BILLS-111hr4173enr.pdf.

20. Trice, *Reengineering*, 2–11.

21. Ibid., 12.

22. T. Sowell, *The Housing Boom and Bust* (New York: Basic Books, 2010), 23, 25, 145.

23. T. Wood, *The Commercial Real Estate Tsunami: A Survival Guide for Lenders, Owners, Buyers, and Brokers* (Hoboken, NJ: John Wiley & Sons, 2010), xvii.

Chapter 7: Mixed Signals

1. Rhinesmith, *Is There a Ticking Time Bomb in Commercial Real Estate?* (Washington, DC: Congressional Oversight Panel, 2010), 1.

2. Ibid., 5. Office space is the largest form of commercial property in the United States. The commercial real estate sector also includes health care, self-storage, senior living, restaurant, timberland, and parking properties.

3. The internal rate of return, or IRR, represents the annual profitability of an investment as a percent rate of return. It shows how much a deal's return can fall in percentage terms *before* the investor's capital is at risk. Not to get too technical, an IRR calculation starts with the net operating income (NOI) pro-

duced by a property and then solves (through a trial-and-error method) for the rate at which the initial cost of the investment has compounded (appreciated). Put another way, the calculation results in the annual rate of return that equates the present value of the NOI with the initial cash invested—the investment's effective yield (benefit) from start to finish.

4. Deutsche Bank Research, *Commercial Real Estate Loans Facing Refinancing Risk* (Frankfurt: Deutsche Bank, 2010), 3.

5. Rhinesmith, *Ticking Bomb*, 7.

6. Ibid., 12.

7. According to the MIT Center for Real Estate, the Moody's/REAL monthly Commercial Property Price Index (CPPI) was at a peak of 192 in October 2007, falling to 108 in October 2009 (a decline of 43.8 percent). See http://web.mit.edu/cre/research/credl/rca.html for the methodology of deriving the monthly CPPI.

8. Shlomi Ronen, "Raising Capital during Tough Times," *Urban Land*, January–February 2011, 72.

9. Ibid.

10. Ibid., 73.

11. Ibid.

12. The new Basel III regulations that are to be phased in by the Bank for International Settlements require that the capital base of banks must be raised.

13. Urban Land Institute and PricewaterhouseCoopers, *Emerging Trends in Real Estate 2011* (Washington, DC: ULI and PwC, 2010), 1.

Chapter 8: Violating the Law of the Lever

1. S. Berges, *The Complete Guide to Real Estate Finance for Investment Properties* (Hoboken, NJ: John Wiley & Sons, 2004), 61.

2. A. Elgonemy, "Debt-Financing Alternatives: Refinancing and Restructuring in the Lodging Industry," *Cornell Hospitality Quarterly* 43 (2): 10.

3. Ibid., 21.

4. S. Johnson and J. Kwak, *13 Bankers: The Wall Street Takeover and the Next Financial Meltdown* (New York: Vintage Books, 2011), 137.

5. Ibid.

6. Ibid.

7. Ibid., 138.

8. Aline van Duyn, Michael Mackenzie, and Richard Milne, "Credit markets: Paper weight," *Financial Times*, October 31, 2010, http://www.ft.com/cms/s/0/d7abb7c2-e51d-11df-8e0d-00144feabdc0,dwp_uuid=81bff92e-b744-11df-839a-00144feabdc0.html#axzz1EKkZnDNM, (accessed January 7, 2011).

9. Ibid.

10. International Monetary Fund, *World Economic Outlook: Recovery, Risk, and Rebalancing* (Washington, DC: IMF, 2010), 21.

11. Ibid.

12. Ibid.

13. Guhan Venkatu, "Out of the Shadows: Projected Levels for Future REO Inventory," Federal Reserve Bank of Cleveland, October 19, 2010, http://www.clevelandfed.org/research/commentary/2010/2010-14.cfm, (accessed December 19, 2010).

14. M. Thompson and I. Broff, "A Missed Assessment of Real Estate Debt Risk: How the Credit Rating Agencies and Commercial Bank Regulators Missed the Assessment of Real Estate Debt Risk, Creating the Largest Real Estate Bubble in US History," *Real Estate Issues* 34 (3): 32.

15. Ibid., 26.

16. Ibid.

17. Ibid., 27.

18. Ibid., 28.

19. Ibid.

20. Ibid.

21. Ibid.

22. Ibid.

23. Ibid.

24. Ibid.

25. Ibid.

26. Ibid. This book focuses on the single-family residential segment, which is separate from the condominium (condo) market. The condo form of ownership is a niche in the overall homeownership market. Cooperative sales (co-ops) are also generally lumped together in this segment of the residential sector. Although severely impacted by the mortgage crisis, condo ownership represents an alternative to both apartment rental and other forms of single-family homeownership, including townhomes and second (vacation) homes. This market has not only expanded in the traditional resort and recreational areas, but also in the mature suburbs and central business districts of larger cities across the United States.

   As a distinct market segment, condos have only been in existence in the United States since 1960. Increased condo development began around 1970, with the momentum in terms of numbers having been realized between 2003 and 2008. According to the *Economics & Business Journal*, approximately 5 percent of the existing housing supply in the country is in the form of condominium or co-op ownership.

27. Ibid.

28. Ibid.

29. Ibid.

30. Ibid.

31. Urban Land Institute and PricewaterhouseCoopers, *Emerging Trends in Real Estate 2011* (Washington, DC: ULI and PwC, 2010), 1.

32. Ibid., 4.

33. Andrew Palmer, "Bricks and slaughter," *The Economist* (a special report on property), March 5, 2011, 16.

34. B. Graham and D. Dodd, *Security Analysis* (New York: The McGraw-Hill Companies, 1934), 79, 117.

35. Monetary policy is the process by which the monetary authority of a country, such as the Fed, controls the supply of money, often targeting a rate of interest to attain a set of objectives oriented toward the growth and stability of the overall economy.

36. Sebastian Mallaby, "Romney can turn private equity into political capital," *Financial Times*, February 3, 2012, 9.

Chapter 9: Fiddling With the System

1. R. Shiller, *Irrational Exuberance* (New York: Broadway Books, 2005), 157–159.

2. R. Shiller, *The Subprime Solution: How Today's Global Financial Crisis Happened, and What to Do About It* (Princeton, NJ: Princeton University Press, 2008), 47.

3. R. Shiller, *Market Volatility* (Boston: MIT Press, 1989), 371–400.

4. D. Samuel, "The Subprime Mortgage Crisis: Will New Regulations Help Avoid Future Financial Debacles?" *Albany Government Law Review* 2 (1): 224.

5. Stephen Labaton, "SEC Concedes Oversight Flaws," *New York Times*, September 27, 2008, A1.

6. S. Johnson and J. Kwak, *13 Bankers: Wall Street Takeover and the Next Financial Meltdown* (New York: Vintage Books, 2011), 134.

7. Ibid.

8. Ibid.

9. J. Stiglitz, "Capitalist Fools: Five Key Mistakes That Led Us to the Collapse," in Carter, *The Great Hangover: 21 Tales of the New Recession from the Pages of Vanity Fair* (New York: Harper Perennial, 2010), 145–152.

10. J. Bexley, J. James, and J. Haberman, "The financial crisis and its issues," *Research in Business & Economics Journal* 3: 44.

11. Mark Brickell, "Lessons gleaned from housing sector's flawed risk assessments," *Financial Times*, April 14, 2011, 24.

12. Ibid.

13. Ibid.

14. Ibid.

15. Stephen King, "Greenspan's Delphic message on US deficit," *The Independent* (London), February 7, 2005, http://www.independent.co.uk/news/business/comment/stephen-king-greenspans-delphic-message-on-us-deficit-531556.html, (accessed November 17, 2010).

16. Johnson and Kwak, *13 Bankers*, 88. Comments made by Alan Greenspan on July 16, 2003.

17. M. Zandi, *Financial Shock: A 360° Look at the Subprime Mortgage Implosion, and How to Avoid the Next Financial Crisis* (Upper Saddle River, NJ: FT Press, 2008), 77.

18. Ibid.

19. Ibid.

20. Joe Reeser, "The Real Cause of the Current Financial Crisis," September 27, 2008, http://www.opednews.com/articles/The-Real-Cause-of-the-Curr-by-Joe-Reeser-080926-83.html, (accessed November 21, 2010).

21. In May 2011, Congress unveiled legislation to replace government-sponsored enterprises Fannie Mae and Freddie Mac with at least five private companies that would issue mortgage-backed securities with explicit federal guarantees. The proposed bill would require the new entities to hold more capital than Fannie and Freddie and would only issue federal guarantees to the mortgage-backed securities rather than the entities themselves, meaning that they would operate as public utilities. Advocates say taxpayers will be less exposed to losses because of the higher standards on both sides of the loan. Additionally, the firms would pay a fee for government backing to finance a catastrophic insurance fund, much as the FDIC levies fees and handles bank failures.

22.   The full proposal for the regulations requiring issuers of MBSs to retain an economic interest in the credit risk for securitized assets can be viewed at http://www.fhfa.gov/webfiles/20688/QRMFedReg33111.pdf.

23.   The Volcker rule is a proposal by economist and former Federal Reserve chairman Paul Volcker to restrict US banks from making certain kinds of speculative investments, if they are not on behalf of their customers. Volcker has argued that such speculative activity played a key role in the financial crisis.

24.   Kurt Schacht, "US financial reform bill 'not enough' to avoid systemic risk," *Financial Times* (FTfm supplement), September 12, 2010, 18.

25.   Ibid.

26.   Ibid.

27.   Comments made by Andrew Lo, Professor of Finance at MIT's Sloan School of Management, in a panel discussion titled "Re-Engineering Real Estate: Top Minds Weigh In" during the MIT Center for Real Estate's 25th Anniversary Conference, October 26, 2010, http://web.mit.edu/cre/events/anniversary/reengineering-real-estate.html, (accessed November 22, 2010).

28.   Quantitative easing (QE) is an unconventional monetary policy used by some central banks to stimulate their economies. The central bank creates money that it uses to buy government bonds and other financial assets in order to increase the money supply and the excess reserves of the banking system; this also raises the prices of the financial assets bought, which lowers their yields.

      Expansionary monetary policy normally involves a lowering of short-term interest rates by a central bank. However, when such interest rates are either at (or close to) zero, normal monetary policy can no longer function, and quantitative easing may be used by the monetary authorities in order to lower interest rates further out on the yield curve to further stimulate the economy. Risks include the policy being more effective than intended, or not being effective enough if banks simply opt to sit on the additional cash in order to increase their capital reserves in a climate of increasing defaults.

29. H. Paulson, *On the Brink: Inside the Race to Stop the Collapse of the Global Financial System* (New York: Business Plus, 2010), 70.

30. The Basel Accords refer to the banking supervision accords (recommendations on banking laws and regulations)—Basel I and Basel II, as well as Basel III, which is under development—by the Basel Committee on Banking Supervision (BCBS). They are called the "Basel Accords" as the BCBS maintains its secretariat at the Bank for International Settlements in Basel, Switzerland, with the committee normally meeting there.

31. The purpose of Basel II, which was initially published in 2004, was to create an international standard that banking regulators could use when creating regulations about how much capital banks needed to put aside to guard against the types of financial and operational risks that they faced. Advocates of Basel II believed that such an international standard could help protect the international financial system from the types of problems that arise when a major bank or a series of banks collapse. Basel II attempted to accomplish this by setting up risk and capital management requirements designed to ensure that a bank holds capital reserves appropriate to the risk the bank exposes itself to through its lending and investment practices. Generally speaking, these rules mean that the greater risk to which the bank is exposed, the greater the amount of capital the bank needs to hold to safeguard its solvency and financial stability. The 2008 financial crisis proved that Basel II was largely ineffective.

32. Tier 1 capital is the core measure of a bank's financial strength from a regulator's point of view. It is composed of "core capital," which consists primarily of common stock and disclosed reserves (or retained earnings), but may also include non-redeemable (non-cumulative) preferred stock.

To be considered well-capitalized, a bank must have a Tier 1 capital ratio that is at least 6 percent of its risk-adjusted assets. The ratio is calculated as follows:

$$\frac{\text{Common Stock} + \text{Non-redeemable Preferred Stock} + \text{Retained Earnings} + \text{Disclosed Reserves}}{\text{Total Assets}}$$

33. Jonathan Rosenthal, "Chained but untamed," *The Economist* (a special report on international banking), May 14, 2011, 11.

34. R. Rajan, *Fault Lines: How Hidden Fractures Still Threaten the World Economy* (Princeton, NJ: Princeton University Press, 2010), 158.

35. Ibid.

36. Gillian Tett, "Why the public wants its pound of bankers' flesh," *Financial Times*, March 12–13, 2011, 8.

37. Rajan, *Fault Lines*, 161.

Chapter 10: The Seeds of Risk

1. S. Johnson and J. Kwak, *13 Bankers: The Wall Street Takeover and the Next Financial Meltdown* (New York: Vintage Books, 2011), 75.

2. Ibid.

3. Ibid., 76.

4. Ibid., 75.

5. Ibid., 129. The joint-acquisition of Energy Future Holdings by Kohlberg Kravis Roberts & Company and TPG Capital in 2007, with more than $40 billion in debt, was the biggest LBO ever for a non-single firm deal.

6. US Bankruptcy Code, 11 U.S.C. § 548(2); Uniform Fraudulent Transfer Act, § 4. This is because the company usually gets no direct financial benefit from the transaction, but incurs the debt for it nevertheless.

7. W. Lasher, *Practical Financial Management* (Mason, Ohio: Thomson South-Western, 2008), 695.

8. Standard & Poor's, *The Leveraging of America: LBOs—The Good, the Bad, and the Ugly* (New York: Standard & Poor's Credit Research, 2007), 3.

9. Johnson and Kwak, *13 Bankers*, 72.

10. C. James, "Mortgage-Backed Securities: How Important Is Skin in the Game?" *FRBSF Economic Letter*, December 13, 2010 37: 1.

11. The Dodd-Frank act generally requires credit risk retention of 5 percent of any asset included in a securitization, or less than 5 percent if the assets meet underwriting standards established by regulation.

    Risk retention will also be required for collateralized debt obligations (CDOs), commercial mortgage-backed securities (CMBSs), securities collateralized by CDOs, and similar instruments collateralized by other asset-backed securities (ABSs). To provide clarification for the reader, mortgage bonds are sometimes classified as "asset-backed securities" (ABSs)—along with bonds that are backed by credit card loans and auto loans—and not as "mortgage-backed securities" (mortgage bonds). That is because the securities are backed by loans, which are financial assets to the *creditors*. However, the conventional practice of the real estate sector is to classify mortgage bonds as mortgage-backed securities (MBSs), as discussed in chapter 2. According to F. Fabozzi and F. Modigliani's *Mortgage and Mortgage-Backed Securities Markets* (Boston: Harvard Business School Press, 1992), 312, ABSs are "securities collateralized by assets that are not mortgage loans."

Under Dodd-Frank, underwriting standards and the amount of risk retention may be different for different asset classes. Dodd-Frank specifies the
asset classes to be treated separately as residential mortgages, commercial
mortgages, commercial loans, auto loans, and any other asset class that the
Office of the Comptroller of the Currency (OCC), the FDIC, and the SEC
deem appropriate.

Dodd-Frank exempts "qualified residential mortgages," or QRMs,
from the risk retention provisions. Regulators have been tasked to define
what exactly constitutes a QRM, providing that the definition is not
broader than the definition of the same term under the Truth in Lending
Act (TILA) of 1968.

As background, in 2010 Dodd-Frank required banking, securities,
and housing regulators to come up with a "gold standard" for home mortgage pools in securitizations that would signify low risk for lenders and
investors. Loans that do not meet the agencies' key tests for minimal risk
would be designated as "non-qualifying." For these loans, originators and
sponsors of mortgage-backed securities would need to put some of their
own skin in the game into reserve—5 percent of loan principal balances—
so that they could bear at least part of the risk of loss in the event of
delinquencies.

Under the new system, non-qualifying loans would come with extra
costs to originators, who presumably would pass them along to borrowers
in the form of higher interest rates—anywhere from 75 basis points and
upwards, according to analyst estimates.

After months of negotiations, the following six agencies—the Federal
Reserve, HUD, the FDIC, the Federal Housing Finance Agency, the OCC,
and the SEC—produced some 300 pages of proposed rules. The following
are their key criteria for home mortgages to meet the QRM standard:

- Minimum down payments of 20 percent for purchases and 30 percent for refinancings (the specific amount of the down payment is highly controversial and is still being negotiated as of this writing);
- Maximum permissible debt-to-income ratios of 28/36—no more than 28 percent of monthly gross income can go for mortgage-related debt, and no more than 36 percent for *all* household debt payments; and
- No sixty-day delinquencies in the twenty-four months preceding application.

Lastly, proposals from regulators also include QRM equivalents for commercial real estate loans, known as "qualified commercial real estate" loan standards, or QCRE. The underwriting standards for commercial loans that may be included in an exempt commercial mortgage-backed security (CMBS) transaction are designed to ensure that the property securing the loan is stable and provides sufficient net operating income to repay the loan. The commercial loans of companies with a debt service coverage ratio of 1.7 or greater would generally be eligible for inclusion in a CMBS transaction exempt from Dodd-Frank risk retention requirements. In certain limited circumstances, a 1.5 debt service coverage ratio would suffice to qualify a company's commercial loan for the risk retention exemption. (A debt service coverage ratio of 1.5 means that for every $1.00 in principal and interest payments, there is $1.50 available in net operating income).

12. Annie Lowry, *The Washington Independent,* http://washingtonindependent.com/93795/the-return-of-the-1000-down-mortgage, (accessed February 27, 2011).

13. S. Meister, *Commercial Real Estate Restructuring Revolution: Strategies, Tranche Warfare, and Prospects for Recovery* (Hoboken, NJ: John Wiley & Sons, 2011), 158.

14.   Keith Jurow, "FHA Insured Mortgages: A Disaster in the Making, Part 1,"
       Seeking Alpha, http://seekingalpha.com/article/219558-fha-insured-mort-
       gages-a-disaster-in-the-making-part-1, (accessed February 23, 2011).

15.   Ibid.

16.   Ibid.

17.   Ibid.

18.   The purpose of the Section 203(b) Mortgage Insurance Program is to pro-
       vide insurance to purchase or refinance a main residence. The mortgage
       loan is funded by a lending institution, such as a mortgage company, bank,
       or a savings and loan association, and the mortgage is insured by HUD.
       The specific eligibility requirements are as follows: The borrower must
       meet standard FHA credit qualifications; the borrower is eligible for 96.5
       percent financing; the borrower is able to finance the upfront mortgage
       insurance premium into the mortgage; and the borrower will be responsi-
       ble for paying an annual premium. Eligible properties are one-to four-unit
       residential structures.

19.   The minimum FICO score requirement for FHA-insured loans is 580 for
       a 3.5 percent down payment. Since mid-2010, anyone purchasing a home
       with a score that's lower than 580 is required to provide a 10 percent down
       payment, which is still too low for such risky homebuyers. In addition,
       seller help for closing costs has been reduced from 6 percent to 3 percent.

       FICO risk scores range from 300–850, with 711 being the median
       FICO score of Americans. The objective of the FICO risk score is to predict
       the likelihood that a consumer will go ninety days past due (or more) in
       the subsequent twenty-four months after the score has been calculated.
       The higher the consumer's score, the less likely they will go ninety days past
       due in the subsequent twenty-four months.

20.   Lender Processing Services, *LPS Mortgage Monitor* (Jacksonville, FL: LPS,
       2010), 19.

Chapter 11: Facing the Music

1. To simplify an extremely complex topic, when a country's money supply rises its exchange rate is expected to depreciate (weaken) because the markets are flooded with its own currency (think over-supply). To bring down the total national debt and to pay for rising interest costs, the US Treasury would need to print more money (or sell more bonds) to finance the country's deficits, thus causing the value of the dollar to decline. For a detailed discussion on exchange rates, see D. Moss, *A Concise Guide to Macroeconomics: What Managers, Executives, and Students Need to Know* (Boston: Harvard Business School Press, 2007), 125–139.

2. Carmen Reinhart and Kenneth Rogoff, "Growth in a Time of Debt," (working paper, National Bureau of Economic Research, Washington, DC, 2010), 25.

3. Government Accountability Office, "The Federal Government's Financial Health: A Citizen's Guide to the 2008 Financial Report of the United States Government," February 13, 2009, 7.

4. Ibid., 8.

5. P. Angelides et. al., *The Financial Crisis Inquiry Report* (New York: PublicAffairs, 2011), xvii.

6. Ibid., xix.

7. Fareed Zakaria, "Restoring the American Dream," *Time*, November 1, 2010, 33.

8. Ibid.

9. Edward Luce, "Goodbye, American Dream," *Financial Times* (Life & Arts section), July 30, 2010, 1.

10. Jon Hilsenrath, "Fed Economist: Housing Is a Lousy Investment," *Wall Street Journal*, January 5, 2010, http://blogs.wsj.com/economics/2010/01/05/fed-economist-housing-is-a-lousy-investment/.

11. Ibid.

12.   Joseph Gyourko, "5 myths about home sweet homeownership," *Washington Post*, November 15, 2009, B3.

13.   "Common Myths about Home Ownership Versus Renting," http://www. associatedcontent.com/article/460432/common_myths_about_home_ ownership_versus.html, (accessed January 4, 2011).

14.   Ibid.

15.   Suzanne Kapner, "US housing: Sunset Boulevard," *Financial Times*, August 17, 2010, 7.

16.   M. Zandi, *Financial Shock: A 360° Look at the Subprime Mortgage Implosion, and How to Avoid the Next Financial Crisis* (Upper Saddle River, NJ: FT Press, 2008), 1–5.

17.   C. Herbert, *Report to Congress on the Root Causes of the Foreclosure Crisis* (Washington, DC: US Department of Housing and Urban Development, 2010), 18.

18.   Ibid.

19.   Ibid.

20.   Ibid.

21.   Ibid.

22.   J. Krainer and S. LeRoy, "Underwater Mortgages," *FRBSF Economic Letter*, October 18, 2010 31:1.

23.   Andrew Palmer, "Bricks and slaughter," *The Economist* (a special report on property), March 5, 2011, 9.

24.   Krainer and LeRoy "Underwater," 2.

25.   Ibid. In Phoenix and Las Vegas, the 2011 share of underwater mortgages was 52 percent and 61 percent, respectively.

26.   Herbert, *Report*, 19.

27.   Ibid., 29.

28.   Ibid.

29.   Ibid.

30. Wenli Li and Michelle White, "Mortgage Default, Foreclosures, and Bankruptcy," (working paper, Federal Reserve Bank of Philadelphia, University of California, San Diego, and the National Bureau of Economic Research, 2009), 18.

31. Ibid., 20.

32. Ibid., 21.

33. Anthony Downs, "Overbuilding and High Debt Could Cause Real Estate to Obstruct Economic Growth for Years," *National Real Estate Investor*, October 2010, 50.

34. "Robo-signing" is a term used by consumer advocates to describe the robotic process of the mass production of false and forged execution of mortgage assignments, satisfactions, affidavits, and other legal documents related to mortgage foreclosures and legal matters being created by persons without knowledge of the facts being attested to. It also includes accusations of notary fraud wherein the notaries pre- and/or post-notarized the affidavits and signatures of so-called robo-signers.

35. The research titled "Forced Sales and House Prices" was published in the *American Economic Review* in August 2011. In the study, MIT economist Parag Pathak and Harvard researchers John Campbell and Stefano Giglio examined 1.8 million home sales in Massachusetts from 1987 through 2009.

36. Palmer, "Bricks and slaughter," 8.

37. While the trend of the shadow inventory is improving, the current level and distressed months' supply remain high. (An inventory of 4.5 months is considered normal). The short-term weakness in prices and longer-term weakness of the drivers that affect the housing market imply that excess supply will remain high for an extended period of time. CoreLogic's research suggests that although a portion of the shadow inventory would be good candidates for loan modifications, it would in all likelihood only be a small share of the total US single-family residential inventory.

38. Tanya Marsh, "Understanding the Commercial Real Estate Debt Crisis," *Harvard Business Law Review* 1: 35.

39. Ibid.

40. Ibid.

41. Ibid., 36.

42. Ibid.

43. Ibid., 37.

44. Ibid., 38.

45. Ibid.

46. Deutsche Bank Research, *Commercial Real Estate Loans Facing Refinancing Risk* (Frankfurt: Deutsche Bank, 2010), 3.

47. International Monetary Fund, *Global Financial Stability Report: Navigating the Financial Challenges Ahead* (Washington, DC: IMF, 2009), 32.

48. F. Hubert, *Germany's Housing Policy at the Crossroads* (Berlin: Freie Universität Berlin, 1993), 22.

Chapter 12: An American Renewal

1. J. Broome, "Expensive Tuition," *The RMA Journal*, February 2009, 13.

2. Ibid.

3. Ibid., 14.

4. Ibid.

5. Ibid.

6. Ibid.

7. Ibid.

8. Ibid.

9. Ibid., 15.

10. Ibid., 16.

11. Ibid.

12. Based on an interview with Michael Burrichter, a Principal with CBRE Investors, in November 2010.

13. Alyssa Katz, "The Rent Trap," *The American Prospect*, March 2011, vol. 22, no. 3, 25–28.

14. S. Simon, "The Advantages of Renting," National Public Radio, February 21, 2009.

15. Katz, "The Rent Trap," Ibid.

16. Ibid.

17. Ibid.

18. Ibid.

19. Ibid.

20. Suzanne Kapner, "US housing: Sunset Boulevard," *Financial Times*, August 17, 2010, 7. The comparison calculated by Robert Shiller doesn't account for dividends or the use of leverage.

21. Christina Rexrode, "Mortgage deduction under renewed scrutiny," *Washington Post*, March 12, 2011, E9.

22. Ibid.

23. A. Downs, *Real Estate and the Financial Crisis: How Turmoil in the Capital Markets is Restructuring Real Estate Finance* (Washington, DC: Urban Land Institute, 2009), 47.

24. CBRE, *Capital Markets Multi-Housing 2011 Annual Market Report* (Boston: CB Richard Ellis National Multi-Housing Group, 2011), 5.

25. William Wheaton, "A Proposal to Repair the US Mortgage Mess," (working paper, Department of Economics, MIT Center for Real Estate, 2010), 1.

26. Ibid.

27. Ibid.

28. According to William Wheaton, the owner's gain of $40,000 is derived as follows: (The property's future selling price of $140,000 – the value of the mortgage of $60,000 = $80,000) x (the claim of the future appreciation of 50%) = $40,000.

29. Wheaton, "A Proposal," Ibid.

30. Ibid, 2.

31. Ibid.

32. Ibid.

33. *Wall Street Journal*, "Is Slashing Mortgage Principal the Answer?" January 17, 2010, http://blogs.wsj.com/developments/2010/01/17/is-slashing-mortgage-principal-the-answer/.

34. "Second-Liens and Other Barriers to Principal Reduction as an Effective Foreclosure Mitigation Program," US House of Representatives Hearing Before the Committee on Financial Services—Second Session (Washington, DC: US Government Printing Office, April 13, 2010), 11.

35. *Wall Street Journal*, "Is Slashing," Ibid.

36. Edward Pinto, "The Future of Housing Finance," *Wall Street Journal*, August 17, 2010, 1.

37. Ibid.

38. Ibid.

39. D. Clune and J. Hosey, *The Foreclosure Crisis in Kent County: A Call for a Comprehensive Response* (Grand Rapids, MI: Dyer-Ives Foundation, 2009), 25.

40. Daniel Indiviglio, "The Mortgage of the Future," *The Atlantic*, http://www.theatlantic.com/business/archive/2010/08/the-mortgage-of-the-future/61859/, (accessed January 9, 2011).

41. Ibid.

42. The ratchet mortgage is patented by banking consultant Bert Ely and debt management specialist Andrew Kalotay.

43. Urban Land Institute and PwC, *Emerging Trends in Real Estate 2011* (Washington, DC: ULI and PwC, 2010), 1.

44. T. Wood, *The Commercial Real Estate Tsunami: A Survival Guide for Lenders, Owners, Buyers, and Brokers* (Hoboken, NJ: John Wiley & Sons, 2010), 111.

45. Ibid., 123–141.

46. Ibid., 123.

47. Ibid., 121.

48. Ibid., 45.

49. Ibid., 176.

50. Based on Anthony Downs, "Commercial Property Equity Gap: How to Cope," *Urban Land*, November 11, 2010, http://urbanland.uli.org/Articles/2010/Nov/DownsCope, (accessed March 3, 2011).

51. Mara Der Hovanesian and Dean Foust, "Why This Bust is Different," *BusinessWeek*, November 16, 2009, 45.

52. H. Paulson, *Best Practices for Residential Covered Bonds* (Washington, DC: The US Department of the Treasury, 2008), 9.

53. The Covered Bond Act would establish the following eligible asset classes: residential mortgages, home-equity loans, and commercial loans.

54. Richard Rydstrom, "The Great Mortgage Financing Hand-Off: Securitization, Private-Label, and Covered Bonds," US Covered Bond Council, http://www.scribd.com/doc/49714806/1-Covered-Bond-Council-Mortgage-Loan-Securitization-FINAL-1, (accessed Feb-ruary 10, 2011).

55. Paulson, *Best Practices*, 7–8.

56. Charles Bryan, Cadwalader, Wickersham & Taft, LLP, "New US Covered Bond Legislation Introduced," March 25, 2010, http://www.cadwalader.com/assets/client_friend/032510NewCoveredBond.pdf, (accessed February 15, 2011).

57. W. Bonner and A. Wiggin, *Financial Reckoning Day: Surviving the Soft Depression of the 21ˢᵗ Century* (Hoboken, NJ: John Wiley & Sons, 2003), 224.

Epilogue

1. George Magnus, "Financial bust has bequeathed a crisis of capitalism," *Financial Times*, September 13, 2011, 22.

2. Ibid.

3. R. Scheer, *The Great American Stickup* (New York: Nation Books, 2010), 5.

4. N. Prins, *It Takes a Pillage: An Epic Tale of Power, Deceit, and Untold Trillions* (Hoboken, NJ: John Wiley & Sons, 2011), 63–64.

5. C. Morris, *The Two Trillion Dollar Meltdown: Easy Money, High Rollers, and the Great Credit Crash* (New York: PublicAffairs, 2008), 160.

6. A. Sorkin, *Too Big to Fail: The Inside Story of How Wall Street and Washington Fought to Save the Financial System—and Themselves* (New York: Penguin Books, 2010), Author's Note.

7. Richard Milne, "Follow the line of debt to spot a coming crisis," *Financial Times*, (Risk Management special report), March 22, 2011, 3. The term "black swan" was coined by author Nassim Nicholas Taleb.

8. Steven Rattner, "Green shoots are piercing through the gloom," *Financial Times*, November 7, 2010, 20.

9. Robert Rubin, "How America can withstand the headwinds," *Financial Times*, November 1, 2010, 11.

Index

The headings of the Index reference pages 1–388.

About the Author

Anwar Elgonemy draws on over twenty-five years of experience in real estate acquisitions, developments, financings, and valuations. Elgonemy speaks four languages and has advised real estate clients throughout the United States, the Caribbean, Europe, the Middle East, Latin America, and Southeast Asia.

Currently, he is director of acquisitions for Equinox Hospitality Group, a San Francisco-based private equity firm that focuses on the lodging sector. Previously, Elgonemy was a senior vice-president with Jones Lang LaSalle (NYSE: JLL). In addition, he was employed by PKF Consulting (valuations), Marriott International (feasibility and development), Laventhol & Horwath (advisory), and Hilton (accounting and operations).

Elgonemy is a Certified Commercial Investment Member (CCIM), Counselor of Real Estate (CRE), Fellow of the Royal Institution of Chartered Surveyors (FRICS), and a Member of the Appraisal Institute (MAI). Widely published, he has also attained top-tier media coverage in the *New York Times, Wall Street Journal, Financial Times,* and *Time* magazine.

Elgonemy holds an MBA from The Thunderbird School of Global Management in Arizona. In 2012, he will become an alumnus of the Harvard University Graduate School of Design.